DIRECTORY OF ISLAMIC FINANCIAL INSTITUTIONS

This is the first reference book to address itself to Islamic banking and finance and it offers comprehensive information on all major institutions who have commercial or banking interests in this field.

It includes an analysis of the principles behind interest-free banking and indicates its relationship with financial institutions in both Islamic countries and Western ones. It also lists the laws governing interest-free banking in countries where it is extensively in operation and provides essential information for all international financial institutions.

The Directory lists all banks and financial institutions by country, giving details of their specific role and areas of operation.

JOHN R. PRESLEY, Banking Centre and Department of Economics, Loughborough University, for the International Centre for Islamic Studies.

DIRECTORY OF ISLAMIC FINANCIAL INSTITUTIONS

Edited by
JOHN R. PRESLEY

CROOM HELM
London • New York • Sydney

© 1988 International Centre for Islamic Studies
Croom Helm Ltd, Provident House, Burrell Row,
Beckenham, Kent, BR3 1AT
Croom Helm Australia, 44-50 Waterloo Road,
North Ryde, 2113, New South Wales

Published in the USA by
Croom Helm
in association with Routledge, Chapman & Hall, Inc.
29 West 35th Street,
New York, NY 10001

British Library Cataloguing in Publication Data
Presley, John R.
    Directory of Islamic financial institutions.
    1. Financial institutions — Islamic
    countries — Directories
    I. Title
    332.1'025'17671   HG187.3
    ISBN 0-7099-1347-8

Library of Congress Cataloging-in-Publication Data

A Directory of Islamic financial institutions/edited by John R.
    Presley for ICIS.
        p.   cm.
    Bibliography: p.
    Includes index.
    ISBN 0-7099-1347-8
    1. Banks and banking — Islamic countries — Directories. 2. Banks
and banking — Islamic countries. I. Presley, John R.
II. International Centre for Islamic Studies.
HG3368.A5D57   1988
332.1'025'17671 — dc19   87-30403

Printed and bound in Great Britain by Mackays of Chatham Ltd, Kent

Contents

Preface

It was a great honour for me to be asked by Mr Muazzam Ali, Vice-Chairman of the International Association of Islamic Banks, to edit this first directory of Islamic banking. I have long been a student of Islamic economics and banking and shared many debates, particularly with my Muslim friends in the Arab Gulf States and Pakistan. I was particularly pleased to accept the invitation because it gave me an opportunity to further the understanding of Islamic banking in the West. There is much ignorance both in the United States and in Europe as to what constitutes Islamic banking; the primary objective of this directory is to begin to correct this ignorance, to give detailed information on the principles, theory and institutions of Islamic banking and to explore the progress which has already taken place in many Muslim states towards the introduction and operation of Islamic financial institutions.

Of course much still needs to be done, particularly in relation to the refinement of Islamic banking practices, its functions alongside Western commercial banking practices and in the adjustments to the operations of money markets and monetary policy which are necessary. This Directory shows that it is no longer possible to ignore the progress of Islamic finance; increasingly commercial banks are being called upon to work with new Islamic institutions and to conform to the Islamic banking procedures which exist in most Muslim countries. It is already impossible to do business in Iran and Pakistan without some expertise in Islamic banking; now over 50 Islamic financial institutions function effectively in more than 17 different countries including Sudan, Kuwait, Egypt, Jordan, Bahrain, Turkey, Pakistan and Iran. Twenty years ago only one Islamic bank existed. Now 1,000 million Muslims around the world are beginning to question the principles upon which traditional banking has operated in the West and are supporting the eventual move towards an Islamic approach in their financial markets, systems and institutions. There is now a determination that Islamic banking will succeed and this is enhanced by the support from the organisation of Islamic Conferences, a succession of Islamic Summits and the work of the International Association of Islamic Banks. Never before has such an effort been put into the development of an international and national Islamic economic order.

This is the first directory of Islamic financial institutions. It is divided into three parts. Part One addresses the framework and principles of Islamic banking, explores the nature and growth of the major international Islamic financial organisations and institutions and examines some important theoretical considerations relating to Islamic banking. Part Two presents a directory of Islamic banks and financial institutions; this Directory gives details of the area of operation of each bank, background information, contact addresses, a list of directors, the level and growth of assets, capital structure and profitability together with some indication of likely future developments. Each entry has been checked by the bank, although no independent audit of the accounts has been undertaken by the Directory. Part Three examines in more detail the process of Islamisation of the financial system in both Pakistan and Iran; it also includes a survey of the major Islamic banking laws which have been introduced in Iran, Pakistan, Malaysia, and Turkey.

The contents of this Directory have been taken from many different sources. As Editor, I wish to express my sincere thanks to all the banks and financial institutions who have assisted in bringing together this information. Numerous individuals have also contributed to the written word; in particular I wish to thank Prince Mohammad Al Faisal Al Saud and Muazzam Ali, President and Vice-President respectively of the International Association of Islamic Banks and Ahmad Mohammed Ali, President of the Islamic Development Bank. I am grateful to all the members of the Middle East and Research Departments of the International Monetary Fund who contributed to the preparation of *Islamic Banking* (IMF Occasional Papers, February 1987) which is incorporated in various sections of this Directory.

John R. Presley

Acknowledgements

I am particularly grateful to Zubair Iqbal for obtaining permission from the IMF for me to use the IMF paper in this Directory. The list of contributors is almost endless; it would be impossible to mention all by name but I would especially wish to thank the following for their effort in assembling this Directory: Mr Nawazish Ali Zaidi, Dr Ahmed El Naggar, Dr Ziauddin Ahmed, Mr D M Qureshi, Dr Mehmud El Ansari, Mr Jalaluddin Ahmed, Mr Ibnul Hassan, Mr Mukarram Ali, Mr N H Jaffery, Mr Ahmed Amin El Fouad, Mr Bagkir Youssef Al Mudawi, Mr Zafar Ahmad Khan, Dr Ashrafuzzeman, Mr Mukhtar Zaman, Mr M W Farooqi, Mr Jalees Ahmed Faruqui, Ms Kerra Soker, Ms Kit Lawson, Dr Mahmoud M El Helw, and Mr H Kabbara.

Finally I wish to express my gratitude to my secretary, Laura Walmsley, for her excellent work in typing this Directory and to Gary Watson for his work in organising the entries to Part II.

Part One

Islamic Banking: The Background

1

A Framework of Islamic Banking[1]

Inevitably the study of the Islamic economic system has proceeded through a comparison with the existing international economic order. In comparing one with the other the most obvious difference is that one is Riba (interest)-free and the other is Riba-orientated. Yet emphasising the differing approaches to interest over-simplifies the description of the Islamic financial system and the Islamic economic order. The elimination of Riba is not a very simple task in view of its pivotal role and its total integration in the current economic order. Even so, the elimination of Riba does not automatically convert a non-Islamic financial system into an Islamic one or the present International Economic Order into the Islamic Economic Order in any real sense.

The Islamic Economic Order is based upon a set of principles found in the Quran. No matter what aspect of the Islamic Economic Order is introduced, for practical operations it has to base itself on the Qur'anic concept of social justice. The Islamic financial system, therefore, cannot be introduced merely by eliminating Riba but only by adopting the Islamic principles of social justice and introducing laws, practices, procedures and instruments which help in the maintenance and dispensation of justice, equity and fairness.

The nature of the operations of banking is central to the functioning of any financial system, Islamic or otherwise. Until the early part of the 20th century, Islamic banking was the subject of mainly theoretical discussions. It was not possible to initiate a programme of practical implementation of Islamic Banking on a scale which could produce a solution of the economic problems confronting the contemporary world and yield greater social benefits to the Islamic world.

Most efforts to introduce Islamic banking in earlier years were through isolated private and individual initiatives. These efforts, in the midst of the huge and extremely powerful operations of the non-Islamic banks, were unable to make a significant impact upon established banking practices. Small beginnings, however, often develop into projects of promise and more elaborate, large-scale

---

1. Written by Muazzam Ali, Vice-Chairman, International Association of Islamic Banks.

3

undertakings. The individual and private initiatives in the field of Islamic banking thus provided an excellent working example on which the infrastructure of interest-free banking could subsequently be built.

Some pioneering Islamic banks, on a very modest scale, were established in Egypt in the decade of the 1960s and operated as rural social banks along the Nile Delta. The operation of interest-free banking in these rural areas, where banking, as such, had not previously existed, proved to be an initiative well worth pursuing. Such an initiative in a remote corner of Egypt and on a very small scale has acted as an inspiration to others to promote a more substantial movement towards a new Islamic economic and financial system.

NEW INITIATIVES

The late King Faisal bin Abdul Aziz Al-Saud of Saudi Arabia can be credited with the postive realisation of the Ummah's responsibility for creating an Islamic economic system at state level. This initiative led to the Organisation of Islamic Conferences being established. Major attempts were made to initiate collective efforts towards uniting Muslims in pursuit of common objectives. The elimination of Riba and the creation of Islamic financial and economic institutions were amongst these objectives. It was the belief of His Majesty King Faisal that, since the Qu'ran prohibited Riba and laid down specific principles for an Islamic economic society, it was incumbent on every Muslim to comply with these principles. He felt that the Islamic nations must evolve a structure which would be a blend of the Sharia (Islamic Law) and modern financial techniques in order to produce a new and viable financial alternative, free of what is prohibited in Islam and pursuing what is enjoined in it.

The Islamic conference

In December 1970, when the second Islamic Conference of Foreign Ministers was held in Karachi, Pakistan and Egypt jointly sponsored a proposal which called for a study of the establishment of an International Islamic Bank for Trade and Development together with a Federation of Islamic Banks. Experts from 18 Islamic countries examined the proposal and prepared their report. This recommended that the interest-based financial system should be replaced by a system of participation schemes linked with profit-and-loss sharing. Consequently it was agreed that a federation of Islamic banks, together with an international Islamic bank should be established.

It was proposed that the international Islamic bank should act to:

(1) finance commercial transactions among Islamic countries.
(2) finance development and investment institutions as its affiliates.

(3) undertake the necessary transfers, clearing and settlement among the central institutions of the Islamic banks in Muslim countries as a beginning towards building up an integrated Islamic economy.

(4) set up central institutions in Muslim countries. These should offer short- and long-term loans for the commercial and development needs of the country concerned.

(5) support the efforts of these central institutions in the Muslim countries in pursuing their objectives within the framework of Islamic directives.

(6) administer and utilise Zakat funds.

(7) administer the surplus liquidity of these central institutions.

The establishment of a specialised agency was also recommended to be called the Investment and Development Body of Islamic Countries. Its main function was to pursue the following objectives:

(1) investment of Islamic capital.

(2) balancing the investment and development operations of the Muslim countries.

(3) selection of suitable fields for investment and the undertaking of research in these areas.

(4) extending technical advice and assistance for projects designated for regional investment in Islamic countries.

In addition to these recommendations it was proposed to establish a further specialised agency, the Association of Islamic Banks, as a consultative body in the field of Islamic economy and banking. Its mandate included the provision of technical advice to those countries wishing to establish Islamic banks and financial institutions and the encouragement and support for their efforts. This was to involve the Association in sending experts to those countries, extending the knowledge of Islamic banking and allowing for an exchange of information and experience between Islamic countries.

Establishment of an Islamic financial window

In March 1973, in the third Islamic Conference of Foreign Ministers held in Bengazi in Libya, these proposals were further examined and it was decided that a financial and economic department should be set up within the Islamic Secretariat. This was to serve the Muslim world in undertaking research and giving advice on economic matters, particularly the establishment of Islamic banks. This department was expected to act as the nucleus of a specialised agency in financial and economic fields of interest, serving the member states of the Organisation of Islamic Conferences. Subsequently a committee of experts representing the oil-producing Islamic countries met in Jeddah in July

5

1973 to further the establishment of an Islamic bank. The bank's charter, its rules and regulations were drafted and submitted to a second meeting of experts which was held in May 1974. This was followed by the second Islamic Conference of Finance Ministers in Jeddah, where a draft agreement was approved for the establishment of the Islamic Development Bank with an authorised capital of two billion Islamic Dinars (equivalent of two billion SDRs). The member states of the Organisation of Islamic Conferences became members of the bank. Established in 1975, the Islamic Development Bank has been serving the financial and investment needs of Islamic countries, especially those which are short of capital and where international credits are needed for development projects.

The early years of the bank's operation were characterised by setbacks and restrictions caused by adverse political events; in spite of this, its membership increased from 22 to 43 countries. Without doubt the Bank has played an important role in meeting the development needs of the Islamic world. It has provided interest-free loans for infrastructure projects and financed member countries on the basis of equity participation. Funds not needed immediately for longer-term operations are used to finance foreign trade, using the systems of Murabaha and leasing (see p. 51). By 1985 85 projects in over 30 member countries had received loans from the Bank amounting to 493 million dinars and 60 projects had been given financial assistance via equity participation, amounting to 260 million dinars. Leasing aid had been given to 50 projects and 250 foreign trade transactions, amounting to 3,379 million dinars had been carried out.

The Bank helped to establish a number of Islamic banks in various countries and set up a Research and Training Institute to conduct and promote research and impart training in the field of Islamic economics, banking and finance.

The International Association of Islamic Banks

One of the important recommendations of the study group which was commissioned by the Islamic Conference of Foreign Ministers was to create the Association of Islamic Banks; this was to co-ordinate and to develop a close relationship between the Islamic banks and other financial institutions and to promote Riba-free banking internationally. His Royal Highness Prince Mohamed Al Faisal Al Saud became the leading figure in the promotion of Islamic financial institutions in various parts of the world. The International Association of Islamic Banks was established under his Chairmanship in August 1977, with the Presidents of the member banks or their nominees as its Board of Directors.

The Association is providing Islamic countries with the technical assistance and expertise necessary for the establishment of their own Islamic banks; it is promoting the activities of Islamic banks, fostering their growth and representing their interests; it is creating co-operation among Islamic banks in their operations and encouraging an exchange of expertise. It is also carrying out training and research in the field of Islamic financial systems. Membership of the Association is open to all national Islamic banks in all Muslim countries and to all financial institutions, private and public, which are Riba-free. As such, the Association has the potential of becoming a singularly active and viable organisation for the pursuit of its objectives on a worldwide basis, particularly as it enjoys the recognition and authority conferred on it by the ninth Islamic Conference of Foreign Ministers. It has been given an observer status at the OIC and, besides having been recognised by the central banks and monetary authorities of the Islamic countries, its status is accepted by all the major international organisations. These include the United Nations Conference on Trade and Development (UNCTAD), the United Nations Industrial Development Organisation (UNIDO) and the Economic and Social Council of the United Nations.

The Association has also established a Higher Religious Supervisory Board. This is composed of a group of experienced Grand Ulema of Islamic jurisprudence who have a knowledge of international stock markets and related subjects. The Board's function is to supervise and control the financial transactions of Islamic banks and to see that they are strictly in accordance with the Sharia. It makes decisions and issues decrees (fatwas) which are binding on member banks. In addition, the Board has the authority to call seminars and conferences of Islamic jurisprudents and economics scholars from all over the world to make decisions and to lay down a basis for any new economic situations and questions which may arise. The Board has already requested all banks and financial institutions to appoint a board of not less than 13 jurisprudents and scholars whose decisions will be binding within their own organisations. Any bank which does not implement the tenets of the Board cannot claim to be working within the framework of the Sharia.

Two categories of institutions

As a result of the initiatives which have been mentioned earlier, the central banks and the monetary authorities of several Islamic countries have become increasingly interested in Islamic financial institutions. Consequently, an expert committee has been set up to examine and prepare guidelines on the promotion, regulation and supervision of Islamic banks. This committee has examined specific issues and problems relating to the promotion of Islamic banking, including liquidity problems, access to capital markets, fiscal treatment of income from partial or total ownership of Islamic banks, minimum capital requirements, the building up of reserves, and several other related issues. In 1981, when the fourth meeting of the Central Bank Governors held in Khartoum, the report of the experts' group was duly approved. A training structure for the manpower requirements of the Islamic banks was also established.

Many Islamic financial institutions are now functioning in various parts of the Muslim world. Most of these institutions were established in the second half of the 1970s and early 1980s in Egypt, Sudan, the Gulf countries, Pakistan, Iran, Malaysia, Bangladesh, and Turkey. Most owe their existence to private initiative. They fall into two broad categories; they are either Islamic commercial banks or Islamic investment and international holding companies. The first category includes, among others, the Faisal Islamic Banks in Egypt and Sudan, the Kuwait Finance House, the Dubai Islamic Bank, the Jordan Islamic Bank for Finance and Investment, the Bahrain Islamic bank, and the Islamic International Bank for Investment and Development, Egypt. The second category, having either a national or an international mandate, includes Dar Al-Maal Al-Islamic (Geneva), the Islamic Investment Company of the Gulf, the Islamic Investment Company (Bahamas), the Islamic Investment Company (Sudan), the Bahrain Islamic Investment Bank (Manama), and the Islamic Investment House (Amman).

The objectives of these institutions include the undertaking of all financial operations required by Muslims in the framework of the principles and precepts of the Sharia; this embraces the investment of funds within the islamic context, the generation of Halal profits, and the consolidation, promotion and co-operation of Islamic financial operations internationally.

Private initiative has been responsible for much of the progress to date but this has inspired interest at state level as well. Several Islamic countries have now taken steps towards the introduction of Islamic banking and financial systems on an evolutionary basis. In Sudan, Malaysia, Pakistan, Turkey, the United Arab Emirates and Iran, specific legislation has been introduced to facilitate the operations of Islamic financial institutions on a national scale (see Part Three, p. 215).

Achievements in Islamic banking: some examples

The task of listing all achievements relating to Islamic banking over recent years would be too exhausting. What follows is merely a selection of some major developments and achievements that have taken place:

On a worldwide basis it is important to appreciate the Dar Al-Maal Al-Islami (DMI). (For more details see p. 34) This was set up in 1981 with His Royal Highness Prince Mohamed Al Faisal Al Saud as Chairman, and with heads of states and prominent businessmen from all over the Islamic world as its founders. It was designed to act mainly as a holding company and advisory agency geared towards the setting up of Islamic banks, investment and Takafol (insurance) companies, and subsidiaries to conduct Islamic financial activities. It is organised as a legal entity in the form of a Trust under the laws of the Commonwealth of the Bahamas. DMI has absorbed the Islamic Investment Company and its two affiliates, the Sharia Investment Services (Geneva) and the Islamic Investment Company (Sharjah), and has established a network of Islamic financial institutions in various parts of the Islamic world. It has subsidiaries in Guinea, Senegal and Niger and has started trading activities in Nigeria, Mali and Burkina Faso. It is currently negotiating for DMI subsidiaries to be set up in other parts of Africa. Its future intentions include the setting up of institutions in Asia and the expansion of the Massraf Faisal Al-Islami of Bahrain by opening branches in Pakistan. Eventually, it expects to expand into America, Europe and the Far East. At the country level, the following activities indicate the strength of movement to Islamic banking:

Pakistan

Pakistan has always been at the forefront in pioneering Islamic banking. As early as July 1979, interest was eliminated from the operations of three of its institutions: the National Investment (Unit) Trust, the House-Building Finance Corporation and the Mutual Funds of the Investment Corporation of Pakistan. In 1979-80, the Government also introduced a scheme for the provision of interest-free loans to farmers cultivating subsistence holdings and this scheme was later extended to fishermen. In 1980–1, the Small Business Finance Corporation and the Investors' Scheme of the Investment Corporation of Pakistan were also put on an entirely interest-free basis.

In January 1981, following the Mudaraba Companies and Mudaraba (Flotation and Control) Ordinance of 1980, all 7,000 branches of the Pakistan nationalised commercial banks started business based on profit-and-loss sharing (PLS) and a scheme was introduced to provide interest-free loans (Qard Hassan) to students to finance their studies. In 1981–2, housing finance began on a rent-sharing basis. By June 1984, Rs 22,000 million had been deposited in PLS accounts. At the beginning of 1985, the entire banking system of Pakistan was converted to the new system.

The Investment Corporation of Pakistan has, from 1980, offered its investors a Sharing Accounts Scheme under which a small investor can buy shares in limited companies and get a return on 1.5 times his contribution. This is the only scheme of its kind in the country and is operated by the Corporation through its eight branches, at Karachi, Lahore, Peshawar, Quetta, Rawalpindi, Faisalabad, Multan and Hyderabad. By June 1984, there were 9,800 accounts under this scheme. The ICP also offers Mutual Funds for small investors to share in the benefits of a large investment portfolio, and in June 1984, the dividends on the Mutual Funds were between 11.5 and 28 per cent. ICP portfolios constituted nearly a quarter of the turnover of the Karachi Stock Exchange for 1982–3.

The Small Business Finance Corporation promotes growth in the private sector among small enterprises and has 23 offices throughout the country working in close association with 103 branches of the nationalised banks. During

9

1985, it began providing start up capital for young professional tradesmen in order to ease the unemployment problem in Pakistan.

Bankers' Equity is a private limited company sponsored by the State Bank of Pakistan and the nationalised commercial banks to meet the needs of industrial financing in the private sector. The National Investment (Unit) Trust's net investment for the years 1984–5 was over three times greater than in 1982–3. The House-Building Finance Corporation had assets in excess of Rs 7,800 million by 1985, over 75% higher than in 1981.

Egypt

The Faisal Islamic Bank of Egypt is the foremost interest-free bank in the country, having started operating in 1978. It has an impressive performance, with total assets in excess of $2 billion by 1986 and net profits of $106 million. The Islamic International Bank for Investment and Development is a joint stock Egyptian company engaged in operations as an investment bank, a merchant bank and a commercial bank and uses all the Islamic financial instruments, providing a wide range of banking services.

Cyprus

The Faisal Islamic Bank of Kibris commenced business in March 1983. It established the Faisal Islamic Investment Corporation and opened two branches in Kibris and a branch in Istanbul, Turkey. In ten months it financed Murabaha operations amounting to TL 450 million. Musharaka and Mudaraba operations were also carried out at a reasonable profit. It has encouraged savings by visiting villages, factories and schools with a mobile bank car to collect savings. It operates other Islamic funds, including Qard Hassan and Zakat.

Kuwait

Kuwait Finance House was established in 1977 and operated on a interest-free basis from the beginning. It has eight branches in Kuwait. It made rapid progress, deposits rising from KD 149 million in 1980 to KD 474 million in 1982. By 1985 its total assets exceeded KD 803 million and net profit stood at KD 17 million.

Bahrain

The Massraf Faisal Al-Islami of Bahrain began operations in December 1982. By 1985 its total assets had grown to US $677 million, with profits of US $2.6 million.

United Arab Emirates

The Dubai Islamic Bank was a pioneer of Islamic banking, having opened in 1975. Its investment fields include housing, industrial projects and commercial activities. In some years, its depositors have received returns well above those of conventional banks.

Qatar

The Qatar Islamic Bank is one of the most recently established Islamic banks. But although it only started in 1983, it has already attracted sizeable deposits. Its total assets were then devalued between 1983–6, to over QR 883 million.

Malaysia

The Bank Islam Malaysia was the first Islamic bank to open in South East Asia. It was established in July 1983 and 30 per cent of its equity was taken up by the Federal Government. It has one office in the capital and plans to open branches in all the constituent states.

Iran

Islamic banking came into force in Iran in January 1984, following a Bill approved by the Government in August 1983. Pending approval of the Bill, banking transactions amounting to over 100 billion rials had been handled according to the new system and, by October 1983, 20,000 bank employees had already attended training courses.

Turkey

In December 1983, Islamic banking in Turkey was sanctioned by a Decree of the Government which dealt with the founding and operation of Special Finance Institutions working according to Islamic principles under the jurisdiction of the Central Bank of Turkey. The Decree came into effect in February 1984.

Variety of operations

The various Islamic financial institutions functioning today are carrying out a variety of banking, financing and investment operations on a competitive basis. The banking system handles current accounts, savings accounts, systematic savings accounts, fixed investment accounts and call investment accounts. Financing is being done in a variety of ways. On a short-term basis, it is being carried out for trade, acceptance and hire purchase. On a medium-term basis, it covers loans, business development credits and lease financing. On a long-term basis, it is extended to mortgages, equity financing and project financing. An international banking service is also available with these institutions for foreign exchange transactions, purchase and sale of currencies, purchase and sale of commodities, transfer of funds, export financing, letters of credit and letters of guarantee.

There are some other miscellaneous services also; these include safe deposit boxes, security safekeeping services, management of private investment portfolios and trustee functions. It is thus evident that the financial and banking operations, within a short period of no more than seven years or so, have covered a fairly wide field and it may be hoped that, after the national initiatives taken by various countries mature, Islamic financial operations will include practically all the aspects of business, commerce and investment known to the modern world.

The Massraf Faisal Al-Islami may be quoted as a typical example of how an Islamic financial institution obtains funds. Its main sources include demand deposits, where repayments are guaranteed, and investment deposits, which are held on a fiduciary basis. In this, the operation of investment account deposits in particular may be noted. They are offered on a fixed-term or a call basis and are due as to principal and profit in 90 days, 180 days or one year after deposit. The call investment accounts are due 7 days or 30 days after call. The MFI receives 80 per cent of any profits generated by the investment of assets held for investment accounts. All the funds of MFI are invested in the investment areas and forms approved by the Religious Supervisory Board in conformity with the Islamic laws and the Sharia. Among the Islamic instruments which are being used at present, the most important are Mudaraba or financing participation, Musharaka or mutual financial participation, Qard Hassan or Islamic loan financing for commercial use, Murabaha or financing the sale of goods, Ijara or lease financing, Ijara wa Iktina or lease purchase financing, and Takafol or the Islamic alternative to contemporary Western insurance.

It is not necessary here to go into the detailed working and the technicalities of all these forms and financial instruments (see p. 20 for details). They have already been accepted as the most familiar instruments in the field of Islamic finance and banking. Together, these instruments provide the Islamic alternative for the operation of a complete finance system, based upon the principles of equity, fairness, justice and human consideration. It has to come through an evolutionary process. While various countries are making their own national efforts to produce a working machinery of their own, the principles and practices have to be standardised and will have to be made universally applicable. For this purpose, a very close co-ordination and constant exchange of information and experience will have to be maintained between the countries and the private agencies involved in this evolutionary process. What is important and worth valuing is the fact that a number of countries have taken national decisions to evolve such a system. The expression of such a national desire would have been unimaginable a decade ago; now it is a reality.

The next decade will represent the stage of implentation. There has been much progress to date but there is a great deal more still to be done. The Islamic economic order has to be sound not only in its techniques and methods but also in its moral and ethical principles and practices; the period of evolution will necessarily be a lengthy one.

2

The Islamic Economic System: An Overview

PROPERTY AND WEALTH

Islam is not a religion in the limited sense of the word but covers all aspects of human life and wants. It seeks to develop a new moral personality in man, an integrated social existence and a new socio-economic and political order. It has its own approach to economics — concepts, objectives, methods, laws and instruments. The Islamic economic system is not directly related to either capitalism or any variants of socialism or communism. The fundamental difference is that the Islamic economy rests upon Divine guidance whereas capitalistic and socialist economics propose particular human action without reference to religion. The Islamic concept of economics originates from the basic principles governing property. The Almighty Allah is the real Owner of everything. Man is no more than His trustee. Man in Islam is Allah's Khalifa (vicegerent) and representative on earth. As His trustee, man is obliged to obey the instructions of the One who appointed him in this capacity.

There are clear and precise laws laid down by Allah about wealth and property. They concern the acquisition, use and disposal of property and relate to all forms of property whether it is for private use, trade, agriculture, industry or for any other purpose. The rules governing the acquisition of property are summarised in the expression Halal. Property can only be acquired through legitimate means. According to the Quran no part of property must have any doubtful association.

The owner of property is under an obligation to show his gratitude to Allah for purifying his wealth by paying Zakat, an obligatory tax. In addition to Zakat there are Sadaqaat; these are alms and charity over and above Zakat, paid voluntarily in order to express man's high sense of gratitude to Allah. It is evident from tradition and Islamic preaching that those who refuse to pay Zakat put themselves in the category of rebels who must be opposed. Zakat, like Salat (prayers five times a day) and fasting during the month of Ramadan, is a fundamental part of Islam representing the third of the five pillars of Islam. Muslims possessing property and wealth have a responsibility to the poor.

Payment of Zakat is a test of the believer's faith, distinguishing him from the faithless. It is a bond between man and his Creator, purifying the person of his selfishness, discouraging him from holding wealth and encouraging him to share it with others. In so doing Zakat offers security to the giver and a source of satisfaction and comfort.

Islam protects and safeguards the dignity of the individual in all circumstances, especially in relation to Sadaqaat. The poor are not to be degraded or despised for having to receive alms. In a truly Muslim society Sadaqaat are considered more beneficial to the giver than the receiver. The giver is rewarded in this world and in the Hereafter. Sadaqaat helps the poor in so far as it provides subsistence. The richer member of Islamic society is guided by the following rules in the Quran:

(1) You should not feel proud of your wealth.
(2) In managing your wealth you should seek the pleasure of Allah and the reward in the Hereafter.
(3) You must be kind and good to others (by giving) as Allah has been good to you (in bestowing upon you vast riches).
(4) You should not aim at causing corruption as Allah does not like those who cause corruption.

At the same time the Quran argues strongly against those who try to dispossess the rich of their wealth through extortion or other forcible means. The Quran uses the severest expression to describe usurers: 'Those who swallow usury shall stand in front of you only like a person who had been mad through the touch of Satan. That is, because they say trade is like usury. (But Allah has permitted trade and forbidden usury.) Whosoever receives admonition from Allah and gives up his error, his past sins shall be forgiven and his affairs committed to Allah. But whosoever reverts (to bad habits) shall suffer eternal hellfire'. The Quranic instructions about usury are clear: 'O you who believe, fear Allah and give up what remains of your claims of usury if you are truly believers. If you don't then take notice of war from Allah and His apostle. But if you repent then you shall be entitled to your capital sums so that no injustice is committed by you and no injustice suffered by you'.

ECONOMIC DEVELOPMENT IN ISLAMIC COUNTRIES

The question of economic development has assumed unprecedented importance. The world is dominated by countries which have achieved outstanding economic and technological advances and they co-exist with a multitude of countries exhibiting economic backwardness and the poverty associated with it. The search for a new international economic order to eliminate the economic gap dividing nations is today the primary objective of the United Nations. In the group of more than one hundred countries, representing two thirds of the world's population which suffers from a state of under-development and deprivation, the Muslim countries occupy a position of prominence. They are not only confronted with the all too familiar problems of development, they are also faced with the all-important question of finding a development model which suits their religious and ideological beliefs.

Although there is no strong argument against using external finance to foster development, there remains a strong desire for self-reliance in seeking economic progress. An Islamic society necessarily calls for all the population to supply both an individual and collective effort in the search for progress; self-discipline and personal sacrifice are required for the common good of society. In the case of Muslim countries the development efforts must reach over national boundaries; the Muslim World seeks a development model which is all-embracing.

There is a general recognition that the resources for development do exist in Muslim countries. There is sufficient human wealth and local raw materials to bring about development and to rid these countries of social imbalances and inadequate infrastructure. Currently Muslim countries typically import manufactured goods from the West, even when raw materials are available locally for domestic production. Utilising their energy resources and putting a greater emphasis upon improving the labour skills of Muslim countries through education and training, it is possible for infrastructure to be developed and for industry to flourish.

One crucial issue in the development process is clearly that of how investment can be financed. Although the Muslim World is able to accept many of the financial practices prevalent in the Western World, it is opposed to fixed interest payments on investments; equally Islam is against the hoarding of money. Consequently an alternative form of funding development needs to be organised such that neither interest or hoarding is present in the financial system.

Certainly this will take time to accomplish. The Muslim World has so far been unable to develop its own institutional framework. It has a history of colonialism, division and disintegration. Only in recent years has the Islamic consciousness been awakened and the possibilities of evolving an Islamic institutional framework been explored.

In selecting the development model most appropriate for the Muslim World three basic features are emerging as essential. The model should be compatible with the Islamic environment, it should have the ability to encourage people to mobilise and to use their abilities to foster development, and it should have flexibility. The development model employed in the Western World was primarily dependent upon a materialistic environment, with little spiritual basis whatsoever. Consequently the end product of development was assessed according to the material advancement achieved. Although the socialist world transferred the vehicle of development to the government and away from the entrepreneur and the market place, it nevertheless also sought material advancement. At the other extreme some capitalist societies were of the view that healthy economic development was only possible with the free participation of both consumers and producers and with limited government interference.

It cannot be denied that in Western Europe the development model employed has been successful; it has allowed participation in the development process and has, to a large extent, led to the realisation of their hopes and the economic conditions which they aspired to. In its extreme, the model has been based upon human desires and instincts, particularly the desire for money, possessions and power. The model allowed for these desires and instincts to persist and through them material advancement has taken place.

Whatever model in adopted, it must be flexible: it must be able to adapt to changing circumstances, economic or otherwise. It is evident that even though the economic society in the Islamic World may be in a state of backwardness, its concept of progress and advancement remains constant and continues to be associated with a Divine Constitution, namely the Holy Quran. This concept renders the Islamic society fundamentally different from other societies in their approach to life, the universe and humanity. The values determining the development approach of Islamic societies come from Allah. This wordliness is not the be-all and end-all of the Divine value system. For the Islamic society this world is a part of the Hereafter. Consequently, for the Islamic society, the material aspects of life must be closely linked with spiritual and moral factors. A purely materialistic model, whether capitalistic or socialistic, will not be acceptable in a truly Muslim society.

Growth and development are not one and the same thing. Growth is a simple and natural phenomenon, whereas development is a planned operation directed to the attainment of certain goals. Development is necessarily a collective function and can be at a national or regional level. If the entire development process could occur in a uniform pattern producing uniform results for the entire human society, the task of development would be without problems. In reality such success never exists and it becomes the function of planning to harmonise the process of change and to guarantee, as far as possible, a dynamic equilibrium as economic, social and political conditions change.

The experience of the developing world has been that the development plans which have been handed over to them have proved excessively ambitious; to meet the expense of such plans they have incurred a heavy burden of international debt. Consequently the gap between their living standards and those of the rich, developed countries has widened. Increasingly developing countries are resorting to pruning their development goals and making their development plans more modest. They are trying to adopt appropriate intermediate technology and are encouraging local small enterprises alongside the essential large-scale projects. They now feel it is necessary for them to invest in labour-intensive projects and to improve the quality of those of their products which can be internationally marketed. However, detrimental effects are resulting from this process. Consumption is increasing but urban congestion and pollution is becoming a problem in a world of poverty amid plenty.

There is no doubt that full comprehensive planning, which could allow for precautions against problems of disequilibrium and maladjustments, is the most effective pattern of development. It is only after many years of accumulating social costs and increasing moral laxity that economists have recognised that the maintenance, if not improvement, of moral values, and the achievement of social objectives are equally as important as the quest for economic objectives in the development process. In recent years economic progress has been linked to social goals. Ultimately the United Nations, in seeking a New International Economic Order, has outlined a charter of economic rights and duties for individuals and societies which exhibits certain moral standards. Many would agree that this has its foundation in Islamic principles; the creation of a sound economy must rest upon fairness and justice, social welfare and an equitable distribution of income and wealth.

The divisions which have existed in the Islamic World cannot be denied; but they are not the result of conflicts over Islamic ideology. More commonly they stem from the introduction of varieties of Marxist or liberal competition into Muslim countries, not always as result of a free choice within the countries concerned. In general the Muslim World is composed of countries which have gone through periods of Western colonialism or domination. Consequently the educational system imposed often had little relationship to the Islamic heritage of thought and belief.

A true Islamic educational system begins with the concept that man was created to worship Almighty God and therefore all man's activities should represent deeds performed in the service of God. To worship God in Islam is to devote all life's activities to God; this would include the pursuit of economic development and the fulfilment of social obligations. The form which economic development takes therefore and the social implications of that development must be approved not only by man but by God. Worshipping God in Islam is not by prayer and fasting alone, but is the way in which a society or individual conducts every aspect of life.

The development model applicable in the case of Muslim countries must conform with Islam's attitude to many aspects of life, in particular knowledge, work, capital, production and consumption. In Islam the road to increased knowledge is endless. A man of knowledge and learning is held in the highest esteem. But, unlike in other societies, in an Islamic society knowledge is recognised not just for the sake of knowledge but for building life. A person should not conceal his knowledge from others. People must be deliberate in speech and at the same time refrain from discussing subjects of which they do not have full knowledge. Idle talk of misinformation is un-Islamic. Work is also a virtue in Islam; again it represents a form of worship. Man is regarded as productive so long as he is able to work; Islam does not recognise a retirement age; provided man is capable of serving society he should continue to do so. This attack on idleness has its parallel in relation to money. Muslims are required to invest their money and not to squander it; they must promote production and invest in capital, refraining from excessive and wasteful consumption. Extravagances and miserliness are both undesirable.

Given that man is God's vicegerent on earth, his life must be devoted to developing earth; from this the Muslim should gain the highest motivation to work for economic progress. All men are created equals; all people must be treated alike; stability and order are pre-requisites for development; Islam orders its followers to be devoted to the community, to obey law and lawful authority. By doing so, a socio-political stability and security can be achieved and a platform for economic development established.

It is upon these general principles that the Islamic development model must be founded. If greater efforts are made to interpret these abstract motives in terms of the daily routine of economic life there will be an opportunity for the Muslim World to reach for fairness and justice, for the full participation of the individual and the community in economic life and for the security and stability it desires for society.

3

Islamic Banking Operations

DEPOSIT TAKING

Deposit taking is the major source of funds in the Islamic banks. Its importance is underlined by the fact that it is virtually cost-free as the Islamic banks do not pay interest on deposits but depositors share in the profit, if any, of the fund users.

Islamic banks currently offer the following types of deposit account: (1) Deposits payable on demand, such as current accounts, saving accounts, and ordinary deposits at call or short notice. (2) Investment deposit accounts.

Current accounts

Islamic current accounts are a service offered mainly to Islamic bank depositors to process bank transfers and pay cheques drawn on them through the normal national and international clearing systems. These accounts are payable on demand, and no interest or profit is received on such accounts. The value date system as known in conventional banks is not applicable to these accounts. The capital of the Islamic bank is fully subject to the claims of holders of Islamic current accounts. This type of account is considered as an interest-free loan (Qard Hassan) from the acount holder to the bank, the first being a lender (when money is deposited) and the second a borrower. When cheques are drawn on the account, the account holder becomes a borrower and the bank a lender.

Current accounts in foreign currency, mainly US dollars, may be opened in many Islamic banks, eg Faisal Islamic Bank (Egypt), Faisal Islamic Bank (Sudan), Islamic Bank International (IBI). This is, of course, in addition to the opportunity of opening current accounts in the domestic currency where the bank is located. Recently it has been possible in IBI-Denmark to open a current account in three major foreign currencies, namely, the US dollar, deutsche mark, and pound sterling. The minimum funds accepted for the opening of these accounts must not be less than US$ 10,000 or equivalent.

Bonus and fees on current accounts

Normally most Islamic banks do not charge fees or pay interest on current account balances. However, in Al-Baraka International Limited (ABIL), a licensed London-based deposit taker, a slightly different situation arises; when a 'bonus current account' is opened, in either pounds sterling or US dollars, a bonus is paid on the average balance in excess of £2,500 (the bonus level) or equivalent. To qualify for the bonus, the balance should be maintained for at least six consecutive months. The debtor is allowed to give a bonus to the creditor either in the form of an increase on the amount of the debt or any other sign of gratitude in compliance with the Prophet's saying: 'The best from among you are those who discharge their debts in the best way possible'. However, Islamic jurists have put two restrictions on this practice: (1) the amount of compensation should not be stipulated in the loan contract, and (2) this act must not become a common practice; otherwise it will not be more than a remuneration of capital in a straightforward loan which is forbidden under Islamic law.

Although some banks advocate charging customers for current account services other banks do not, provided a minimum balance is maintained. Such services may be free of charge since the benefits accruing to the bank from investing the floating balance more than offset the cost. For this reason a free service is considered by some jurists as some kind of compensation by the bank to the account holder. As such it is regarded as a disguised interest and therefore should not be permitted.

Savings accounts

In a commercial investment Islamic bank, ordinary saving accounts (excluding term deposits) are payable on demand. The procedures and formalities of depositing and withdrawing are almost identical in both systems. An exception is noted when a saving account is opened in an Islamic bank. The depositor may (if he wishes) assign to the bank the right to invest the deposited sum. Since interest is forbidden, profits (or losses) are realised upon investing a certain portion of these types of deposits in short-term financing. If the depositor chooses not to assign that right, the saving account would be similar to a current account, although a passbook may still be used.

Profits of saving accounts are normally less than profits of fixed investment deposit accounts, the reason being that saving deposits can be withdrawn on demand as in the Kuwait Finance House and in some other institutions within a few days' notice.

Investment deposit accounts

Investment deposit accounts are called 'Islamic participating accounts'. In practice, there are two main kinds of investment accounts; specified and unspecified.

In the first category the depositor authorises the bank to invest the deposited sum in particular projects or sectors. For this reason these accounts are sometimes called 'conditional' or 'limited investment accounts' because they are geared to a specific sector(s) or project(s). The Islamic banks may invest part of their own funds along with the depositor's and in this case they would share the profit/loss with the account holder. In the second category the depositor gives the Islamic bank an unconditional authorisation to invest the deposited sum without any restriction as to sector or project; provided, that is, that all financing deals are in compliance with Islamic principles and fall within the bank's investment criteria. These accounts are held for short-term periods ranging from three, six, nine or twelve months irrespective of their type. They are also held for longer-term periods of up to five years.

Eligibility for profits differs from one bank to another. To encourage small savers, the Faisal Islamic Bank of Egypt's profits are paid on one-month deposits, whereas in the Faisal Islamic Bank of Sundan and the Dubai Islamic Bank profits are paid on three- and twelve-month deposits respectively. However, in the Islamic banks of Pakistan profits are calculated on a points product method.

In Al-Baraka International Limited (ABIL), a fixed-term deposit (of not less than £5,000 or equivalent) may be opened in the name of a UK resident or non-resident. The minimum term is one month or a multiple of one month. To comply with the Bank of England's regulations concerning the depositors right to a secured return on fixed-term deposits, ABIL undertakes to invest these deposits in 'a manner calculated to give a minimum return' which could be anything from 0.5 to 2 per cent of the deposited sum. In cases where the actual profit exceeds this rate, a bonus would be credited to the account to cover for the difference between the minimum and the actual return. A withdrawal notice of not less than seven days before maturity must be given; failing this, the account is renewed for another term on the same conditions as before.

FORMS OF FINANCING OPERATIONS

Introduction

In the conventional banking system, personal or corporate loans are performed through a simple financing mechanism. The banks, acting as financial intermediaries, accept deposits from the public and lend them to the borrowers, regardless of whether these borrowers are individuals or corporate entities. The banks' profits are mainly attributed to the difference between interest expended (paid) to depositors, and interest earned (received) from borrowers.

In the Islamic banking system the issue is rather more complicated. Money does not earn money without a collaboration between capital and effort. Therefore depositors do not earn an automatic fixed return on their deposits as in the conventional system. A link has to be introduced so that the expected earnings of depositors are directly related to, and constitute a proportion of, the profits earned by entrepreneurs. None the less, financing or participating instruments vary to suit the financial needs in the market and to provide short-, medium- and long-term funds. These Islamic instruments take one or more of the following forms: Mudaraba, Musharaka, Murabaha and Ijara wa Iktina. The definitions and mechanism surrounding each type are discussed below.

Mudaraba

Mudaraba (capital trust) was a pre-Islamic custom used to finance a significant portion of the caravan trade in Arabia. Orientalists believe that 'commenda', as it came to be known in the Medieval West around the tenth century, was adopted from the Islamic commercial practice that was in operation as early as the sixth century.

In jurisprudence terms, Mudaraba is a contract in profit sharing, with one party providing funds and the other the work. In other words, Mudaraba (or Qirad) is a contract between two parties: an Islamic bank as an investor (Rab al-Mal) who provides a second party, the entrepreneur (Mudareb) with financial resources to finance a particular project. Profits, if any, are shared between the two parties in a proportion agreed in advance. Losses, if any, are the liability of the Islamic bank, and the Mudareb loses only his efforts and his expected share in the profits.

Mudaraba is best adopted in project and trade financing. Some Hanbali jurists (or Fuqaha) allow its usage in financing agriculture and in financing small businesses or workmanships. In pursuing this type of financing an Islamic bank may use its own funds, its depositors' funds or both. The contractual relationship between the Islamic bank and depositors or between the bank and entrepreneur varies with respect to the source of funds utilised.

(1) If the bank uses its own funds, it is said to be an investor (Sahib al-Mal) and the entrepreneur a Mudareb;
(2) If the bank employs the depositors' funds without committing any of its own, the bank would be acting as an agent for the depositors from the time the deposits are accepted to the time when the money is invested in a Mudaraba contract. At this stage the bank becomes a Mudareb with respect to the depositors, and a Sahib al-Mal (investor) with respect to the entrepreneur. It is conceivable, however, that this dual identity can be eliminated if the bank acts in its fiduciary capacity from the time deposits

23

are accepted to the time when the Mudareb contract is terminated.

(3) If the bank utilises a mixture of its own funds and that of the depositors, the bank would act as an agent for the depositors, whereas between the bank and the entrepreneur the former acts in its own capacity as an investor.

The application of Mudaraba in financing current Islamic banking operations is very limited owning to the restrictions of Mudaraba transactions. These restrictions inhibit its wider application to cover many sectors in the economy. For instance, the majority of Islamic scholars argue that Mudaraba should be limited to self-liquidating transactions. Here the assets of the Mudaraba are easily recognisable and must be realised and liquidated so that the proceeds can be easily distributed between the partners at the termination of operations, completion of deal, or the achievement of the Mudaraba objectives. If the partners want to renew the Mudaraba a new contract must be negotiated, but only after the old one has been terminated and the rights and liabilities of the parties concerned have been recognised and settled. The argument for this rather stringent rule is based on the terms and conditions applied in Mudaraba contracts. The most important of these, according to the majority of Islam jurists, are that:

(1) Mudaraba should be limited to trading activities such as buying and selling.
(2) The entrepreneur has no right to mix the Mudaraba funds and his own funds.
(3) Before liquidation and distribution of profits, the Mudareb possesses an uncontested right not only to his share in the profits but also to any gains or appreciation in the value of output or assets of the joint venture that might occur during the life of the Mudaraba contract. Furthermore the determination of the partners might require detailed calculation which is time-consuming, especially if such an exercise has to be done several times a year.
(4) The Mudaraba accounts must be recorded properly and audited independently, a rather awesome task especially for small businesses when the cost involved is not justifiable.

However, a broader definition of Mudaraba - that may be applied in various economic activities - needs further research and thorough analysis. For one thing, the majority of Islamic jurists hold the view that Mudaraba contracts are confined to commercial activities. None the less, this does not mean that new ideas or modern concepts have to be shelved. On the contrary, the evolution and continuation of Islamic banking are largely dependent on new and innovative approaches to finance. Trying to assign old labels to new financial instruments serves only to confuse the issue and may not be applicable given the new realities

24

of business finance and its complexities. After all, Islamic banking and finance is a new concept in many respects; it will not be impaired if new approaches are adopted, provided always that they serve the needs of modern societies, and comply with the Sharia.

Musharaka financing (participation finance)

Musharaka financing is a well established partnership contract in Islamic law and was operative in the early Islamic period. It is also one of the most popular means of financing, outside banking systems, among commercial or small industrial sectors in Arabic and Islamic cities.

In the context of Islamic banking, Musharaka is described as a joint venture between an Islamic bank and a customer or business entity geared for certain operations and may terminate within a specified period of time, or when certain conditions are met. Contrary to Mudaraba, the two partners in Musharaka participate in the capital of the venture. Profits are allocated according to an agreed proportion, allowing for managerial skills to be remunerated. However, if losses occur, they are borne by the partners in proportion to their contribution to the capital. For example, the bank may participate in 60 per cent of the capital, though its share in profits might not exceed 50 per cent. Whilst in the case of losses the bank's liability must not be less than 60 per cent. The bank's right to ask for collateral or surety is limited by Sharia for this type of financing.

The Islamic bank may finance industry, trade, real estate, contracting and almost all legal enterprises through equity or direct participation. Musharaka is well suited for financing private or public companies and particularly in project financing for short-, medium- and long-term periods. The Faisal Islamic Bank in Sudan, for example, finances selected projects and assists in the procurement of production equipment on a Musharaka basis for periods of up to three years. In all cases projects are evaluated; if they are economically feasible and expected to be profitable, and if the would-be partner has adequate experience, the extent of the Bank's participation is then negotiated.

There are two main types of Musharaka agreement: (1) Musharaka related to certain projects or deals and terminating with the project's completion, and (2) Redeemable Musharaka. In the latter category, the bank recaptures the committed investment progressively with the project's ability to generate profits and an adequate cash flow sufficient to pay back the bank's initial investment and the agreed shares in profits. This type of deal is similar to redeemable participation in conventional banking systems.

Musharaka financing is characterised by the following features:

(1) First and foremost the Islamic bank is not guaranteed a fixed return on its participation.
(2) Equity participation of venture capital in the conventional system does not

preclude the project from borrowing and incurring interest payments. In the Islamic system, borrowing at a fixed interest rate from a commercial bank is forbidden. Clearly circumstances may arise when Musharaka financing may be set alongside fixed interest borrowing; should this happen, the Islamic bank may be prepared to take steps to renew the interest borrowing. This is the case, for example, with the International Islamic Bank for Investment and Development in Egypt; it is prepared to inject fresh money to buy out other banks or creditors for projects, and by so doing it clears the balance sheet of any interest-bearing debts.

(3) Whether a bank steps in to finance fixed assets, working capital or both, the bank's benefits lie in the profit-sharing scheme between the bank and the venture.

(4) Profits are shared *pro rata* with equity (total shareholders' rights) and are calculated for this purpose, after allowing for management fees and before depreciation and provisions, as non-cash items.

(5) At the outset it appears that using leverage (mainly overdraft) with equity participation is not advocated in the Islamic banking system. However, an Islamic bank may extend free interest participation to alleviate liquidity shortages on a short-term basis.

None the less, the extent of Musharaka financing ranges from 7 to 10 per cent of the total financing package of Islamic banks.

Murabaha (mark-up on sale)

Murabaha is available for financing the purchase or import of capital goods, consumable goods or raw materials. Under the agreement, the customer provides the bank with the specifications and quotations of the goods to be purchased. The Islamic bank studies the documents with reference to the price, specification and conditions for payment. In many instances the bank may be able to obtain the same goods from a different supplier at more favourable conditions than those obtained by the customer. When the bank and its customer have agreed on the terms of the deal, the former purchases the goods or commodities and passes the title to the customer at a later date. The profit accruing to the bank is mutually agreed as mark-up on the cost of purchase. There are certain fundamental principles attached to Murabaha which are overlooked in the existing literature and should be emphasised here:

(1) The purchase price should be declared to the client, especially where the bank succeeds in obtaining a discount or rebate. Since the mark-up is calculated on the net purchase price, any discount or rebate obtained has to be acknowledged and accounted for to the benefit of the client. This procedure is a strict application of Murabaha rules.

(2) The goods themselves must be classified and clearly identified according to international or commonly accepted standards or classifications, otherwise Murabaha contracts are void.

(3) The third element relates to whether the original agreement between the Islamic bank and the customer is binding or not.

There are two methods of dealing with this third element. In Dar Al-Maal Al-Islami the customer requests the bank to purchase the goods and submits an intent to buy same on arrival; this promise is binding. In the Kuwait Finance House the customer gives a non-binding promise to buy the commodities that were purchased by KFH on his behalf. Some scholars argue that the promise to buy the goods, before the title is transferred and the goods are in the bank's custody, must not be binding for two reasons: (a) if the promise were binding, then the transaction would be similar to an ordinary letter of credit and the mark-up would not be more than a disguised interest; (b) the occidental principle in Islamic contracts prohibits binding agreements whereby a party promises to deliver or sell goods he does not own.

However, the problem is resolved within Sharia principles as follows: (a) the promise or intent to buy is not binding as long as the goods are not purchased; and (b) custody of the goods is not always necessary since it is widely accepted that the bill of lading is the document of title in international trade. Once issued, an Islamic bank would be able to sign the sales agreement with the customer. The transfer of title would be affected by endorsing the bill upon arrival of the goods at the port of destination.

Nevertheless, when the shipping documents are received by the bank, the accounts party is notified and requested to honour his promise to buy within two weeks at most. The amount to be paid by the accounts could be paid by the bank as an interest-free loan from the bank to the latter until the settlement date. In cases where the client has a credit balance in the bank which is less than the value of the transaction, the latter may finance the gap to conclude the deal. When the goods are sold, profits will be distributed in proportion to the parties' contributions.

The same basic principles of Murabaha as outlined above, particularly the transfer of title and the physical custody of the goods, apply to domestic trade and finance by means of an instrument called 'international Murabaha'. Here, although the client must open an account in the bank prior to opening the letter of credit, it is not uncommon for the bank to require a cash cover from the client to ensure payment, in addition to endorsing commercial papers in favour of the bank as in the conventional banking system.

There are some arguments that the service fee must not be proportional to the amount of the letter of credit, on the grounds that the paper and administrative work are not related to the value of the letter of credit. It is difficult to quantify exactly the actual expenses related to each letter. A minimum charge rate of ½ per cent, as recommended by the Kuwait Finance

House Religious Supervisory Board, is considered fair and common.

As far as repayment terms are concerned, they are flexible and simple. Once the purchase price plus the bank's margin have been agreed, repayment can be stretched over a period of 6 to 24 months and sometimes 36 months, depending on the market pattern of the commodity and the terms of trade. In any case, repayment may be discharged by instalment or on a lump sum basis.

Sometimes a client may finance the purchase of the goods by using his own funds. In this case, the bank acts merely as an agent charging a service fee, but no commission is charged for the extension of the letter of credit. In Islamic law this operation is called Mutajara.

In summary, Murabaha financing has gained momentum in Islamic banking operations. For example, Al-Rajhi Group, London branch, a subsidiary of Al-Rajhi Islamic Bank of Saudi Arabia has so far confined its operations to Murabaha with a turnover of US$ 3 billion in the first three years of operation! In the Islamic Bank in Luxembourg, Murabaha financing reached around 37 per cent of its total financing in the year ending 30 June 1984.

Ijara (lease financing)

The exact meaning of the term Ijara is 'reward' or 'recompense'. Its use started before Islam, was regularised during the early expansion of Islam and has now been adapted to modern needs. Under its terms, a business or individual client may request the bank to purchase machinery or equipment with the intention of renting it to the client. Ijara financing is based upon valuing the financial position of the client and the expected direct cash flow of the lease contract in the same manner as in ordinary lease financing decisions in a conventional bank, though without taking interest into consideration.

This instrument of financing has gained momentum in the conventional banking system owing in part to its tax advantages. In many countries the rental payments are tax deductible. In Islamic finance there are two forms of leasing:

(1) Direct leasing finance, whereby the Islamic bank allows the customer to use capital assets owned by the bank for a limited period of time ranging from a few days to a few months or years depending on the type of asset in question. In return the lessee pays a monthly or annual rental fee.

(2) Lease and purchase finance (Ijara wa Iktina), whereby the Islamic bank rents the assets to the customer who promises to purchase the asset within a specified period. The rental payment could be a fixed amount or a percentage directly related to the cash flow of the project and consists of the bank's share in the net profit attributable to the asset plus the rental charges. According to this profit-sharing method, when the total rental charges equal the cost of the asset, the asset ownership will be transferred to the customer.

Alternatively, the leasee may open a savings account in the bank which will be credited with each payment. The funds in this account would be invested by the bank and the proceeds credited to the account as well. Once the total amounts accumulated in the account equal the purchase price of the asset, the lessee pays the bank and acquires the asset.

The transfer of title depends on the nature of the deal. If a lump sum payment is agreed upon, the title will be transferred to the customer upon exercising his option and paying the agreed price. While if the payment was made by tranches and spread over a period of time, the transfer of title, in this case, will be gradual and the bank's title to the property decreases proportionally, as well as the rental fees, with the successive payments of the tranches.

SOCIAL SERVICES OF ISLAMIC BANKS

Social services are considered to be an integral part of Islamic banking operations. In many Islamic banks it is an important function and not merely secondary to the operations discussed above. These services may be classified into three main areas: benevolent loans (Qard Hassan) and overdrafts, collection and distribution of Zakat fund, Sadaqaat (donations) and activities associated with the preservation of the Islamic culture and heritage.

Benevolent loans

The act of lending money is not prohibited in Islam. On the contrary, Islamic teachings urge that assistance be given to the needy in the alleviation of hardships. Consequently, an Islamic bank may lend money on an interest-free basis to a number of beneficiaries which might include:

(1) Depositors who maintain regular accounts.
(2) Shareholders in certain circumstances.
(3) Companies or clients who have already been financed by the bank. The purpose of the interest-free loan, in this case, varies according to the circumstances; it may for example be to meet a liquidity crisis or to pay a foreign correspondent in lieu of a documentary letter of credit. The amount paid by the bank is considered an interest-free loan from the time of payment until the settlement date.
(4) For education, marriages and other social purposes.

All these loans are payable within a specified period either by instalment or lump sum amount.

However, inter-bank loans on a mark-up basis, as currently practised in Pakistan, are not permitted. It is evident that the banks are permitting themselves what they forbid to their customers, which is in principle unjustifiable.

29

Overdrafts

The Islamic Banking Conference decided, in Dubai in 1979, that it is perfectly acceptable for a customer to overdraw his current account. This is looked at normally as an overdraft in the conventional system. However the Islamic bank does not charge interest or fees on overdrafts, which are treated as interest-free loans. There are, however, two conditions to be observed: first, the overdraft should be for short-term periods; second, they must not exceed an upper limit to be decided upon by each bank separately.

The Islamic Development Bank has laid down the terms and conditions associated with benevolent loans:

(1) Adequate legal and economic considerations of the transaction in question must be met;
(2) Adequate securities and guarantees and other safeguards must be secured;
(3) The requested loan must be for productive and not consumption purposes;
(4) The loan amount must be small and fall within the limits laid down by the Board regarding duration and value.

GUARANTEES, TRANSFERS AND COLLECTIONS

These services include performance bonds, letters of guarantee, letters of credit, travellers cheques, money transfer, foreign exchange transactions and safe deposits etc. The Islamic bank may collect a service fee corresponding to the exact expenses incurred by the bank on the services rendered. However, when the transaction involves the sale and purchase of gold or precious metals on behalf of a customer, the Islamic bank may charge a commission in its capacity as an agent; this is perfectly legal under Islamic law.

Letters of guarantee (LG)

Principally, the issuance and acceptance of letters of guarantee are not a matter of dispute in Islamic banks. The controversy amongst Islamic jurists relates to a situation where the fees charged on this service are proportional with the amount of the guarantee. The crux of the matter rests on the fact that the guarantee according to traditional Islamic jurisprudence is a non-profit contract which means that it must be given free of charge as a 'human service'. According to the traditional views, Islamic banks are prevented from taking proportional fees and concurrently they are prevented from rendering this service as it involves risks which are not remunerated. However, whilst these jurists do not allow the bank to make commission and assume uncovered risk, by contrast, they allow the bank to accept proportional or lump sum commission if the LG is partially or totally covered by the customer. A second group of jurists classify the guarantees into profitable and non-profitable and consider LGs as profitable and as such allow the Islamic banks to charge fees and commissions in compensation for the risk involved. On the other hand, some banks have required the customer to cover about 20–30 per cent of the guarantee and in return they issue the LG free of charge. A new approach has looked at the guarantee, according to Gamal Attia, as 'a kind of finance' to be remunerated by a share of the profit generated by the transaction for which the LG was issued.

The religious boards in all Islamic banks supervise the authenticity of these services and sanction the rate of the service charge or fees, advising on the conformity of these service charges with Shariah.

Advisory and financial banking services

Advisory and financial services offered by Islamic banks are numerous and designed to widen the scope of convenient operation for the customers and facilitate their business. Amongst these services are financial planning, consulting, property management, preparation of feasibility studies and project evaluation, stock issues and collection of call issues, trustee services and finally agency operations.

Foreign remittances

Money transfer may be affected by a number of forms and means of payment. The more widely accepted and used are cheques, drafts and money orders (whether by mail or telex).

A few centuries ago money transfer in the Islamic world was quite common in financial transactions across boarders. Suftadja, literally a draft, is a financial instrument used for transmitting money from one place to another. Suftadja principles are well established and clearly defined in both the Islamic and commercial laws of many Arab and Islamic countries. Such drafts are used both at individual and institutional levels, especially for transferring money from the Central Government to provinces and vice versa. Few Islamic jurists are inclined to discourage its acceptance on the grounds that the transmitter, or the money changer, guarantees the remittance against the 'risks of the road'. They argue that when the sender pays in advance a sum of money to the money changer who issues the Suftadja, a debtor/creditor relationship has ensued. Thus the sender, who becomes a creditor, has made an unlawful benefit represented by the safety of the transferred money without an apparent corresponding benefit to the transmitter. Therefore, they allege this kind of transaction ought to be declined to avoid the doubt of Riba. However, the Encyclopaedia of Islamic Law (1970) has pointed out that the transfer of money benefits both parties and not

31

only the sender and as such it is a lawful service. Moreover, securing money against the risks of the road is a normal and legitimate benefit and is not similar to a pure monetary gain enjoyed by the lender in a loan contract which is said to be usury. The money transfer is an absolute necessity for tourists, students and non-residents who have to remit funds to their families etc. What must be observed, however, is that the issue of a draft or money should be made simultaneously and the spot exchange rate has to be used.

Transfer of debts and bills collection

The transfer of debt was not known in Roman law as it was not possible to transfer the debt to a new debtor or creditor without liquidating the old debt and establishing a new debtor/creditor relationship with a new debt. Although it was possible to appoint a proxy to collect the debt, it was not an efficient disposition since the principal had the full power to cancel the proxy before the effective collection of debt.

Hawala, or the transfer of debt, dates back to the sixth century and became the basis for other financial instruments. While the transfer of credit was not known in the European community until the enactment of the old French law of 1803 it was first introduced in the civil law in Germany in 1886, and in England partly in 1875 and finally in 1925.

Collection of bills through the Islamic bank is a legal act since collection is only a service rendered by the bank on behalf of the owner or endorser of the bill. The bank is entitled to obtain a fee or service charge for such works.

Bills discounting

Discounting is an act of endorsing a bill of exchange by the beneficiary to a bank. In consideration thereof, the bank pays the beneficiary the amount of the bill, in advance, less the discount proportion. Normally the discount rate includes commissions and endorsement fees plus the interest rate on the value of the bill from the discount date to maturity. As explained earlier, there is no question regarding the validity of the service fee. As for the interest charged by the bank, the Islamic Law Encyclopaedia in Kuwait rules that discounting of bills by a bank is not valid in Islamic jurisprudence for the following reasons.

(1) The transfer of debt from the endorser to the bank is not valid due to the inequality between the transferred debt and the debt to be collected.
(2) By the same token, it is not a loan either, since the amount paid by the bank is less than that to be collected from the debtor.
(3) It is not also a selling of debt due to the fact that the selling of pecuniary assets for same is only valid if an equal value of a currency were

exchanged for an equivalent value of the same or of another currency; otherwise the transaction would lead to Riba al-Fadl.

However, there is virtually no harm in requesting the Islamic bank to collect the bills for certain reasonable fees to be agreed upon. The absolute banning of these types of transactions by the Islamic Encyclopaedia is most probably related to the normal discounting practices applied by conventional banks. Consequently the Islamic banks have found it proper to extend interest-free loans to their customers by holding the bills as collateral.

Types of notes and means of payment

There are virtually three recognised types of notes or bills in Islamic financial dealings: the cheque, the bill of exchange and the promissory note. A cheque is a note by which a drawer advises the drawee, normally a bank, to pay a specified sum of money to a third person called the beneficiary. A bill of exchange is a commercial paper by which the drawer (the creditor) orders another person (the debtor) to pay a sum of money at a certain date to a designated beneficiary or to bearer. A promissory note is an undertaking by the signatory to pay a specified sum of money, at a certain date, to a second person called the beneficiary.

MONEY AND CAPITAL MARKETS

In principle, an Islamic bank is able to underwrite securities and to be active in trading and selling. Portfolio selection or equity participation is governed by certain rules and regulations that should be strictly adhered to, such as (1) the company issuing the shares should not deal or trade in banned operations and should not be a financial institution whose main activities are directly related to trading interest-based securities, or syndication, underwriting and management of interest-bearing bonds; (2) dividends or yields must not be guaranteed or stated in advance; and (3) in retrospect, dealings in preference shares are not allowed on the grounds that they entitle the holder to preferential rights as to dividends and they bear a fixed rate of return.

Money market transactions are confined and restricted in the conventional banking system. Money market instruments such as banker's acceptance, inter-bank loans (except benevolent loans), short sales, trading on the margins and currency option are entirely forbidden in their present form under Islam due to the interest factor and fixed yield as well as to the unwarranted risk inherent in these instruments.

By the same token, trading and issuing of certificates of deposit and bonds, whether yielding fixed or floating rates of interest and whether convertible to shares or not, are not allowed in Islamic banks. The issuance of these certificates is permissible when the yields are related to the profits of the project. Zero-coupon bonds which are bought at discount are also banned on the grounds that the discount is merely the difference between the face value and the purchase price and represents the accumulated interest on the purchase price.

ISLAMIC CERTIFICATES OR SUKUKS (BONDS)

To attract deposits and mobilise savings, the Islamic banks have issued various types of bonds for different transactions. In 1981 DMI Trust introduced the DMI equity participation certificate (EPC). The DMI/EPC was launched in order to increase DMI capital by US $210m. In the first phase of this issue, closed in January 1981, 2 million units were issued at US $105 each excluding a fee of US $5. The minimum subscription was set up at ten equity units totalling US $1,100. Interestingly DMI had undertaken to buy back these certificates from selling participants if the sale fell within the criteria established by DMI to control risks and costs of market dealing activities, though the prospectus for this particular issue was vague regarding the overall limits and sub-limits for such repurchase. Nonetheless, DMI has committed itself to act as market maker pledging at the same time not to support the price, if it was held within sustainable levels! The Islamic Investment Company of the Gulf (IIC), a subsidiary of DMI, has issued several Mudaraba Certificates including the 'Islamic Institutional Reserve' Mudaraba (IRM), several issues of 'Islamic Mudaraba for current Investment' (MCI), and Islamic Mudaraba for Investment Savings and Solidarity among Muslims.

As the titles imply, these certificates are based on the same principle as Mudaraba or trust fund where the subscriber is the 'beneficial owner' and IIC is the 'managing trustee'. The objective of Islamic institutional reserves Mudaraba (in denominations of US $100,000) is to create a vehicle through which the Islamic institutions and businessmen may invest on a short-term or medium-term basis on Islamic principles. Holders of IRMs are entitled to two benefits excluding the profits from the certificates. First, IIC may issue, upon request, letters of credit in values that may equal up to four times the institution's portfolios, provided that the institution's credit ratings are satisfactory. Second, IIC may consider financing the total cost of an acceptable trade transaction. The profits of the deal would be shared between IIC and the holder of IRMs. In both cases the investor would receive profits on his investments. Ninety per cent of the declared profits go to the certificate holder and the rest to the investment company, in addition to management fees of not less than one dollar per one thousand dollars invested.

DMI is also trying to establish an 'inter-institutional market' for Equity Participation Certificates through its subsidiaries and to list it on the leading stock exchange.

The Islamic Mudaraba for Current Investment (MCI) works on the same basis as IRMs except that the minimum subscription is US $500. Withdrawal from the scheme is permissible either partially or totally and is effective in the first five days of the month following the investor's instructions. As the Mudaraba is managed monthly by using computer financial systems, profits may be calculated and recorded on a monthly basis.

The Islamic Mudaraba for Investment Savings and Solidarity among Muslims (MIS) is the Islamic counterpart to life insurance. The instalment paid by each participant in addition to the profit, if any, will be accumulated until the insured reaches the age of 60. Insurance compensation will be paid in case of death out of the profits of each participant (as a gratuitous contribution to Islamic solidarity) to the heirs of the deceased before the age of 60. For each certificate issued, the heirs receive: (1) an amount equivalent to the total instalments paid prior to the date of death; (2) any profit earned on these investments; and (3) a solidarity benefit in the form of a contribution out of the profits of surviving participants equal to the outstanding balances less any arrears.

For example, if a 40-year-old participant applies for four certificates of US $10,000 each, and dies after paying five annual instalments, the total compensation will amount to:

5 annual instalments paid	US $10,000
Profits earned	$2,000
15 unpaid instalments	$36,000
Total	$48,000

The Saudi based Islamic Development Bank (IDB) issues certificate of deposits to individuals and institutions in a minimum denomination of US $250,000. The proceeds of these certificates are employed in financing foreign trade activities among member countries or their institutions.

The Islamic Jordanian Bank is authorised by its charter to issue two types of Muqarada (trust) bonds. The joint Muqarada bonds are fixed-term bonds ranging normally from one to ten years. The participants in the joint Muqarada bonds receive an annual yield equivalent to a share in the net profits of the bank in the year following the issue date. The specified Muqarada bonds are lined with specified investment enterprises managed separately by the bank. The investors in the specified Muqarada bonds are not entitled to a share in the net profit of the bank. They share only in the net profits of each Muqarada bond on a percentage basis.

The Bahrain Islamic Bank is entitled, according to the articles of association, to issue a negotiable profit-sharing investment certificate. However, it does not appear that the bank has utilised this privilege yet. Pakistan was the first Islamic country that regularised the issuance of Mudaraba certificates by a special law called the Mudaraba Companies and Mudaraba Flotation and Control Ordinance, 1980. Four types of Mudaraba Certificates are allowed: multi-purpose perpetual Mudaraba, multi-purpose fixed period Mudaraba, specified purpose perpetual Mudaraba and specified purpose fixed period Mudaraba.

COMMUNITY TRADING

Generally the Islamic banks are currently involved in spot cash markets. Future contracts are permissible within the following boundaries:

(1) Future (Baya-li-Ajal) sales require the transfer of the goods to the possession of the buyer, while payment will be due in the future and would be higher than in cash sales.
(2) Al-Salam (forward buying) requires cash payments in consideration for goods, that will be delivered in the future. Salam contract stipulates the specific identification and determination of the commodities in terms of weight, measurement index, and duration of the contract.

The following types of sale are also allowed.

(3) Tawliya (break-even sale), 'to sell at cost'.
(4) Wadi'a, 'to sell at a discount'.

It is worth noting that options in commodities and shares are permissible, in principle, if they are between two parties alone since the permissibility of selling or transferring the option to a third party is currently debatable among Islamic jurists.

4

The International Association of Islamic Banks (IAIB), The Higher Religious Supervisory Board and Dar Al-Maal Al-Islami

THE INTERNATIONAL ASSOCIATION OF ISLAMIC BANKS (IAIB)

The International Association of Islamic Banks was established on 6 Ramadan 1397 (20 August 1977) and received immediate acceptance from the Islamic Conference of Foreign Ministers. The Conference recommended that the member states of the Organisation of Islamic Conferences (OIC) fully support the Association. The text of the agreement to establish the Association was deposited with the OIC which in turn distributed the text to all its member states in 1978. The Association was given an observer status by the OIC. Consequently, the Association has been represented at all the conferences of Islamic Foreign Ministers since the ninth conference, and has also attended the Islamic Summits from the third onwards as an observer. It has played an active role in the meetings of the Central Banks and monetary agencies of Islamic countries as well as in the meetings of specialised bodies of the OIC in the field of banking and insurance.

Aims and activities

In broad terms the Association aims to strengthen ties between the Islamic financial institutions, fostering co-operation, co-ordinating their activities and monitoring their operations to ensure that they conform with Islam. The Association provides technical assistance and expertise to Islamic communities wishing to establish Islamic banks and assists in the development of such banks both at national and international levels. It co-ordinates information and data about clients with absolute confidentiality and helps to overcome obstacles likely to be faced by member banks without interfering with their executive affairs. It also represents the common interests of Islamic banks at national and international level, arranges capital movement between Islamic banks and unifies operating procedures. It develops and runs programmes to improve the efficiency of employees of Islamic banks, provides advice, conducts studies relating to Islamic projects and prepares proposals for securing financial resources. It also conducts publicity campaigns to disseminate knowledge about Islamic business concepts and dealings.

The board of directors

The Board of Directors is the highest authority of the Association and comprises the presidents of the member banks or their nominees. An entrance fee and an annual subscription is paid to the Association by the member banks.

The Board's term of office is five years. However, if any member bank fails to honour its financial obligations, disregards any of its other constitutional obligations or commits any act which may harm the Association, it may be deprived of its membership by the Board.

The Board holds six-monthly meetings which may be attended by representatives of regional and international Islamic bodies and other experts who have the right to participate in the discussions but not to vote. Resolutions of the Board are adopted by a simple majority of those present, a quorum being a simple majority of the members of the Association. In the event of a deadlock, the President has a casting vote.

The powers of the Board of Directors include the following:

(1) Amendment of the constitution.
(2) Election of the President and Vice-President of the Association.
(3) Approval of the rules and procedures of the Association.
(4) Appointment of the Secretary General.
(5) Determination of member banks' entrance fee and subscription.
(6) Adoption of annual budget estimates and closing accounts.
(7) Consideration of reports of the Secretary General on the activities of the Supreme Legal Supervisory Body concerning the extent of member banks' adherence to the Sharia in the conduct of their business.
(8) Appointment of auditors, approval of their fees and consideration of their reports.

The term of office of the President and the Vice-President is five years and is renewable. The President convenes and chairs meetings of the Board and generally presides over the meetings of the Association, assuming also any powers that may be entrusted to him by the Board.

General Secretariat

The General Secretariat is the technical and administrative body of the Association; it may also be affiliated with any other special body if that affiliation is considered necessary for the achievement of the aims and objectives of the Association. The Secretary General, who is appointed on nomination of the President for a five year renewable term, is the executive agent of the Board. The official language of the Association is Arabic. The Association has its own independent budget with its financial year beginning on the first of Muharram and ending on the last day of Dhu'l Hajja.

Supreme Legal Supervisory Body

The Supreme Legal Supervisory Body (SLSB) of the Association comprises the heads of the legal departments of each member bank; the Board may also appoint additional experts and scholars to the SLSB. The function of this body is to ensure that member banks conduct their respective businesses in conformity with the rules of the Sharia and to consider submissions made by any Muslim individual or organisation as to the extent of this conformity by any member bank.

Offices

Headquarters:
PO Box 4992, Jeddah, Kingdom of Saudi Arabia
Telephone: 68 90 804 - 64 48 364
Telex: 401430 FOCUS SJ

IAIB Office, Cairo:
47 Oruba Street, Helipolis
PO Box 2838, Helipolis, Houria's, Cairo, Egypt

IAIB Gulf Office, Dubai:
PO Box 1080 Deira, Dubai
Telephone: 2298 71
Telex: 45 889 EM

IAIB Asian Office, Karachi:
PO Box 5410, Karachi
Telephone: 528 183
Telex: 24 646 PPI PK

IAIB European Office, London:
144–6 King's Cross Road, London WC1X 9DH
Telephone: 01 833 8275

THE HIGHER RELIGIOUS SUPERVISORY BOARD

The Higher Religious Supervisory Board was established by the IAIB in order to implement a decision of the Conference of Foreign Ministers of Islamic countries. This decision recognised the desire for the Heads of Governments of Islamic States to establish Islamic banks and financial institutions, working within the framework of the Sharia. The Board is comprised of long-experienced Grand Ulema of Islamic jurisprudence who have a thorough understanding of international commodity markets and stock exchanges. It is responsible for the supervision and control of Islamic banks and financial institutions, enforcing their strict adherence to Islam. It can make 'fatwas' or directives on the appropriate procedures for dealings and transactions in money markets.

Article 2 of the Higher Board's statute stipulates that the Board is entrusted with the following:

(a) To study the 'Fatwas' previously issued by the religious supervisory boards of member banks, in an attempt to make decisions identical.
(b) To study the previously issued 'fatwas' to see how far they conform with the rulings of Islamic Sharia.
(c) To supervise the activities of the Islamic banks and financial institutions and members of the Association to ensure their conformity with the rulings of the Islamic Sharia. In addition it has to draw the attention of the concerned parties to any potential violation of these activities. In discharging its duties, the Board has the right to go through the laws and by-laws of member banks and financial institutions and to draw their attention to whatever violation might have been made in this respect. In so doing, utmost confidentiality must be observed.
(d) To issue legal religious opinions on banking and financial questions in response to requests by member Islamic banks and financial institutions, or their religious supervisory boards or the secretariat general of the Association.
(e) To study matters related to financial and banking operations in response to requests for advice from Islamic financial institutions.
(f) Decisions and 'fatwas' of the Board are obligatory and binding on member banks and financial institutions in cases where these are already approved by all members. However, any member bank or financial institution is entitled to ask for re-consideration of any decision. A detailed note must then be submitted in cases of disagreement as any bank is entitled to follow either course of action in the disagreement unless it is otherwise enforced by the Board.
(g) To clarify legal religious rulings on new economic questions.

This article shows the vast authority enjoyed by the Higher Board in verifying and supervising the dealings of Islamic banks and financial institutions such that they are within the framework of the rulings of Islamic Sharia. In addition, the Higher Board has the authority to call for seminars and conferences to be attended by jurisprudents and scholars of the Islamic economies from all over the world, in order to ascertain the correct Islamic approach to any new economic questions arising.

In confirming the above-mentioned objectives, Article 2 of the Board's statute also stipulates the following: 'The Board is to base all of its decisions and Fatwas on the general and particular principles and teachings of the Sharia, as stipulated in the Holy Book and Sunna, regardless of any doctrine or any specific sect'. All the HIgher Board's decisions are binding on member banks and financial institutions as mentioned in Para (e) of Article 2.

The Higher Board has requested that the agreements of association of all banks and financial institutions should call for the establishment of religious supervisory boards consisting of Muslim jurists. It is not enough that a bank should appoint an adviser, in the belief that he alone can handle the entire work of the Board. The Higher Board recommends that each Islamic bank and financial institution should form a board of not less than 13 jurisprudents and Islamic economy professors who should have the final decision in all matters.

The Higher Religious Supervisory Board has been and is still carrying out its duties in accordance with the decision of the conference of Foreign Ministers of Islamic countries and the by-laws governing its work. As such, a bank cannot be 'working within the framework of the rulings of Sharia', without implementing the tenets of the Higher Religious Board. It is the right of the International Association of Islamic Banks to publicise the name of any bank which is not observing the Sharia.

THE ROLE OF DAR AL-MAAL AL-ISLAMI IN THE PROMOTION OF AN ISLAMIC FINANCIAL SYSTEM

The Dar Al-Maal Al-Islami (DMI) was incorporated in July 1981 within authorised capital of $1 billion. Its operations began with a paid up capital of $3 million subscribed by a group of prominent businessmen and personalities in the Muslim world and by the general public worldwide. The founders of DMI include, amongst others, The Heads of State of Bahrain, Guinea, Pakistan, Sudan and the United Arab Emirates. His Royal Highness Prince Mohamed Al-Faisal Al-Saud, son of the late King Faisal of Saudi Arabia, is the Chairman of DMI and the person responsible for its formation. Having instigated the establishment of the International Association of Islamic Banks in 1977, he actively campaigned in various Islamic centres for support in the creation of DMI.

Though not incorporated until July 1981, the basic principles of DMI had been pronounced as early as February of that year in a declaration referred to as the 'covenant' and the 'call' to the Ummat al-Islami (the Islamic World Fraternity). Through this 'covenant' and 'call' the founders of DMI reaffirmed the principles emerging from the teachings of the Holy Quran and the Islamic Sharia. These principles bind all Muslims to the religious obligation to regulate their life such that the material bounty bestowed on them by Allah is used to promote and meet the objectives set in Islam. The founders acknowledged the dissatisfaction expressed by Muslims with the Riba system and supported the public demand for the development of Islamic financial institutions and instruments which are compatible with the economic and social conditions of the Ummat al-Islami. Thus, from the conceptional stage of the 1950s and 1960s, the formation of DMI represented a physical step towards the introduction of a new international financial order based upon Islam and the application of the Sharia to economic and financial transactions.

The objectives of DMI are:

(1) To undertake financial operations required by Muslims within the framework of the principles and precepts of Sharia.
(2) To implement its various activities through subsidiaries established or to be established in Islamic and other countries.
(3) To invest, within an Islamic context, the funds of Muslims to generate Halal profits.
(4) To promote and consolidate co-operation between Muslims.

DMI is designed to act mainly as a holding company and a management adviser for the setting up of Islamic banks, investment companies and Takafol companies (the Islamic alternative to Western insurance). It also envisages organising and operating subsidiaries to conduct other financial or business activities.

DMI has been in operation for five years and in this period has established a network of Islamic financial institutions in various parts of the Islamic world. These institutions embrace Massaref (Islamic banks), investment companies and Takafol companies. In the future it has plans to develop activities relating to leasing, trading, contracting, consulting and shipping.

Most of the target countries of DMI are in the Islamic world, principally in the Middle East, North Africa and sub-Saharan Africa. It is pioneering the establishment of Islamic financial institutions in Africa and it has already established subsidiaries in Guinea, Senegal and Niger which are functioning satisfactorily. In addition, DMI has established business and investment relationships with other African countries. Trading and investment activities based on Sharia principles have been undertaken in Nigeria, Mali and Burkina Faso. During the coming years new DMI operations will be established in other African countries where protocols have already been signed or where negotiations are in progress.

Similar steps will be taken to establish DMI institutions in Asia. Its future expansion programme includes the opening of branches of Massraf Faisal Al-Islami of Bahrain in Pakistan and The Faisal Finance Institution in Turkey. At a later stage DMI will expand outside the Ummat Al-Islami, to America, Europe and the Far East. This will help the mobilisation of Muslim funds available in these areas for Halal financial transactions.

Operations

In order to finance projects, trade, commerce, industry and agriculture etc, DMI has successfully devised a set of basic types of Islamic contracts based upon Murabaha (cost plus financing), Musharaka (profit sharing), Mudaraba (trust financing), Ijara (lease), Ijara wa Iktina (lease purchase) and Qard Hassan (interest-free loans). It has proved through experience that these Islamic forms of contract can adapt to new economic situations. In formulating its contracts it has ensured, through its Religious Board, that contracts are compatible with the precepts of Sharia.

In the field of investment, DMI has provided appropriate opportunities and investment channels by using the Massaref and investment companies that it has established. Through the Islamic Investment Company of the Gulf (the Managing Trustee), it has so far successfully floated several Mudarabas. At present, the Mudaraba funds under management of the DMI investment group exceed $1 billion. DMI and its associates are now examining possibilities of creating new Islamic financial instruments such as leasing, Real Estate and Haj Mudarabas.

Investors' funds are being employed for the Islamic financing of projects, trade, commerce and other operations. Islamic contracts have been developed to meet the requirements of different types of financing. These have been utilised in projects relating to construction, transport, shipping, road-building, fishing, food, agriculture, specialised equipment and real estate. Computerised project analysis and accounting methods have been developed by DMI to suit customers' needs and to ensure the speedy handling of financing requests which adhere to Sharia requirements.

The Massaref operated by DMI function is in accordance with instructions prepared after counselling the leading Sharia authorities. Current accounts are payable on demand and are debited by bank transfer or bank cheque. Since a DMI Massaref assumes all risk with respect to current accounts, the holder receives no profit or earnings of any nature with respect to current account balances. The Massaref also offer ancillary client services such as foreign exchange transactions, transfer of funds, safe deposit boxes/lockers, individually managed discretionary accounts, letters of credit, letters of guarantee, export financing facilities etc.

The Massaref also maintains clients' investment accounts on a profit and loss sharing basis for fixed term or on call basis. The funds received from clients in investment accounts are employed in one or more accepted investments according to Islam, having no element of Riba. All operations of DMI Massaref are subjected to the supervision of the Religious Boards which ensure that each

Islamic bank operates in conformity with the Islamic principles forbidding Riba.

Islamic Takafol Companies (ITC) have been set up to utilise Mudaraba arrangements, in accordance with Islam, as a substitute for insurance services. The ITC acts as a management company, admitting participants, collecting instalments, providing management services, investing funds and paying Takafol benefits. Whenever needed, it provides for the support of the fund through an Islamic Retakafol company which pools Takafol contributions from different companies.

The difference from Western insurance lies in the manner of distribution of assets and profits from the investment of assets to the subscribing of the public. It is not based on a system of proportionality to the amount invested by each member of the public, but rather on a system of sharing the financial consequences of defined loss, according to the principles of co-operation among Muslims articulated by the Sharia. Each subscriber pays his share in the Takafol company and this is invested in profit-yielding projects on behalf of subscribers. The Takafol company receives a fee to cover actual handling expenses, it does not share in profits.

Details of operations since 1981

In accordance with its aim to expand throughout the Ummah thus serving as many Muslims as possible, Dar Al-Maal Al-Islami has established or taken participations in Massaref, Investment, Takafol and other business ventures in 13 countries in the Muslim world and a few international financial centers.

During the financial year 1982–3, five investment companies were established in Bahrain, Guinea, Niger, Senegal and Sudan in addition to five Massaref in the Bahamas, Bahrain, Guinea, Niger and Senegal and a Takafol Company in Luxembourg. Also, during the same year, a majority owned business company, Spacetronics S.A., was established to develop and market Islamic clocks and watches. During the following financial year, 1983–4, one Takafol company was incorporated in Bahrain and one Re-Takafol company in the Bahamas. During the same year, DMI acquired an important participation in Faisal Islamic Bank of Egypt and Faisal Islamic Bank Sudan. Together with the Faisal Islamic Bank of Egypt it launched the Islamic Investment and Development Company in Egypt.

Thus, during the first four years after its incorporation, DMI established or acquired substantial participations in eight Massaref (including participations taken in Faisal Islamic Bank of Egypt and Faisal Islamic Bank Sudan), seven investment companies, three Takafol companies and three business companies; altogether 21 entities investing a total of $98.6 million.

Funds under management

The major achievement of DMI Group in its first four years was the mobilisation of $1.4 billion of clients' funds by its various subsidiaries. (See Table 1.4.1)

Table 1.4.1: Funds under management

June 30	Gulf	West Africa	Europe/ North Africa	Takafol	Other	Total
1979	12.0	—	—	—	—	12.0
1980	29.9	—	—	—	—	29.9
1981	113.1	—	—	—	—	113.1
1982	453.0	—	—	—	—	453.0
1983	872.5	0.6	—	—	—	873.1
1984	1,095.3	11.8	2.5	1.1	—	1,110.7
1985	1,315.0	10.7	5.7	3.0	32.7	1,367.1

Unit: US$ million

Mobilisation of funds began in early 1979 by the Islamic Investment Company, operating mainly in the Arabian peninsula. The concept of an Islamic system for the investment of funds met with an immediate and enthusiastic response by Muslim clients, and funds under management grew rapidly. By the end of July 1981, when DMI was created, they stood at $137 million. Since then, the network of subsidiaries has been expanded and funds managed for clients have grown substantially.

The way forward

Service to the Umma imposes a broad Islamic role upon DMI, which has been playing a modest but important role in helping to bring closer together those Islamic communities which are separated geographically. In the years to come, with necessary support in the Islamic countries, DMI is prepared to play an even more dynamic role in promoting Islamic financial institutions in various parts of the Muslim World, and to prove that banking according to the principles of Sharia is not only feasible but also profitable. The setting up of DMI was a bold initiative in the search for further development in Islamic banking and investment.

The task, however, is not an easy one. It needs help, assistance and co-operation both from governments and from central banks. The policy-making agencies in the governments of the Islamic countries have a very important role to play in this respect. DMI has faced many hurdles in its negotiations with the fiscal and banking authorities concerning the establishment of its institutions.

Table 1.4.2: Group Balance Sheet

	1985	1984
Current Assets		
Cash and bank balances	8,822	10,007
Short-term investments	119,039	121,805
Accounts receivable	13,750	9,528
Accrued income	6,026	8,049
	147,637	149,389
Less Current Liabilities		
Accounts payable	12,768	17,130
Massaref customer accounts	20,431	15,604
Proposed distribution	3,166	
Contingency reserve	3,546	
	39,911	32,734
Net Current Assets	107,726	116,655
Investments	98,044	76,275
Fixed Assets	25,485	27,179
Intangible Assets	48,740	51,700
Net Assets	279,995	271,809
Represented by:		
Trust capital	279,995	271,809

Unit: US$ '000

The major obstacle in most Islamic countries is that the existing banking, licensing and regulation laws are modelled on Western statutes designed to regulate Riba banks. The contractual nature of an Islamic bank's relationship with its clients and the nature of assets held by Islamic banks often make it technically impossible for an Islamic bank to operate within such requirements. In particular, methods of borrowing from the Central Bank and the ability to earn profit on the Massaref's surplus funds deposited with the Central Bank are still in the process of negotiation in most countries.

The Islamic banking system depends upon participation in profit and loss. The Islamic banks can develop only if such payments of profit participations are granted fiscal equality with the payment of interest. Thus, changes in legislation need to take place where necessary, to ensure that profit participations and similar payments made by a person or corporation to an Islamic bank are deductible in computing the taxable income of the payer under local law as a business expense. Similarly, such profit participations paid or credited by an Islamic bank to depositors should be deductible in computing the taxable income of an Islamic bank. Profit participations received by depositors at an Islamic bank can be subject to the normal tax regimes of the Islamic countries.

DMI has established an appropriate financial foundation and, through its financial institutions, has begun to provide savings and deposit accounts as well as investment and monetary operations which are right and lawful according to Islam. It is upon this solid base that future progress must be made and DMI must continue to play a catalytic role in encouraging the growth of Islamic financial institutions throughout the world.

Offices

Dar Al-Maal Al-Islami Trust
Nassau, The Bahamas, PO Box N. 7130
Telephone: (809) 32-213312
Telex: 0297/20312

Dal Al-Maal Al-Islami (DMI) SA,
84, Avenue Louis Casai,
Geneva, Switzerland, PO Box 161
Telephone: (022) 98-40-40
Telex: 28391 SHAR CH
HIFAX: 988990–988991

Board of Supervisors

Mohamed Al-Faisal Al-Saud, Chairman
Abdulaziz Abdullah Alfadda
Abdullah Othman Al-Hussaini
Muazzam Ali
Abdullah Ahmed Zainal Alireza
Ibrahim Khalifa Al-Khalifa
Mohamed Abdullah Abdulkarim El-Khereiji
Fahd Alabdallah Al-Owaidah
Youssef Fadel Al-Sabbah
Saud Al-Abdullah Al-Faisal Al-Saud
Hassan Abdallah Al-Turabi
Mohamed Abdulaziz Al-Wazzan
Omar Abdul Rahman Azzam
Haydar Mohamed Ben Ladin
Haji Aminu Dantata
Ibrahim El-Tayeb Elrayah
Ahmed Mohamed Salah Jamjoom
Faisal Islamic Bank, Egypt (Represented by Mahmoud Mohamed El-Helw)
Faisal Islamic Bank, Sudan (Represented by Al-Bagkir Youssef Mudawi)

Executive Committee

Mohamed Al-Faisal Al-Saud, Chairman
Abdulaziz Abdullah Alfadda
Muazzam Ali
Abdullah Ahmed Zainal Alireza
Youssef Fadel Al-Sabbah
Saud Al-Abdullah Al-Faisal Al-Saud
Omar Abdul Rahman Azzam

Religious Board

Mohamed Khater Mohamed, Chairman
Al-Siddick Mohamed Al Amin Al-Darir
Youssel Al-Karadawi
Mohamed Karam Shah
Malek Abdul Aziz Sy
Abdallah ben Mani'e

Senior Management

Omar Abdi Ali (Chief Operating Officer)

Executive Vice-Presidents
Mohamed Fouad El-Sarraf (Assistance and Coordination)
Moustafa Hosny (General Counsel and Board Secretariat)
Zafar Ahmed Khan (Controller General)
Dariush Oskoui (Corporate Affairs)
Moustafa Mohamed Sakkaf (Treasury)

Corporate auditors
Price Waterhouse & Co

5

The Role of the Islamic Development Bank (IDB): The First Ten Years[1]

The Islamic Development Bank came into being in October 1975. It was set up in recognition of the need to foster the well-being of the peoples of the participating countries and to achieve a harmonious and balanced development of these countries. It is based on the conviction that such development can be best advanced through mutual financial and economic co-operation among the states which are members of the Islamic Conference. It is designed to promote and strengthen co-operation among its members in economic, social and other fields of activity. The Bank is orientated towards development, investment and welfare and it seeks to mobilise financial and other resources both within and outside the member countries. It is expected to promote domestic savings and investment and a greater flow of development funds into the member countries.

Its functions are to:

(1) Participate in the equity capital of productive projects and enterprises in member countries.
(2) Invest in social infrastructure projects in member countries by way of participation or other financial arrangements.
(3) Make loans to the private and public sector for the financing of productive projects, enterprises and programmes in member countries.
(4) Establish and operate special funds for specific purposes.
(5) Operate trust funds.
(6) Accept deposits and raise funds in any other manner.
(7) Assist in the promotion of foreign trade, especially in capital goods, among member countries.
(8) Invest funds not needed in its operations in an acceptable manner.
(9) Provide technical assistance to member countries.
(10) Extend training facilities for personnel engaged in development activities

---

1. Based upon an article by Mr Ahmad Mohammed Ali, President of the Islamic Development Bank, and on extracts from the Tenth Annual Report of the IDB.

in member countries.

(11) Undertake research to enable the economic, financial and banking activities in Muslim countries to conform to the Shariah.

(12) Co-operate, subject to the Agreement, in such a manner as the Bank may deem appropriate, with all bodies, institutions and organisations having similar purposes, in pursuance of international economic co-operation.

(13) Undertake any other activities which may advance its purposes.

(14) Conduct its operations in accordance with the principles of Shariah.

The present membership numbers 43 countries compared to 22 founding member countries. The Bank is a completely independent institution operating in accordance with its Articles of Agreement and has its own Board of Governors and Executive Directors.

The authorised capital of the Bank is two billion Islamic Dinars (ID) and the subscribed capital is ID 1,952 million. The Islamic Dinar, which is the unit of account, is equal to one Special Drawing Right of the International Monetary Fund. Unlike other international development banks, the Islamic Development Bank is also authorised to accept deposits from individuals, institutions and governments. The Bank is also empowered to set up special funds and to manage trust funds.

In the months following its establishment, the Bank had to tackle the task of completing the necessary physical arrangements, laying down its organisational structure and the recruitment of professional staff. It also had to devote considerable time to the formulation of its policy guidelines in view of the fact that it was required to function on the basis of Islamic principles. It had to find its own path as there existed no readily applicable format to follow. This was indeed a difficult and complex task as it not only involved interest-free financing but new ideas about development objectives which, in turn, had implications of a far-reaching character for every aspect of its activities. The absence of interest income on a fixed basis in the case of the Islamic Development Bank (unlike other international banks) calls for a highly sophisticated, organised and quantitatively precise approach in its operations.

Usually there is a long interval between the establishment of an international development bank and the start of its financing operations, as the assembling of professional staff and laying down of the initial guidelines take considerable time. However, the Islamic Development Bank was anxious to make the quickest possible start with its financing operations. With this end in view, it took the rather unusual step of preparing a comprehensive document on its policies and operations and setting out its initial ideas. The object was to acquaint the member countries with the Bank's thinking, so that they could assume the initiative in offering possibilities for financing, thereby saving the time which is taken up in project-identification through the mounting of special missions. The President of the Bank visited and made direct contacts with almost all the member governments. All this greatly expedited the preparation of a sizeable stockpile of projects.

Ten years is not a long time in the life of an international institution. In dealing with development finance, this is really a short period for the institution to make its mark; more so where, as in the case of the Islamic Development Bank, it has no precedents to follow and no analogous institutions from which to learn. For more than ten years, the developing countries, of which the IDB member countries are a sub-group, have experienced a most hectic period of socio-economic difficulties. Out of 36 countries that have been declared least developed by the United Nations, 19 are members of the Islamic Development Bank. As the socio-economic needs of the member countries have expanded and even become more complex, the Bank has increased the volume of its operations and introduced new forms of financing. This has been necessitated by the need to cater to the requirements of its member countries, within its limited resources.

Various indices can be used to demonstrate the progress that the Bank has made in these past ten years:

— At its inauguration in 1395H, there were 22 member countries. The membership now stands at 43.
— The staff strength has grown from 30 in 1396H to the present number of 449, embracing both professional and supporting staff.
— In 1396H, only two projects valued at ID 13.0 million were approved while, by the end of 1405H, a cumulative total of 579 projects valued at almost ID 5.0 billion had been approved. Meanwhile, disbursement had increased to about ID 3.5 billion by the end of 1405H.
— At its inception, the Bank had only two modes of financing, while today seven exist.
— During the first year of it operations, the Bank had one co-financed project while, by the end of 1405H, there had been as many as 91 co-financing arrangements which, through their catalytic effect, enabled more funds to be spread over many more projects in many more member countries than would otherwise have been possible.
— In order to facilitate the co-ordination of assistance, the Bank has had co-operative agreements with nine international or regional institutions and seven Arab funds, all of whom undertake operations in the Bank's member countries.

During this period, the Bank introduced and increased its Special Operations for assistance to Muslim communities and for specific instances of member countries suffering from certain natural and other calamities. These Special Operations involved, at the end of 1405H, a cumulative total of ID 158 million, for projects that ranged from drought relief, aid to refugees, assistance during periods of natural disasters, to the distribution of Hajj sacrificial meat to refugees and other needy persons within the Muslim Ummah.

There have been institutional innovations too, the most important of which

Table 1.5.1: The Islamic Development Bank: The record for the first ten years (1396–1405H/1976–85)

	1396H		1397H		1398H		1399H		1400H		1401H		1402H		1403H		1404H		1405H		Total (since 1396H)	
	No.	Amount	No.	Amount	No.	Amount	No.	Amount	No.	Amount	No.	Amount	No.	Amount	No.	Amount	No.	Amount	No.	Amount	No.	Amount
Operations:																						
Loan	1	6.00	11	55.41	5	25.46	6	33.74	9	52.68	6	28.12	9	48.03	11	73.45	12a	71.46	15	98.62a	85	492.97a
Equity	1	7.45	8	38.23	5	29.36	8	39.79	10	39.04	10	45.98	8	28.70	5a	15.61	1	6.00	4	9.87a	60	260.03a
Leasing	–	–	1	5.22	1	10.00	2	16.25	5	36.47	3	30.69	8	73.53	10a	86.43	12a	125.27	9	92.10a	50	462.04
Instalment Sale	–	–	–	–	–	–	–	–	–	–	–	–	–	–	–	–	–	–	7	65.90	7	65.90
Profit Sharing	–	–	–	–	1	4.27	–	–	–	–	–	–	–	–	1	3.06	–	–	–	–	2	7.33
Technical Assistance	–	–	3	0.84	3	0.82	3	1.37	3	3.38	10	6.83	8	4.44	12	5.99	7	2.96	13	6.63	64	33.25
Total Projects	2	13.45	23	99.70	15	69.91	27	91.14	27	131.57	29	111.62	33	154.70	38	184.54	32	205.70	48	373.11	268	1,321.53
Foreign Trade Financing	–	–	5	43.61	14	127.44	25	262.45	33	352.67	32	370.24	28	359.77	28	480.61	47	714.31	38	668.21	250	3,379.31
Total Ordinary Operations	2	13.45	28	143.31	29	197.35	46	353.59	60	484.24	61	481.86	61	514.47	66	665.15	79	920.01	86	941.32	518	4,700.84
Special Assistance Account	–	–	–	–	–	–	1	0.71	7	8.46	9	5.33	8	9.25	7	7.85	14	62.65	11	63.90	57	158.15
Grand Total	2	13.45	28	143.31	29	197.35	47	354.30	67	492.70	70	487.19	69	523.72	73	673.00	93	982.66	97	1,005.22	575	4,858.99
Disbursement		–		12.73		92.94		212.86		362.78		479.79		391.28		487.35		722.81		731.83		
Gross Income		–		–		2.97		9.75		19.65		26.13		30.23		26.18		34.83		62.69		
Net Profit		–		–		(–2.19)		2.28		10.14		14.72		16.93		2.45		18.37		43.61		
Reserves:																						
capital		–		16.64		16.64		16.46		16.64		16.64		16.46		16.64		16.64		16.64		
special		–		–		–		–		90.53		129.78		166.67		200.66		235.55		264.28		
general		–		–		–		–		–		10.23		24.96		41.88		44.33		52.70		
Balance on Investment Deposit Scheme		–		–		–		–		–		43.81		50.04		155.39		77.10		67.70		
Subscription		750.00		765.00		767.50		780.00		790.00		1,820.17c		1,822.67		1,822.67		1,850.17		1,952.07		
Number of Member Countries (at end)		26		32		34		36		40		41		42		42		43		43		

– Nil
a Includes projects for which two types of financing were approved.
b Totals may not add up due to rounding.
c Jump due to response to resolution adopted at Fifth Annual Meeting of Board of Governors.
Unit – ID million

were the establishment of the Islamic Research and Training Institute (IRTI), a library and a computer centre.

The Bank, as it has evolved, has had to face various challenges, most of which have arisen and continue to arise mainly because the resource needs of the member countries are expanding at a much faster pace than the resources available to the Bank. One of the persistent issues engaging the attention of the Bank, therefore, is that of examining feasible ways and means for the mobilisation of additional financial resources, including innovative monetary instruments and modalities that are consistent with the Islamic Sharia. The IDB cannot resort to the resources of existing capital markets, since these do not conform to Islamic principles.

The Bank finances only projects/enterprises which are technically sound and economically viable. All projects/enterprises to be financed by the Bank are subject to rigorous appraisal and evaluation by the Bank. A project/enterprise with a high financial rate of return and a high economic rate of return is preferred. Preference is accorded, as far as possible, to all sub-regional and regional projects/enterprises and to those projects which promote complementarity in the economies of member countries. Priority is also accorded to loans for projects which demonstrate clear efforts towards self-help and have a strong social orientation. For financing purposes the Bank gives priority to those countries which are least developed economically among its members. Special consideration is shown to those countries which have the largest commitment to economic development as reflected in their resource mobilisation effort, development programmes and the orientation of their economic and financial policies. The Bank is proximate to the projects it finances. It exercises its right of full access to all information pertaining to the working of an enterprise which it has financed.

One of the leading objectives of the Bank is to organise itself to facilitate a transfer of technology and skills from within its membership and also to serve as a clearing house for the mobilisation of outside technical assistance. This service is particularly welcome to those members who have provided large financial resources to the Bank. Their real need is to be able to utilise the huge capital resources that they have with the help of modern technology. A transfer of technology and skills from amongst member countries also has the indirect effect of bringing them closer and clearing the way for economic co-operation and integration.

Developing new financial instruments

Conventionally, international development banks invest funds not needed in operations in government securities, government guaranteed securities, time deposits and certificates of deposits. However, having surveyed the various alternative possibilities existing for the placement of funds, and bearing in mind

Table 1.5.2: Projects Approved by Country and by Type of Financing during the First Ten years (1976–85)

	Loans	Equity[a]	Leasing[b]	Instalment Sale[c]	Profit Sharing	Technical Assistance	Total
Algeria	23.64	—	—	11.75	—	—	35.39
Bahrain	4.44	3.05	15.29	—	—	—	22.78
Bangladesh	33.60	5.25	27.68	—	—	—	66.53
Benin	4.70	—	—	—	—	2.32	7.02
Burkina Faso	9.89	5.42	3.51	—	—	3.69	22.51
Cameroon	19.85	13.76	—	—	—	1.00	34.61
Chad	11.05	—	—	—	—	—	11.05
Comoros	6.75	—	—	—	—	1.41	8.16
Djibouti	4.90	—	—	—	—	0.95	5.85
Egypt	10.30	—	—	—	—	—	10.30
Gabon	5.00	—	—	—	—	—	5.00
Gambia	—	—	—	—	—	0.61	0.61
Guinea	14.97	4.07	6.15	—	—	1.09	26.28
Guinea-Bissau	—	—	—	—	—	0.46	0.46
Indonesia	15.00	16.84	8.56	3.12	—	—	43.52
Iraq	19.72	—	—	—	—	—	19.72
Jordan	14.00	29.38	42.09	9.10	—	0.53	95.10
Lebanon	7.44	—	—	—	—	0.09	7.53
Libya	—	—	26.06	—	—	—	26.06
Malaysia	23.64	10.80	10.00	—	—	—	44.44
Maldives	1.67	—	5.34	—	—	0.09	7.10
Mali	22.86	2.65	—	—	—	2.37	27.88
Mauritania	27.63	7.67	18.89	—	—	1.36	55.55
Morocco	13.00	36.08	3.53	—	3.06	—	55.67
Niger	20.90	9.22	—	—	—	2.98	33.10
Oman	12.50	7.01	28.66	7.01	—	0.24	55.42
Pakistan	13.25	22.66	68.33	—	—	—	104.24
Palestine	—	—	—	—	—	0.72	0.72
Senegal	20.85	15.33	9.31	—	—	3.11	48.60

Sierra Leone	6.00	—	—	—	—	1.87	7.87
Somalia	8.90	4.00	—	—	—	0.55	13.45
Sudan	13.00	7.25	—	—	—	—	20.25
Syria	14.65	—	25.00	10.43	—	—	39.65
Tunisia	33.68	20.61	17.59	24.49	—	3.05	82.29
Turkey	7.25	24.78	102.49	—	—	—	162.06
Uganda	8.76	—	6.00	—	—	1.19	15.95
UAE	—	12.52	—	—	4.27	—	16.79
Yemen AR	21.90	1.70	37.58	—	—	2.85	64.03
Yemen PDR	17.31	—	—	—	—	0.72	18.02
Total	492.97	260.03	462.04	65.90	7.33	33.25	1,321.53

— Nil
a Includes line of equity
b Includes line of leasing
c Commenced in 1405H
Unit: ID million

the requirement of the Islamic Development Bank in terms of security, liquidity and a return based on performance and the avoidance of a pre-determined interest rate, it was apparent that the IDB needed to seek and develop new alternatives for the placement of its uncommitted funds. Consequently, new uses of funds are often radically different from those being currently employed by other institutions.

One of the methods which the Bank applies is the financing of foreign trade of member countries. The first experiment which the Bank undertook in this respect was the financing of raw material imports (coke and copper) to Algeria. The Bank was successful in concluding an agreement for the purchase of US$ 13 million worth of such material and its subsequent resale to Algerian companies. The payment of the resale value was made within 21 months. A similar deal was approved about the same time for Turkey for the purchase of coke with US$ 15 million as an initial step. By 1985 foreign trade financing of this kind had amounted to over ID 3.3 billion.

In recent years the IDB has sought to reduce its dependence upon subscribed capital as a source of funds. In pursuance of its commitment to conform to the Sharia in its activities, the Bank has consulted a number of prominent economists and Sharia scholars regarding the Sharia base for developing both new instruments and a secondary result. The following guidelines have emerged: (1) The Sharia permits, in principle, the issuance and circulation of shares. (2) However, the issuance, circulation and trading of shares should not contravene, intentionally or otherwise, any principle of Islamic Sharia. Furthermore, the income generated by such issuances must not be directly linked with any lending operation. (3) From an Islamic point of view, the owner of shares can obtain liquidity through one of two methods; through sales or through obtaining a loan against the share certificate, which represents ownership in real assets.

The question of liquidity in the above context has received conscious attention in the Bank. In issuing the prospective Islamic financial certificates, the Bank is considering among other measures the possibility of indicating — on each occasion that it issues certificates — its willingness, with certain conditions, to repurchase these certificates. A major feature of this procedure is that the Bank will not be bound by a predetermined purchasing price. Indication of the Bank's willingness to repurchase the certificates will provide the prospective investor with the liquidity element required by him as an owner of assets. This measure is expected to continue at least until the development of an organised secondary market.

The Bank is presently engaged in an in-depth study to determine the types of certificates which may be issued as well as the terms and conditions of their issuance. Two types are receiving consideration: (1) Islamic Certificates of Deposit (ICDs); (2) Islamic Investment Certificates. The main distinction between these two categories of certificates is that the ICDs do not revolve around a specific project or activity, and the issuing bank can use the funds it raises in any Mudaraba profit-sharing activities and in any area that it deems most appropriate. The investor in this case will participate in the overall profits of the Bank and the amount of profits will be based on the maturity of the ICD itself.

The Investment Certificates, on the other hand, are meant for investment in a specific project or activity. In short, the investor in Investment Certificates has a choice as to the way his funds are to be placed, while the investor in the Certificates of Deposit does not have this option. However, due to the complexity of operating a system for the Islamic Certificates of Deposit, the Bank intends to start with the second category of certificate, that is, the Investment Certificates.

There is no doubt that the successful utilisation of the above certificates to mobilise sufficient funds depends, to a large extent, on the existence of a system to provide them with liquidity. An investor should be able to dispose of his certificates when he needs liquidity. The ideal solution is the development of an organised Islamic financial market to deal with all issuances of Islamic banks and other Islamic investment and financial institutions. This would, however, require a relatively long period of time to develop and would also require major structural changes. The Bank is therefore considering a number of interim measures to be utilised, on a temporary basis, as a substitute for the organised market mentioned above. Some of these measures are:

(1) The use of the stock exchange markets presently existing in some member countries (Egypt, Jordan, Kuwait, Pakistan etc), provided that operations relating to these certificates do not violate the Shariah.

(2) A scheme which involves an understanding that IDB will endeavour to purchase the certificates when presented to it by the investor, within certain constraints.

(3) Establishment of a new organisation (Islamic Financial Investment Company), to be established jointly by various Islamic banks, to perform certain functions related to the certificates issued by all Islamic banks, such as underwriting, floating, trading etc. It may also be possible for IDB to perform voluntarily the functions mentioned above, on an interim basis, until the establishment of the Islamic Financial Investment Company.

In the continuous search for innovative modes of financing conforming to the Sharia, recent studies in the Bank have indicated two new ones, namely Instalment Sale and Declining Participation. The first has already been implemented by the Bank, while the second is under further study.

Instalment sale

For several years, the Bank has been financing fixed assets for its member countries through leasing arrangements. In this connection, it was recently felt that a single mode did not provide the necessary flexibility to the Bank for the financing of assets. For example, the asset in question may not be eligible for leasing either because it is not separately identifiable or because of its short useful life span. On the other hand, the legal or tax regulations of the prospective lessee may not make leasing an attractive, or even a feasible proposition. Moreover, many prospective lessees (mainly in the private sector) fail to get a commercial bank guarantee in case of leasing because they do not hold ownership of the assets leased.

As a result of the above limitation in the leasing mode, IDB has introduced the new mode of Instalment Sale. This is a contract of sale whereby the ownership of the asset is immediately transferred to the buyer, while the purchase price (which is higher than the original cost) is payable by instalments. Though this will mean, on the one hand, that IDB cannot repossess the asset if the buyer defaults in any instalment; it also means, on the other, that the Bank does not have to worry about the risks associated with ownership of assets. This mode of financing fully conforms to Sharia and falls within the Deferred Sale Scheme (Al-Baya li Ajal) which the majority of Muslim jurists have held to be a lawful and valid scale.

The declining participation mode of financing

This mode of financing which is also in full conformity with the Sharia and has been successfully implemented by some other Islamic banks, is at present under study. Declining participation is a type of financing whereby IDB would enter into a full or partial financing arrangement with the sponsor of a project, on the basis that a share, in proportion to its investment, of the net profit actually realised would be received by IDB as profit accruing to its investment; an agreed part of the sponsor's share of the net profit would also pass to IDB to enable it to recoup the funds advanced by it. After IDB has recouped all of the funds invested by it, the full title of the project would be transferred to the sponsors.

In considering this mode of financing, the Bank realises the need for identifying projects with a high level of profitability and a regular flow of income since returns and repayments would be tied to projects and not restricted to contractual obligations and guarantees. Furthermore, the Bank realises that this mode of financing requires close follow-up to ensure that revenues and costs are properly accounted for. On the other side of the coin, the declining participation mode of financing deviates from the classical concept of profit-sharing in that IDB retains the right of redeeming all its investment profits in the initial year of the life of the project, while the sponsor gets his returns at a later stage.

Conclusion

While the Islamic Development Bank is designed to assist its members, the activities it is expected to undertake are by no means devoid of interest for developing countries generally. In many ways its work and operations have significant implications for the development financing process and its conceptual framework. For one thing, the Bank undertakes interest-free financing from its ordinary resources. In a situation where the existing institutions providing concessional finance are finding replenishment of resources increasingly difficult, this represents a big stride in the field of concessional financing and opens a way of mitigating the interest burden problem. Moreover, the Bank focuses primarily on equity financing — an area which has remained grossly neglected with its difficulties and complexities as well as its implications by way of involvement in ownership, management and supervision. Again, the Bank's participation in productive projects and enterprises on the basis of profit-sharing requires a rather decentralised and different organisational structure than is the case with the other international development banks. The fact that the Bank cannot charge or receive interest has significant implications. This factor acts as a catalyst forcing the Bank to be active and to operate on the basis of the minimum surplus and this results in the funds being used more actively for development financing. At the same time, it obliges the Bank to seek new modes and instruments of placement of its surplus finds so that the funds not needed immediately in the Bank's operations are utilised for the economic development of its member countries instead of finding their way onto the international money markets.

It has to be noted that from its very inception the Bank has been alive to the need to forge the closest ties with other international development financing agencies and also national development banks and institutions, so as to be able to make the largest contribution to the development of its member countries. With this objective in view, the Bank decided to move in the direction of joint financing arrangements with other co-lenders which enabled it to make the quickest possible start. In doing so, the Bank's attitude and operations were conditioned by two main requirements. In the first place, it sought to ensure that the aggregate flow of resources to its member countries was enlarged and that the co-financing arrangement had the effect of providing additionally to the resources available to its member countries. This was judged with reference to the country's programme or in terms of ensuring that the financing effort by the Islamic Development Bank called forth some additional resources from its co-lenders. Secondly, while in the initial stage having to rely more on the technical appraisal of its partners the Bank did not hesitate to influence their judgement and to interest them in projects for which the Islamic Development Bank has a higher priority. In any case, it consciously guards against the risk that the co-financing and parallel-financing arrangements lead to any complacency on its part to develop its own technical apparatus. In fact, the Bank has been striving to equip itself rapidly for independent operations in the shortest possible time. What is more, where it is co-financing arrangements or independent operations, the Islamic Development Bank seeks to operate on the principles which are enshrined in its Article of Agreement and which give it a personality of its own.

6

The Evolution of Islamic Banking

In the last 20–24 years Islamic banking has been passing from a conceptual to a realisation phase. There is now no longer any doubt that methods, policies and tried practices are in place which show how a complete Islamic system can function internationally, more securely and beneficially to all savers and investors in Muslim countries.

It would be wrong to assume that in the Western banking system no risk-sharing is undertaken by the owners of money. This applies to all borrowing but particularly to country borrowing. Western financial institutions have allowed individuals, enterprises, countries and even parts of the world to rise to debt levels which are beyond their capacity to repay. This has been a very short-sighted development and is neither in the interest of the debtor nor the creditor. The end product is a wastage of resources as banks fail in their responsibility to warn borrowers of the pitfalls of their projects and investments. Projects remain incomplete, short of finance and resources. This situation is partly the result of lenders, because of fixed interest charges, not seeing themselves as fully sharing the risks of project failure and therefore not devoting sufficient energy to assessing risk. Had the banking system been more rigorous in its approach to risk assessment and taken much more responsibility in terms of an efficient and profitable utilisation of funds, many of the current problems of international debt may well have been avoided. As a last resort there has been an attempt to throw the burden of debt relief upon the international development agencies, but the scale of the problems is so great that they have not been able to provide a total solution to international debt and economic development.

This is undoubtedly one of the main strengths of an Islamic banking system in which the risk is borne by the investor and the financier. It is therefore in the financier's own interest to pay particular attention to the viability of the project in which the financial support is vested.

No claim can be made that the framework of Islamic banking is yet complete. Certainly it is approaching completion with regard to the possibilities placed before savers/investors, but that in itself is not adequate. The next phase is to strengthen the support of the system internationally and nationally through well-developed Islamic substitutes for classical monetary regulation and central bank practices, coupled with greater collaboration between banks directly and through the International Association of Islamic Banks (and the other groups that link them together).

There are other important transitional problems to address. In particular the legal and practical relationship between the Islamic banking system and the current, capitalistic banking system must be evolved. External trade between Islamic and non-Islamic countries must necessarily involve some working relationship between interest-free and interest-based banking; it is still not clear what relationship that might be.

THE ROLE OF CENTRAL BANKS AND MONETARY AUTHORITIES

Major initiatives must be taken in the near future regarding the prudential regulation of Islamic banks and monetary control. Central banks clearly have a responsibility in this context; not only is it necessary to establish appropriate regulatory and supervisory procedures but an environment must be created in which the growth and development of Islamic banks can take place.

Some of the problem areas which the central banks and policy-making authorities in Islamic countries can help resolve are:

(1) Islamic banks are at a considerable disadvantage in facing competition with conventional banks because they do not have access to the money markets and may even face hostility from the conventional banks in these markets. The conventional banks can always resort to other banks and to the central bank when they face a difficult liquidity situation; this is not often the case for Islamic banks. A solution to this problem is to make provision for central bank assistance to the Islamic banks on a basis compatible with the Sharia. (DMI Trust is studying this function for members of the Group.)

(2) There is a need for central banks to foster the development of financial instruments which are interest-free to enable the Islamic banks to meet statutory liquidity requirements; they also need short-term profitable investment opportunities for excess liquidity. Development of an efficient market for such instruments would greatly facilitate the growth and profitability of Islamic banks.

(3) Existing banking laws in most Islamic countries do not cater for the functioning of Islamic banks. Thus there is need to re-consider banking laws with the aim of extending the coverage of such laws to the operations of Islamic banks based on Sharia.

(4) There is a need for the creation of specialised departments in central banks to guide and supervise the operations of Islamic banks and particularly the different new functions that are undertaken by these banks.

(5) Suitable methods must be adopted to govern the relation between the Islamic banks and the central banks and monetary authorities. In particular there is a need to:

    (a) explore appropriate methods for extending the same support in terms of financing and re-financing facilities to the Islamic banks on a non-interest basis;

    (b) explore appropriate methods for facilitating short-term investments of excess liquidity in Islamic banks on a profit-sharing basis;

    (c) extend investment returns distributed by the Islamic banks to their depositors with privileges identical to those enjoyed by depositors of conventional banks, eg extending to such investment returns the same tax exemptions and incentives which are available to returns on deposits with conventional banks.

The Islamic banks for their part should adapt to modern business practices through:

(1) The expansion of the range of dealings in the financial markets through comprehensive banking services.

(2) The improvement of the means to attract funds and closer attention to the direction of these funds towards investments in accordance with the provisions of the Sharia.

(3) The provision of necessary funds to meet the requirements of all sectors including the welfare sector (Zakat Waki). Banks need also to recognise and address their international as well as national roles.

This is not to say that progress has not already been made — the appearances of this directory is testimony to that fact — but obviously much more must be done. The activities of DMI are a good example of steps taken in the right direction; it, and its subsidiaries, provide finance at the local level; through its investment and holding companies it also has an international orientation; at a third level it and other Islamic banks act together in the syndication of loans and joint venture business activities. Co-ordination and co-operation amongst Islamic banks is essential for future progress; whilst competition is a part of the Islamic economy, unhealthy rivalry must be avoided.

THE ORGANISATIONAL STRUCTURE OF A TYPICAL ISLAMIC BANK

An Islamic bank can be a private company, a government-owned institution or a mixture of both. No preference is stated for any particular form, provided the bank functions according to Islamic principles and beliefs. An Islamic bank is no different from any other bank in the sense that it must operate with a General Assembly, or Board of Directors, which is ultimately responsible to the owners of the bank in ensuring that the bank functions efficiently and profitably.

Since the objectives of an Islamic bank are quite different from those of traditional banks this may be well reflected in its overall organisation. The most important divisions within an Islamic bank are as follows:

Sharia supervisory board

An Islamic bank does not only have to have a board of directors but it also has to have a Shariah advisory board. This is most important where Islamic banks operate in a society which does not fully apply Shariah laws. The board should possess a high degree of independence both internally and externally.

The main function of the Sharia supervisory board is to make sure that the operations of an Islamic bank are undertaken according to Sharia principles. If an Islamic bank works within a society which applies Sharia laws, the existence of an advisory board would be unnecessary. In these circumstances the state would have a central institution which gave 'fatwas' or Sharia rulings on banking operations. Currently this is predominantly not the case and, given that the practical daily economic and social life of the community does not conform with Islam, such an advisory board remains an essential feature of Islamic banking.

The social department

The Islamic bank lays special emphasis on the welfare of the society in which it operates. As a minimum its objective must be to prevent any exaggeration in the income and wealth differentials of members of the community and it should work towards the alleviation of poverty. This can be achieved in two ways; firstly by financing projects with a social dimension and secondly by taking some responsibility for raising Zakat and distributing this to needy individuals. The bank itself must pay Zakat on bank capital and profits and this again should be used to alleviate poverty.

The social department of an Islamic bank has therefore to organise the collection of Zakat donations, it has to identify the sectors of the community where these donations can best be utilised and it has to create a preference in the bank for those investments which best serve the community rather than a restricted group of people.

The investment department

The automatic consequence of the fact that an Islamic bank provides finance on the basis of participation — that is, sharing losses as well as profits — is that it must take a greater involvement in the projects that it finances. The bank must act so as to avoid losses from project financing and to make sure that its funds are utilised effectively. An investment department takes this prime responsibility; its staff must be skilled in the analysis and appraisal of projects and in a position to offer sound advice to potential bank customers.

Although traditional banks can to some extent get involved in the projects which they finance, the existence of loan agreements based upon fixed-interest payments does not subject them to the same degree of risk. Interest payments are made irrespective of whether a particular project is loss-making or profit-making and therefore the need to get involved in projects is less pressing.

The follow-up department

This may be a part of, or separate from, the investment department. Clearly there must be an analysis and appraisal of projects before finance is offered. Having sanctioned financial support however, the performance on the project needs to be monitored; indeed there is justification for substantially more than monitoring taking place: given a potential share in loss making projects, the banks have a need to identify possible problem areas and to take remedial action. Active participation can not only avoid losses being incurred, but can substantially improve the rate of return on project finance.

Recruitment and training department

One particular disadvantage for Islamic banks has been a dearth of personnel trained in Islamic banking activities. The traditional recruiting ground has been in other commercial banks and therefore it has been necessary for the Islamic banks to embark upon comprehensive training programmes. The importance of this is enhanced by the educational background of most employees. As yet in most of the countries where Islamic banks operate, the educational system remains heavily influenced by Western educational practices and less by the economic and social implications of Islam. For a time such training was supported by the International Institute of Islamic Banking and Economics established in Cyprus. This was actively used by way of the Islamic financial institutions and it was successful in bringing forward a cadre of personnel capable of working in Islamic banks.

The legal department

The operations of Islamic banks do not always come under the existing civil laws. For this reason a legal department is essential for the drawing up of constraints based upon the Sharia. In the event of any dispute between the bank and its customers the existing countries may be unable to act. Therefore a sound and comprehensive contract is a pre-requisite for effective Islamic banking business.

Of course this list of departments is not exhaustive; it merely highlights the differing structure between Islamic and other banks because of the major dissimilarities in their respective operations. In the current financial climate Islamic banks face additional burdens because of the nature of government activity and the prudential and monetary regulations of ministries of finance and central banks. In particular it is often the case that central banks issue directives and regulations which are relevant to traditional banks but not applicable in Islamic banking. On occasion this may damage the operation of the Islamic bank or, indeed, make it impossible for the Islamic bank to function properly. In this situation the machinery needs to exist for a dialogue to take place between the Islamic bank and the central bank. The requirements to cope with this type of event are the establishment of good relationships between bank and central authorities, and the abilities to be able to persuade those authorities of the case of the Islamic bank *vis-à-vis* traditional banking.

By the very nature of its operations an Islamic bank faces a less certain future than a traditional bank. Its participation in the risk process places heavy demands upon staffing requirements not only in quantity but also in quality terms. Added to this is the need to operate in an environment which is moulded by central authorities to the requirements of traditional banks and not Islamic banks. This makes the placing of Islamic banking operations more problematical; target setting is less applicable and greater flexibility is the order of the day as the economic environment in which the bank operates changes.

But this is the essence of Islamic banking. The Quran opposes the more certain environment for the bank created by fixed-interest payments. It requires the banks to offer time, effort and active participation in projects; only by so doing can they expect to share in the profits available.

7

The Islamic Financial System and Banking: Some Theoretical Considerations

Islam possesses its own paradigm of economic relations within the context of an entire Islamic system based on injunctions and norms called the Sharia. The Sharia specifies, *inter alia*, rules that relate to the allocation of resources, property rights, production and consumption, the workings of markets, and the distribution of income and wealth. Similarly, rules and requirements have been specified that define the framework within which the underlying monetary and banking system can be designed. The central requirement of this framework is the replacement of the rate of interest with the rate of return on real activities as a mechanism for allocating financial resources. For this purpose a variety of methods and instruments, based on risk- and profit-sharing, are suggested to give effect to the requirements of such a system.

The Sharia provides a blueprint of how a society is to be organised and how the affairs of its members are to be conducted. However, the system itself has not been applied in its entirety, with the exception of a brief period at the inception of Islam. Only in recent decades have some Muslims again become interested in the society-wide implementation of Islamic teachings. Accordingly, analysis of an Islamic economic system, its implementation in present-day economies and its economic consequences is still relatively undeveloped. In partial analyses that have been undertaken thus far, the idea of a banking system operating on a non-interest basis, as the most visible characteristic of an Islamic economic system, has received by far the greatest amount of attention. A few Muslim societies have chosen it as a point of departure towards Islamisation.

Although the elimination of interest is a central characteristic of an Islamic financial system, it is by no means its only characteristic. Once interest is eliminated, questions arise as to the features of the new system, how it is to be implemented, how it will function, and what are its economic implications. In what follows, an attempt is made to provide answers to some of these questions. Because so far there has been little systematic analysis of the implications of implementing an Islamic financial system as part of a complete Islamic system, the preliminary nature of this attempt at theoretical analysis needs emphasis.

EXPLANATION OF PROHIBITION OF INTEREST

In the Quran the charging of interest is considered an injustice. However, although this theme has constituted the cornerstone of Muslim writers' rationalisation of the prohibition of interest, their economic analysis has, to a great extent, placed major emphasis on the alleged lack of satisfactory theory of interest in the Western economic tradition. (See Bashir, 1982, pp. 24–5.) Muslim writers see the existing theories of interest as attempts to rationalise the existence of an institution that has become deeply entrenched (Qureshi, 1985, p. 8) in modern economies and not as an attempt to justify, based on modern economic analysis, why the money lender is entitled to a reward on the money he loans out (Uzair, 1980, Abu Saud, 1980). For example, the notion that interest is a reward for savings does not in their view constitute a moral justification for interest, since in their view such a justification only arises if savings are used for investment to create additional capital and wealth. When an individual saves, however, his saving may take the form of hoarding or the purchase of a financial asset without a simultaneous increment in new investment. In the view of these analysts, the mere act of abstention from consumption should not entitle anyone to a reward.

Similarly, these writers argue that it is an error of modern theory to treat interest as the price of, or return for, capital. Money, they argue, is not capital, not even representative capital, it is only 'potential capital' which requires the service of the entrepreneur to transform the potentiality into actuality; the lender has nothing to do with this conversion of money into capital and with using it productively (Ahmad, 1985, pp. 13–27).

To the closely related notion that interest arises as an inevitable consequence of the difference between the values of capital goods today and a year hence, they argue that the so-called 'pure rate (or own rate) of interest', resulting from the time factor in valuation, may never enter into the calculation of the suppliers of fund and it seldom, if ever, is paid as such. When forced into a position of identifying the 'pure rate of interest', the theorists always refer to the rates of return on 'riskless assets' such as those paid on high quality government securities or the rate of return on debentures of highly successful corporations. But this is a rate of interest on debt, not a rate of return on capital assets. In the case of most successful companies' debentures, the rates of interest are determined on the basis of the long-term success of these businesses, and if these corporations face difficulties and their profit declines, the 'pure rate' ceases to prevail because their debentures are no longer considered as 'riskless'. Hence the 'pure rate of interest' is only a theoretical construct that does not correspond to the actual return on capital assets. Muslim writers argue that even if the basis for time preference is the expected difference between the value of commodities this year and next, it seems more reasonable to allow next year's economic conditions to determine the extent of the reward.

Muslim writers also maintain that when a person lends money, the funds are either used to create a debt or an asset (ie through investment). In the first case, Islam considers that there is no justifiable reason why the lender should receive a return simply through the act of lending *per se*. Nor is there a justification, either from the point of view of the smooth functioning of the economy or from the point of view to any tenable scheme of social justice, for the State to attempt to enforce an unconditional promise of interest payment regardless of the use made of the borrowed money. If, on the other hand, the money is used to create additional capital wealth, the question is raised as to why the lender should be entitled only to a small fraction (represented by interest rate) of the exchange value of the utility created from the use made of his funds; he should be remunerated to the extent of the involvement of his financial capital in creating the incremental wealth.

Islam, the Muslim writers argue, does not object to, in fact encourages, true profit as a return to entrepreneurial effort and to financial capital. Only the identification of money with capital and the justice of interest as a reward for the mere act of refraining from consumption is denied. The lender of money advanced for the purpose of trade and production can be contracted to receive a share of the profit because he becomes part-owner of capital, sharing in the risk of enterprise, and is thus entitled to receive a share of the profits of the firm. He is a partner in the enterprise and not a creditor. There is a fundamental difference between an ordinary shareholder who is one of the proprietors of the enterprise, liable for its debts to the extent of his investment, and receiving a dividend only when a profit is earned, and a creditor who, as a debenture holder, lends money without the risk of owning and operating capital goods and who claims interest irrespective of the profit or loss position of the enterprise. He runs a risk, but this risk is not of the enterprise but of the solvency of the borrower.

Islam permits a wide freedom of contract, assuming that the terms of the contract are not in violation of the precepts of the Shariah; in particular, it permits any arrangement based on the consent of the parties involved so long as the shares of each are contingent upon uncertain gains. This aspect of the arrangement is crucial, since the Shariah condemns even a guarantee by the working partner merely to restore the invested capital intact, not only because it removes the element of uncertainty needed to legitimise the bargain for possible profits, but also because the lender will not be remunerated to the extent of the productivity of his financial capital in the resulting profit.

The law prohibiting interest may perhaps be clarified by considering Islam's position on individual property rights and obligations, and its conception of economic justice. Islam recognises two types of individual claims to property: (1) property that is a result of the combination of individual's creative labour and natural resources; and (2) property whose title has been transferred by its owner as a result of exchange, remittance of rights of others in the owner's property, outright beneficient grants by the owner to those in need, and finally, inheritance.

Money represents the monetised claim of its owner to property rights created by assets obtained either through (1) or (2). Lending money, in effect, is a transfer of this right and all that can be claimed in return is its equivalent and no more. Funds lent are used either productively, in the sense that they create additional wealth, or unproductively in the sense that they do not lead to the creation of incremental wealth by the borrower. In the latter case, since no additional wealth, property, or asset is created by the borrower, the money lent — even if it is legitimately acquired — cannot claim any additional property rights, since none are created. In the former case, when it is used in combination with the creative labour of the entrepreneur to create additional wealth, the lender may bargain for a portion of this incremental wealth but not for a fixed return, irrespective of the outcome of the enterprise.[1]

PERMISSIBLE FORMS OF TRANSACTION

In disallowing interest and permitting profits, the Shariah has developed two specific forms of business arrangements, Mudaraba and Musharaka, as means of earning profits without resort to charging interest. In the case of Mudaraba, one party provides the necessary financial capital and the other supplies the human capital needed for successful performance of the economic activity undertaken. Mudaraba traditionally has been applied to commercial activities of short duration. Musharaka, on the other hand, is a form of business arrangement in which a number of partners pool their financial capital to undertake a commercial-industrial enterprise. Musharaka is applicable to production or commercial activities of longer duration. These profit-sharing arrangements may be applied either to the whole enterprise, where each partner takes an equity position, or to a particular line of activity within an enterprise; ie they can have either whole-firm, or project-specific orientation.[2]

It is expected that projects will be selected for funding through partnerships primarily on the basis of their expected profitability rather than the creditworthiness or solvency of the borrower. This factor, along with the fact of predominance of equity markets and absence of debt markets, has led to the general conclusion that, potentially, in an Islamic system there will be (a) more varied and numerous investment projects for which financing is sought; (b) more

---

1. This property right explanation of prohibition of interest also helps to clarify not only the emphasis which the Quran places on the injustice of interest but also its exhortations to Muslims to provide interest-free loans to the needy (Qard al-Hasanah) for which the Quran promises manifold returns from Allah. The Quran suggests that such loans are made to Allah and it is He who will guarantee manifold returns to the lender.

2. Musharaka and Mudaraba are primarily partnership arrangements in the commercial-industrial sector of the economy but have their counterparts in farming (called Muzar'ah) and in orchard-keeping (called Musaqat), where the harvest is shared between and among the partners based on a pre-specified percentage of profit-sharing.

cautious, selective, and perhaps more efficient project selection on the part of the suppliers of funds; and (c) greater involvement of the public in investment and entrepreneurial activities, particularly as private equity markets develop, than in the traditional fixed-interest-based system.

In the Islamic profit-sharing arrangement, while the profit is shared between the agent-entrepreneur and the owner of financial capital based on a predetermined share parameter, the loss is borne only by the owners of the funds and not by the entrepreneur. This fact affords human capital (as representative of present work and effort) a status on a par with financial capital (as representative of monetised past labour and work); therefore, if the owner of financial capital risks the loss of his funds, the agent-entrepreneur is recognised as risking his time, effort, and labour, but no more.

THE BANKING SYSTEM

In an Islamic system, banks, although constrained to carry out their transactions in accordance with the rules of the Sharia, essentially perform the same functions as they do in a conventional system. That is, they act as administrators of the economy's payments system and as financial intermediaries. The need for them in the Islamic system arises precisely for the same reason as in a conventional system. That is, generally, their *raison d'être* is the exploitation of the imperfections in the financial markets (Stigler, 1967). These imperfections include imperfect divisibility of financial claims, imperfect information, transaction costs of search and acquisition, diversification by the surplus and deficit units, and existence of expertise and economies of scale in monitoring transactions. Financial intermediaries in an Islamic system can reasonably be expected to exhibit economies of scale with respect to these costs, as do their counterparts in the traditional system. Just as in the traditional system, the Islamic depository financial intermediaries transform the liabilities of business into a variety of obligations to suit the tastes and circumstances of the surplus units.

One major difference between the two systems is that, owing to prohibition against interest and the fact that the banks will have to rely primarily on profit-sharing, Islamic banks will have to offer their asset portfolios of primary securities in the form of risky, open-ended 'mutual fund' type packages for sale to investors/depositors. In contradistinction to this system, the banks in a conventional system keep title to the asset portfolios they originate. These assets are funded by banks through issuing deposit contracts, a practice that results in solvency and liquidity risks, since their asset portfolios and loans entail risky pay-offs and/or costs of liquidation prior to maturity, while their deposit contracts are liabilities that are often putable instantaneously at par.

In an Islamic system, due to the fact that the return to banks' liabilities will be a direct function of the return to their asset portfolios, and also because the assets are created in response to investment opportunities in the real sector, the return to the lender is removed from the cost side of a company's income and expenditure statement and becomes instead an allocation of profit, thus allowing the rate of return to financing to be determined by the productivity in the real sector.

Muslim scholars and economists have developed alternative schemes or models of a proposed banking system within the framework of Islamic requirements. The most widely accepted of these integrates the asset and liability sides based on a principle called the Two-Tier Mudaraba (Siddiqi, 1982). This model envisages depositors entering into a contract with a banking firm to share the profits accruing to the bank's business. The bank, on its asset side, enters into another contract with an agent-entrepreneur who is searching for investible funds and who agrees to share his profit with the bank in accordance with a predetermined percentage stipulated in the contract. The bank's earnings from all its activities are pooled and are then shared with its depositors and shareholders according to the terms of their contract. The profit earned by the depositors is thus a percentage of the total banking profits. According to this model, the banks are allowed to accept demand deposits that earn no profit and may be subjected to a service charge. This model, though requiring that current deposits must be paid on the demand of the depositors, operates on a fractional-reserve basis. It further stipulates 'that the bank is obligated to grant very short-term interest-free loans (Qard Hassan) to the extent of a part of the total current deposits' (Chapra, 1982).[1]

In this model, the losses incurred as a result of investment activities by the banks would be reflected in the depreciation of the value of deposits. However, the probability of losses is minimised through diversification of the investment portfolios of the banks and by careful project selection, monitoring, and control. The proponents of the model have suggested loss-compensating balances built up by the bank out of its earnings in good times and deposit insurance schemes launched in co-operation with the central banks as a means by which the probability of such losses could be reduced (Siddiqi, 1982). In addition, and perhaps more importantly, what will further reduce the probability of losses by the depositors is the fact that the banks have direct and indirect control over the behaviour of the agent-entrepreneur through both explicit and implicit contracts.

---

1. Recently Mohsin Khan (1985) has suggested a different model of Islamic banking. This model, also based on profit-sharing, divides the liability side of the bank balance sheet into two windows. One contains demand deposits (transaction deposits) and the other contains investment balances. The choice of window will be left to the depositor. Khan's model requires a 100 per cent reserve for demand deposits, on the presumption that such deposits are placed as Amanah (safe-keeping) and therefore must be fully backed by reserves because the bank does not have the right to use these deposits belonging to depositors as the basis for money creation through fractional reserves. Money deposited in investment accounts, on the other hand, is placed with the depositor's full knowledge that they will be invested in risk-bearing projects; therefore no guarantee is justified and the model stipulates no reserve requirements for the second window.

The banks can exert control through both the formal terms of their contract and through an implicit reward-punishment system in the sense of refusing further credit or blacklisting the agent-entrepreneur. The nature of the contract permits the banks to focus their attention on the probability of default, expected rate of return, and promotion and control of the firms in which they invest.

FINANCIAL MARKETS

One difficulty that might arise in an Islamic financial system is that with the division of the liability side of the balance sheet of the banking system into investment deposits and demand deposits, wealth owners would channel only part of their savings into the accumulation of physical capital and the remainder would be allocated to the accumulation of idle balances. To be sure, the build-up of idle balances runs counter to the Islamic exhortation against the hoarding and accumulation of money (ie keeping money idle without corresponding transactions demand for it). (See Chapra, 1985.) Moreover, these balances not only cannot earn any return, but also, if kept for a full year, they become subject to a compulsory levy of 2.5 per cent, thus imposing relatively high opportunity cost on idle balances (Abu Saud, 1980). None the less, since the alternative to idle balances is risk-bearing deposits, it may be worthwhile for the depositors to maintain a considerable portion of their savings in the form of either money or demand deposit balances.

Perhaps the most challenging issue in the implementation of an Islamic financial system is how to devise risky return-bearing instruments that can provide the investors with a sufficient degree of liquidity, security, and profitability to encourage their being held. Proposals along this line rely on the development of instruments corresponding and parallel to the permissible forms of transactions. These include such instruments as Mudaraba and Musharaka certificates, short-term profit-sharing certificates, and leasing certificates (Al-Jahri, 1983). Additionally, proposals have been made for the development of specific instruments that may be issued by the central bank as well as by the government, particularly relating to its specific investment projects (Siddiqi, 1982). Generally, any risk-bearing instrument reflecting a position in a real asset and earning a variable rate of return that is tied to the performance of the asset, is considered to be consistent with Islamic law.

Once appropriate instruments are designed, markets are required in order that these instruments can be traded. For this reason, Muslim writers have pointed out the desirability of primary, secondary, and money markets (Siddiqi, 1982). Given that a proper securities underwriting function is performed by some institutions in the system (eg the banks) firms could directly raise the necessary funds for their investment projects within the stock market, which would provide them with a second source of funding other than the banks.

The development of a secondary market is important and essential to the development of a primary market. All savers, to some degree or another, have a liquidity preference, in the Islamic system as in any other system. To the extent that savers can, if necessary, sell securities quickly and at low cost, they will be more willing to devote a higher portion of their savings to long-term instruments than they would otherwise. Since primary securities in the Islamic system are normally tied to particular projects and enterprises, there are various risks that must enter into the portfolio decisions of the investor. Therefore, creation of a secondary market will stimulate investment in such securities by giving investors the option to buy or sell at any time.

Furthermore, and in order to facilitate the provision of needed liquidity through financial intermediaries, a money market in the form of interbank financial intermediation is desirable (El-Sarraf, 1984). In the traditional interest-based system the money market becomes a source through which financial institutions adjust their balance sheet positions, as a correction for the imperfect synchronisation between payments and receipts. The money market, in this case, becomes a source of temporary financing in which transactions are mainly short-run portfolio adjustments. In an Islamic financial system, a principal activity of money markets would be the channelling of surplus funds of one financial institution into profit-sharing projects of another. Since banks in an Islamic system acquire assets within the constraints imposed by the structure of their liabilities, it is conceivable that some banks may, at times, have excess funds available but no assets — or no assets attractive enough in terms of their risk-return characteristics — on which they can take a position. At the same time, there may be banks with insufficient financial resources to allow them to fund all available investment opportunities or with certain investment opportunities for which they may prefer risk-sharing with other banks. There should therefore be the opportunity for the development of a market for inter-bank funds.

EFFECTS ON SAVING AND INVESTMENT

Concerns have been expressed that the adoption of an Islamic financial system may lead to a reduction of saving and retardation of financial intermediation and development. One argument to support this assertion has been that increased uncertainty in the rate of return affects savings adversely (Pryor, 1985). The few studies that have considered this question have tended to compare the effects on saving of a fixed and certain rate of return with those of a more uncertain rate of return, implicitly assuming the same mean rate of return with greater variability. The result, obviously, shows a reduction in saving. This conclusion is, however, far from obvious when both risk and return are allowed to vary.

The results of an analysis in which risk and return variability have both been taken into account depend on assumptions regarding the form of the utility function and its risk properties eg the degree and the extent of risk aversion, the degree to which the future is discounted (Sandmo, 1970) whether or not increased risk is compensated by higher uncertainty, and finally the income and substitution effects of increased uncertainty. It has been shown, for example, that when future non-capital income is subjected to risk, decreasing temporal risk aversion is a sufficient condition for increased uncertainty about future income to decrease consumption and increase saving (Phelps, 1967). With respect to capital income, the combined substitution and income effect of increased uncertainty is shown to be indeterminate (Hanson and Menezes, 1978). Other studies have shown that under reasonable assumptions, in the face of uncertainty households will increase their saving for precautionary reasons (Leland, 1968). Theoretical analysis has not, therefore, provided a clear-cut testable hypothesis in this regard, and it becomes an empirical question whether saving will increase or decrease in an Islamic system. It can, however, be reasonably expected that a 'rational planner may take more provision for the future when the future becomes more uncertain' (Hahn, 1969). There is thus no strong theoretical reason to believe that on balance savings will decline as a result of introducing an Islamic economic system.

Numerous difficulties impede the development of a financial system in most developing countries. Such difficulties include discrimination against small and indigenous entrepreneurs (Bhatia and Khatkhate, 1975), shallowness of financial markets, and limited availability of asset choices for savers. These difficulties will not be automatically eliminated by the introduction of an Islamic financial system. Studies of the financial repression hypothesis have emphasised the need for a positive and relatively high rate of return in order to mobilise savings and to integrate financial markets. While the integration of financial markets should present no special difficulties in the Islamic system, provision of a positive high rate of return, although not requiring any arbitrary decision by the authorities to increase the nominal yield, necessitates mobilisation of entrepreneurial ability through efficient project selection and allocation of financial resources based primarily on the expected profitability of projects (Chapra, 1985; Siddiqi, 1982). If the existing bias against small entrepreneurs persists, financial resources continue to flow to well-established and large entrepreneurs, financial markets remain narrow, and asset choices are limited, the adoption of an Islamic financial system can be expected to have no more than limited success in promoting economic development.

CENTRAL BANKING AND MONETARY POLICY

The main task of central banking in an Islamic financial system is the provision of an institutional framework necessary for the smooth operation of financial markets in compliance with the rules of the Shariah. The central bank needs to take the lead in promoting financial institutions, deposit and loan instruments, and a yield structure conducive to the efficient mobilisation of savings and allocation of resources. In particular, the central bank has the task of fostering the development of primary, secondary, and money markets. As explained above, mere adoption of Islamic rules of finance will not necessarily create the impetus for financial and economic development where the shallowness of financial markets and lack of attractive financial instruments limit the scope of financial intermediation.

Another possible function of the monetary authorities is the enforcement of Islamic regulations concerning contracts and property rights, as they apply to financial and capital markets. Such enforcement is desirable in order to reduce the uncertainties that tend to discourage private investments, and to encourage lending of funds primarily on the basis of the viability and profitability of investment projects rather than the solvency, creditworthiness, or collateral strength of entrepreneurs.[1] The reduction of uncertainty in the structure of contract and property rights is desirable because prohibition of interest by itself creates a moral hazard problem embedded in principal-agent contracts; without a stronger legal framework, such contracts will involve an increase in the cost of monitoring investments and reduction in overall investment itself (W.M. Khan, 1984). In fact, one may venture the opinion that, if the Islamic rules regarding contracts and property rights are not enforced, the main risk of adopting an Islamic financial system, particularly in the initial stages, would not be lower savings but lower investment.

Muslim writers have stressed the need for policies to maintain the stability of the value of currency (Siddiqi, 1982). They envisage an activist role for monetary policy, not only in maintaining a stable value of the currency but also in promoting full employment and growth (Chapra, 1985). They expect that these objectives can be fostered by monetary and credit policies conducted by the central bank (Siddiqi, 1982). Much of the effectiveness of monetary policy in an Islamic economy will depend on which of the schemes for Islamic banking is adopted. Under a fractional reserve system, monetary policy would operate as under a conventional banking system, and the formulation of a financial policy package for stabilisation purposes would be akin to the traditional stabilisation programmes typically supported by the IMF. In the model requiring a 100 per cent reserve requirement, the effectiveness of monetary policy would be weakened as the central bank would be unable to alter the reserve requirements. To that extent, stabilisation targets would have to be realised through control of the monetary base rather than credit.[2]

---

1. It is reasonable to expect that in the long run the latter set of factors is closely correlated to the viability and profitability of investment projects undertaken by the entrepreneurs. Hence, the distinction drawn here relates more to the initial phases of implementation.

2. Those favouring the adopting of the model requiring a 100 per cent reserve requirement argue that it would make the system more efficient because: (a) whereas any switch from high-powered money to deposit money and vice versa in the fractional reserve system creates an inherent instability, such a switch in the 100 per cent reserve system will only change the composition of money, thus leaving the total supply constant; (b) in a fractional reserve system it is more costly to maintain or to increase the existing stock of real balances as a result of changes in money supply arising from deposit creation or from substituting deposit and cash. It is argued that a 100 per cent reserve system contributes to the stability of the economy as a whole. By eliminating any differences between the monetary base and the money supply, thus making the money multiplier equal to unity, the 100 per cent reserve system forces the banking system to be fully liquid. This model would preclude the central bank from using variation in the reserve ratio as a policy instrument. (See M. Khan, 1985.)

Moral suasion will remain an instrument of policy to be exercised by the central bank. Moreover, the suggestion has been made that the central bank can regulate the ratios for profit sharing between banks and enterprises on the one hand and between banks and their depositors on the other. While the adoption of this policy instrument would undoubtedly strengthen the control of the monetary authorities over the volume of credit creation, it would have implications for resource-allocation (Siddiqi, 1982) and represent limitations on the freedom of contract and on the sharing of losses by partners (as laid down in the Sharia). There may also be problems of equity if the profit-sharing rules imposed by the central bank require a lower proportional share in profits than the prescribed share in losses.

The usual regulation, supervision, and control functions of the central bank *vis-à-vis* the banking system can be expected to be continued and reinforced in an Islamic financial system. A further opportunity for enhancement of the control of the banking system is available to the central bank through its purchase of equity shares not only of the banks but also of other financial institutions. This possible instrument, together with those already discussed, should leave the central bank in a position to carry out its traditional leadership role in the financial system.

Selected Bibliography on Islamic Economics and Banking

Abbasi, Masud A., 'Comments on the draft of zakat order', *Industrial Accountant* (Karachi, July–Sept. 1979), pp. 50–4.
——— 'Interest: an economic study on the three economic systems', *Islamic Review* (London, March–April 1969), pp. 28–32.
Abd Al-Bari, M., 'Islam and socialism', *Islamic Literature* (Aug. 1951), pp. 21–7.
Abdul Rauf, M., 'The Islamic doctrine of economics', *Journal of the Rabitah* (Feb.–March 1979), pp. 22–7.
Abdullah, A., 'Islamic banking', *Journal of Islamic Banking and Finance* (Karachi) vol. 4, no. 1, (Jan. 1987).
Abdullah, S. M., 'Zakat and poverty: a comment', *Voice of Islam* (Karachi, Jan. 1976), pp. 194–8.
Abdus-Salam, M., 'The role of fiscal and accounting thought in applying zakat', Unpublished: presented at First International Conference on Islamic Economics (Makkah, 1976).
Abu Ali, S., 'Comments on "Fiscal Policy in an Islamic Economy",' *International Seminar on Monetary and Fiscal Policy of Islam* (Islamabad, 1981).
——— 'Comments on "Implications of Islamic consumption patterns for savings, growth and distribution in a macroeconomic framework", by Fahim Khan', *Second International Conference on Islamic Economics* (Islamabad, 1983).
Abu Saud, M., 'Economic policy in Islam', *Islamic Review* (London, May 1957), pp. 7–14.
——— 'Islamic view of riba', *Islamic Review* (London, Feb. 1957), pp. 9–16.
——— 'The Economic order in the general conception of the Islamic way of life', *Islamic Review* (London, Feb.–March 1967), pp. 11–14, 24–6.
——— 'The exploitation of land and the Islamic law', *Islamic Review* (London, Sept. 1952), pp. 6–10 (Oct. 1952), pp. 5–10.
——— 'Economic policy in Islam', *Islamic Review* (London, May 1957), pp. 7–15.
Abu Saud, 'Money, interest and qirad' in Khurshid Ahmad (ed.), *Studies in Islamic economics* (Jeddah, 1980), pp. 59–83.
Abu Sulaiman, A.H., 'The Theory of the Economics of Islam', *Proceedings of the Third East Coast Regional Conference MSA* (1970).
Abu Zahra, M., 'The zakat', *Second Conference of the Academy of Islamic Research* (Cairo, 1965), pp. 123–65.
Agabany, Fouad, 'Faisal Islamic Bank (Sudan): a promising experience in comprehensive Islamic banking', Unpublished: presented at International Seminar on Monetary and Fiscal Economics of Islam (Islamabad, 1981).
Aghnides, Nicholas P, *Mohammadan theories of finance* (Lahore, 1961).
Ahmad, Afazuddin, 'Economic significance of zakat', *Islamic literature* (Lahore, Aug. 1952), pp. 5–11.
Ahmad, Ausaf, 'Some basic issues of fiscal policy in Islamic economy', *International Conference of Muslim Scholars* (Islamabad, March 1981), vol. I, pp. 1–54.
——— 'A macro theory of distribution in Islamic economy', presented at Second International Conference on Islamic Economics (Islamabad, 1983).
Ahmad, Ilyas, 'Ibn Taimiyah on Islamic economics', *Voice of Islam* (Karachi, Aug. 1961), pp. 557–69.
Ahmad, K., *Towards the monetary and fiscal system of Islam* (Islamabad, 1981).

———— *Monetary and fiscal economics of Islam: an outline of some major subjects of research*, (Jeddah, 1977).

———— (ed.) *Studies in Islamic economics* (Leicester, 1980).

Ahmad, Mahfuz, 'Distributive justice and fiscal and monetary economics in Islam', Unpublished: papers presented at International Seminar on Monetary and Fiscal Economics of Islam (Makkah, 1978).

Ahmad, Mahmud, 'Semantics of theory of interest', *Islamic Studies* (Rawalpindi, June 1967), pp. 171–96.

Ahmad, Rafiq, 'The origin of economics and the Muslims', *Economist*, (Punjab University, June 1969), pp. 17–49.

Ahmad, Sh M., 'Semantics of the theory of interest', *Islamic Studies* (June 1967), pp. 171–95.

———— 'Social justice without tears', *Economist* (Punjab University, June 1969), pp. 71–84

———— 'Man and money', *Islamic Studies* (Islamabad, Sept. 1970), pp. 217–44.

———— 'Interest and unemployment', *Islamic Studies* (Islamabad, March 1969), pp. 9–46.

———— 'Monetary theory of trade cycles', *Islamic Studies* (Islamabad).

———— 'Islamic socialism in Pakistan: an overview', *Islamic Studies* (Islamabad, Summer 1976), pp. 111–21.

———— *Social justice in Islam* (Lahore, 1975).

———— '*Can an economy work without profit and money?*' Unpublished (1981).

———— 'Banking in Islam', *Journal of Islamic Banking and Finance* (Karachi), vol.2 (April–June 1985), pp. 13–27.

Ahmad, S. Wasim, 'Comment on "Fiscal Policy of an Islamic State",' Unpublished: presented at International Seminar on Monetary and Fiscal Economics of Islam (Islamabad, Jan. 1981).

Ahmad, Ziauddin, 'Socio-economic values and Islam and their significance and relevance to the present-day world', *Islamic Studies* (Islamabad, Dec. 1971), pp. 343–55.

———— 'Dr Najjar's introduction to economic theories in Islam', *Islamic Studies* (Islamabad) pp. 269–80.

———— 'The theory of riba', *Islamic Studies*, (Islamabad, Winter 1978), pp. 171–85, reprinted from *Islamic Quarterly* (London, Jan.–June 1978).

———— 'Zakat and economic wellbeing', *Islamic Studies* (Islamabad, Summer 1981).

———— 'Nisab of zakat', *Islamic Studies* (Islamabad, Autumn 1981), pp. 239–59.

———— 'Financial policies and the Prophet', *Islamic Studies* (Islamabad, Spring 1975), pp. 10–25.

———— 'Ushr and ushr lands', *Islamic Studies* (Islamabad, Summer 1980), pp. 76–94.

———— 'Economic co-operation among Islamic countries: implications and modalities of a free trade area', Unpublished: presented at First International Conference on Islamic Economics (Makkah, 1976).

———— 'Comments on "Economics of profit sharing"', Unpublished: presented at International Seminar on Monetary and Fiscal Economics of Islam (Islamabad, Jan. 1981).

———— 'Comments on "Effects of elimination of riba in the distribution of income" by Ali A Rushdi', *Second International Conference on Islamic Economics* (Islamabad, 1983).

———— *Money and banking in Islam* (Jeddah, 1983).

———— 'Interest free banking in Pakistan', *Journal of Islamic Banking and Finance*, (Karachi) vol. 4, no. 1 (Jan. 1987).

Ahmed K. and Ansari, Z.A, *Islamic perspectives: studies in honour of S. A. Maududi* (Leicester, 1979).

Ahmed, Sh M., *Economics of Islam: a comparative study* (Lahore, 1977).

Ahmed Ziauddin and Khan, M.F., *Money and banking in Islam* (Rawalpindi, 1983).

Ahsan, Manazir, 'Baiytul-Mal and its role in the Islamic economy', *Criterion* (Karachi).

Ajijola, A.D., *The Islamic Concept of social justice* (Lahore, 1977).

Akhtar, Ramzan, 'Islamic concept of economic development', *Science, Technology and Development* (Islamabad, July 1982), pp. 8–16.

Al-Arabi, M.A., 'Private ownership of property', *Islamic Review* (London).

—— 'Economics in the social structure of Islam', *Voice of Islam*, (Karachi, Oct. 1958), pp. 5–15, reprinted *World Muslim League* (Singapore) (July–Aug. 1966), pp. 10–25.

—— 'Investment of capital in Islam', *Second Conference of the Academy of Islamic Research*, pp. 103–21.

—— 'The Islamic economy and contemporary economy', *Third Conference of the Academy of Islamic Research* (Cairo, 1966), pp. 201–369.

—— 'Private property and its limits in Islam', *First Conference of the Academy of Islamic Research* (Cairo, 1964).

—— 'Contemporary banking transactions and Islam's view thereon', *Second Conference of the Academy of Islamic Research* (Cairo, 1965), reprinted in *Islamic Review* (London, May 1966), pp. 10–16.

Al-Husaina, Ishaq M., 'Hisba in Islam', *First Conference of the Academy of Islamic Research* (Cairo, 1964), pp. 255–75, reprinted in *Islamic Review* (London, Feb. 1969), pp. 30–6.

Al-Jahri, M.A., 'A monetary and financial structure for an interest-free economy: institutions, mechanisms and policy' in Z. Ahmed et alia (eds), *Money and banking in Islam* (Jeddah, 1983).

—— 'Towards an Islamic macro model of distribution', *Second International Conference on Islamic Economics* (Islamabad, 1983).

Al-Khafif, Sh A., 'Individual property and its limits in Islam', *First Conference of the Academy of Islamic Research*, (Cairo, 1964), pp. 79–103.

Al-Labban, Ibrahim, 'Islam and the problem of poverty', *Islamic Review* (London, Aug. 1967), pp. 14–19.

—— 'The right of the poor to the wealth of the rich', *First Conference of the Academy of Islamic Research* (Cairo, 1964), pp. 167–86.

Al-Masri, Rafiq, 'Banking system in Islam', (Imran Khan Nayaree trans.), *Second International Conference on Islamic Economics* (Islamabad, 1983).

Al-Naggar, Ahmad, 'The healthy path towards economic development: the Islamic alternative', *International Seminar on Islamic Social Justice* (ABU Zaria, Nigeria, Jan. 1978).

Al-Najjar, A.H.A., 'Comments on "Guarantee of a minimum level of living in an Islamic state" by M. N. Siddiqi', *Second International Conference on Islamic Economics* (Islamabad, 1983).

Al-Nisra, Rafiq, *Development finance and distribution in Islamic perspective* (Islamic University, Islamabad, 1984).

Al-Nowaihi, M., 'Fundamentals of economic justice in Islam', *Proceedings of the Third East Coast Regional Conference MSA* (1970), reprinted in *Voice of Islam* (Oct.–Nov. 1972).

Al-Ramadi, Gamal Edin, 'Social security in Islam', Al-Azhar (Cairo, March 1965), pp. 9–12.

Al-Rasul, A.S. Ibrahim, 'Courses of economics with Islamic perspective', *Second International Conference on Islamic Economics* (Islamabad, 1983).

Al-Sayis, M.A., 'Ownership of land and its benefits in Islam', *First Conference of the Academy of Islamic Research* (Cairo, 1964), pp. 127–50.

Al-Syed, Abdul Malik, 'Financial and administrative institutions in the Islamic state', Unpublished: presented at the First International Conference on Islamic Economics (Makkah, 1976).

Al-Tahawi, Ibrahim, 'Principles of economic theory in Islam', *Sixth Conference of the Academy for Islamic Research* (Cairo, 1971), pp. 689–714.

Alam, S., 'Modern economics and ethics', *Muslim News* (April 1985).

Alan, Hasmat, 'Distribution theory under Islamic law' (George Town University, 1953).

Alavi, Q.A., Rahman, 'An introduction to the economic philosophy of Islam', *Islamic Literature* (Lahore, April 1950), pp. 25–34.

Alexander, A.P., 'Industrial entrepreneurship in Turkey, its origin and growth', *Economic development and cultural change* (1960), pp. 349–65.

Ali, Abdul Kadir, 'Land property and land tenure in Islam', *Islamic Review* (London, Dec. 1959), pp. 20–3, also printed in *Islamic Quarterly* (London, April–July 1959), pp. 4–11.

Ali, Ausaf, 'Political economy of the Islamic state', PhD thesis (University of Southern California, 1970).

Ali, Muazzam, 'Islamic banking comes of age', *Conference on Islamic Banking* (London, September 1984).

———— 'Pakistan moves towards its Islamic identity', Presented at the Pakistan Society at Burlington House, London, 15 May 1986. Printed in the Society's Bulletin.

———— *Papers on Islamic Banking* (London, 1984).

———— *Islamic banks and strategies of economic co-operation* (London, 1982).

Ali, S. Aftab, 'Risk bearing and profit sharing in an Islamic framework: some allocational considerations', Unpublished: Presented at International Seminar on Monetary and Fiscal Economics of Islam (Islamabad, Jan. 1981).

Ali, Shaukat, *Administrative ethics in a Muslim state* (Lahore, 1975).

Ali, Syed Ahmad, *Economic foundations of Islam: a social and economic study* (Calcutta, 1961).

Amedroz, H.F., 'The Hisba jurisdiction in the Ahkam Sultaniyyah of Mawardi', *Journal of the Royal Asiatic Society* (London, 1916), pp. 77–101, 287–314.

Ansari, Ageel A., 'An institutional framework for capital formulation in an Islamic economy', *Second International Conference on Islamic Economics* (Islamabad, 1983).

Ariff, M., 'Islamic ethics and economics', *Proceedings of Seventh Annual Conference of AMSS* (USA, 1978), pp. 1–20.

———— 'Comments on "Monetary policy in an Islamic economy"', Unpublished: Presented at International Seminar on Monetary and Fiscal Economics of Islam (Islamabad, Jan. 1981).

———— 'The role of monetary policy in an Islamic economy', Unpublished: Presented at International Seminar on Monetary and Fiscal Economics of Islam (Makkah, 1978).

———— 'Comments on "The economics of poverty in Islam with special reference to Muslim countries" by M A Mannan', *Second International Conference on Islamic Economics* (Islamabad, 1983).

———— *Monetary and fiscal economics of Islam*, (Jeddah, 1978).

Ashtor, Eliahu, 'Banking instruments between the Muslim East and the Christian West', *The Journal of European Economic History* (Winter 1972), pp. 553–73.

Atuallah, Sh, *Revival of zakat* (Lahore, 1949).

Austruy, J., 'Islam's key-problem: economic development', *Islamic Review* (London, 1967–8).

Ayyad, M., Gamaluddin, 'The merits of labour of Islam', *Al-Azhar* (Cairo, April 1966), pp. 7–10.

Banisdar, *Work and the worker in Islam* (Hasan Mashhadi, trans.), (Tehran, 1980).

Bashir, B.A., 'Portfolio management of Islamic banks', PhD thesis (Lancaster University, 1982).

———— 'Portfolio management of Islamic banks: certainty model', *Journal of Banking and Finance*, vol. 7 (1983), pp. 339–54.

Beg, M.A., Jabbar, 'A contribution to the economic history of the caliphate', *Islamic*

Quarterly (July–Dec. 1972), pp. 140–67.

—— 'The status of brokers in Middle Eastern society in the pre-modern period', *The Muslim World* (April 1977), pp. 87–90.

Berger, Morroe, *The Arab World Today* (London, 1962).

Bhatia, Rattan J., and Deena R. Khatkhate, 'Financial intermediation saving mobilisation and enterpreneurial development: the African experience', *International Monetary Fund Staff Papers* (Washington, DC, 1975) vol. 22, no. 1.

Bin Jamal, Mohammad, 'Zakat: a socio-economic power for development and progress of the Muslim community', *World Muslim League* (Singapore, May 1964), pp. 47–52.

Cattan, H., 'The law of Waqfs', *Law in the Middle East* (1955), pp. 203–22.

Chapra, M.A., 'Monetary policy in an Islamic economy', Unpublished: Presented at International Seminar on Monetary and Fiscal Economics of Islam (Islamabad, Jan. 1981).

Chapra, M.U., 'Money and banking in an Islamic framework', Unpublished: Presented at International Seminar on Monetary and Fiscal Economics of Islam (Makkah, 1978).

—— *Objectives of Islamic economic order* (Leicester, 1979).

—— *The economic system of Islam* (London, 1970).

—— *Towards a just monetary system* (Leicester, 1985).

—— 'Money and banking in an Islamic economy' in M. Ariff (ed), *Monetary and fiscal policy of Islam* (Jeddah, 1982).

Chawdury, M.A., *Interest rate and intertemporal efficiency in an Islamic economy: issue revisited* (Jeddah, 1982).

Chowdhury, M.A., 'Foundations of Islamic economics', *Criterion* (Karachi, Jan. 1974).

—— 'Islamic political economy and the human investment revolution', Al-Ittihad (Indiana, April 1978), pp. 31–5.

—— 'The doctrine of riba', *The Journal of Development Studies*, vol. 2. (Peshawar, 1979), pp. 47–68.

—— 'Principles of Islamic economics', *Islamic Studies* (Islamabad, Summer 1981), pp. 89–107.

—— 'The rate of capitalisation in valuation models in an Islamic economy', Unpublished: Proceedings of International Seminar on Monetary and Fiscal Economics of Islam (Islamabad, Jan. 1981).

—— 'A mathematical formulation of mudarabah', *Proceedings of Third National Seminar of Association of Muslim Social Scientists* (Gary, Indiana, 1974).

—— 'A social service model in the Islamic economy', *Proceedings of the Seventh Annual Conference of AMSS* (Indiana, USA, 1978), pp. 31–42.

Conn, Harvie M., 'Islamic socialism in Pakistan: an overview', *Islamic Studies* (Islamabad, Summer 1976), pp. 111–21.

Cook, M.A., (ed.), *Studies in the economic history of the Middle East* (London, 1970).

Cragg, K, 'The intellectual impact of communism upon contemporary Islam', *The Middle East Journal* (Washington, Spring 1954), pp. 127–38.

Daley, J.W., and Puligandia, 'Islam and the concept of progress', *Islamic Review* (London, Feb. 1970), pp. 31–6.

Dannet, Daniel C., *Conversion and the poll tax in early Islam*, (Lahore, 1962).

Dawalibi, Maruf, 'Islam versus capitalism and Marxism', *World Muslim League* (Singapore, May 1966), pp. 14–24.

De Somogyi, J., 'Economic theory in classical Arabic literature', *Studies in Islam* (New Delhi, Jan. 1965).

—— 'Trade in classical Arabic literature', *The Muslim World*.

―――― 'State intervention in trade in classical Arabic literature', *Studies in Islam* (New Delhi, July 1967), pp. 61–4.

―――― 'Economic fundamentals in classical Arabic literature', *Studies in Islam* (New Delhi, July 1966), pp. 115–8.

―――― 'The part of Islam in oriental trade, *Islamic Culture*, (Deccan, 1956), pp. 179–89.

―――― 'Trade in the Quran and Hadith', *The Muslim World* (April 1962), pp. 110–14.

De Zayas, F.G., 'The functional role of zakat in the Islamic social economy', *Islamic Literature* (Lahore, March 1969), pp. 5–10.

―――― 'Tithe lands, kharaj lands and the law of zakat', *Islamic Literature* (Lahore, May 1967), pp. 5–9.

Donohue, J and Esposito, J (eds), *Islam in Transition* (New York, 1982).

El-Alfi, Ezzat S., 'Production, distribution and exchange in khaldun's writings', PhD thesis (University of Minnesota, 1968).

El-Din, S., Ibrahim T., 'Comments on "Implications of Islamic consumption patterns for savings, growth and distribution" by Fahim Khan', *Second International Conference on Islamic Economics* (Islamabad, 1983).

El Naggar, Ahmed, *One hundred questions and 100 answers concerning Islamic banks* (London and Geneva, 1980).

El-Sarraf, F. M., Money market dealings within the framework of the Islamic law, *Journal of Islamic Banking and Finance* (Karachi), vol. 1, no.2, (Spring 1984), pp. 57–64

Farid, Q.M., 'Is interest obsolete?', *Voice of Islam* (Karachi, July 1964), pp. 495–502.

Faridi, F.R., 'On wages in an Islamic economy', *Islamic Though* (Aligarh, April–June 1960), pp. 61–6.

―――― 'The problem of industrial peace', *Islamic Research Circle Bulletin (Rampur, Oct. 1953), pp. 5–18.*

―――― *'Economic development and Islamic values', Islamic Thought* (Aligarh, April 1964), pp. 9–53.

―――― 'Need for a scientific study of Islamic economy', *Islamic Thought* (Aligarh, Sept.–Oct. 1955), pp. 34–5.

―――― 'A theory of fiscal policy in an Islamic state', Unpublished: Presented at International Seminar on Monetary and Fiscal Economics of Islam (Islamabad, Jan. 1981).

―――― 'Public budgeting, capital accumulation and economic growth in Islamic framework', *Second International Conference on Islamic Economics* (Islamabad, 1983).

Fatmi, S., *Economic survey of the Muslim countries* (Islamabad, nd).

Faure, A., 'Trade guilds in Islamic countries in the Middle Ages', *Islamic Review* (London, Jan. 1968), pp. 9–17.

Fisher, S.N., (ed.), *Social forces in the Middle East* (Ithaca, NY, 1955).

Gaiani, A., 'The juridical nature of the Moslem qirad', *East and West* (Rome, 1953), pp. 81–6.

Gardener, G.H., and Sami, A.H., 'Islamic socialism', *The Muslim World* (April 1966), pp. 71–86.

Ghaznavi, S.A.B., *Circulation of wealth in Islam*, Engineering University Islamic Society (Lahore).

Ghoraba, Hammoudah, 'Islam and slavery', *Islamic Quarterly* (London, Oct. 1955), pp. 153–9.

Gibb, H.A.R., 'The fiscal rescript of Umar II', *Arabica* (1955), pp. 1–16.

Goitein, S.D., 'Letters and documents on the Indian trade in medieval times', *Islamic Culture* (Decca, July 1963), pp. 188–205.

―――― 'Commercial and family partnership in the countries of medieval Islam', *Islamic Studies* (Islamabad, Sept. 1964), pp. 315–7

―――― *A Mediterranean society*, vol.1; *Economic foundation: the Jewish communities of the Arab World as portrayed in the documents of the Cairo Geniza* (Berkeley, California, 1967).

Haffar, Ahmad R., 'Economic development in Islam in western scholarship', *Islam and the modern age* (Delhi, May 1975), pp. 5–22 (Aug. 1975), pp. 5–29.

Hahn, Frank, 'Savings and uncertainty', *The Review of Economic Studies* (1970), vol. 37, no. 109, pp. 20–4.

Hakim, K.A., *Islam and communism* (Lahore, 1953).

Halpern, M., 'The implications of communism for Islam', *Muslim World* (Jan. 1953), pp. 28–41.

Hamid, Habeeb, 'On problems of Islamic research in economics', *Islamic Thought* (March–April 1958), pp. 31–2, (May–June 1958), pp. 19–20.

Hamidullah, M., 'Budgeting and taxation in the time of the Holy Prophet', *Islamic Literature* (Lahore, Feb. 1956), pp. 75–84.

——— 'Islam's solution to the basic economic problems: the position of labour', *Islamic Culture* (Deccan, April 1936), pp. 213–33.

——— 'Islam and Communism', *Islamic Review* (London, March 1950), pp. 11–26.

——— 'A suggestion for interest free Islamic monetary fund', *Islamic Review* (London, June 1966), pp. 11–2.

——— 'Islamic insurance', *Islamic Review* (London, March–April 1951), pp. 45–6.

Hamoud, Sami H., 'Islamic banking in theory and practice', *The Universal Message* (Karachi, Oct. 82), pp. 15–17.

Hans, J., 'Islamic law and Western monetary thinking', *Islamic Review* (London, Dec. 1949), pp. 24–6.

Hanson, David and Carmen F. Menezes, 'The effect of capital risk on optimum saving', *Quarterly Journal of Economics*, vol. 92 (Nov. 1978), pp. 653–70.

Haq, Inamul, *Principles and philosophy of democratic socialism in Islam* (Karachi, 1966).

Haque, M. Anzarul, 'A critical study of Jalal al-Din al-Dawwani's contribution to social philosophy', PhD thesis (Aligarh Muslim University).

Haque, M., Atiqul, 'An outline of Islamic banking: its short history and its contrasts with Western banking', *Shefa Welfare Trust* (Dakka).

Haque, M., Riyazul, 'The Islamic economic system: policy implication for its introduction in Pakistan', Unpublished dissertation for MA (Eco) Development Studies (University of Manchester, 1980).

Haque, Ziaul 'Inter-regional and international trade in pre-Islamic Arabia', *Islamic Studies* (Islamabad, Sept. 1968), pp. 207–32.

——— 'Metayage and tax farming in the medieval muslim society', *Islamic Studies* (Autumn 1975), pp. 219–37.

——— 'Origin and development of Ottoman timar system', *Islamic Studies* (Islamabad, Summer 1976), pp. 123–4.

——— 'Riba, interest and profit', *Pakistan Economist* 24 May 1980, pp. 14–35, 31 May 1980, pp. 13–30.

——— Review of 'Studies in Islamic economics', *Hamdard Islamicus* (Karachi, Spring 1982), pp. 93–108.

——— 'The theory of mudarabah (profit sharing) in Islamic jurisprudence', Unpublished: Presented at International Seminar on Monetary and Fiscal Economics of Islam (Islamabad, Jan. 1981).

——— *Islam and feudalism: the economics of riba, interest and profit* (Vanguard Books, Lahore, 1985).

——— *Landlord and peasant in early Islam* (Islamabad, 1977).

Hasan, A., 'Social justice in Islam', *Islamic Studies* (Islamabad, Sept. 1971), pp. 209–19.

Hasan, Hasan Ibrahim, *Islam: a religious, political, social and economic study* (Beirut, 1967).

Hasan, M. Syed, 'The Quranic way out of the present economic tangle, *Islamic Thought* (Aligarh, May–June 1954), pp. 17–19.

Hasan, Najmul, *Social security system of Islam with special reference to zakah* (Jeddah, 1984).

Hasan, Riaz, 'The nature of Islamic urbanisation : a historical perspective', *Islamic Culture* (July 1969), pp. 233–7.

Hasan, Zubair, 'Distributional equity in Islam', Presented at Second International Conference on Islamic Economics (Islamabad, 1983).

Hasanuzzaman, S.M., 'A glossary of classical Islamic terms', *Islamic Order* (Karachi, Jan. 1979), pp. 61–8.

———— 'Zakat, taxes and estate duty', *Islamic Literature* (Lahore, July 1971).

———— 'Zakat and fiscal policy', Unpublished: Presented at First International Conference on Islamic Economics (Makkah, 1976).

———— 'Comments on "The Theory of Mudarabah in Islamic Jurisprudence"', Unpublished: Presented at International Seminar on Monetary and Fiscal Economics of Islam, (Islamabad, Jan. 1981).

———— 'Comments on "Economic Implications of Islamic land Ownership and Land Cultivation" by Mustafa and Askari', Presented at Second International Conference on Islamic Economics (Islamabad, 1983).

———— 'Issues relating to zakat and ushr', *Second International Conference on Islamic Economics* (Islamabad, 1983).

———— 'Economic functions of the Islamic state (up to the end of the Umayyad period)', PhD thesis (Edinburgh University, 1973).

Hassanein, M., 'Towards a model of the economics of Islam', *Proceedings of the Third East Coast Regional Conference* (MSA, 1970).

Hoda, Mir Shamsul, 'Islamic economy', *Islamic Literature* (Lahore, May 1953), pp. 17–25.

Huda, M.A., 'Economics accepting Islam', *World Muslim League* (Singapore, Jan. 1964), pp. 10–17.

Huq, Ataul, 'Poverty, inequality and the role of some Islamic economic institutions', *Second International Conference on Islamic Economics* (Islamabad, 1983).

Hussain, Muzaffer, *Motivation for Economic Achievement in Islam* (Lahore, 1974).

Hussain, S., Mushtaq, 'Interest on money and Islam: a suggested analysis', Report of First Regional Conference of the MSA of US and Canada (Stanford, California, June 1966).

Hussain, Zahid, 'Prohibition of interest in an Islamic state', *Pakistan Economist* (17 Nov. 1979), pp. 17–21, 26.

Ibn Khaldun, *The Mugaddimah: an introduction to history* (London, 1958), pp. 481.

Ibrahim, M., 'The standard of business morality in Islam', *Islamic Literature* (Lahore, May 1971), pp. 281–9.

Idris, Gaafar, 'Economics Sans Man Sans Purpose', Review of J. K., Galbraith's 'Economics and the Public Purpose', *Impact* (London, 28 June, 11 July 1974).

Imamuddin, S.M., 'Maritime trade under the Mamluks of Egypt', *Hamdard Islamicus* (Karachi, Winter 1980), pp. 67–7.

———— 'Al-Hisba in Muslim Spain', *Islamic Culture* (Deccan, Jan. 1963), pp. 25–9.

———— 'Bayt al-Mal and banks in the medieval Muslim world', *Islamic Culture* (Jan. 1960), pp. 22–30.

Imran, M., 'Islamic social justice: the alternative to the curse of capitalism and socialism', *Criterion* (Karachi, Jan.–Feb. 1970), pp. 21–31.

———— *A survey of issues and a programme for research in monetary and fiscal economics of Islam* (Islamabad, 1981).

Iqbal, M., 'Comments on "Effects of the elimination of riba on the distribution of income" by A. A. Rushdi', *Second International Conference on Islamic Economics* (Islamabad, 1983).

Irshad, Sh Ahmed, 'Islamic economy and the elimination of interest', *Voice of Islam* (Karachi, Nov. 1963), pp. 78–85.

—— *Interest Free Banking*, (Karachi, nd).

Irving, T.B., 'Ibn Khaldun on agriculture', *Islamic Literature* (Lahore, Aug. 1955), pp. 31–2.

Ishaque, Khalid M., 'Islamic approach to economics', *Criterion* (Karachi, Oct. 1977), pp. 11–28 (Nov. 1977), pp. 20–32 (Dec. 1977), pp. 17–28.

—— 'Problem of taxation: its Islamic solution', *Muslim News International* (Aug. 1972), pp. 23–6 (Sept. 1972), pp. 13–16.

Islahi, Abdul Axim, *Economic thoughts of Ibn al-Qayyim* (CRIE, Jeddah, 1984).

Islam, Zafarul, 'Aurangzeb's farman on land tax', *Islamic Culture* (Deccan, 2 April 1978), pp. 117–26.

Izadi, Ali M., 'The role of az-zakat in the Islamic system of economics in curing the poverty dilemma', *Proceedings of Third National Seminar of AMSS* (Gary, Indiana, 1974), pp. 9–18, reprinted in *Voice of Islam* (Karachi, June 1975), pp. 436–43.

—— 'The role of az-zakat (an institutionalised charity) in the Islamic System of economics in curing the poverty dilemma', *Proceedings of Third National Seminar of AMSS* (Gary, Indiana, May 1974).

Javed, Mahmud, 'Capitalism and socialism', *Criterion* (Karachi, Sept. 1973), pp. 25–35 (April 1974), pp. 14–31.

Jawed, Nasim A., 'Islamic socialism: an ideological trend in Pakistan in the 1960s', *The Muslim World* (July 1975), pp. 196–216.

Kahf, Monzer, 'Islamic economic system: a review', *Al-Ittihad* (Indiana, Jan. 1978), pp. 39–50.

—— 'Savings and investment functions in a two sector model of Islamic society', Unpublished: Presented at the International Seminar on Monetary and Fiscal Economics of Islam (Makkah, 1978).

—— 'A model of the household decisions in an Islamic economy', *Proceedings of the Third National Seminar of AMSS* (Gary, Indiana, 1974), pp. 19–28.

—— 'Fiscal and monetary policy in an Islamic economy: a theoretical analysis of a three sector model', Unpublished: Presented at International Seminar on Monetary and Fiscal Economics of Islam (Makkah, 1978).

—— 'Taxation policy in an Islamic economy', Unpublished: Presented at International Seminar on Monetary and Fiscal Economics of Islam (Islamabad, Jan. 1981).

—— 'Comments on "Economics of Profit Sharing"', Unpublished: Presented at International Seminar on Monetary and Fiscal Economics of Islam (Islamabad, Jan. 1981).

—— *The Islamic economy* (MSA, Gary, Indiana, 1979).

—— *The calculation of zakat for Muslims in North America* (MSA, Indiana, 1978).

—— *The economic views of Taquiddin Taimeyah (1263–1328): the great radical reformist of the Islamic middle ages* (1973).

—— *A contribution to the study of the economics of Islam* (University of Utah, SLC, July 1973).

—— *Challenges confronting Islamic economics* (University of Utah, SLC, July 1972).

Kamali, A.H., 'Banks and loans under Islamic economic order' *Pakistan Economist* (Karachi, 2–8 Dec. 1978), pp. 32–3 (9 Dec. 1978), pp. 32–3 (16 Dec. 1978), pp. 19–20 (6 Jan. 1979), pp. 33–5.

Karpat, Kemal H. (ed.), *Political and social thought in the contemporary East* (New York, 1970).

Kemal, A.R., 'Comments on ''Risk bearing and profit sharing in an Islamic framework''', Unpublished: Presented at International Seminar on Monetary and Fiscal Economics of Islam (Islamabad, Jan. 1981).

Kerr, M.H., 'Islam and Arab socialism', *Muslim World* (Oct. 1966), pp. 276–81.

Khalifa, A.H., *Islam and communism* (Lahore, Institute of Islamic Culture).

Khan A.J., Wassy M.A., and Siddiquie K., 'Interest-free commercial banking framework', Mimeo (Karachi, 1978).

—— 'Some queries and replies on interest-free banking framework', Mimeo (Karachi, 1978).

Khan, Abdul Jabbar, 'Elimination of riba from the banking system, *Journal of Islamic Banking and Finance* (Karachi), vol. 1, no. 3 (Summer 1984), pp. 22–44.

Khan, Fahim M., 'Macro consumption function in an Islamic framework', *Journal of Research in Islamic Economics*, vol. 2, no.1.

—— 'Factors of production and factor markets in Islamic perspective', International Centre for Research in Islamic Economics.

—— 'Comments on ''Economics of project evaluation in Islamic perspective''', *International Seminar on Monetary and Fiscal Economics of Islam* (Islamabad, Jan. 1981).

—— 'A report on the Islamic banking as practised now in the world', *International Seminar on Monetary and Fiscal Economics of Islam* (Islamabad, Jan. 1981).

—— 'Implications of Islamic consumption patterns for savings, growth and distribution in a macroeconomic framework', *Second International Conference on Islamic Economics* (Islamabad, 1983).

Khan, Ihsan Mohammad, *World Problems and Muslim Economies* (Karachi, 1952).

Khan, M., 'Comments on ''An institutional framework for capital formulation in an Islamic economy'''. *Second International Conference on Islamic Economics* (Islamabad, 1983).

Khan, M. A., 'Islamic economics: an outline plan for research', *Criterion* (Karachi, April 1979), pp. 27–35.

—— 'Jizyah and Kharaj', *Journal of the Pakistan Historical Society* (Karachi, Jan. 1956).

—— *Islamic economics: annotated sources in English and Urdu* (The Islamic Foundation, Leicester, 1983).

Khan, M. Ajmal, 'Islam and usury', *Studies in Islam* (New Delhi, April 1964), pp. 86–92.

Khan, M. Akram, 'The theory of employment in Islam', *Islamic Literature* (Lahore, April 1968), pp. 5–16.

—— 'The economics of fatah', *Criterion* (Karachi, March 1976), pp. 13–20.

—— 'Economic implications of tawhid, risala and akhira', *Criterion* (Karachi, June–July 1977), pp. 22–43.

—— 'Economic values in Islam', *Criterion* (Karachi, Feb. 1977), pp. 14–24.

—— 'Ideological dimensions of the theory of inflation', *Criterion* (Karachi, Jan.–Feb. 1978), pp. 7–38.

—— 'A survey of contemporary Islamic thought in the institution of interest', *Islamic Education* (Lahore, July–Aug. 1973).

—— 'Interest-free banking: some further questions', *Islamic Education* (Lahore, March–June 1972), pp. 129–47.

—— 'Interest-free banking', *Islamic Studies* (Summer 1977).

—— 'Stock exchanges: their functions and need for reform', *Criterion* (Karachi, Jan. 1972), pp. 28–38.

—— 'Modern taxation and zakat', *Islamic Education* (Lahore, May–June 1974), pp. 7–15.

—— 'International monetary crisis: causes and cure', *Criterion* (Karachi).

────── 'Types of business organisation in Islamic economy', *Islamic Literature* (Lahore, Aug. 1971), pp. 5–16.

────── 'Fiscal system of Islam: a review article', *Islamic Education* (Lahore, July–Aug. 1975), pp. 35–42.

────── 'Theory of employment in Islam', *Islamic Literature* (Lahore, April 1968), pp. 5–16.

────── 'International monetary crisis: causes and cure', *Criterion* (Karachi, Mar.–Apr. 1971), pp. 5–19.

────── 'A profile of riba-free banking', Unpublished: Presented at International Seminar on Monetary and Fiscal Economics of Islam (Makkah, 1978).

────── 'Al-hisba and the Islamic economy', *International Conference of Muslim Scholars* (Islamabad, March 1981), vol. 1, pp. 68–80.

────── *A survey of contemporary economic thought in Islam*, Mimeo.

Khan, M. Ali, 'Non-interest pricing of capital and general equilibrium in an Islamic economy', Unpublished: Presented at the International Seminar on Monetary and Fiscal Economics of Islam (Islamabad, Jan. 1981).

Khan, M.E., 'Is Islam against family planning?', *Islam and the Modern Age* (New Delhi, May 1975), pp. 61–72.

Khan, M. Ihsanulla, 'Communism and Islam contrasted', *Islamic Literature* (April 19512), pp. 11–21.

Khan, M., Shabbir, 'A suggestion to the students of economics', *Islamic Thought* (Aligarh, July–Aug. 1955).

Khan, Mohsin S., 'Interest-free banking: a theoretical analysis', *Staff Papers, IMF* (Washington), vol. 33 (March 1986), pp. 1–27.

Khan, Mohsin S., and Abbas Mirakhor, 'The financial system and monetary policy in an Islamic economy', (1985) unpublished, IMF.

Khan, M.Z., *Islam: its meaning for modern man* (London, 1962).

Khan, Mir Sa'adat Ali, 'The Mohammadan laws against usury and how they are evaded', *Comparative Legislation* (1920), pp. 233–44.

Khan, S. Rafi, 'Comments on 'Poverty, inequality and the role of some Islamic economic institutions' by A Huq', *Second International Conference on Islamic Economics* (Islamabad, 1983).

Khan, Shahrukh R., 'Profit and loss sharing: an economic analysis of an Islamic financial system', Unpublished: PhD thesis (University of Michigan, 1983).

────── 'An economic analysis of a PLS model for the financial sector', *Pakistan Journal of Applied Economics*, vol. 3, no. 2 (Winter 1984), pp. 89–106.

Khan, Waqar Masood, 'Toward an interest-free Islamic economic system: a theoretical analysis of prohibiting debt financing', PhD thesis (Boston University, 1984).

Khurshid, Ahmad, 'Method of approach to economics', *Islamic Thought* (Aligarh, Mar.–Apr. 1955).

Kifayatullah, 'Economic thought in the eighth century: the Muslim contribution', *Voice of Islam* (Karachi, March 1976), pp. 301–4.

Kilingmulier, E., 'The concept and development of insurance in Islamic countries', *Islamic Culture* (1969), pp. 27–37.

Kister, M.J., 'The market of the Prophet', *Journal of the Economic and Social History of the Orient* (Leiden, Jan. 1965), pp. 272–6.

────── 'The social and political implications of three traditions in the "Kitab al-Kharaj" of Yahya B., Adam', *Journal of the Economic and Social History of the Orient* (Leiden, Oct. 1960), pp. 326–34.

Knoun, Sh Abdullah, 'Private property and its limits in Islam', *Proceedings of the First Conference of the Academy of Islamic Research* (Cairo, 1964).

Labib, Subhi, 'Capitalism in medieval Islam', *The Journal of Economic History*, vol. 29

(1969), pp. 79–96.

Laliwala, Jaferhusen I., 'Inflation in an Islamic economy', *International Seminar on Monetary and Fiscal Economics of Islam* (Makkah, 1978).

Latham, J.D., 'Observations on the test and translation of Al-Jarsifi's treatise on "Hisba"', *Journal of Semitic Studies* (1960), pp. 124–43.

Leland Hayne, E., 'Saving and uncertainty: the precautionary demand for saving', *Quarterly Journal of Economics*, vol. 82 (1968), No. 3, pp. 465–73.

Lewis, Archibald R., (ed), *The Islamic world and the West* (London, 1970).

Lewis, Bernard, 'Communism and Islam', *International Affairs* (London, 1954), pp. 1–12.

Lokkegaard, F., *Islamic taxation* (Lahore, 1979).

Lombard, M., *The golden age of Islam* (Amsterdam, 1975).

Mahmoud, Mabid, 'Frictions, power rationing and al-Zakat', *Proceedings of Third National Seminar of AMSS* (Gary, Indiana, May 1974).

Majid, A.A., 'A strategy of economic co-operation among the Islamic countries', Unpublished: Presented at First International Conference on Islamic Economics (Makkah, 1976).

Majid, Abdul, 'Islam, Christianity and monopoly', *Islamic Review* (London, Aug. 1940), pp. 287–90.

Malik, Muhammad Shafi., 'Wages in an Islamic economy', *Islamic Thought* (Aligarh, July–Sept. 1960), pp. 62–7.

Malik, Zahid, *Re-emerging Muslim world* (Lahore, 1974).

Mamuddin, S.M., 'Commercial relations of Spain with Ifriqiyah and Egypt in the tenth AC', *Islamic Culture* (Deccan, Jan. 1964), pp. 9–14.

Mannan, M.A., 'Indexation in an Islamic economy: problems and possibilities', *The Journal of Development Studies* (Peshawar, 1981), pp. 41–51.

—— 'Consumption loan in Islam', *Islamic Review* (London, Mar. 1970), pp. 19–22.

—— 'Islam and trends in modern banking: theory and practice of interest-free banking', *Islamic Review* (London, Nov.–Dec. 1968), pp. 5–10 (Jan. 1969), pp. 28–33.

—— 'A Muslim world bank: urgent need', *Criterion* (Karachi, Jan.–Feb. 1971), pp. 15–20.

—— 'Review of "Risk bearing and profit sharing in an Islamic framework"', Unpublished: Presented at International Seminar on Monetary and Fiscal Economics of Islam, (Islamabad, Jan. 1981).

—— 'The economics of poverty in Islam with special reference to Muslim countries', *Second International Conference on Islamic Economics* (Islamabad, 1983).

—— *Islamic economics, theory and practice* (Lahore, 1970).

—— *Islamic perspectives on market prices and allocation* (Jeddah, 1982).

—— *Abstracts of researches in Islamic economics* (Jeddah, 1984).

—— *Why is Islamic economics important? Seven reasons for believing* (Jeddah, 1982).

Manzar, Abdul Moiz, 'On economic development and Islamic values', *Islamic Thought* (Aligarh, Jan. 1965), pp. 66–70.

—— 'Economics needs a reconstruction', *Islamic Thought* (Aligarh, Mar.–April. 1955).

Mawdudi, A.A., 'Principles and objectives of Islam's economic system', *Criterion* (Karachi, Mar.–Apr. 1969), pp. 44–58.

—— 'Birth control' (Lahore, 1974).

—— 'The economics problem of man and its economic solution' (Lahore, 1975).

Meenai, S.A., *Money and banking in Pakistan* (Karachi, 1984).

Merk, J., 'Socialist ideas in the poetry of Muhmmad Iqbal', *Studies in Islam* (New Delhi, June 1968), pp. 167–79.

Metawally, M.M., 'Fiscal policy in the Islamic economy', Unpublished: Presented at

International Seminar on Monetary and Fiscal Economics of Islam (Islamabad, Jan. 1981).

Meyer, A.J., 'Entrepreneurship and economic development in the Middle East', *Public Opinion Quarterly* (1959), pp. 391–6.

―――― 'Economic thought and its application in the Middle East', *Middle East Economic Papers* (Beirut, 1956), pp. 66–74.

―――― 'Entrepreneurship, the missing link in the Arab state', *Middle East Economic Papers* (Beirut, 1954), pp. 24–8.

―――― *Middle Eastern capitalism* (Cambridge, Mass, 1959).

Mintjes, H., 'The shariah and social justice', *Al-Mushir* (Rawalpindi, Apr.–June 1977), pp. 99–105.

―――― *Social justice in Islam* (Amsterdam, 1977).

Mohiuddin, Ghulam, 'On market mechanism under the influence of Islamic spirit', *Islamic Thought* (Aligarh, Jan.–Feb. 1958).

Mohsin, M., 'Problems and development of Islamic banks', *Journal of the Rabitah* (Makkah, May 1979), pp. 22–7.

―――― 'Comments on "Monetary policy in an Islamic economy"', *International Seminar on Monetary and Fiscal Economics of Islam* (Islamabad, Jan. 1981).

―――― *Assessment of corporate securities in terms of Islamic investment requirements* (CRIE, Jeddah, 1983).

Mukherji, Badal, *Theory of a firm in a zero interest rate economy* (CRIE, Jeddah, 1984).

Maradpuri, A.M., *Conflict between socialism and Islam* (Lahore, 1970).

Muslehuddin, M., 'Islamic commonwealth and Muslim world bank', *Muslim News International* (Karachi, Jan. 1971), pp. 15–18.

―――― 'Interest-free banking and feasibility of mudarabah', Unpublished: Presented at First International Conference on Islamic Economics (Makkah, 1976).

―――― *Economics and Islam* (Lahore, 1974).

―――― *Banking and Islamic law* (Karachi, 1974).

―――― *Insurance and Islamic law* (Lahore, 1969).

―――― *Sociology and Islam* (Lahore, 1977).

―――― *Islamic socialism: what it implies* (Lahore, 1975).

―――― *Banking and Islamic law* (Karachi, 1974).

Muslim, A.G., 'Islam and the problem of inflation', *Criterion* (Karachi, Jan. 1977), pp. 5–10.

―――― 'The early development of the Islamic concept of riba', *Current British Research in Middle Eastern and Islamic Studies* (Durham, 1971).

―――― 'The theory of interest in Islamic law and the effects of interpretation of this by the Hanafi school up to the end of the Mughal Empire', Unpublished: PhD Thesis (University of Glasgow, 1974).

Mustafa, A., and Askara, H.G., 'Economic implications of Islamic land cultivation', *Second International Conference on Islamic Economics* (Islamabad, 1983).

Nabhani, S.T. Din, 'The economic system of Islam', *Islamic Review* (London, July 1953), pp. 28–32 (Aug. 1953), pp. 7–13.

Nadvi, S.H.H., 'Al-Iqta: a historical survey of land tenure and land revenue administration in some Muslim countries, with special reference to Persia', *Proceedings of the Third East Coast Regional Conference MSA (USA), 1970* (1973), pp. 125–56, reprinted in *Islamic Studies* (Islamabad, 1971).

Naqvi, K.A., 'Comments on "The economics of poverty in Islam with special reference to Muslim countries", by M.A., Mannan', *Second International Conference on Islamic Economics* (Islamabad, 1983).

Naqvi, S.N.H., 'Ethical foundations of Islamic economics', *Islamic Studies* (Islamabad, Summer 1978), pp. 1–35.

——— 'Economics of human rights: an Islamic perspective', *Hamdard Islamicus* (Karachi, Summer 1981), pp. 31–51.

——— 'Islamic economic system: fundamental issues', *Islamic Studies* (Islamabad, Winter 1977), pp. 327–46.

——— 'Misunderstanding axiomatic approach: an author explains', *The Universal Message* (Karachi, Nov. 1982), pp. 24–5.

——— 'Interest rate and inter-temporal allocative efficiency in an Islamic economy', Unpublished: Presented at International Seminar on Monetary and Fiscal Economics of Islam (Makkah, 1978).

——— *An agenda for Islamic economic reform* (Islamabad, 1980).

——— *Individual freedom, social welfare and Islamic economics* (Islamabad, 1981).

——— *Ethics and economics: an Islamic synthesis* (Leicester, 1981).

——— *On replacing the institution of interest in a dynamic Islamic economy* (Islamabad, 1982).

Nazeer, M.M., *The Islamic economic system: a few highlights* (Islamabad, 1981).

Neinhaus, V., 'Role of Islamic banks in national development and international co-operation: a Western view', *The Universal Message* (Karachi, Aug. 1982), pp. 8–10, (Sep. 1982), pp. 18–19.

——— *Literature on Islamic economics*, (Cologne, 1982).

Oksay, Ilhan U., 'International monetary order and OPEC's surplus fund: the implications for the Islamic world', *Second International Conference on Islamic Economics* (Islamabad, 1983).

Otiti, A.O.G., 'Comments on "International monetary order and OPEC's surplus funds", by I.U. Oksay', *Second International Conference on Islamic Economics*, (Islamabad, 1983).

Parwez, G.A., *Quranic Economics* (Lahore, nd).

Pellat, C.L., 'Some remarks on "A problem of taxation in medieval Islam"', *Hamdard Islamicus* (Karachi, Spring 1981), pp. 15–22.

Perwez, G.A., '*The Quranic economics*', *Islamic Review* (London, Jan. 1960), pp. 26–30.

Phelps, Edmond, 'The accumulation of risky capital: a sequential utility analysis' in D.D. Hestor and James Tobin (eds), *Risk aversion and portfolio choice* (New York, 1967), pp. 137–53.

Poliak, A.N., 'Classification of land in Islamic law and its technical terms', *American Journal of Semitic Languages and Literatures* (1957), pp. 50–62.

Pryor, Frederick L., 'The Islamic Economic System', *Journal of Comparative Economics* (New York), vol. 9 (1985), pp. 197–223.

Qadir, A., 'Comments on the "Rate of capitalisation in an Islamic economy"', Unpublished: Presented at International Seminar on Monetary and Fiscal Economics of Islam, (Islamabad, Jan. 1981).

——— 'Comments on "Fiscal policy in an Islamic economy"', Unpublished: Presented at International Seminar on Monetary and Fiscal Economics of Islam, (Islamabad, Jan. 1981).

Qadri, Anwar A., 'The shariah and other economic systems', *Criterion* (Karachi, Sept.–Oct. 1959), pp. 39–53.

Quraishi, Marghoob A., 'Investment and economic development in Muslim countries' *Proceedings of Third National Seminar of AMSS* (Gary, Indiana, May 1974).

Qureshi, A.H., A critical study of Wellhausen's theory of land and poll-tax under Muslims', *Islamic Literature* (Lahore, Jan.–Feb. 1959), pp. 45–56.

——— 'Assessment and collection of jizyah under Umar I', *Voice of Islam* (Karachi).

——— 'The terms kharaj and jizya and their implications', *Journal of Punjab Historical Society* (June 1961), pp. 27–38.

Qureshi, A.I., 'Views of Islam on interest', *Islamic Review* (London, July 1957), pp. 5–10.

───── *Islam and the theory of interest* (Lahore, 1974 (1946)).

───── *Economic and social system of Islam* (Lahore, 1979).

───── *Fiscal system of Islam* (Lahore, 1978).

Qureshi, A.M., 'Wages in an Islamic economy' *Islamic Thought* (Aligarh, Mar.–Apr. 1959), pp. 24–8.

───── 'On "Wages" in an Islamic economy, *Islamic Thought* (Aligarh, Oct.–Dec. 1960), pp. 40–5.

Qureshi, D.M., 'The religious import and rationale', *Islamic Order* (Karachi, 1980).

───── 'Some aspects of the introduction of zakat', *Industrial Accountant* (Karachi, July–Sep. 1979), pp. 11–15.

───── 'Investment financing on the basis of shared risk', *Journal of Islamic Banking and Finance* (Karachi), vol. 2, no.2 (April–June 1985), pp. 7–12.

Qureshi, M.A., 'Investment and economic development in Muslim countries', *Proceedings of Third National Seminar of AMSS* (Gary, Indiana, 1974), pp. 1–8.

Qureshi, M.L., *Problems and prospects of development and economic co-operation among Islamic countries* (Islamabad, 1974).

Qutb, Sayyid, 'The basis of social justice in Islam', *Criterion* (Karachi, July–Aug. 1968), pp. 5–18.

Rafiuddin, M., *The fallacy of Marxism* (Lahore, 1969).

Rafiullah, 'Birth control in the light of', *World Muslim League* (Singapore, July–Aug. 1966), pp. 26–31.

Ragab, Ibrahim A., 'Islam and development', *World Development*, vol. 8 (London, 1980), pp. 512–21.

Rahf, M., 'Contemporary challenges to Islamic economists', *Al-Ittihad* (Gary, Indiana, April 1978).

Rahman, A., *Economic doctrines of Islam* (Lahore, 1975–6, 3 vols, pp. 224, 273, 275.

Rahman, Anisur, 'A methodology for the formulation of urban development plans in the Islamic context with an application to al-Madina al-Munawwara', *Second International Conference on Islamic Economics* (Islamabad, 1983).

Rahman, Fazlur, 'Economic principles of Islam', *Islamic Studies* (Islamabad, Mar. 1969), pp. 1–8.

───── 'Riba and interest', *Islamic Studies* (Karachi, March 1964), pp. 1–43.

Rahman, Fazlur (Gunnavri) 'A study of commercial interest in Islam', *Islamic Thought* (Aligarh, July–Oct. 1958), pp. 24–46.

───── *Banking and insurance: economic doctrines of Islam* (London).

Rashad, Shah M., 'Land ownership and tenure in Islam', *Islamic Thought* (Aligarh, 1959), pp. 29–34.

Rasul, G. and Khan, A.M., *Patterns of trade among Muslim countries* (Islamabad).

Ready, R.K., 'The Egyptian municipal savings bank project', *International Development Review* (June 1967), pp. 2–5.

Richards, D.S., (ed), *Commercial techniques in early medieval Islamic trade* (Oxford, 1970).

Rodinson, Maxime, *Islam and capitalism* (Paris, 1966).

Rozenthal, Franz, *Ibn Khaldun: the Muqaddimah, an introduction to history*, vol. I (London, 1958).

Rushdi, A.A., 'Effects of the elimination of riba on the distribution of income', *Second International Conference on Islamic Economics* (Islamabad, 1983).

Rycx, Jean-Francois, *Islamic investment companies: questions regarding the Islamic investment company (Bahamas) and Dar Al-Maal Al-Islami.*

Sabzwari, M.A., 'System of zakat, *Dawn* (Karachi, April 21, 28, 1978; May 5, 12, 19, 1978).

───── *A study of zakat and ushr with special reference to Pakistan* (Karachi, 1979).

Sahibzada, M.I., 'The economic implications of an Islamic state', *Journal of University of Peshawar* (Dec. 1953), pp. 96–125.

Saiyigh, Y.A., *Entrepreneurs of Lebanon: the role of the business leader in a developing economy* (Cambridge, Mass, 1962).

Salama, A.A., 'Fiscal policy of an Islamic state', Unpublished: Presented at International Seminar on Monetary and Fiscal Economics of Islam (Islamabad, Jan. 1981).

───── 'Fiscal analysis of zakat with special reference to Saudi Arabia's experience in zakat', Unpublished: Presented at International Seminar on Monetary and Fiscal Economics of Islam (Makkah, 1978).

Saleem, M., 'Ethical justification of family planning', *Islamic Studies* (Islamabad, Sept. 1969), pp. 253–64.

Sandmo, A., 'The effect of uncertainty on savings decisions', *The Review of Economic Studies* (July 1970), vol. 37, no. 111, pp. 353–60.

Sarkar, Abdul Bari, *The concept of Islamic socialism* (Dacca, 1964).

Sattar, M.A., 'Ibn Khaldun's contribution to economic thought', *Proceedings of the Third East Coast Regional Conference, MSA (US) 1970* (1978), pp. 157–68.

Sattar, S.A., 'Interest-free banking', *Pakistan Management Review* (Karachi, 1974), reprinted in *Criterion* (Karachi, June 1974), pp. 15–26.

Schacht, J., 'Early doctrines on waqfs', *Mel Koprulu* (1953), pp. 443–52.

Schacht, J., and Bosworth C.E., (eds), *The Legacy of Islam* (Oxford, 1974).

Schieffelin, Olivia (ed), *Muslim attitudes towards family planning* (New York, 1973).

Shafi, M.M., 'Distribution of wealth in Islam', *Muslim News International* (Karachi, Feb. 1969), pp. 5–10 (Mar. 1969), pp. 3–8.

───── *Islamic jurisprudence* (Lahore, 1971).

Shan, S.Y., 'Islam and productive credit', *Islamic Review* (London, March 1959), pp. 34–7.

───── *Islamic jurisprudence* (Lahore, 1971).

Shahidi, Tafaz, 'Insurance in Islam and the Imamate's opinion, Unpublished: Presented at the First International Conference on Islamic Economics (Makkah, 1976).

Shakir, A.M.A., 'Individual and social responsibility in Islamic thought', PhD thesis (New York University, 1966).

Sharif, M. Raihan, 'Ibn Khaldun: the pioneer economist, *Islamic Literature* (Lahore, May 1955), pp. 33–40.

───── 'The concept of economic development in Islam', *Second International Conference on Islamic Economics* (Islamabad, 1983).

───── *Islamic social framework* (Lahore, 1970).

Sheikh, N.A., *Some aspects of the constitution and the economics of Islam* (Woking, 1961).

Sherwani, H.K., 'Ibn-e-Khaldun and his politico-economic thought', *Islamic Culture* (April 1970), pp. 71–80.

───── 'Ibn-e-Taimyah's economic thought', *Islamic Literature* (Lahore, Jan. 1956), pp. 9–23.

Siddiqi, A.H, 'Comments on "Taxation policy in an Islamic state"', Unpublished: Presented at International Seminar on Monetary and Fiscal Economics of Islam (Islamabad, Jan. 1981).

───── *A bibliography of Islamic banking* (Karachi University).

Siddiqi, Amir H., *The origins and development of Muslim institutions* (Karachi, 1969).

Siddiqi, Aslam, *Modernisation menaces muslims* (Lahore, 1974).

Siddiqi, Kalim, 'Islamic development plan', *Al-Islam* (Singapore, Jan.–Mar. 1974), pp. 24–30.

Siddiqi, M.A.M., 'Riba-usury and interest: Quran's verdict is clear', *Islamic Order* (Karachi, 1980).

Siddiqi, Mazlaruddin, *Marxism or Islam?* (Lahore, 1975).

Siddiqi, M.M., 'Islam and economic exploitation', *Islamic Literature* (Lahore, June 1968), pp. 25–40.

—— 'Socialistic trends in Islam', *Iqbal* (Karachi, April 1952), pp. 65–82.

—— 'Economics of Islam', *Islamic Thought* (Aligarh, 1970), pp. 22–3.

—— 'A model of interest-free banking', *Criterion* (Karachi, July–Aug. 1961), pp. 19–33, reprinted *Journal of Islamic Studies* (Cairo, Oct. 1969), pp. 1–22.

—— 'Problems of Islamic research', *Islamic Thought* (Aligarh, Oct.–Dec. 1957), pp. 1–8.

—— 'Industrial peace', *Islamic Thought* (Aligarh, Oct.–Dec. 1959), pp. 24–8.

—— 'A survey of contemporary Islamic literature on money, banking and monetary policy', Unpublished: *International Seminar on Monetary Economics of Islam* (Makkah, 1978).

—— 'Comments on '' The elimination of interest from the economy''', *International Seminar on Monetary and Fiscal Economics of Islam* (Islamabad, Jan. 1981).

—— 'Economics of profit sharing', Unpublished: Presented at International Seminar on Monetary and Fiscal Economics of Islam (Islamabad, Jan. 1981).

—— 'An Islamic approach to economics', *Seminar on Islamisation of Knowledge* (Islamabad, 1982).

—— 'Guarantee of a minimum level of living in an Islamic state : basis in shariah rationale and contemporary implications', *Second International Conference on Islamic Economics* (Islamabad, 1983).

—— *Issues in Islamic banking* (Leicester, 1983).

—— *Insurance in an Islamic economy* (Leicester, 1985).

—— *Banking without interest* (Leicester, 1983).

—— *Economic enterprise in Islam* (Lahore, 1972).

—— *Contemporary literature on Islamic economics* (Leicester, 1978).

—— *Some aspects of Islamic economy* (Lahore, 1970).

—— *Banking without interest* (Leicester, 1983).

—— *Rationale of Islamic banking* (Jeddah, 1980).

—— *Muslim economic thinking* (CRIE, Jeddah, 1981).

—— *Recent works on history of economic thought in Islam: a survey* (CRIE, Jeddah, 1982).

—— 'Muslim economic thinking: a survey of contemporary literature' in Khurshid Ahmad (ed.), *Studies in Islamic economics* (Jeddah, 1980).

—— 'Islamic approaches to money, banking and monetary policy: a review in M. Ariff (ed.), *Monetary and fiscal economics of Islam* (Jeddah, 1982), pp. 25–38.

Siddiqi, S.A., *Public finance in Islam* (Lahore, 1975).

Siddiqui, A.R., *Islamic studies: a select guide to bibliographic and reference material* (Leicester, 1979).

Spengler, J.J., 'Economic thought of Islam: Ibn Khaldun', *Comparative studies in society and history* (The Hague, 1964), pp. 268–306.

Stigler, George J., 'Imperfections in the capital market', *Journal of Political Economy* (Chicago) vol. 75 (June 1967), pp. 287–92.

Suhrawardi, A. Al-Mamoon, 'The wakf of moveables', *Journal Proceedings of the Asiatic Society of Bengal N S*, 7 (1911), pp. 323–40.

Sutcliffe, Claud R., 'Is Islam an obstacle to development?', *The Journal of Developing Areas* (Illinois University, Oct. 1975), pp. 77–81.

Syed, J.W., 'Islam and material progress', *Islamic Literature* (Lahore, July 1954), pp. 15–19.

Tabakoglu, A., 'Labour and capital concepts in Islamic economics', *Second International Conference on Islamic Economics* (Islamabad, 1983).

Taher, A., 'Comments on "Public budgeting, capital accumulation and economic growth in Islamic Framework", by F.R., Faridi', *Second International Conference on Islamic Economics* (Islamabad, 1983).

Tahir, Sayyid, 'Comments on "A macro theory of distribution in Islamic economy", by Ausaf Ahmed', *Second International Conference on Islamic Economics* (Islamabad, 1983).

Tritton, A.S., 'Notes on the Muslim system of pensions', *Bulletin of the School of Oriental and African Studies* (1954), pp. 170–2.

Tug, Salih, 'The centralisation of the zakat and individual freedom', Unpublished: Presented at International Conference on Islamic Economics (Makkah, 1976).

Tuma, E.H., 'Early Arab economic policies', *Islamic Studies* (Islamabad, March 1965), pp. 1–23.

Udovitch, A.L., 'Labour partnerships in early Islamic law', *Journal of Economic and Social History of the Orient* (Leiden, 1967), pp. 64–80.

—— 'Credit as a means of investment in medieval Islamic trade', *Journal of the American Oriental Society* (July–Sept. 1967), pp. 260–4.

—— *partnership and profit in medieval Islam* (New Jersey, 1970).

Ulgener, S.F., 'Monetary conditions of the economic growth and the Islamic concept of interest', *Islamic Review* (London, Feb. 1967), pp. 11–14.

Uzair, M., 'Some conceptual and practical aspects of interest-free banking', *Islamic Studies* (Islamabad, Winter 1976), pp. 247–69.

—— 'Interestless banking: will it be a success?', *Voice of Islam* (Karachi).

—— 'Comments on "Fiscal policy in an Islamic state"', Unpublished: Presented at International Seminar on Monetary and Fiscal Economics of Islam (Islamabad, Jan. 1981).

—— 'Comments on " A methodology for the formulation of urban development plan in the Islamic context with an application to Madina Al-Munawwara", by Anis Ur Rehman', Discussion paper for the Second International Conference on Islamic Economics (Islamabad, 1983).

—— 'Comments on "Economic implications of Islamic land ownership and land cultivation", by Mustafa and Askari', *Second International Conference on Islamic Economics* (Islamabad, 1983).

—— *Interest-free banking* (Karachi, 1978).

—— 'Central banking operations in an interest-free banking system' in M. Ariff (ed.), *Monetary and fiscal economics of Islam* (Jeddah, 1982), pp. 211–36.

Wafi, A.A., 'Economics integration in Islam', *Sixth Conference of the Academy of Islamic Research* (Al-Azhar, Cairo, 1971)

Wafi, A.A.W., 'Islamic socialism: the best guard against communism', *Al-Islam* (Singapore, Jan.–Mar. 1974), pp. 24–30.

Wickers, G.M., 'Al-Jarsifi on the hisba', *Islamic Quarterly* (London, 1956–7), pp. 176–87.

Wohlers-Scharf, T., *Arab and Islamic banking: new business partners for developing countries* (Paris, 1983).

Yusuf, M.M., *Law and philosophy of zakat* (Damascus, 1960).

Yusuf, S.M., *Studies in Islamic history and culture* (Lahore 1970).

Zaidi, N., 'Pakistan: restructuring the laws for Islamic banking', *Journal of Islamic Banking and finance* vol. 4, no.1 (Karachi, Jan. 1987).

Zaim, Sabahaddin, 'Comments on "The concept of economic development in Islam", by M.R., Sharif', *Second International Conference on Islamic Economics* (Islamabad, 1983).

Zaman, Raquibuz, 'Workability of an Islamic economic system in the modern world, *Proceedings of the Seventh Annual Conference of AMSS* (Indiana, 1978), pp. 21–30.

Zarqa, A., 'Capital allocation, efficiency and growth in an interest-free Islamic economy', *Journal of Economics and Administration* no. 16, (Jeddah, Nov. 1982), pp. 43–55.

————— 'Stability in an interest-free Islamic economy', Unpublished mimeo (Feb. 1983).

Zarqa, A. and Alkaff, S.H., 'Financing of durable consumer products under Islamic banking', *The Universal Message* (Karachi, Feb. 1983), pp. 11–12.

————— 'International Islamic Bank Ltd, Dacca', *The Universal Message* (Karachi, Feb. 1982), pp. 23–5.

Zarqa, M.A., 'Economics of project evaluation in Islamic perspective', Unpublished: Presented at International Seminar on Monetary and Fiscal Economics of Islam (Islamabad, Jan. 1981).

Zerruq, H.R.M., 'Islam and family planning', *Islamic Literature* (Lahore, Aug.–Sept. 1958), pp. 71–4.

Part Two

Directory of Islamic Financial Institutions

Introduction

This directory has been compiled from the annual reports of the institutions concerned and from their responses to a questionnaire sent out by the International Association of Islamic Banks. There has been no independent audit of the figures provided. Most Islamic financial institutions are included in the directory (see index below); a few, however, have been omitted, either because their annual reports were not available, or the questionnaire was not completed and returned, or because several institutions are in their infancy and sufficient information was not forthcoming. Those seeking further information should write to the editor at The Banking Centre, Loughborough University, Loughborough, Leics LE11 3TU.

The publishers wish to apologise for the incorrect placement of Tadamon Islamic Bank (p. 124). This should be listed under Sudan.

Index

Islamic Banks and Financial Institutions

	United Bank Limited
Qatar	Qatar Islamic Bank (SAQ)
Sudan	Islamic Bank for Western Sudan
	Islamic Co-operative Development Bank
	Faisal Islamic Bank (Sudan)
Turkey	Faisal Finance Institution
UAE	Dubai Islamic Bank
UK	Al Rajhi Company for Islamic Investments Limited

BAHAMAS

Massraf Faisal Al-Islami (Bank and Trust) Bahamas Limited

Norfolk House, Third Floor
Frederick Street
PO Box N-9935
Nassau
Bahamas

Head Office

Dar Al-Maal Al-Islami (DMI) SA
84 Avenue Louis-Casai
PO Box 161
1216 Cointrin
Geneva
Switzerland

Telephone/Telex/Cable

Tel: (809) 322 14 61, 322 14 62, 322 14 63, 322 14 64
Telex: (20) 274 MASSRAF

Other Branches: N/A

Date of formation

Massraf Faisal Al-Islami (Bank and Trust) Limited (MFI/Bahamas) was incorporated on 9 December 1982 and was granted a licence by the Government of the Bahamas on 23 December 1982 to conduct banking and trust business.

Background

Massraf Faisal Al-Islami is one of the many subsidiaries of Dar Al-Maal Al-Islami Trust and is subject to the banking laws of the Bahamas. However, all of its transactions completed as well as those contemplated are fully in accordance with the tenets of the Sharia.

Areas of operation

MFI Bahamas began its operations on 1 February 1984, and is now managing a portfolio of investment funds in excess of US$ 600 million which essentially are invested in parallel purchase and sale of currency transactions with a wide forum of Middle and Far Eastern, Swiss, French, Canadian and Scandinavian banks.

It is the international arm of all Dar Al-Maal Al-Islami (DMI) bodies. Its responsibilities include tasks such as: management of international flow of funds; co-ordination of foreign exchange transactions; investment in international markets through parallel purchase and sale transactions. These activities make MFI Bahamas the cornerstone of DMI's international banking activities.

It is hoped that MFI Bahamas will shortly become involved in other areas of Islamic banking and financing.

Directors

HRH Prince Mohamed Al-Faisal Al-Saud (President & Director)
HE Dr Omar Abdul Rahman Azzam (Vice-President & Director)
HRH Prince Abdullah Al-Faisal Al-Saud (Director)
Sheik Abdullah Ahmed Zainal Alireza (Director)
Mr Omer Abdi Ali (Director)
Mr Moustapha Sakkaf (Director)
Mr Frank A G Davis (Director)
Dr Moustafa Hosny (Secretary)
Mrs Beryl Hanna (Assistant Secretary)

Objectives

The aim of the MFI Bahamas is to provide modern banking services and facilities in strict accordance with the Islamic Sharia and to mobilise and channel investment into projects and business operations to obtain Halal profits for clients.

It attempts to act as an intermediary between the DMI and other international Islamic financial institutions.

Level and growth of assets (US$)

	Total assets
1984	1,594,865
1985	2,470,054 (+54.9 per cent)

Profitability (US$)

	Accumulated profit (deficit)
1984	(437,000)
1985	362,467

103

Capital Structure

Paid-up capital is US$ 2 million.

Future developments

DMI has expanded its Massaref network into Turkey and Pakistan.

BAHRAIN

Albaraka Islamic Investment Bank BSC (EC)

Head office

Al Hedaya Building
7th and 8th Floor
Al Khalifa Road
PO Box 1882
Manama
Bahrain

Telephone/Telex/Cable

Tel: 259641, 254269, 254278, 251828 (General Manager)
Telex: 8220 BARAKA BN, 8994 BARAKA BN

Other branches: N/A

Date of formation

21 February 1984.

Background

Albaraka Islamic Investment Bank (AIIB) was established in Bahrain and registered as a closed shareholding company. It was officially declared at the meeting of the constituent General Assembly held by the founders in Manama, State of Bahrain, on 20 Jumada al-Awal 1404/21 February 1984. The Bank operates under a licence issued by the Bahrain Monetary Agency, No MNM/14/83 dated 8 Safar 1404/12 November 1983, in accordance with the investment banking regulations. The share capital of AIIB is owned by a group of prominent businessmen in addition to a number of Islamic banks.

Areas of operation

The main activities of AIIB are taking demand and investment deposits, providing finance on the basis of Murabaha (cost plus profit margin), Musharaka (profit participation investment), leasing and introducing Islamic capital instruments. All transactions are in accordance with Islamic principles. The Bank tends to focus its operations on investment in Arab and Islamic countries.
    Murabaha and Mudaraba have been particularly well utilised by the AIIB.

Both operations have witnessed major expansion in the first two years of operation of the Bank as seen from the figures below (all given in terms of US$):

	1984	1985
Mudaraba investment	6,600,000	7,350,000
Murabaha investment	114,588,765	252,450,474

The Bank has so far provided joint investment deposit accounts and specific investment deposit accounts.

Founder members

Shaikh Saleh Abdulla Kamel
Shaikh Hussein Mohsin Al Harthy
Dr Nasser Ebrahim Al Rasheed
Haj Saeed Ahmed Lootah
Dr Hassan Abdulla Kamel
Shaikh Omar Abdulla Kamel
Mr Abdul Aziz Abdulla Kamel
Dr Mohammed Abdou Yamani
Mr Abdul Latif Abdul Rahim Janahi
Mr Mahmoud Jameel Hassoubah
Shaikh Saleh Abdul Aziz Al Rajhi
Shaikh Suliman Abdul Aziz Al Rajhi
Shaikh Abdulla Abdul Aziz Al Rajhi
Shaikh Mohamen Abdul Aziz Al Rajhi

Directors

Shaikh Saleh Abdulla Kamel (Chairman and Managing Director)
Shaikh Hussein Mohsin Al Harthy (Director)
Albaraka Investment and Development Company, Jeddah. Represented by:
    Dr Hassan Abdulla Kamel (Director)
    Dr Mohammed Abdou Yamani (Director)
    Haj Saeed Ahmed Lootah (Director)
    Mr Abdul Latif Abdul Rahim Janahi (Director)
    Mr Mahmoud Jameel Hassoubah (Director)

Supervisory board

Dr Sami Homoud (General Manager)
Mr Abdulla Abolfatih (Assistant General Manager: Banking and Financing)

Objectives

As the Bank is registered as an Exempt Company, it seeks to carry on its business activities outside of Bahrain. The Bank focuses its attention principally on investment in Arab and Islamic countries. Its main concern is with providing

105

finance and banking services on an Islamic basis in strict conformity with the principles of Sharia.

Level and growth of assets (US$)

	Total assets
1984	125,737,070
1985	274,674,387 (+118 per cent)

Profitability (US$)

	Total profit
1984	4,833,548
1985	4,427,649

Number of employees

1984	15
1985	26

Capital structure

The Bank's authorised and subscribed capital is US$ 200 million divided into 2 million shares of $100 each. The paid-up capital on the date of registration is $50 million which equals 25 per cent of the total nominal value of the subscribed shares.

Future developments

The AIIB hopes to establish four fully owned companies in Bahrain dealing with Murabaha, Mudaraba, Salam and projects which will be used as the nucleus for the secondary Islamic capital market.

Bahrain Islamic Bank (BSC)

Head Office

Bahrain Islamic Bank (BSC)
Government Avenue
Government Road
PO Box 5240
Manama
Bahrain

Telephone/telex/cable

Tel: 231402 (10 lines)
Telex: 9388 BESMEH BN, 9390 BESMEH BN
Cable: ISLAMI BANK

Other branches

Muharraq — Tel: 330728/330729
Gudaibiya — Tel: 270458/250927/245446

Date of formation

The Bahrain Islamic Bank (BSC) was incorporated in accordance with the Amiri Decree No 2 of 1979, issued on 7 March 1979. The Bank started its activities on 22 November 1979.

Background

The Bahrain Islamic Bank (BSC) is considered to be the first Islamic bank to be incorporated in Bahrain, and the third to conduct this type of business in the Gulf area. The aim in establishing the Bank was to implement Islamic principles in the banking and economics field for the benefit of the community and country as a whole.

The Bank complies strictly with the rules of Sharia in all its dealings and banking services by avoiding everything that has been forbidden by religion. In all its activities and investments the Bank adheres to the principles laid down by the members of the Sharia Control Committee. The latter works closely with the Bank's executive management in order to oversee the practical aspects of the Bank's dealings and to help them lay down legal restrictions ensuring the soundness of such transactions and profits gained for the benefit of customers and the community.

Areas of operation

The Bank's operations cover current and savings accounts, investment deposit accounts, mutual participation financing, participation financing leading to acquisition, letters of credit and guarantee and the provision of foreign exchange services.

The Bank has also helped to promote other financial institutions in the Gulf. It has contributed in the equity participation of the following establishments and extended its support and full co-operation to develop further economic activities in the Gulf:

Bahrain Islamic Investment Co, Bahrain
Albaraka Islamic Investment Co, Bahrain
Al Tadamon Islamic Bank, Sudan
Islamic Bank of Western Sudan, Sudan
Albaraka Turkisa Finance House, Turkey
Bangladesh Islamic Bank, Bangladesh
Varnish and Paints Project, Egypt
The Islamic Insurance and Reinsurance Co, Bahrain

Founder members

The State of Bahrain	Shares
Individual financiers and businessmen	500,000
Ministry of Justice and Islamic Affairs (Minors Directorate)	100,000
General Corp'n for Social Insurance	500,000
The State of Kuwait	
Kuwait Finance House	500,000
Ministry of Wafqs and Islamic Affairs	250,000
Ministry of Justice	250,000
Ministry of Finance	500,000
Kingdom of Saudi Arabia	
Islamic Development Bank	750,000
United Arab Emirates	
Dubai Islamic Bank	250,000

Directors

Shaikh Abdul Rahman Bin Mohamed Bin Rashid Al Khalifa (Chairman)
Mr Khalid Rashid Al Zayani (1st Deputy Chairman)
Mr Mohamed Yousuf Al Roumi (2nd Deputy Chairman)
Mr Abdul Latif Abdul Rahim Janahi (Managing Director)
Mr Ibrahim Mohamed Zainal (Deputy Managing Director)
Mr Mohamed Abdulla Al Hamed Al Zamil (Member)
Mr Mubarak Qassim Kanoo (Member)
Mr Ahmad Mansour Al Aly (Member)
Mr Mohamed Bardan Mohamed (Member)
Mr Yousuf Mohamed Saleh Al Awadi (Member)
Mr Yousif Abdulla Mudo (Member)
Sheikh Said Ahmed Lotah (Member)
Mr Ibrahim Ahmed Yalli (Member)

Supervisory board

Sheikh Yousif Ahmed Al Sidiki
Sheikh Mohamed Abdul Latif Al Saad
Sheikh Abdul Amir Mansour Al Jamri
Sheikh Abdul Hussain Khalaf Al Asfoor
Sheikh Ibrahim Mohamed Al Mohmood

Objectives

The Bank complies strictly with the rules of Sharia in all its dealings and banking services by avoiding everything that has been forbidden by religion. It follows the advice of its supervisory board on such issues to ensure the soundness of transactions on a religious basis and to help distribute profits on a socially beneficial and equitable manner.

Types of deposit account

The Bank offers three types of account:

(1) *Current account:* A normal cheque book account for which the customer is not charged.
(2) *Saving account:* A profit sharing account for which the customer is issued with a passbook.
(3) *Investment deposit account:* Such an account is fixed, continuing fixed or specific.

Level and growth of assets (BD)

	Total assets
1984	42,010,402
1985	64,576,905 (+34.9 per cent)

Profitability (BD)

	Net profit
1984	2,755,938
1985	2,697,540

Capital structure (BD)

Authorised capital	23,000,000
Subscribed capital	11,500,000
Paid-up capital	5,750,000

(The total subscribed capital has been divided into 5,750,000 shares each of a face value of 2 BD of which 50 per cent has been paid up.)

Sharekat Al-Takafol Al-Islamiah (Bahrain) EC

Head office

PO Box 2856
Manama
Bahrain

Telephone/telex/cable

Tel: 257822 Manama
PO Box 20246
Riyadh 11455
Saudi Arabia
Telex: 204173 DMI

Other branches

PO Box 9707
Jeddah 11423
Saudi Arabia
Telex: 403763 DAR MAL

Date of formation

23 August 1983.

Background

STI Bahrain is a subsidiary of the Dar Al-Maal Al-Islami Trust whose aim is to promote the development of an integrated Islamic financial and economic system. This is being achieved by the establishment of a network of Islamic Takafol (an alternative to contemporary insurance) and Islamic business institutions.

Areas of operation

The network of STIs serves as a managing trustee of various Takafol Mudarabas, the equity of which is subscribed by the public and invested for their profit.

Founder members

Dar Al-Maal Al-Islami Trust Limited
HRH Prince Mohamed Al Faisal Al Saud

Directors

Dr Abdul Aziz Al Fadda (Chairman)
Mr Mohamed Khairy (Member and General Manager)
Mr Gamal El Khatib (Deputy General Manager)
Mr Mohamed Fawzi Amer (Member)
Mr Khider Mohamed Ali (Member)
Mr Omar Abdi Ali (Member)

Supervisory board: N/A

Objectives

The aim is to provide individuals and financial institutions with all type of Takafol services in accordance with the Sharia as the Islamic alternative to contemporary insurance. The Company provides insurance services on a co-operative basis and its role is just as a manager of funds and not a risk bearer; claims are made out of the contributions of the participants.

Islamic insurance operations limited

The company offers two types of mudarabas:

(1) Mudarabas for Takafol among Muslims (alternative to life insurance).
(2) Mudarabas for Takafol pertaining to assets of Muslims (alternative for non-life insurance).

Profitability

As yet the Company has not become profitable, having only started operations in late 1984.

Capital structure

Paid-up capital of the Company is US$ 10 million.

Future developments

After the establishment of the New Saudi Company 'The National Co-operative Insurance Company', which is fully supported by the government, STI Bahrain is expecting an official recognition.

Massraf Faisal Al-Islami of Bahrain (EC)

Head office

Chamber of Commerce Building
PO Box 20492
Manama
Bahrain

Telephone/telex/cable

Tel: 275040
Telex: 9270 FAISBX BN, 9411 FAIFX BN
Telefax: 277305
Cable: MASFASLAM

Other branches (Kingdom of Saudi Arabia)

Offices of HRH Prince Mohammed Al Faisal Al Saud

Al Baroom Center
11th Floor
Hail Street
PO Box 9707
Jeddah 21423
Tel: 651 2728, 651 7032, 651 6900, 651 2496
Telex: 403763 DARMAL SJ (603 763)
Telefax: 651 6552

Junction of Prince Mohamed and Dhahran Streets
Al Moajil Centre
PO Box 7447
Dammam 31462
Tel: 833 8426, 833 8554
Telex: 802454 DARMAL SJ
Telefax: 833 8622

King Faisal Foundation 8th Fl R/Tower
Al Olaya Street
PO Box 352
Riyadh 11411
Tel: 465 2255 Ext 5083, 6798, 6799
Telex: 201180 FAISAL SJ (401180)
Telefax: 463 3895

Al Kaki Building
Almansour Street
Near Al Ghazawi Square
Makkah Mukarama
Tel: 542 7059, 542 7841
Telex: 403763 DARMAL SJ
Telefax: 542 8205

Sultana Street
Jamjoom Building, 3rd Floor
Flat No 3
PO Box 3152
Madinah Munawara
Tel: 823 2912, 823 267, 823 2308
Telex: 403763 DARMAL SJ
Telefax: 823 2128

Date of formation

The Massraf Faisal Al-Islami of Bahrain (EC) was incorporated in Bahrain on 14 July 1982 as an exempt joint stock company and holds an offshore banking licence issued by the Bahrain Monetary Agency.

Background

The Massraf Faisal Al Islami of Bahrain (EC) is a subsidiary company of the Dar Al-Maal Al-Islami Trust. Its marketing area is based in Saudi Arabia with offices in Jeddah, Makkah, Madinah, Riyadh and Dammam so far. More such offices are hoped to open shortly.

The Massraf functions strictly in accordance with the principles of Sharia. In order to ensure strict and continuous conformity with Islamic principles, all operations of the Massraf are checked by its religious supervisory board to whom the management reports periodically. In the case of new operations and activities, approval of the board is invariably obtained prior to their implementation.

Areas of operation

Services offered: Current accounts, savings accounts, investment accounts, private investment portfolio managaement; Islamic financing: Mudaraba (trust financing), Musharaka (participation financing), Murabaha (cost-plus trade financing), Ijara (lease financing), Ijara wa Iktina (hire-purchase financing), Qard Hassan (loan free of profit/loss), Composite financing (blend of various forms of Islamic financing) and Syndication with other Islamic financial institutions; Letters of credit (opening, confirming and negotiating); Letters of guarantee (bid bonds, performance, advance payment etc); Foreign exchange transactions and fund transfers; Commodities and metals.

Directors

Sheikh Abdullah Ahmed Zaynel Alireza (Chairman)
HRH Prince Saud Alabdallah Al Faisal (Deputy Chairman)
Mr Zafar Ahmed Khan (Director)
Mr Khedfer Mohamed Ali (Director)
Sheikh Mohamed Abdullah El Khereiji (Director)
Mr Omar Abdi Ali (Director)
Mu Moustapha Mohamed Sakkaf (Director)

Senior management

Nabil A Nassief (General Manager)
Imtiaz Pervez (Deputy General Manager)
Ahmed A Suleiman (Assistant General Manager)
Salim Abdul Sattar (Operations Manager)
Abdul Rahman Shebab Ahmed (Senior Assistant Manager)
Ali Abdulaziz Al Hemaidi (Assistant Manager)
Abdulaziz Al Mutlaq (Assistant Manager)
Mousa A Hussein (Assistant Manager)

Supervisory board

Dr Yousuf Al Karadawi (Chairman)
Sh Abdulaziz Al Masnad (Member)
Sh Abdulrahim Al Mahmoud (Member)

Objectives

The objectives of MFI Bahrain and of the DMI Group are threefold:

(1) To facilitate Islamic banking services and to make them readily available across the Muslim world. Thus Muslims can use normal banking services

without contravening their holy laws.
(2) To serve all Muslims in the community by allocating finance and profits to the most desirable and needy projects.
(3) To promote the faith and economic development on an Islamic basis.

Level and growth of assets (US$)

	Total assets
1983	143,504,000
1984	272,367,000 (+90 per cent)
1985	677,113,000 (+149 per cent)

Profitability (US$)

	Net profit
1983	881,000
1984	2,629,000

Capital structure

The Massraf Faisal Al Islami of Bahrain has an authorised and paid-up capital of US$ 30 million wholly owned by Dar Al-Maal Al-Islami Trust (DMI).

BANGLADESH

Islami Bank Bangladesh Limited

Head office

75 Motijheel Commercial Avenue
PO Box 233
Dhaka
Bangladesh

Telephone/telex/cable

Tel: 252921, 235183, 235184
Telex: 642525 IBANK BJ
Cable: ISLAMIBANK

Other branches

Dhaka Main Branch
75 Motijheel Commercial Area
Dhaka

Agrabad Branch
105 Agrabad Commercial Area
Chittagong

Sylhet Branch
288 Taltola
Sylhet

Chawk Mogultully Branch
95 Chawk Mogultully
Dhaka

Khatungonj Branch
119 Amir Market
Khatungonj
Chittangong

Khulna Branch
7 Sir Iqbal Road
Khulna

Narayangonj Branch
40 S M Maleh Road
Tanbazar
Narayangonj

Foreign Exchange Branch
41 Dilkusha Commercial Area
Dhaka

Islampur Branch
12 Islampur Road
Dhaka

Barisal Branch
87/88 Hemayetuddin Road
Barisal

Bogra Branch
Kazi Nazrul Islam Road
Bogra

Rajshahi Branch
162 A K M Fazlul Haque Road
Rajshahi

Moulvi Bazar Branch
402 Central Road
Moulvi Bazar

Pabna Branch
Sonapatti
Pabna

Cox's Bazar Branch
209 Main Road
Cox's Bazar

Rangpur Branch
Zilla Parishad Super Market
Rangpur

Date of formation

13 March 1983.

Background

Islamic Bank Bangladesh Limited (IBBL) is run in strict accordance with Islamic principles. Formed in 1983, it was sponsored jointly by: Kuwait Finance House, Kuwait; Investment and Exchange Corporation, Qatar; Bahrain Islamic Bank, Bahrain; Banking System International Holding, SA Luxembourg; Al Raj Company, KSA; Dubai Islamic Bank, UAE; The Public Institute for Social Security, Kuwait; Ministry of Waqf and Islamic Affairs, Kuwait; Ministry of Justice, Kuwait; Islamic Development Bank; Jordan Islamic Bank, Jordan; HE Sheikh Fouad Abdul Hameed Al Khateeb; HE Sheikh Ahmed Salah Jamjoom, KSA.

These were the major sponsors together with two local institutions and 19 local individuals.

IBBL is thus a joint venture between foreign sponsors (70 per cent) and locals (30 per cent). The Bank was incorporated with an authorised capital of 500 million taka and a paid-up capital of approximately 80 million taka.

The Bank has a network of 16 branches including a foreign exchange branch at Dilkusha Commercial Area in Dhaka.

Operation

IBBL accumulates its funds through four major accounts: current account, PLS special note deposit account, PLS deposit account and PLS term deposit account. The current account holders do not share profit or loss. However, all PLS account holders share the profit or loss of the Bank's business.

All of the Bank's business is performed in strict accordance with Islamic principles. Other areas the Bank concentrates on inlcude Murabaha, Musharaka, leasing, hire purchase and Bai Muajjal.

In the first three and a half years more than 115 industrial projects and about 2,500 commercial parties were financed, none of which have proved unwise investments.

Directors

Mohammad Abdur Razzaque Laskar (Chairman)
Sheikh Abdullah Sulaiman Al Rajhi (Vice-Chairman and representative of Al
   Rajhi Company for currency exchange and commerce, KSA)

Mohammad Bashiruddin (Vice-Chairman)
Mohammad Younus (Director)
Mohammad Abdullah (Director)
Abul Quasem (Director)
Mohamed Mosharraf Hossain (Director)
Mohammad Malek Minar (Director)
Abdulana Mohammad Shamsuddin (Director)
M A Rasheed Chowdhury (Director)
Mahbubur Rahman Khan (Director) (Representative of the Bangladesh Government)
Dr Abdul Razzaq Kamil (Director) (Representative of Islamic Development Bank)
Ahmed Bazie Al-Yaseen (Director) (Representative of the Kuwait Finance House)
Mir Quasem Ali (Director) (Representative of the Bangladesh Islamic Centre)
Commodore (Retd) Ataur Rahman (Director) (Representative Ibne Sina Trust)
M Sekander Ali (Director) (Representative of Investment Corporation of Bangladesh)
Saeed Ahmed Lootah (Director) (Representative of the Dubai Islamic Bank)
A Latif A Rahim Janahi (Director) (Representative of the Bahrain Islamic Bank)
Moulana Abdul Jabbar (Director) (Representative of Baitush Sharaf Foundation Ltd)
Hamad Al-Hageri (Director) (Representative of Public Institute for Social Security, Kuwait)
Abdul Wahab A Al-Houti (Director) (Representative of Ministry of Awqaf and Islamic Affairs)
Fouad Abdul Hameed Al-Khateeb (Director) (Kingdom of Saudi Arabia)
Ahmed Salah Jamjoom (Director (Kingdom of Saudi Arabia)

Sharia council

Maulana Mohammad Abdul Jabbar (Chairman)
Maulana Syed Muhammad Ali (Member-Secretary)
Maulana Mufti Abdur Rahman (Member)
Maulana Syed Kamaluddin Jafri (Member)
Maulana Delawar Hussain Sayeedi (Member)
Maulana Kamaluddin Khan (Member)
Janab M Khaled (Member)
Janab Abdul Asad Ali Ahmed Rushdi (Member)
Janab Advocate Mozammel Huq (Member)

Level and growth of assets (Taka)

	Total assets
1983	223,252,636
1984	1,043,186,241 (+367 per cent)
1985	2,237,052,130 (+114 per cent)

Profitablity (Taka)

	Net profit
1983	(2,557,675) (loss)
1984	7,829,727
1985	8,865,668

Number of employees

1983	127
1984	291
1985	535

Capital structure (Taka)

Authorised capital   500 million
Paid-up capital   79.5 million

Future developments

Islami Bank Bangladesh Limited hopes to expand rapidly at home and abroad. Applications are pouring in from the general public for IBBL to open in different parts of the country.

DENMARK

Islamic Bank International of Denmark

Head office

7 Jernbanegade
DK-1608 Copenhagen V
PO Box 271
Denmark

Telephone/telex/cable

Tel: +45 1 11 47 77
Telex: 16478 isbank dk
Fax: +45 1 32 07 14

Other branches: N/A

Date of formation

18 April 1983.

Background

Some Ministries of Awqaf together with Islamic institutions and Islamic banks joined a number of Muslim individuals who saw the need for an Islamic bank outside the Muslim world. Such a Western Islamic bank was to act as correspondent bank and provide Halal banking services in accordance with applying the Sharia principles when providing alternative banking services needed by Muslims.

The Islamic Bank International (IBI) is a Halal operating commercial bank fully authorised under the Danish Banking Act with a licence from the Central Bank in Denmark. Denmark, a member of the EEC, was seen as an ideal place to locate an Islamic bank to provide the West with investment opportunities in strict accordance with Islamic principles. The bank has not been granted any special concessions with regard to existing Danish legislation. However, it has succeeded in creating a number of contracts — including short-term investment programmes — being strictly Halal as verified with the bank's Sharia adviser.

Areas of operation

At present, investments by IBI focus on leasing, Murabaha, and an international trade financing of Danish exports and imports to and from Islamic countries in particular.

The existing set of financial instruments is limited and characterised by being somewhat inflexible and without an organised secondary market for Sharia-based financial instruments if the need for a diversification of the portfolio should occur.

Directors

Gunner Thorlund Jepsen (Chairman)
Paul Moller (Vice-Chairman)
Syed Ghulam Us Syedain (Director)
Barry Clayton Noton (Director)
Luay Hashim Allawi (Director)
Peter Jerichow (Director)

Management

Poul Tage Madsen (General Manager)

Supervisory board

Abdul Sattar Abu Ghuddah (Sharia Adviser and Internal Auditor)

Objectives

The IBI of Denmark has several objectives: (1) to demonstrate that banking activities based on Islamic Sharia can work within the existing framework of Western legislation relating to banking and financial services to the benefit of

119

the clients and the bank; (2) to promote and finance trade between the EEC countries and the Islamic countries (particularly the Gulf Arab countries and Egypt); (3) IBI will finance Halal activities in Denmark and in other EEC countries where the bank possesses the necessary credit evaluation expertise to secure a low risk investment portfolio. A final objective is to provide a strong and reliable link for the transfer of knowledge and capital between Western Europe and the Islamic countries.

Level and growth of assets (DKK)

	Total assets
1983	207,086,000
1984	339,935,303 (+64.15 per cent)
1985	239,796,251 (−29.41 per cent)

Profitability (DKK)

	Net profit
1983	840,000
1984	876,049
1985	(5,825,597)

Number of employees (average)

1984	15 full-time
1985	16 full-time

Capital structure

IBI is fully owned by Islamic Finance House Universal Holding SA in Luxembourg. The bank's equity amounts to DKK 40,000,000 and the paid-up reserves amount to DKK 5,000,000.

EGYPT

Faisal Islamic Bank (Egypt) SA

Head office

1113 Cornish el Nil
PO Box 2446
Cairo
Egypt

Telephone/telex/cable

Tel: 753109, 753165, 742113, 743364
Telex: 93877, 93878 F BANK UN
Cable: FAISAL BANK CAIRO

Other branches

El Azhar:
1 Souk El Kahira El Fatimi
El Azhar Square
Tel: 911280, 916341

Ghamra:
259, 261 Ramsiss Street
Cairo
Tel: 825217, 830182

Heliopolis:
15 El Hegaz Street
Heliopolis
Cairo
Tel: 587519, 581256

Alexandria:
7 Victor Passily Street
El Azarets
Alexandria
Tel: 4928018, 4911653

Damenhour:
Irrigation Management Building
Behind Omar Effendi
Damenhour
Tel: 24000

Tanta (1):
73 El Gaish Street
Tanta
Tel: 324336, 321808, 328338

Banha:
El Bahr Street
Banha
Tel: 23877, 23820

Suez:
Port Said Street,
Suez
Tel: 2834
Cairo direct: 767145

Assuit:
No 1 Awkaf Building El Asher of Ramadan
Project Assiut
Tel: 323739, 326006

13 more branches under establishment.

Date of formation

The Faisal Islamic Bank of Egypt was formed on 27 August 1977, in accordance with law 48 of the year 1977. On 3 October 1977, the Ministry of Waqf issued a Ministerial Decree enacting the statutes of the Bank and on 5 July 1979 the Bank was officially inaugurated.

Background of the bank

Faisal Islamic Bank of Egypt is an Egyptian joint stock company which operates in strict accordance with the principles of the Sharia.

Areas of operation

The Bank performs activities in investment and commercial operations by means substitutional to the conventionally practised interest system (usury), either independently or in partnership with others sharing any profit or loss according to equity participation.

The Bank also undertakes Mudaraba as another form of activity in which one side places the capital and the other manages the partnership. It also participates in the establishment of medium- or long-term projects whether commercial, industrial or agricultural by sharing in their capital. The Bank undertakes research in this respect to ensure the feasibility of the project in question and whether such a project's financing would be in accordance with Islamic principles.

These are by no means the only activities of the Bank. In addition it provides all the more mundane services such as letters of credit, letters of guarantee and foreign exchange transactions.

Directors

Prince Mohamed Al Faisal Al Saud (Chairman)
Mr Hamed Mahmoud Habib (Vice-Chairman)
Eng Ahmed Helmy Abdel Maggid (Member)
Dr Ahmed Thabet Ewaida (Member)
Dr Ahmed Abdel Aziz El Nagar (Member)
Dr Tawfik Mohamed El Shawi (Member)
Sheikh Hidar Ben Laden (Member)
Dr Abdel Sabour Abdel Moumen Marzouk (Member)
Dr Abdel Aziz Abd Allah Al Feda (Member)
Mr Ali Ahmed Hamdi (Member)

Dr Omar Abdel Rahman Azam (Member)
Dr Mahmoud Mohamed El Helw (Member)
Dr Youssef Abd Allah El Karadawy (Member)
Egyptian Waqf's Authority (Member)
Dar Al-Maal Al-Islamic (Member)

Governor: Dr Mahmoud Mohamed El Helw

Deputy Governor: Mr Ahmed Adel Kamal

Supervisory board

His Eminence Sheikh Mohamed Khater Mohamed El Sheikh (Chairman)
Dr Mohamed El Taib El Naggar (Member)
Sheikh Salah Abou Ismail Mohamed (Member)
Dr Ali Hassan Youness (Member)
Mr Mohamed Hamed Abdel Aal (Member)

Objectives

The objective of the Faisal Islamic Bank of Egypt is to perform all types of banking and financial activities and to promote and participate in all industrial, economic and urbanisation developments at home and abroad in accordance with Sharia.

Types of deposit account

There are three types of account broadly available to customers although the actual range of specific accounts is far in excess of these.

Excluding current accounts we can concern ourselves firstly with general investment accounts. A minimum investment of US$ 200 is required to open such an account or the equivalent in another currency. The length of the deposit is six months, one year or more, all funds being invested in activities in accordance with Islamic principles. Profits of investments are distributed on a shared basis according to the amount and length of deposit.

Secondly, the Bank offers specific investment accounts in the fields of industry, agriculture and services. Thirdly, savings accounts can be opened for which an unlimited amount of money can be deposited and withdrawn at any time.

Islamic banking operations

(1) Financing through partnership; (2) Murabaha sales; (3) Mudaraba operations; (4) Direct investment in projects; (5) Participation in the establishment of other companies.

Level and growth of assets (US$)

	Total assets
1985	1,776,568,000
1986	2,105,418,000 (+18.52 per cent)

Profitability (US$)

	Net profit
1985	104,970,000
1986	106,982,000

Capital structure

The Bank's authorised capital is US$ 500 million and its issued capital 100 million; 51 per cent belonging to Egyptian shareholders and 49 per cent to Muslims of other Islamic countries.

Tadamon Islamic Bank

Head office

Parliament Avenue
PO Box 3154
Khartoum
Sudan

Telephone/telex/cable

Tel: 81877, 74432, 70417, 73145, 73146
Telex: 22158, 22687, 22688 DAMAN SD
Cable: BANKDAMAN

Other branches

Capital branches

Khartoum:
PO Box 3154
Khartoum
Tel: 81877, 74432, 70417, 73145, 73146
Telex: 22158, 22687, 22688 DAMAN SD
Cable: BANKDAMAN

Omdurman:
PO Box 846
Omdurman
Tel: 54130, 55733
Telex: 28062 DAMAN SD
Cable: BANKDAMAN

Saggana:
PO Box 155
Saggana
Tel: 47365, 47366

Country branches

Port Sudan:
PO Box 475
Port Sudan
Tel: 5045, 5007
Telex: 70035 TADM SD

Nyala:
Tadamon Islamic Bank
Nyala
Tel: 2445

Gedarif:
PO Box 156
Gedarif
Tel: 2284, 2285

Sinnar:
PO Box 163
Sinnar
Tel: 2277

Managil:
Tadamon Islamic Bank
Managil

Karima:
Tadamon Islamic Bank
Karima
Tel: 22061, 22062

Date of formation

The Tadamon Islamic Bank (TIB) was promoted on 22 November 1981 and commenced operations on 24 March 1983.

Background

Tadamon Islamic Bank came into being when a number of Muslim Sudanese businessmen took the initiative on 22 November 1981 to form an Islamic bank dealing without interest. The Articles and Memorandum of Association were thus drawn up and the necessary arrangements were taken to float shares in and outside Sudan. The Bank was then inaugurated on 24 March 1983.

Areas of operation

Tadamon Islamic Bank has three main activities: (1) All types of banking operations; (2) Investment according to Islamic modes of finance; (3) Financing of exports and imports.

TIB is specially interested in developing national wealth and international trade in accordance with Islamic principles. The Bank is involved in short-term investment providing all possible services to its customers. The Bank hopes to expand into the fields of medium- and long-term financing in the near future.

Founder members

Faisal Islamic Bank (Sudan)
Kuwait Finance House
Ministry of Enduments and Religious Affairs
Sheikh Salih Abdalla Kamel
Mohamed and Abdalla Ibrahim El Subaie
Dubai Islamic Bank
Bahrain Islamic Bank
Others (including 2,700 shareholders)

Directors

Syd Khidir Hassan Kambal (Chairman)
Syd Dr Ibrahim Obiedulla El Hussein (Director)
Ibrahim Abdul Salam (Director)
Syd Ahmed Alnaw Mohamed Ali (Director)
Hamid Abdul Salam
Syd Altigani Hassan Hilal (Director)
Syd Al Sheikh Abdulbasit Ali (Director)
Kuwait Finance House (Director, representation, KFH)
Syd Sayed Omer Hassan Kambal (Director)
Syd Abdul Rahim Mohamed Makawi (Director)
Syd Abdul Gadir Hussein Jaffar (Director)
Syd Abdulla Ibrahim Al Subaie (Director)
Syd Osman Abdul Galil Abuzaid (Director)
Syd Hashim Elias Bashir (Director)
Aljalsi Trading, Marketing and Contracting Co
Syd Dr Yousif Hamid Al Alim (Director)

Senior management

Syd Salah Ali Abu El Naja (General Manager)
Syd Dr Awad Ahmed El Jazz (Deputy General Manager)
Syd El Rasheed Saad El Sufi (Assistant General Manager)
El Sheikh Ahmed Ali Abdullah (Manager, Fatwa and Research Dept)

Supervisory board

Tadamon Islamic Bank does not have a supervisory board as such but its Fatwa and Research Dept corresponds to such a body.

Sheikh Ahmed Ali Abdullah (Manager, Fatwa & Research Dept)
Sheikh Makhawi Modawi Makhawi (Head of Sharia Dept)
Dirdiry Mohamed Ahmed (Head of Legal Affairs Dept)
Syd Musaad Mohamed Ahmed (Head of Economic Research Dept)

Objectives

The objectives of TIB are twofold: (1) To conduct financial, commercial and investment operations and to contribute in the industrial, agricultural and construction development programmes; (2) To promote the growth of Islamic financial institutions in a variety of ways.

Type of deposit accounts

The main categories of accounts available are the current, investment and deposit (savings) accounts.

Islamic banking operations utilised

The Bank utilises Musharaka, Murabaha, and Mudaraba operations. The use of these operations over the last two years is shown below.

1984	*Amount* (Ls million)	*Number*	*Percentage*
Murabaha	23.0	495	61.5
Musharaka	13.9	206	37.4
Mudaraba	0.5	4	1.3
TOTAL	37.4	705	100
1985			
Murabaha	43.0	677	66.3
Musharaka	19.0	137	30.3
Mudaraba	2.2	16	3.4
TOTAL	65.4	830	100

Asset growth (Ls million)

December 1983   57.4 million
December 1984   80.0 million
December 1985   137.8 million

Asset structure

(1) Cash and balances with banks; (2) Commercial paper and other debit balances; (3) Investments; (4) Fixed assets. (See balance sheet.)

127

Profitability (Ls)

Net distributed profit
1984   913,183
1985   1,373,293

Number of employees

	Officers	*Workers*
1984	141	58
1985	206 (+46 per cent)	88 (+51 per cent)

Capital structure (US$ million)

Authorised capital   50.0
Paid-up capital   13.2

Future developments

Major future developments include entering the field of long-term investment and expanding banking services provided within Sudan and in other countries. Further, the Bank wishes to participate in the economic development and growth of the country. This will be aided by the Islamisation of the banking system in helping to create an Islamic economic society.

INDIA

Al-Ameen Islamic Financial and Investment Corporation (India) Limited

Head office

Millia Building
109 NR Road
Bangalore-560 002
Karnataka
India

Telephone/telex/cable

Tel: 226412
Telex: 0845-8218 ACIC

Other branches

The Institution has four branches, one in each of the four states of South India.

Crescent Building II Floor
Cherutty Road
Calicut-673 032
Kerala

111 D Devaraj Urs Road
Mysore-570 001
Karnataka

No 32 Nungambakkam High Road
Madras-600 034
Tamil Nadu

No 4-1-7/A/2 Tilak Road
Ramkote
Hyderabad-500 001
Andhra Pradesh

Date of formation

The Company has been registered under the Companies Act, 1956 with Certificate of Incorporation No 7217/85-86 dated 16 October 1985. It commenced business on 12 April 1986.

Background

Al-Ameen is the first interest-free financial company to be set up in India according to Sharia principles. It has been registered under the Indian Companies Act as a Public Limited Company and the necessary approvals have been obtained from the Reserve Bank of India to function as a non-banking financial company.

Founder members

Dr Mumtaz Ahmed Khan is the founder member and is at present the Chairman of the Institution.

Directors

Dr Mumtaz Ahmed Khan, Doctor (Chairman)
Mr K Rahman Khan, Chartered Accountant (Managing Director)
Mr Ateeq Ahmed, Businessman (Finance Director)
Mr Abdul Gaffar Haji Latif, Businessman (Director)
Mr Ziaulla Shariff, Engineer and Builder (Director)
Mr M K Kamaluddin, Chairman, New Model Indian High School, Dubai (Director)
Mr P A Ibrahim Haji, Industrialist, Dubai (Director)

Senior management

Dr Mumtaz Ahmed Khan, M.B.B.S, (Chairman): prominent social worker
Mr K Rahman Khan, B.Com. F.C.A. (Managing Director): chartered accountant and Member of Karnataka Legislative Council
Dr Asif Raza Chida, M.Com., P.Phil., Ph.D. (Chief Executive, Projects): experienced Projects and Financial Consultant

Mr A Rafeq, B.Com., A.C.A. (Chief Accounts Officer): chartered accountant
Mr S A Koya, M.Sc. (Agri) (Regional Manager, Calicut): experienced banker
Miss Farida Yasmin, M.B.A. (Project Officer): projects assistant
Mrs Tahera Sultana, B.Tech., M.B.A. (Project Officer): projects assistant
Imtiaz Ahmed, M.Com. (Executive, Business Development): sales executive
Mr Hafizulla, B.Com., C.A. (Final) (Manager, Mysore Branch): accounts
assistant
Mr Mohd Faizur Rahman, M.A. (History) (Manager, Madras Branch):
experienced banker.

Supervisory board

The members of the Board of Directors are also members of the Supervisory
Board for the Head Office. A Regional Board, with local members, has been
constituted for the overall supervision of branches. The members of this Board
are:

Madras branch:
Mr T T P Abdulla: Indian Foreign Service (Former Ambassador to Saudi
Arabia)
Mr Habeebulla Badsha: senior advocate
Mr Ahmed Mohammed Sait: industrialist and garment exporter
Mr A J Razakh: advocate; Member of Tamilnadu Waqf Board
Mr P K Shabbir Ahmed: engineer and architect; prominent social worker
Mr E P Mohammed Ismail: former Principal, Jamal Mohammad College,
Trichy
Mr Kaka Mohammad Zubair: Correspondent, Islamic College, Vaniyambadi.

Calicut branch:
Mr T P A Koya: engineer and architect
Dr Mohammad Koya: doctor
Mr K P Hassan Haji: secretary, J D T Islam Orphanage
Dr Moidu: doctor
Mr K V Kunhammed: businessman
Mr P S Abdul Rahman: businessman.

(List of members for Mysore and Hyderabad branches is being finalised.)

Objectives

(1) To inculcate the savings habit among the poor.
(2) To assist in the socio-economic upliftment of poor Muslim brethren, in
the form of interest-free advances to the poor, to set up business.
(3) To assist entrepreneurs to function on Islamic principles and invest in
productive ventures.
(4) To undertake or participate in the formation, management, supervision or
control of socially relevant projects.

(5) To provide re-finance facilities to those vehicle owners who have hypothecated their vehicles/equipments at exorbitant rates of interest.

(6) To channel deposits for investment on Islamic principles.

(7) To propagate the concept of Islamic banking among both Muslims and non-Muslims.

(8) To participate in ventures on a profit and loss sharing basis.

Types of deposit account

There are at present four types of deposits:

(1) *Term deposit:* Under this scheme deposits can be made for a period ranging from six months to 36 months. The deposits are entitled to bonus as and when declared by the Company, payable monthly, quarterly, half-yearly or yearly.

(2) *Housing deposit:* Deposits of a fixed monthly amount for a minimum period of 36 months are to be made, which entitle the depositor to a maximum of double the amount of his/her deposit to be used for purchase/construction of a house. The deposit is not entitled to interest nor is any interest charged on the loan.

(3) *Haj deposit:* Any person desirous of performing Haj and willing to save daily/weekly/monthly can deposit under this scheme for a period ranging from one to three years. The deposits accumulated are refunded to meet Haj expenses.

(4) *Interest-free deposit:* Any philanthropic individuals, charitable trusts or institutions can make deposits under this scheme for a period ranging from six to 36 months, on which no interest is payable. Such type of deposits are utilised for granting interest-free loans (Kardhassana).

Islamic banking operations utilised

The following Islamic banking operations are utilised by the Institution: leasing (Ijara), interest-free advances (kardhassana), project finance (mudaraba), venture finance (musharaka), financial and technical consultancy on Islamic principles.

Level and growth of assets

Not applicable since the Company only commenced operations on 12 April 1986.

Profitability

The Company earned an operating profit of Rs 44,554/- (US$ 3,427) and a net profit of Rs 8,606/- (US$ 662) in three months between April and June 1986.

Number of employees

Number of employees on 30 November 1986 was:

Office staff

Postgraduates	14
Graduates	22
Undergraduates	14
	50

Field officers

Graduates	10
Undergraduates	25
	35

Total staff 85

Capital structure (Rs)

Authorised capital	
(10,000,000 equity shares of Rs 10/- each)	100,000,000
Issued, subscribed and paid-up	
(49,985 shares of Rs 10/-)	499,850
(Share application money pending allotment)	1,218,000

Future developments

The Company is at present carrying on the following business activities: (1) Leasing; (2) Investment in joint ventures; (3) Three-wheeler autorickshaw re-finance; (4) Interest-free advances.

It was confident of achieving business worth Rs 200 lakhs (US$ 1,538,461) during 1986 with a turnover of Rs 15 crores in the fifth year (US$ 11,538,000). There were also plans to release interest-free advances of Rs 20 lakhs (US$ 153,846) in 1986 and of more than Rs 1.5 crore (US$ 1,153,846) in 1987–92.

Being the first non-banking finance company in India to function on the principles of Islamic Sharia, AIFIC has met with overwhelming response from all quarters. The Company has an ambitious plan for a nationwide network with branches in all major states of India. As a result of the growing demand for lease of fixed assets and other activities, the Company is poised to achieve new heights in its business activities on the basis of Islamic Sharia. Project finance, venture finance and financial and technical consultancy services are the areas that the Company is expected to enter in a big way.

A scheme specially designed for non-resident Indians is to be launched in January 1987. The scheme offers entrepreneurial assistance to non-resident Indians like entrepreneurial development programmes, and financial and technical consultancy services.

JORDAN

Jordan Islamic Bank for Finance and Investment

Head office

PO Box 926225
Shmeisani
Amman
Jordan

Telephone/telex/cable

Tel: 677377, 666325
Telex: 21125, 23993 (ISLAMI JO)
Cable: ISLAMBANK, AMMAN.

Other branches

Shmeisani:
PO Box 925997
Amman
Jordan
Tel: 677107
Telex: 23944/24150 (ISLAMI JO)

Amman:
King Faisal Street
Sharaim Building
Amman
Jordan
Tel: 638306
Telex: 21032/23375 (ISLAMI JO)
Cable: ISLAMBANK, AMMAN

Al Hussain (Amman):
Khalid Bin Al Walid Street
Jabal Al Hussain
PO Box 926943
Amman
Jordan
Tel: 666120, 666121, 672569, 672609
Telex: 22265 (ISLAMI JO)
Cable: ISLAMBANK, AL HUSSAIN, AMMAN

Wahdat (Amman):
Madaba Street
Close to Civil Status Dept
PO Box 16165
Amman
Jordan
Tel: 778101, 778102
Telex: 22192 (ISLAMI JO)
Cable: ISLAMBANK, WAHDAT, AMMAN

Zerqa:
King Hussain Street
PO Box 1973
Zerqa
Jordan
Tel: 981401, 981402
Telex: 41447 (ISLAMR JO)
Cable: ISLAMBANK, ZERQA

Irbid:
Baghdad Street
PO Box 1950
Irbid
Jordan
Tel: 245151, 245152, 245153, 245154
Telex: 51548 (ISLMR JO)
Cable: ISLAMBANK, IRBID

Bayader Wadi Es-Seir:
Main Street
PO Box 394
Bayader Wadi Es-Seir
Wadi Es-Seir
Jordan
Tel: 816152, 816153
Telex: 23265 (ISLAMI JO)
Cable: ISLAMBANK, WADI ES-SEIR

Aqaba:
3rd Commercial Area
PO Box 1048
Aqaba
Jordan
Tel: 314315, 314316, 314317
Telex: 62331 (ISLAMI JO)
Cable: ISLAMBANK, AQABA

Madaba:
Petra Street
PO Box 695
Madaba
Jordan
Tel: 544702, 543267, 542802, 542902
Telex: 42402 (ISLAMI JO)
Cable: ISLAMBANK, MADABA

Sowaileh:
King Hussain Street
PO Box 717
Amman
Jordan
Tel: 841563
Telex: 23843 (ISLAMI JO)
Cable: ISLAMBANK, SOWAILEH

Kerak:
Italian Street
PO Box 220
Kerak
Jordan
Tel: 351267, 351268
Telex: 63002 (ISLAMI JO)
Cable: ISLAMBANK, KERAK

Ma'an:
King Hussain Street
PO Box 204
Ma'an
Jordan
Tel: 41733, 41799, 32235, 32245
Cable: ISLAMBANK, MA'AN

Date of formation

Jordan Islamic Bank for Finance and Investment was established in accordance with Jordan company law and by virtue of its special law No 13 of 1978, which has been replaced by Law No 62 of 1985. The Bank was officially registered as a public limited company on 28 November 1978 and commenced its operations on 22 September 1979.

Background

Jordan Islamic Bank (JIB) was established in Jordan in 1978 to conduct a full range of banking services within the limits permitted by the Islamic Sharia. The

Bank was particularly concerned with providing such financial intermediation to all citizens of Jordan and so adopted a policy of opening as many regional branches as possible.

Within such a policy the Bank, during 1981–6, succeeded in achieving greater deposits and rechannelling them into fruitful and beneficial investments, ie Murabaha, Mudaraba and participation bases, besides other kinds of investments such as housing scheme projects and commodity investments.

Areas of operation

The major activity of the JIB is to provide traditional banking services to the citizens of Jordan. The Bank carries out such activities within the limits of its own resources and within the bounds of civil and Islamic laws. Such activities include:

(1) Accepting cash deposits and opening current and deposit accounts, transferring funds, issuing bank guarantees and letters of credit.
(2) Dealing in the purchase and sale of foreign currencies on the basis of spot rates only.
(3) Giving fixed-term loans as a mere service without interest.
(4) Managing properties on the basis of an agency fee.
(5) Acting as trustee in accordance with Islamic and civil law.
(6) Carrying out special studies on behalf of clients and giving information and consultancy.

Directors

H E Sheikh Saleh Abdulla Kamel (Chairman)
Mr Bader M Sa'eed Hirsh (Vice-Chairman)
Haj Salem Hussein Abu Assaf (Member)
Dr Ahmad Al-Ajam (Member)
Albaraka Investment and Development Co (Member)
Haj Hamdi Mohamed Al Tabba'a (Member)
Mr Kamal Sami Asfour (Member)
Mr Musa A Shihadeh (General Manager)
H E Sheikh Abdul Hamid Essayeh (Sharia Adviser)
Mr Faisal M Rasheed (Deputy General Manager)
Mr Ali Elayan (Banking Relations Manager)
M/S Ibrahim Al Abbsi and Co (Auditors)

Objectives

The Bank aims at meeting the economic and social needs in the fields of banking services, financial and investment operations on a non-usurious basis. In particular the Bank aims to extend dealings with the banking sector by offering non-usurious banking services with special emphasis on introducing services designed to revive various forms of collective social responsibility on a basis of mutual benefit.

The Jordan Islamic Bank also aims to attract funds and to channel them into financing projects not likely to benefit from usurious banking facilities.

Types of deposit account

Accepting deposits is one of the major functions of the Bank. Such deposits include the following:

(1) *Trust deposits:* The Bank is authorised to use the deposits at its own risk and responsibility in respect of profit or loss; deposits are not subject to any conditions regarding deposits or withdrawals.

(2) *Joint investment accounts:* Such deposits receive a certain percentage of the annual net profits realised in accordance with the conditions of the account.

(3) *Specified investment accounts:* For such accounts the Bank acts as agent for investment of the deposit into a specified project on the basis that the Bank will receive a share of any profits that may accrue from the venture.

Islamic banking operations

The major areas in which funds are employed are in Mudaraba, Murabaha and participation. Apart from the more mundane financial activities, the Bank is also active in the field of social welfare where it promotes economically viable and socially beneficial projects and administers funds for various socially worthy programmes.

Level and growth of assets (JD)

	Total assets
1985	116,318,188
1986	145,205,603 (+24.8 per cent)

Profitability (JD)

	Net profit
1984	893,200
1985	664,893

Capital structure (JD)

As at 30 June 1986:

Paid-up capital	6,000,000
Statutory reserve	2,935,092
Voluntary reserve	491,619
Provisions of investment	2,088,634

Future developments

The JIB is in the process of inaugurating more branches in order to further the range of their services throughout Jordan. It also hopes to participate in the formation of other financial institutions to be run on an Islamic basis.

KUWAIT

Kuwait Finance House (KSC)

Head office

Abdulla Al Mubarak Street and Fahd Al Salim Street Junction
PO Box 24989
13110 Safat
Kuwait

Telephone/telex/cable

Tel: 2445050 (10 lines), 2445070 (10 lines)
Telex: 23331 KT
Cable: BAITMAL

Other branches

Jahra:
Behind Jahra Co-op
Jahra
Tel: 4775325, 4775326, 4775327

Riqah:
Near Riqah Co-op
Riqah
Tel: 3941582, 3941583, 3941584, 3949369

Sharq:
Agool Roundabout
Abdelrahman Al Rafei Building
Sharq
Tel: 2426511, 2426536, 2426514

Fahaheel:
Dabbous Street
Fahaheel
Tel: 3911904, 3913400, 3911997, 3911998

Farwaniya:
Sixth Ring Road
Near Public Housing Authority
Farwaniya
Tel: 4746053, 4746054, 4746057

Failaka:
Failaka Street
Ahmed Rabie Building
Failaka
Tel: 2790267, 2790269, 2791805, 2791809

Faiha:
Faiha Co-op
Faiha
Tel: 2520174, 2520175, 2520176, 2520168

Salmiya:
Near Communication Centre
Salmiya
Tel: 5724536, 5724958, 5724356, 5722489

Hawally:
Beirut Street
Mubarak Al Hasawi Building
Hawally
Tel: 2644143, 2644162

Ministries Complex:
Ministries Complex Building
Tel: 2436203, 2439176

Al Muthanna:
Al Muthanna Complex Building
Fahed Al Salem Street
Al Muthanna Complex
Tel: 2414090, 2414095 (6 lines)

Al Sheib:
Near Sheib Co-op
Al Sheib
Tel: 26104439, 2610436, 2610561, 2610562, 2610607, 2610608

Al Ardiya:
Al Ardiya
Tel: 4880347, 4880439

Date of formation

Formed on 23 March 1977, the Kuwait Finance House (KFH) commenced operations on 31 August 1978.

Background

Kuwait Finance House is an Islamic Bank founded in Kuwait in 1977 with the role of conducting banking operations according to Islamic principles and to help finance projects on a non-usurious basis.

Areas of operation

KFH activities consist of current banking transactions, real estate and commercial investments, general investments in various fields and financing of projects, and finance of foreign trade of Islamic countries.

Founder members

Ministry of Finance
Ministry of Justice
Ministry of Awqaf and Islamic Affairs

Directors

Ahmed Bazie Al Yaseen (Chairman)
Faisal A Al Khatrash (Vice-Chairman)
Bader A Al Mukhaizeem (Managing Director)
Adnan A Al Bahar (General Manager)
Khaled A Al Zeer (Member)
Abdul Jalil A Al Gharabally (Member)
Ali A Al Fouzan (Member)
Samir Al Nafisi (Member)
Mohamed A Al Khudairi (Member)
Mohamed Y Al Roumi (Member)
Haza' J Al Husayan (Member)
Ibrahim Al Khamis (Secretary of Board)

Supervisory board

Shaikh Badr Al Mutawali Abd Al Basit
Dr Khalid Al Madhkur
Dr Abd Al Satar Abu Ghuda

Objectives

(1) To offer all banking services and investment activities compatible with the precepts of Islamic principles; (2) To contribute to the economic development of Kuwait by financing viable projects and investing its customers' deposits; (3) To contribute in the field of social welfare activities.

Types of deposit account

Current accounts; savings accounts; unconditional continuous investment deposits; unconditional fixed investment deposits; open time deposit for absolute investment.

Level and growth of assets (KD)

	Total assets
1984	845,754,430
1985	803,956,911 (−5.0 per cent)

Profitability (KD)

	Net profit
1984	—
1985	17,520,115

Capital structure (KD)

1985

Authorised capital	18,750,000
Paid-up capital	18,701,274

Future developments

Regarding banking services themselves, KFH hopes to introduce new technological techniques such as cash points for the benefit of its clients and to provide rent safes for private use. The other area of development will be in the expansion of the branch network for which work has already been started.

LUXEMBOURG

Islamic Takafol Company

Head office

209 Route d'Arlon
1150 Luxembourg
Grand-Duchy of Luxembourg

Telephone/telex/cable

Tel: (00352) 44 10 67
Telex: 3172 TAKAFO LU
HIFAX 44 12 06

Other branches

Service company in UK:
Islamic Investment Company Ltd
144–6 King's Cross Road
London
WC1X 9DH
United Kingdom
Tel. 01-833-8275

Holland branch office:
Islamic Takafol Company (ITC) SA
Vaillantlaan 294
252 6 HT Den Haag
Tel: (070) 807955

Representative office in West Germany:
Islamic Takafol Company (ITC) — Germany
Krefelderstrasse 21
5000 Koeln 1
West Germany
Tel: (0221) 721221

Date of formation
28 December 1982.

Background

Islamic Takafol Company is a member of Dar Al-Maal Al-Islami (DMI) Trust. DMI is a financial institution which has undertaken to put before the Muslim Ummah contemporary Islamic financial services in strict conformity with Islamic Sharia and without contravening the heavenly imposed prohibition of dealing in Riba.

Areas of operation

The Company commenced marketing Mudaraba Al Tadamon (a Takafol and investment Mudaraba) in the UK in November 1983. Subsequently, it extended its marketing operations to West Germany. In March 1985 the Company set up a branch office in Holland after obtaining permission from the authorities for conducting its business there. The Company's field operations are supervised by two experienced marketing managers and a branch manager.

Islamic Takafol Company admits participants, collects the instalments, provides management services, invests the funds and pays Takafol benefits out of the Takafol fund. As a consequence of the mutual system of Takafol, a major portion of profits is distributed among the participants.

ITC administers the Islamically approved financial arrangement known as Mudaraba. Members of the Ummah are solicited to pool their funds in Takafol Mudarabas and the administration of the funds so raised is entrusted to the

Takafol Company as Mudareb. Instalments paid by the participants are split into investment and Takafol portions.

All investments are made in accordance with Islamic principles, thereby ensuring a Halal return on the savings of the participants.

Directors

HRH Prince Mohamed Al Faisal AlSaud (Chairman)
Mr Muazzam Ali (Vice Chairman)
Mr Omar Abdi Ali
Mr Mohamed Fawzi Amer
Mr Mehmet Evdogan Sergici

Religious board

Mohamed Khater Mohamed (Chairman)
Ali Abdel Kader
Ali Siddick Mohamed Al Amin Al-Darir
Youssef Al Karadawi
Dr Mohamed Mahmoud Kassem
Mohamed Karam Shah
Malek Abdul Aziz Sy
Abdallah ben Mani'e (General Manager)
Mehmet Evdogan Sergici (Managing Director)

Objectives

The aim of Islamic Takafol Company is to provide Takafol services to Muslims, in particular those living in Western Europe. Takafol embodies the concept of solidarity and brotherhood among Muslims for mutual aid and assistance, whereby participants agree to share defined losses to be paid out of defined assets.

There is a large potential market which could be interested in Takafol services in Western Europe. Approximately 6 million Muslims form a relatively affluent part of Europe and many are savings orientated. The Takafol programme, as envisaged initially in the Mudaraba Al Tadamon, will have an inherent appeal to them. The Company will also serve as an administrative basis for the Islamic Re-Takafol Company of the Bahamas.

Islamic banking operations utilised

As DMI puts it, the ITC Luxembourg only provides type 1 Takafol services. Thus it will offer: investment and Takafol in case of death of any participant; group Takafol; Takafol among participants for individual and group pension.

Tadamon Mudaraba is the first of this kind and ITC Luxembourg commenced its marketing. It provides investment and Takafol among Muslims whose ages range from 17 to 55. An important feature of this Mudaraba is that it allows the participant to apply for financing of a project (which is not contrary to Islamic principles and which is viable and acceptable) up to five times the participant's share in the investment fund.

Capital structure

The paid-up capital of the Islamic Takafol Company is US$ 3 million. The authorised capital of the parent company DMI Trust is US$ 1 billion of which US$ 320 million has been paid-up.

Future developments

The Company plans to expand into other EEC countries once the law relating to freedom of establishment is implemented (whereby a company established in one EEC country will be authorised to operate in other EEC countries).

PAKISTAN

Agricultural Development Bank of Pakistan

Head office
1 Faisal Avenue
PO Box 1400
Islamabad
Pakistan

Telephone/telex/cable
Tel: 824135, 825516
Telex: 5618 ADBP PK
Cable: AGRIFIN

Other branches
See Appendix 1.

Date of formation

18 February 1961. The Agricultural Development Bank of Pakistan (ADBP) was set up by merging the Agricultural Development Finance Corporation and the Agricultural Bank of Pakistan to provide credit facilities to agriculturalists and persons engaged in cottage industries in rural areas.

Background

The ADBP was set up by the Government of Pakistan to provide credit facilities for the development of agriculture which includes the raising of crops, purchase of implements, reclamation of land, installation of tubewells, plantation of orchards, poultry farming, dairy farming, bee keeping, sericulture, inland and marine fisheries, development of agro-based industries and cottage industries in rural areas.

The charter of the Bank stipulates that preference will be given to small farmers in meeting the credit requirements of the rural sector.

Areas of operation

The Bank provides credit facilities for short-, medium- and long-term loans. Short-term loans are mostly for seasonal farm inputs and are recoverable within 18 months; medium- and long-term loans are given primarily for creating assets on the farms for the development of agriculture and are recoverable within 2–12 years.

Directors

The Agricultural Development Bank Ordinance of 1961 governs the working of the Bank. Its policies and operations are supervised by the Board of Directors consisting of twelve members. The Chief Executive is appointed by the Government of Pakistan and acts as Chairman of the Board. The other members of the Board are as follows: a representative of the Federal Ministry of Food and Agriculture; a representative of the Federal Ministry of Finance; one representative each from the four provincial governments; one non-official member appointed by the provincial governments for each of the four provinces, representing the farmers; one representative (as observer) from the government of Azad Jammu and Kashmir; a representative of the State Bank of Pakistan.

The day-to-day management of the Bank is looked after by the Chairman, who is assisted by a senior executive director and seven divisional heads of the status of executive director or director general. There are 31 departments at the Head Office; each department is headed by a designated director. For operational purposes the entire country is divided into 29 regions; each region is headed by a regional manager. There are 231 branches spread all over the country.

Objectives

The aims of the Bank, as set out earlier, are to provide credit facilities for a wide range of activities relating to the agricultural sector of the economy.

Capital structure (RS million)

Authorised capital   800,000
Paid-up capital   703,901

Bankers' Equity Limited

Head office

State Life Building No 3
Dr Ziauddin Ahmed Road
Karachi
Pakistan

Telephone/telex/cable

Tel: 520186 (4 lines), 514017
Cable: BANQUITY
Telex: 24646 BEL KR PK

Other branches

6–8 Agha Khan Road
Super Market F-6
Islamabad
Tel: 824241

22 Bridge Colony
Abid Majeed Road
Lahore Cantt
Tel: 370655

2 Arbab Road
Peshawar Cantt
Tel: 73106

IDBP Building
Hali Road
Quetta
Tel: 79020

Date of formation

Bankers' Equity was established in October 1979 and formally started operations on 10 January 1980.

Background of bank

Bankers' Equity was established to meet the diverse requirements of industrial financing and promote and accelerate the industrial development of the private sector. It is sponsored by the State Bank of Pakistan and the nationalised commercial banks. It is incorporate as a private limited company and commenced its activities on 10 January 1980. It was converted into a Public Limited Company in March 1986.

Areas of operation

Bankers' Equity provides industrial finance for the establishment of medium and large-sized projects in the private sector. The two main distinctive features of the Bank's operations are: (1) It aims at accelerating the pace of industrial development in the private sector by offering unified financing packages. The single package financing introduced by the company envisages arrangements of all types of financial requirements of a project at one point; (2) It has played a pioneering role in evolving and promoting the new Islamic modes of financing.

Bankers' Equity provides all types of rupee financing under the arrangement of profit and loss sharing.

Bankers' Equity has made a significant contribution to the process of elimination of Riba from local currency financing for industry and has developed effective and workable alternatives to substitute the economic role played by interest in allocating capital. It has played a pioneering role in promoting the new Islamic modes of financing such as Participation Term Certificates (PTCs), Term Finance Certificates (TFCs), Mudarabas and lease financing under PLS arrangements.

Directors

The overall control and supervision of Bankers' Equity is vested in its Board of Directors which is composed of the Governor the State Bank of Pakistan, the Chairman of the Pakistan Banking Council, presidents of the nationalised commercial banks, an executive director of the State Bank of Pakistan, and the managing director of Bankers' Equity. The Governor of the State Bank of Pakistan is Chairman of the Board.

The current Board is:

Mr V A Jafferty, Chairman (Governor, State Bank of Pakistan)

Directors:

Mr M R Khan (Chairman, Pakistan Banking Council)
Haji Abdul Jabbar Khan (President, National Bank of Pakistan)
Mr Tajammal Hussain (President, United Bank Ltd)
Mr Mohammad Usman (President, Muslim Commercial Bank Ltd)
Mr I D Junejo (President, Allied Bank of Pakistan Ltd)
Mr Sibghatullah (Executive Director, State Bank of Pakistan)
Mr D M Qureshi (Managing Director, Bankers Equity Ltd)
Mr Kassim Parekh (President, Habib Bank Ltd)

Objectives

The prime objective of the Bankers' Equity Limited is to finance the establishment of medium and large-sized industrial projects and to promote and extend Islamic modes of financing in general.

Capital structure

The authorised capital of Bankers' Equity is RS 5,000 million. During the year 1985–6 the company increased its equity base to RS 250 million to RS 1,000 million, subscribed by its shareholders. The equity base, comprising paid-up capital and reserves, amounted to RS 1,390,329 million as at 30 June 1986 as against RS 941,355 million as at 30 June 1985.

Islamic banking operations

During 1985–6, Bankers' Equity syndicate processed and approved 42 requests for a record financing of RS 1,893 million showing a significant rise of around 88 per cent over RS 1,007 million approved for 39 industrial projects in 1984–5. The aggregate approved financing since commencement of financing operations in early 1980 to end June 1986 amounted to RS 7,741 million. Total disbursements during 1985–6 amounted to RS 1,039 million compared with RS 904 million in 1984–5, showing an increase of 14.9 per cent. The cumulative disbursements to end June 986 amounted to RS 3,354 million. The approved projects related to almost all the key industrial sectors of the economy. The sanctioned financing is being provided to these projects in the form of direct equity support, underwriting of public issue of shares on firmed-up to standby basis, PLS and mark-up based short- and long-term investment against purchase of PTCs and TFCs, PLS funds for purchase of local machinery, lease financing, foreign currency loans and guarantees.

Future development

Bankers' Equity proposes to introduce a saving scheme designated as PLC Certificate of Investment (COI). The COI will be issued for fixed term ranging one month to five years in denominations ranging from RS 1,000 to RS one lac. The COI will be both registered and bearer in nature and is proposed to be listed on Stock Exchange. COI will share in the profits of Bankers' Equity. The scheme is expected to be launched in early 1987. Bankers' Equity has been selected by the Asian Development Bank (ADB) for Second Line of Credit, amounting to US$ 100 million. It has also been selected for ADB's Umbrella Line of Equity of US$ 5 million for joint investment in the equity of individual projects.

Number of employees

Total staff as of 30 June 1986 amounted to 178. Of this, the professional staff stood at 109, constituting 61.2 per cent.

Profitability

The operating results of Bankers' Equity for the year 1985–6 continued to show upward trends in income and profits. During 1985–6, the total income of Bankers' Equity increased by 35.4 per cent to RS 262 million compared with RS 192 million in 1984–5. The profits of Bankers' Equity were subjected to corporate tax from the year 1985–6. A summary of profits earned by the Bankers' Equity is as follows (RS million):

	Profit before tax	Net profit
1984–5	119.972	119.972
1985–6	154.465	78.055

Habib Bank Limited

Head office

Habib Bank Plaza
II Chundrigar Road
Karachi
Pakistan

Telephone/telex/cable

Tel: 219111 (50 lines)

Other branches

Branches in Pakistan	1,806
Branches overseas	66
Representative offices (overseas)	6
Subsidiaries	1
Joint ventures	2
Managing agency	1

Date of formation

Habib Bank Limited was established on 25 August 1941 but did not commence full non-interest based banking operations until 1 July 1985.

Background

Habib Bank Limited was established on 25 August 1941 in Bombay as a private limited company. After 1947 its head office was moved to Karachi and since 1974, when it was nationalised, it has been exclusively owned by the government. Besides striving for commercial and monetary objectives, the Bank is making all-out efforts to assist the government in meeting its socio-economic objectives.

Areas of operation

The Bank gives particular attention to the accepting of deposits on savings accounts on varying terms on a profit and loss sharing basis. It also provides funds on the same criterion. The activities of the Bank are now broad-based to cater for the needs of larger segments of the rural and urban population. The Bank, therefore, gives its support to all sectors of the economy, with particular emphasis on exports, industry and agriculture.

Founder members

Mr Ismail Habib (Deceased)

Directors

Mr Kassim Parekh (President)
Mr Sadiq Sayeed Khan (Director)
Mr Safdar A Zaidi (Director)
Mr S Nasim Ahmed (Director)
Mr Fasihuddin Khan (Director)
Mr Himayat Ali Khan (Director)
Mr Tahir Ali Tayebi (Secretary)

Executive board:

Mr Kassim Parekh (President)
Mr S Nasim Ahmed (Member)
Mr Fasihuddin Khan (Member)
Mr Himayat Ali Khan (Member)

Objectives

The stated objectives of the institution are to carry on the business of a banking company, which in Pakistan is done on a non-interest basis.

Types of deposit account

On the non-interest basis the deposit accounts available are: (1) profit and loss sharing saving bank accounts; (2) profit and loss sharing term deposit accounts; (3) profit and loss sharing Khas term deposit accounts; (4) profit and loss sharing special notice time deposit accounts; (5) current deposit accounts (without profit sharing).

Islamic banking operations

All non-interest based banking operations are used as advised from time to time by the State Bank of Pakistan. Three modes of financing are followed: (1) Financing by lending; (2) Trade-related financing; (3) Investment modes of financing.

Level and growth of assets (RS million)

1982   63,881
1983   82,240 (+28.74 per cent)
1984   91,432 (+11.18 per cent)
1985   107,551 (+17.63 per cent)

Profitability (RS million)

1984   828
1985   840

Number of employees

1983   23,106
1984   23,656 (+2.38 per cent)
1985   24,506 (+3.59 per cent)

Capital structure (RS million)

Authorised capital   1,000
Paid-capital   543

Future developments

The Bank is planning to put into operation all permissible Islamic modes of financing.

House-Building Finance Corporation

Head office

Shaikh Sultan Trust Building
10 Beaumont Road
Civil Lines
Karachi
Pakistan

Telephone/telex/cable

Tel: 512581 (5 lines)
Telex: 23851

Other branches

There are four zonal offices, 19 regional offices and 39 district offices.
Zonal office, Karachi:
3rd/4th Floor
Right Front Wing
Civic Centre
Karachi

    Regional office, Karachi:
    Unit No 1, Bungalow NO B-698
    Block No 13, Gulberg F'B' Area
    Karachi
    Regional office, Karachi:
    Unit No 2, Malir
    Regional office, Karachi:
    Unit No 111, 5th Floor
    Shafi Court, Club Road
    Karachi
    Regional office, Karachi:
    Company Cell, 4th Floor
    Civic Centre
    Karachi

Zonal office, Hyderabad:
295-B, Block E
Unit No 9, Latifabad
Hyderabad
  Regional office, Hyderabad:
  295-B, Block E
  Unit No 9
  Latifabad
  Hyderabad
  Regional office, Sukkur:
  Noor House
  Near Ghazi Abdul Rashid Park
  Market Road
  Sukkur
  Regional office, Nawabshah:
  B-350 Behind Firdous Hotel
  Kutchery Road
  Nawabshah
  Regional office, Quetta:
  Muslim Hotel
  Near Imdad Cinema
  M A Jinnah Road
  Quetta
Zonal office, Lahore:
Lake Road
Near Chubargi
Lahore
  Regional office, Lahore:
  Unit (A) Samanabad
  Lahore
  Regional office, Lahore:
  Unit (B) Faisal Town
  Lahore
  Regional office, Faisalabad:
  81-A, Peoples' Colony
  Faisalabad
  Regional office, Multan:
  7-B Gulgishat Colony
  Multan
  Regional office, Bahawalpur:
  Al-Haque
  Opposite Commissioner House
  Bahawalapur

Regional office, Gujranwala:
27-A, Satellite Town
Gujranwala
Zonal office, Islamabad:
8/3 F Shalimar
Street No 10
Bungalow No 10
Islamabad
Regional office, Islamabad:
Shalimar
Islamabad
Regional office, Rawalpindi:
766/F Satellite Town
Rawalpindi
Regional office, Gilgit:
House Building Finance Corporation
Gilgit
Regional office, Peshawar:
36 Defence Officers' Colony
Peshawar
Regional office, Abbottabad:
1st Floor
Supply Bazar
Mansehra Road
Abbottabad

Date of formation

House-Building Finance Corporation (HBFC) was established in 1952.

Background

Established in 1952, HBFC is the only institution in Pakistan which provides long-term finance in the public sector of housing for the construction/purchase of housing units and its credit facilities are available all over Pakistan.

Areas of operation

In 1979 the previous system of interest-bearing loans was replaced. Its successor was introduced in July 1979 and was termed an income sharing investment scheme based on Islamic principles. Under this new scheme HBFC shares in the rental profits of a house in the proportion of its investment made to the total cost of the house which includes the cost of land and construction.

Directors

The affairs of the Corporation are managed by nine members of the Board of Directors. Four members represent each of the four provinces, two represent the

Federal Government, one represents the State Bank of Pakistan and one member is the Managing Director who is also the Chairman of the Board.

Dr F A Rabbani
Managing Director and Chairman
House Building Finance Corporation
Head Office
Karachi

Mr K N Cheema
Joint Secretary
Internal Finance Wing
Ministry of Finance
Government of Pakistan
Islamabad

Mr Ayaz Ali Shah
Joint Secretary
Housing and Environment Division
Government of Pakistan
Islamabad

Mr Syed Sibtul Hasan Shah
Secretary
Housing and Physical Planning Dept
Government of Punjab
Lahore

Mr Naeemullah Khan
Secretary
Housing and Physical Planning Dept
Government of N W F P
Peshawar

Mr Ata Muhammad Jaffer
Secretary
Finance Department
Government of Baluchistan
Quetta

Mr Nazer M Shaikh
Secretary
Finance Department
Government of Sind
Karachi

Mr Fayyaz Ahmed
Director
Banking Control Department
State Bank of Pakistan
Karachi

Mr M Y Siddiki
Deputy Managing Director
House Building Finance Corporation
Head Office
Karachi

Objectives

The purpose of the Institution is to provide financial assistance to house builders for the construction of house units not exceeding 2,250 sq ft of covered area. Investment is made at RS 90 sq ft, subject to a maximum limit of RS 150,000/- in each case and admissibility of the client (recoverable in 15 years).

Level and growth of assets (RS million)

1980–1   4,215.454
1981–2   5,505.997 (+23 per cent)
1982–3   6,652.648 (+17 per cent)
1983–4   7,778.018 (+14 per cent)

Profitability (before tax)

	Income-sharing	*Interest-bearing*	*Total*
1982–3	117.563	11.840	129.403
1983–4	197.871	8.230	206.101

Number of employees

1983–4   1,386
1984–5   1,449 (+4.34 per cent)
1985–6   1,492 (+2.88 per cent)

Capital structure

Besides the share capital of RS 200 million the Corporation's capital resources are made up of a State Bank loan of RS 5,662.2 million and government loans (RS 337.99 million).

Industrial Development Bank of Pakistan

Head office

State Life Building No 2
Wallace Road
Off II Chundrigar Road
PO Box 5082
Karachi — 2
Pakistan

Telephone/telex/cable

Tel: 228535, 228539, 227146, 227149, 227140
Telex: 23722 IDBP PK
Cable: INDEBA Karachi (PAKISTAN)

Other branches

The IDBP has four regional head offices and seven branches:

Regional offices

Karachi:
State Life Building No 2
Wallace Road
Off II Chundrigar Road
PO Box 5078
Karachi — 2
Tel: 228535, 228539, 227146, 227149, 221724
Telex: 23722 IDBP PK
Grams: 'SANATBANK' Karachi

Lahore:
9 Davis Road
PO Box 373
Lahore
Tel: 303155, 303158, 304598
Telex: 44692 IDBP PK
Grams: 'SANATBANK' Lahore.

Peshawar:
2 Arbab Road
PO Box 59
Peshawar (Cantt)
Tel: 72496, 72497, 73379
Telex: 5262 IDBP PK
Grams: 'SANATBANK' Peshawar

Rawalpindi:
State Life Building No 1
The Mall
PO Box 81
Rawalpindi
Tel: 64655, 68035, 68036, 62015
Telex: 5625 IDBP PK
Grams: 'SANATBANK' Rawalpindi
Branches:
Abbottabad:
842 Mansehra Road
Near Jab Bridge
Abbottabad
Tel: 2809, 2478
Grams: SANATBANK, Abbottabad
Gujranwala:
Small Industries Estate
G T Road
PO Box 12
Gujranwala
Tel: 82581
Grams: SANATBANK, Gujranwala
Hyderabad:
Opposite Cantonment Police Station
Saddar
PO Box 204
Hyderabad
Tel: 22636
Grams: SANATBANK, Hyderabad
Mirpur (Azadkashmir):
Allama Iqbal Road
Mirpur (Azadkashmir)
Tel: 3379
Grams: SANATBANK, Mirpur (AK)
Multan:
36 Hassan Parwana Road
PO Box 120
Multan
Tel: 76931
Grams: SANATBANK, Multan

Quetta:
382/3 Shara-e-Hali
PO Box 93
Quetta (Cantt)
Tel: 75614
Grams: SANATBANK, Quetta
Sukkur:
Red Cross Building
Parsi Colony Road
PO Box 62
Sukkur
Tel: 84992
Grams: SANATBANK, Sukkur

Date of formation

1 August 1961.

Background

The Industrial Development Bank of Pakistan was established in August 1961 to meet the needs of the local community in providing medium- and long-term credit requirements in local and foreign currencies for the establishment of small and medium-sized industrial units and for meeting the expansion, modernisation and replacement needs of existing industrial units.

Since its inception the Bank has continued to synchronise its operations with the socio-economic objectives pursued by the Government. During its existence IDBP has developed sufficient professional expertise in development banking. Thus IDBP, one of the two most senior financial institutions in Pakistan, is capable of catering for the diverse needs of the private manufacturing sector.

Areas of operation

In conformity with the recommendations of the Credit Enquiry Commission, 1959, the Pakistan Industrial Finance Corporation (PIFCO) was converted into the Industrial Development Bank of Pakistan in August 1961. The Bank was given extended functions to perform additional financing operations.

IDBP attempts to promote economically desirable, technically feasible and financially viable projects, particularly in the less developed areas. In the acceptance of industrial projects for assistance, it considers not only the credit standing of the entrepreneurs and the commercial profitability of the project but also the economic contribution of projects to the national economy. The Bank operates within the framework of industrial investment schedules formulated by the government.

Directors

Mr Bashir Ahmad (Chairman and Managing Director, IDBP)

Mr Iqbal Mueen (Director, Representing Federal Government)
Mr Zainal Abedeen (Director, Representing Federal Government)
Mr Hafeezullah Ishaq (Director, Representing Government of the Punjab)
Mr Abdullah J Memon (Director, Representing Government of Sind)
Dr D K Riaz Baluch (Director, Representing Government of Baluchistan)
Mr Tanwir Ahmad (Director, Representing Government of NWFP)
Mr D M Qureshi (Director, Representing a Financial Institution)

Senior management

Mr Bashir Ahmad (Managing Director)
Mr Muhammad Wasil Memon (Deputy MD Operations)
Mr S M Yusuf (Deputy MD End-use)

Objectives

The Bank, being one of the major instruments in regulating investment in the private manufacturing sector, endeavours to synchronise its operations with the socio-economic objectives laid down by the government. Some of these objectives relate to the establishment of small projects, diffusion of industrial ownership, setting up industries in less developed areas and search for new lines of manufacture.

Without doubt, IDBP's primary objective is to extend term finance for investment in the private manufacturing sector of the economy.

Types of deposit account

PLS Savings Bank Account; PLS Special Notice 7–29 days and 30 days and over; PLS Term Deposits for 3, 6, and 12 months, 2, 3, 4, and 5 years.

Islamic banking operations

Under government directive to banks and financial institutions, IDBP has shifted its local currency loan operations to permissible non-interest modes of financing from 1 January 1985 to its new loanings to limited companies and from 1 April 1985 to its entire rupee loaning operations. Initially, financing on the basis of 'mark-up' has been chosen and fresh sanctions are being accorded on that basis on the said dates. The Bank's deposit operations are also on a PLS basis.

IDBP completed its first year of loaning operations on a non-interest basis in 1986.

Level and growth of assets (RS million)

	Total assets	Increase
1983	3,565.815	364.110 (11.37 per cent)
1984	4,240.586	674.771 (18.92 per cent)
1985	5,353.986	1,113.400 (26.26 per cent)

Profitability (RS million)

	Profit before tax
1984	50.393
1985	52.969

Number of employees

1983	716
1984	755 (+5.44 per cent)
1985	794 (+5.16 per cent)

Capital structure

The total capital (authorised, issued, subscribed and paid-up) of the Bank was RS 157.00 million as at 30 June 1985.

Future developments

In 1985 the Bank started fully-fledged working capital operations. It contemplates adding the following new business to its existing lines of operation: (1) Underwriting of public issues of shares and bridge financing; (2) Export/import financing; (3) Leasing of machinery and equipments.

Investment Corporation of Pakistan

Head Office

5th Floor
National Bank of Pakistan Building
II Chundrigar Road
PO Box 5410
Karachi
Pakistan

Telephone/Telex/Cable

Tel: 225861 (10 lines)
Telex: 2879 ICP PK, 25223 ICP PK
Cable: 'INVESTCORP'

Other branches

Faisalabad:
Qasr-e-Murmur
Allama Iqbal Road
Faisalabad
Tel: 31874, 31690
Telex: 43438 ICP PK
Cable: INVESTCORP

Hyderabad:
Hotel Fataz
Thandi Sarak
PO Box 347
Hyderabad
Tel: 26676
Cable: INVESTCORP

Islamabad
5-B, F-6/3
Sultan Agha Khan Road (Main Masjid Road)
PO Box 2042
Islamabad
Tel: 811322, 811323, 811714, 811716, 811717, 825681
Telex: 54520 ICPID PK
Cable: INVESTCORP

Karachi:
Standard Insurance House
2nd Floor
II Chundrigar Road
PO Box 5237
Karachi
Tel: 232991 (3 lines), 239837, 239838
Cable: KARINVEST

Lahore:
Shalimar House
2nd Floor
48 Shara-e-Quaid-e-Azam
PO Box 1198
Lahore
Tel: 305429, 305439
Telex: 44891 ICP PK
Cable: INVESTCORP

Multan:
Hussain Agahi Road
PO Box 345
Multan
Tel: 44676, 31571
Telex: 4248 ICP PK
Cable: INVESTCORP

Peshawar:
3 Arbab Road
PO Box 127
Peshawar
Tel: 74957, 74757, 74758
Telex: 5288 ICPPW PK
Cable: INVESTCORP

Quetta:
Shara-e-Iqbal
PO Box 140
Quetta
Tel: 71684, 75380
Cable: INVESTCORP

Rawalpindi:
133 Kashmir Road
PO Box 333
Rawalpindi
Tel: 68097, 65121, 65869, 67608, 68098
Telex: 5813 ICP PK

Date of formation

22 February 1966

Background

The Investment Corporation of Pakistan (ICP) was established in February 1966 through an Ordinance of the Federal Government of Pakistan as a development capital market and as a way of broadening the base of equity investment in Pakistan. Prior to the establishment of the Corporation, the country's capital market did not have any organised investment banking system and issuers found it hard to raise equity capital from the public. Thus, shares of listed companies were concentrated in a few hands.

Areas of operation

The Corporation performs the following functions:

(1)　Underwrites public issues of shares, provides financial assistance through purchase of Term Finance Certificates (TFCs) to enable the entrepreneurs to meet the equity and local currency requirements of funds for financing their projects and also for the purchase of locally manufactured machinery.

(2)　Opens and maintains investment accounts with a view to broad base share ownership and to widening the base of the capital market for the purchase and sale of shares of listed companies.

162

(3) Floats and manages closed-end mutual funds, which besides providing a series of sound scripts for investors seeking a stable return, also serve as a medium for selling seasoned portions of underwriting take-ups of shares and the shares acquired in the process of support operations on the stock market.

(4) Buys and sells shares on the Stock Market in order to provide strength to the Stock Exchange.

Directors

Mr Ghulam Faruque (Chairman)

Mr I H Qarni (Managing Director)

Mr Shamim Ahmed Khan (Joint Secretary, Investment/Finance Division, Government of Pakistan)

Mr Zainal Abedeen (Director General, Investment Promotion Bureau)

Shaikh Irshad Ahmed (Chairman, Turk-Pak International Limited)

Mr Samee-ul-Hasan (Director and Consulting Actuary, State Life Insurance Corporation of Pakistan)

Mr Tajammal Hussain (President, United Arab Bank Limited)

Mr Kassim Parekh (President, Habib Bank Limited)

Mr Muhammad Usman (President, Muslim Commercial Bank Limited)

Mr I D Junejo (President, Allied Bank of Pakistan Limited)

Mr Sibghatullah (Executive Director, State Bank of Pakistan)

Mr A Sami Qureshi (Managing Director, National Investment Trust Limited)

Mr Humayun Akhtar Adil (Member, Executive Board, National Bank of Pakistan)

Senior management

Mr S A Q Haqqani (Deputy Managing Director)

Mr I H Siddiqui

Mr D F Rabadi

Mr Behram Hasan

Mr Muhammad Munawar

Mr Abdul L Uquaili

Mr T A Khan

Mr Kabiruddin Khan

Mr Hashim Khan

Mr Abdul Majeed Qureshi

Mr Haroon I Kahani (all General Managers).

Objectives

The aims of ICP are twofold: (1) To broaden the base of equity investment; (2) To develop the capital market.

Types of investment account

(1) *Profit and loss sharing accounts:* Under the PLS scheme, the Corporation pools its investors' funds with its own funds in the ratio 40:60, subject to a maximum of Rs 45,000 in ICP's case and Rs 30,000 in investors' case in any one account known as a sharing account.

   In case of loss on joint equity investment, it is shared by ICP and investors in the ratio of their present investment, ie 40:60. However, investors are allowed a 60 per cent share in any profit although they contribute only 40 per cent of the capital.

(2) *Non-sharing accounts:* Such accounts are opened by the investors from their own resources, without the participation of ICP.

Islamic banking operations

(1) *Term finance certificates/Participation term certificate (long term):* The Corporation has entered into arrangements for project financing on a long-term basis against purchase of PTCs/TFCs. These are secured by a mortgage of all present and future moveable and immoveable properties of related projects and carry floating charges on their current assets.

(2) *Share issues (medium term):* This represents bridge finance and medium term finance provided to various projects on a participation term/mark-up basis against commitments for underwriting of public issue of shares and against issue of medium-term participation certificates/term finance certificates. The TFCs/PTCs are secured by a mortgage/charge of all the present and future moveable properties and a floating charge on the current assets of the project.

(3) *Loans on mark-up basis against purchase of locally manufactured machinery:* This represents funds provided to various projects for procurement of locally manufactured machinery out of a refinance facility sanctioned by the State Bank of Pakistan. According to the arrangement with the project, the Corporation is entitled to mark-up at 3 per cent on the funds disbursed to the Company.

Level and growth of assets (RS million)

1983   1,983 (+27.3 per cent)
1984   2,072 (+ 4.4 per cent)
1985   2,229 (+ 7.5 per cent)
1986   2,492 (+11.8 per cent)

Profitability (RS million)

1985   9.7
1986   9.1

Number of employees

1985   527 (+4.8 per cent)
1986   532 (+0.9 per cent)

Capital structure (RS million)

Authorised capital	200.0
Issued, subscribed and paid-up	100.0
Long-term loan from the Government of Pakistan	229.3

Future developments

Normally each year ICP floats a mutual fund of Rs 10 million to enable investors of small means to participate in pooled investments. This also helps to broaden the base of equity investments and it is expected that a similar mutual fund may be floated next year.

The investors' scheme of ICP provides a unique opportunity for investment in shares through PLS accounts. This facility is also available to overseas Pakistanis in order to attract foreign exchange into the country. Under the instructions of the Government of Pakistan, ICP is planning to implement the policy of disinvestments of government owned shares in the near future.

Muslim Commercial Bank Limited

Head office

Adamjee House
II Chundrigar Road
Karachi
Pakistan

Telephone/telex/cable

Tel: 224091, 224092, 224093, 224094, 224095, 238535, 238536, 238537, 238538, 238539.
Telex: KAR 887

Other branches

At the end of 1985 the number of branches stood at 1,271. The major ones are:

Main Branch, II Chundrigar Road, Karachi
Corporate Branch, Shaheen Complex, Karachi
Nila Gumbad, Lahore
Circular Road, Lahore
The Mall, Rawalpindi
Peshawar Cantt, Peshawar
Hussain Agahi Road, Multan
Risala Road, Hyderabad

Shara-e-Iqbal, Quetta
Circular Road, Faisalabad

Date of formation

9 July 1947.

Background

Muslim Commercial Bank Limited was established and registered in Calcutta in July 1947. On 10 August the Bank's head office was moved to Karachi. Like all other banks, MCB was nationalised in January 1974 and was merged with Premier Bank in June of the same year. Previously it had been the Bank's policy to consolidate its existing branch network rather than to undertake aggressive expansion. Since 1974, however, expansion has been high up on the Bank's list of priorities and so it has attempted to expand its services to reach the maximum number of people possible.

Areas of operation

Funds are allocated to finance the activities of various economic groups so as to promote economic growth and prosperity. Before it was nationalised the Bank gave credit to selected parties engaged in trade and commerce activities. However, in the period after nationalisation the scope of services offered has increased substantially. The Bank has introduced various credit schemes to finance the needs of farmers and industry in general.

Founder members

Adamjee Haji Dawood
M A Ispahani
A S Ahmed
Abdul Jalil
Abdur Rahman Kasam
M A H Ispahani
F Jehangir Khan

Directors

Mr Mohammed Usman (President)
Mr Masood Akhtar
Mr Iqbal Mueen
Mr M I Gurwara
Mr S Hashim Raza
Mr Iftikhar Ahmed Malik
Mr Mohammad Hamid Ali

Supervisory board

Mr Mohammad Usman (President)

Mr M I Gurwara
Mr S Hashim Raza
Mr Iftikhar Ahmed Malik
Mr Mohammad Hamid Ali
Mr Tameez-ul-Haque (Secretary)

Objectives

(1) Accepting deposits.
(2) Borrowing, raising or taking up money; lending money either upon or without security.
(3) Acting as agents for governments or local authorities or any other person or persons.
(4) Insuring, guaranteeing, underwriting etc.
(5) Acquisition by purchase, lease, exchange, hire or otherwise of any property movable or immovable.
(6) Undertaking and executing trusts.
(7) Undertaking the administration of estates as executor, trustee and otherwise.
(8) Taking, acquiring and holding shares.
(9) Doing all such other things as are incidental or conducive to the promotion or advancement of the Company.

Type of deposit account

(1) Savings accounts; (2) Current accounts; (3) Short notice deposits (7 days and 30 days); (4) Term deposit receipts (maturity between 3 months and 5 years).

Islamic banking operations

The Profit and Loss Sharing scheme was started on 1 January 1981 on a limited scale. However, banks in Pakistan switched over all banking operations to a non-interest based system from 1 July 1985. Under this system financing has been conducted in three major categories: (1) Financing by lending; (2) Trade-related modes of financing; (3) Investment type modes of financing.

Use of Islamic banking operations

Up to December 1984 the following operations were covered on a non-interest basis:

(1) Import bills transactions.
(2) Inland bills.
(3) Investment in National Investment Trust Ltd and the Investment Corporation of Pakistan.
(4) Working capital financing on profit and loss sharing basis.
(5) Housing finance on a rent sharing basis.

From 1 April 1985 all financing has been on a non-interest basis.

167

Level and growth of assets (RS million)

31 December 1984: 19,203
31 December 1985: 22,845

Profitability (RS million)

1984   133
1985   133

Number of employees

1984   12,684
1985   12,591

Capital structure (RS million)

Authorised capital   524
Paid-up capital   262

Future developments

MCB has always played an important role in the economic development of the country. During the sixth Five Year Plan there will be tremendous growth in the industrial and agricultural fields as well as in other sectors. The private sector will also contribute a major role in almost all the fields of economic activity. MCB will play an active role in the development of the country as envisaged in the sixth Five Year Plan. It is worthy of note that MCB has been selected by the World Bank to disburse loans on its behalf.

National Bank of Pakistan

Head office

National Bank of Pakistan Building
II Chundrigar Road
Karachi
Pakistan

Telephone/Telex/Cable

Tel: 226780 (9 lines), 226612 (5 lines)
Telex: 23732 NBP PK, 23733 NBP PK, 2734 NBP PK, 8067 NBP PK
Telegraph: PO Box No 4937, SUMMIT

Other branches

The National Bank of Pakistan has 1,305 domestic offices and 23 overseas offices.

Regional offices

Faisalabad:
69-A Peoples' Colony
Faisalabad
Pakistan

Gujranwala:
Civil Lines (PO Box 202)
Gujranwala
Pakistan

Hyderabad:
2nd Floor
National Bank of Pakistan Building
Fatima Jinnah Road
Hyderabad
Pakistan

Islamabad:
National Bank of Pakistan Building
Civic Centre
Islamabad
Pakistan

Karachi:
1st Floor
National Bank of Pakistan Building
II Chundrigar Road
Karachi
Pakistan

Lahore:
Al-Falah Building
Shara-e-Quaid-e-Azam
Lahore
Pakistan

Multan:
Chowk Shah Abbas
Vehari Road
Multan
Pakistan

Muzaffarabad:
Shaukat Line
Muzaffarabad (AK)
Pakistan

Peshawar:
2 Arbab Road
Peshawar
Pakistan

Quetta:
Staff College Road
Quetta Cantt
Pakistan

Date of formation

9 November 1949.

Background

Established as a semi-commercial bank in 1949, the Bank was nationalised in January 1974 under the Banks Nationalisation Act of the same year. The National Bank also has the distinction of acting as an agent of the Central Bank and operates in areas not served by the State Bank.

Areas of operation

As well as all the normal operations expected of a bank, the National Bank of Pakistan has some special areas and projects which it attempts to fund. It provides substantial amounts of small loans to the agricultural sector and sponsors specialised schemes — including some in the fields of education and small business.

Founder members

Mr Mumtaz Hassan
Mr A Muhajir
Mr Anwer Ali
Mr S Wajid Ali
Mr Khuwaja Muhammad Yusuf
Mr Moazzamuddin Hassain
Mr Mehr Ali Shah Bukhari

Directors

Mr Abdul Jabbar Khan (President)
Mr Muhammad Sher Khan
Mr Mehr A Barlas
Mr S Amjad Ali

Mr Humayan Akhtar Adil
Mr M Saeed Butt

Senior management

Mr Abdul Jabbar Khan (President)
Mr Mehr A Barlas (Member, Executive Board)
Mr S Amjad Ali (Member, Executive Board)
Mr Humayan Akhtar Adil (Member, Executive Board)
Mr Saeed Butt (Member, Executive Board)
Mr Saeed Ahmed Qazi (Senior Exective VP)
Mr Khalid S Hasan (Senior Executive VP)
Mr M Asif Nomani (Senior Executive VP)

Type of deposit accounts

Current accounts; Profit and loss sharing saving account; Term deposits (interest based); Term deposits (non-interest based).

Islamic banking operations

(1) Acceptance of deposits on a PLS basis; (2) Financing on a mark-up basis under a non-interest system of operations.

Banking on a non-interest basis has expanded in the last two years. The first two phases of the project have been successfully completed.

Since 1 January 1985 all financing by banks to government — the public sector corporations as well as the private and public sector companies — has been provided on the new interest-free basis. Accounts/assets now provided on an interest basis will remain as such until maturity. However, since 1 July 1985 the Bank has not accepted deposits on an interest-bearing basis. Savings and term deposit accounts are provided on a PLS basis and current accounts are free of interest, as was the case previously.

Level and growth of assets (RS million)

	Assets
1983	55,812.7
1984	61,654.7 (+10.5 per cent)
1985	75,989.9 (+23.3 per cent)

Profitability (RS million)

	Pre-tax profit
1984	226.4
1985	280.4 (+23.9 per cent)

Number of employees

| March 1985 | 21,736 |
| March 1986 | 21,439 |

Decrease was mainly attributed to retirements and a policy of non-recruitment during the period.

Capital structure (RS million)

Authorised capital   1,000
Paid-up capital   561

Future developments

The Bank is continuing its efforts to streamline and decentralise its operations at local and regional levels. The main purpose being to facilitate the availability of credit at its optimal level by removing bottle-necks for the Bank's customers even in the most remote areas covered by the Bank's extensive branch network.

In order to fulfil the Bank's role of assisting and contributing to the nation's development, future efforts will be directed towards broadening the scope of activities using modern techniques, making use of computers and developing better channels for the Bank's clients.

National Investment (Unit) Trust Limited

Head office

National Bank Building
6th Floor
II Chundrigar Road
PO Box 5671
Karachi
Pakistan

Telephone/telex/cable

Tel: 222056 (4 lines)
Telex: 24476 NIT PK
Cable: WETRUST

Other branches

Faisalabad:
Habib Bank Building (3rd Floor)
Circular Road
Faisalabad
Tel: 27856

Hyderabad:
Ghafoor Chambers
2nd Floor
Market Road
Hyderabad
Tel: 31693

Islamabad:
6-A Super Market
Shalimar Markaz-6
Islamabad
Tel: 828711

Karachi:
158/M 1st Floor
PMC Centre
Opp Shalimar Centre
Tariq Road
Karachi
Tel: 447418

Lahore:
211-212 Alfalah
15 Shara-e-Quaid-e-Azam
Tel: 301810, 301811
Telex: 44594 NIT PK

Mirpur (AK):
Allama Iqbal Road
Bank Square
Mirpur (AK)
Tel: 2237

Multan:
1st Floor, Habib Bank Building
Hussain Agahi
Multan
Tel: 42215

Peshawar:
Saray Plaza No 2
Islamia Road
Near Jan Hotel
Peshawar Cantt
Tel: 74848

Quetta:
Al-Hayat Chambers
M A Jinnah Road
Quetta
Tel: 71304

Rawalpindi:
Al-Ameer Building
46-A/2 Bank Road
Rawalpindi
Tel: 67217

Sukkur:
1st Floor
B-966/1-2 Sir Adamjee Road
Nr Wholesale Cloth Market
Sukkur
Tel: 158547

Date of formation

Incorporated in October 1962 as a joint stock company under the Companies Act 1913.

Background

The National Investment (Unit) Trust Ltd was set up as an open end mutual fund in October 1962 by an agreement between the National Investment Trust Limited as the management company and the National Bank of Pakistan as the trustee. The trust was established for mobilisation of savings to meet the growing needs of the corporate sector and to achieve broad-based corporate ownership. Operations were commenced on 1 January 1963.

Founder members

NIT was established with the sponsorship of the Government of Pakistan in association with the following:

Mr Ahmed Dawood (Industrialist)
National Bank of Pakistan (Statutory corporation)
Pakistan Industrial Credit and Investment Corporation
Industrial Development Bank of Pakistan (Statutory corporation)
Pakistan Insurance Corporation (Statutory corporation)
Habib Bank Limited (Ltd Co)
United Bank Limited (Ltd Co)
Mr Abdul Majid Bawany (Industrialist)
Mr Abdul Hamid Adamjee (Industrialist)

Directors

Mr A Sami Qureshi (Chairman and Managing Director)
Mr K N Cheema (Representing Government of Pakistan)
Mr Abdul Hamid Adamjee (Industrialist)
Mr S M A Ashraf (Pakistan Insurance Corporation)
Mr Ahmed Dawood (Industrialist)
Mr Tajammal Hussain (United Bank Limited)
Mr M W Farooqui (Pakistan Industrial Credit and Investment Corp)
Mian Tajammal Hussain (Industrialist)
Mr Abdul Jabbar Khan (National Bank of Pakistan)
Mr Kassim Parekh (Habib Bank Limited)
Mr I H Qarni (Investment Corporation of Pakistan)
Mr M Usman (Muslim Commercial Bank Limited)
Mr Bashir Ahmed (Industrial Development Bank of Pakistan)

Senior management

Mr Manzoor Ahmed (Deputy Managing Director)
Mr Kabir A Qureshi (General Manager, Investors' Service Dept)
Mr A K M Sayeed (General Manager, Finance and Investment)
Mr Shamshad Ahmed (General Manager, Marketing)
Mr Mohammad Imran (General Manager, Administration)
Mr A D Azhar Khawaja (General Manager, Data Processing Dept)

Objectives

The major objectives of the National Investment Trust are to manage the activities and affairs of National Investment (Unit) Trust Limited. The fundamental aims of the Trust are: (1) To mobilise the savings of the people and to put the pooled funds into productive channels; (2) To meet the growing financial needs of the corporate sector; (3) To broaden the base of equity ownership.

Islamic banking operations

NIT was one of the first institutions chosen for Islamisation of the financial and economic system of Pakistan. Since July 1979 it has made investments in such schemes as are operated on a PLS basis in compliance with the Sharia. Such activities consist of shares in the companies quoted on the Pakistan Stock Exchange, Mudaraba and Participation Term Certificates and under a mark-up system for financing trade and industry. The liquid funds pending investment are kept in PLS accounts of banks.

The net investments made by NIT (at cost) during 1983–4 and 1984–5 were RS 202,265,000 and RS 264,624,000 respectively.

Level and growth of assets (RS million)

Investment	1982–3	1983–4	1984–5
Stock market operations	29.570	19.940	43.156
Purchases from financial institutions	31.795	43.440	54.104
New flotations	9.422	40.180	20.711
Right shares	5.500	104.160	16.949
Mark-up	43.000	26.400	155.000
Participation term certificates	6.700	17.700	37.115
Total	125.987	251.820	327.035

Disinvestment	1982–3	1983–4	1984–5
Stock market operations	32.134	40.183	35.034
Sales to financial institutions	25.586	29.367	37.782
Redemption of shares under buy-back arrangement	00.874	00.945	00.198
Disinvestment under mark-up	13.000	15.260	30.483
Compensation paid by the govt in respect of Multan Electric & Rawalpindi Electric	–	–	1.600
Redemption of Mudaraba certificates	1.961	–	–
Total	73.555	85.755	105.097
Less: capital gains	26.505	36.200	42.686
Net investment at cost	77.937	202.265	264.624

Progressive investments at end of years

At cost	1,116.943	1,319.204	1,583.828
At market value	1,533.533	2,264.896	2,510.653

Profitability (RS million)

Income from dividend and PLS deposits	182.4	219.7
Mark-up and PTCs	1.4	10.3
Element of income and capital gain in price of units sold, less those in repurchase	9.0	11.8
Capital gains	36.2	42.7
Total	229.0	284.5

Number of employees

	1984	1985
Clerical/non-clerical	92	89
Officers	81	80
Total	173	169

Capital structure

The paid-up capital of NIT Limited is RS 1.2 million, subscribed equally by twelve shareholders: the government, four leading banks, four financial institutions and three leading industrialists.

Pakistan Industrial Credit and Investment Corporation Limited

Head office

State Life Building No 1
II Chundrigar Road
PO Box 5080
Karachi-2

Telephone/telex/cable

Tel: 225381 (10 lines)
Telex: 2710 PICIC PK
Cable: PICICORP, Karachi

Other branches

Regional office, Lahore:
PICIC Building
14-A Shara-e-Aiwan-e-Tijarat
PO Box 1830
Lahore
Tel: 305180, 304964, 304965, 306083
Telex: 44512 PICIC PK
Cable: PICICORP Lahore
Peshawar:
10-A Khyber Road
PO Box 166
Peshawar Cantt
Tel: 78480, 79240
Cable: PICICORP, Peshawar
Quetta:
310-B Mafeking Road
Off Staff College Road
Quetta Cantt
Tel: 70644
Cable: PICICORP, Quetta

Islamabad:
Bungalow No 27
Street No 56
Shalimar F-6/4
Islamabad
Tel: 823625, 823626
Cable: PICICORP, Islamabad
Mirpur (Azad Kashmir):
140 Sector D-1
Allama Iqbal Road
Mirpur (AK)
Tel: 3242
Cable: PICICORP, Mirpur (AK)

Date of formation

PICIC was established in 1957.

Background

The Pakistan Industrial Credit and Investment Corporation Limited (PICIC) was
set up in 1957 to give financial and other assistance to the private sector.

Areas of operation

Since 1 July 1985, PICIC has adopted the mechanism of mark-up in its rupee
lending of local currency for the purchase of locally fabricated machinery. This
is done under the Islamic mode of financing as laid down by the State Bank of
Pakistan.

By diversifying into the field of call money market operations the Corporation has managed to improve its profitability.

Founder members

Fakhruddin Valibhai (Director)
M A Rangoonwalla (Director)
Ahmed Dawood (Director)
Amirali H Fancy (Director)
Pir Mohammed Mahfooz (Director)
Sheriar F Irani
I Mahmud

Directors

Pir M Mahfooz (Chairman)
Ahmed Dawood (Deputy Chairman)
M W Farooqui (Managing Director)
G M Adamjee
M Shabbir Ahmad

S M Rafiq Akhtar
Adnan Ahmed Ali (Representing provincial governments)
S M A Ashmof
R G L Barnes (Representing British shareholders)
Zahid Bashir
William E Beam (Representing American shareholders)
Rudolf J Gebert (Alternate Director) (Representing American shareholders)
Khursheed K Marker
I H Qarni
A Sami Qureshi
Ghulam M Samdani (Representing federal government)
Qamaruddin Siddiqi
Jahangir Siddiqui
Athishdam Tharmaratnam (Representing International Finance Corporation)
Keiichiro Ueda (Representing Japanese shareholders)

Objectives

The primary aim is to provide financial support to the private industrial sector of Pakistan. PICIC provides long- and medium-term loans to private industrial sector in the country in foreign and local currencies, as well as underwriting issues of shares and participates in other securities.

PICIC assists Pakistani entrepreneurs to obtain suitable foreign investment in their enterprises and conversely assists foreign investors to locate suitable investment opportunities in Pakistan. The Corporation also assists entrepreneurs in the preparation of investment proposals and acts as a financial adviser to enterprises it has financed. Additionally, it assists in obtaining technical and managerial advice for industries financed by it.

Level and growth of assets (RS million)

	1983	1984	1985	1983–5 growth
Current assets	224	233	265	+18.3 per cent
Long-term advances	3,060	3,566	4,592	+50.1 per cent
Others	554	489	493	−11.0 per cent
Total assets	3,838	4,288	5,350	+39.4 per cent

Profitability (RS million)

	Pre-tax profit
1984	78.69
1985	95.85

Number of employees

	Senior executive vice-presidents	Other officers	Other staff	Total
1984	3	130	166	299
June 1985	3	129	167	299

Capital structure (RS million)

Authorised capital 150.00
Paid-up capital 109.96

Future developments

PICIC is hoping to expand into the field of equity and lease financing for which the prospects appear to be bright in the home country. Such a proposition is likely to further the extent of PICIC's profitability and enhance its cash position.

Pakistan Kuwait Investment Company (Private) Limited

Head office

7th Floor
Sheikh Sultan Trust Building
Beaumont Road
GPO Box 901
Karachi
Pakistan

Telephone/telex/cable

Tel: 51 32 61, 51, 32 80
Telex: 24396 PKIC PK

Other branches: N/A

Date of formation

17 March 1979.

Background

The Pakistan Kuwait Investment Company (PKIC) was established as a result of a Protocol in July 1976 signed by the governments of Pakistan and Kuwait. In strict accordance with the law the Company operates investment opportunities on a profit-orientated basis.

Areas of operation

The Company attempts to promote economic and investment co-operation between Pakistan and Kuwait, and provides finance to both the public and private sectors.

Founder members

President of the Islamic Republic of Pakistan
Amir of Kuwait

Directors

Mr Abdulrehman Al Gaoud (Chairman)
Mr Rishad Haider (Managing Director)
Mr Abdulrehman Ali Al Dawood (Director)
Mr Sibghatullah (Director)
Mr Waleed Al Qattan (Director)
Mr Shamim Ahmad Khan (Director)

Objectives

The major aim is to assist in the establishment of export-oriented or import-substitutional industries in Pakistan. Preference is given to agricultural-based projects as also to those that are profit-orientated.

Islamic banking operations

PKIC is involved in industrial financing in accordance with Islamic banking operations through the use of equity participation, participation term certificates (PTCs) and term financing certificates (TFCs).

Since 1 January 1984 PKIC has adapted its financing procedures in accordance with the Islamic Trend of Financing.

The commitments accordingly made in the years 1984 and 1985 are as follows (RS million):

	1984	*1985*
Equity/co-sponsorship	20.000	4.000
Shares purchase	28.375	—
Bridge loan (TFCs)	—	25.750
Long-term PTCs	27.500	20.884
Short-term PTCs	—	4.000
Underwriting	2.500	—

Profitability (RS million)

	1984	*1985*
Income		
Dividend receipts	22.7	30.8
Interest on loans	15.9	17.1
Interest on deposits	8.7	8.1
Miscellaneous income	7.1	10.1
Total income	54.4	66.1
Expenditure	6.3	8.2
Profit	48.1	58.4

Level and growth of assets (RS million)

Assets			
Capital expenditure	*1983*	*1984*	*1985*
Net fixed assets	3.97	3.78	4.06
Capital work-in-progress	3.58	6.88	22.96
	7.55	10.66	27.02

Investment and loans			
Investments	180.73	213.55	214.92
Loans, debentures and PTCs	128.36	148.84	164.30
	309.09	362.39	379.22

Less			
Overdue instalments	37.86	6.09	14.24
Current maturities	20.83	40.24	36.42
	250.40	316.06	328.56

Current assets			
Overdue instalments and current maturity	58.69	46.33	50.66
Advances, deposits, pre-payments and other receivables	0.32	0.47	0.41
Income receivables	12.17	31.23	24.71
Bank balances	66.99	69.89	51.99
	138.17	147.92	127.77
	396.12	474.64	483.35

Number of employees

	1984	*1985*
Chief executive/managing director	1	1
Senior executives	3	3
Junior executives	8	8
Officers	5	5
Other staff	14	14
	31	31

Capital structure (RS)

Authorised capital	1,000,000,000
Paid-up capital (contributed by):	
State Bank of Pakistan	
6,250 shares of RS 25,000 each	156,250,000
Kuwait Foreign Trading Contracting	
and Investment Company (SAK) (KFTCIC)	
6,250 shares of RS 25,000 each	156,250,000
Total paid-up capital	312,500,000

Future developments

PKIC started its commercial operations in 1979 as a development financing institution. Since then there has been a constant growth in the profitability as well as in the investment portfolio.

Major developments that are likely to take place in the future include commercial banking operations, setting up of regional offices in Pakistan's major cities, introduction of a lease financing company, insurance company, project management institution etc.

Pak-Libya Holding Company (Private) Limited

Head office

3rd Floor
Sheikh Sultan Trust Building (Annexe)
10 Beaumont Road
Karachi
Pakistan

Telephone/telex/cable

Tel: 527407, 510409, 527317
Telex: 25763 PLHC PK
Cable: COINVEST

Other branches: N/A

Date of formation

Pak-Libya Holding Company (PLHC) was incorporated as a private limited company on 14 October 1978.

Background

PLHC was founded as a consequence of an agreement signed in 1974 to promote greater co-operation between the Islamic Republic of Pakistan and the Socialist People's (Libyan) Arab Jamahiriya. Following this accord an inter-governmental agreement was drawn up and signed to set up the Pak-Libya Holding Company Limited.

Areas of operation

PLHC provides a wide range of financial services including local and foreign currency term finances, underwriting and bridge finance of equity issues and other forms of short- and long-term investment financing.

Founder members

The two founder members were the governments of the Islamic Republic of Pakistan and the Socialist People's (Libyan) Arab Jamahiriya, through the State Bank of Pakistan and the Libyan Arab Foreign Investment Company respectively.

Directors

Mr Mohamed Taher Hammuda Siala (Chairman)
Haji Ali Mohammad Shaikh (Managing Director)
Mr Abuzeid Ramadan El Omrani (Director)
Mr M A Kazmi (Director)
Mr Shamim Ahmed Khan (Director)
Mr Nagmeddin G El Bakori (Deputy Managing Director)

Senior management

Haji Ali Mohammad Shaikh (Managing Director)
Mr Nagmeddin G El Bakori (Deputy Managing Director)
Mr Nizar Solehdin (Director, Projects and Finance)
Mr M Sadiq Khan (Secretary)
Mr Mohammad Farooq Khan (General Manager, End-use)
Mr Z I Yazdanie (Chief Manager, Projects)

Objectives

The main objective of the Company is to facilitate industrial investment, particularly in underdeveloped areas of the country, and to raise industrial production to the extent of creating an exportable surplus, import substitution and quicker utilisation of indigenous resources.

In order to achieve these objectives the Company provides financial assistance to prospective entrepreneurs in establishing industrial projects which are viable from financial, technical and economic points of view. In the last five years PLHC has successfully channelled its funds into vital sectors of the economy.

Islamic banking operations

In line with the overall policy framework of the Pakistani Government the Company is supplementing the Islamisation of the economy by transforming its investment operations to the Islamic modes of financing, including PTCs, lease financing and participation in Mudarabas.

PLHC has provided financial assistance to a number of projects on a PLS basis. In addition to equity financing, PTC financing has almost completely replaced the Company's local and foreign currency financing. Other Islamic modes of financing such as mark-up and lease financing have also been adopted in recent years.

Level and growth of assets (RS million)

Total assets at year end
1983   1,216.553 (+4.81 per cent)
1984   1,286.616 (+5.76 per cent)
1985   1,350.942 (+5.0   per cent)

Profitability (RS million)

1984   157.058
1985   157.904

Number of employees

1984   46 (+27.8 per cent)
1985   49 (+6.5 per cent)

Capital structure (RS million)

Authorised capital   2,500
Paid-up capital   1,000

Future developments

The Company's investment policy includes investment particularly in newly established industrial estates in all four provinces. PLHC intends to continue its investment programme and in addition to supplement the Islamisation of the economy by adopting new and innovative forms of financing.

Saudi Pak Industrial and Agricultural Investment Limited

Head office
2nd Floor
44 East Blue Area
Islamabad
Pakistan

Telephone/telex/cable
Tel: 821493, 821494
Telex: 5663-SAPIC-PK
Cable: SAPICO IB

Other branches: N/A

Date of formation

23 December 1981.

Background

SAPICO was set up by the governments of Pakistan and Saudi Arabia to promote investment in the industrial and agro-based industrial fields.

Areas of operation

The Company is concerned with all methods of providing finances to the industrial and agro-based industrial sectors.

Founder members

SAPICO was founded by the Government of Islamic Republic of Pakistan and the Government of the Kingdom of Saudi Arabia.

Directors

Nominees of Kingdom of Saudi Arabia:

Dr Saleh H Humaidan (Deputy Managing Director, Technical Affairs, The Saudi Fund for Development): Chairman

Mohammed Alharbi (Director General, Technical Dept, Real Estate Development Funds): engineer

Jamil Khayat (Budget General Dept, Ministry of Finance and National Economy): engineer

Nominees of the Government of Pakistan:

Qazi M Alimullah (Additional Finance Secretary (EC), Government of Pakistan)

Mr Sibghatullah (Executive Director, State Bank of Pakistan)

Mr Sadiq Sayeed Khan (Additional Finance Secretary (Budget), Government of Pakistan): Deputy Chairman

Senior management

Mr M Ishaq Satti (General Manager/Chief Executive)

Mr Khalid Rashid (Secretary/Chief Accountant)

Mr M Jalil Khan (Chief, Projects Division)

Mr Zaigham Mahmood Rizvi (Deputy Chief, Projects Monitoring Division)

Objectives

The Company has been established to make investment in the industrial and agro-based industrial fields in the Islamic Republic of Pakistan on a commercial basis, through carrying out projects and marketing of their products in Pakistan and abroad.

Islamic banking operations

The following Islamic modes of financing are used: (1) Direct equity participation in industrial financing; (2) Long-term financing on a mark-up basis.

However, other modes of Islamic financing are also being considered. For example, SAPICO is actively considering taking up leasing operations.

Islamic banking operations have been in use since July 1985 although equity participation was utilised from the beginning. SAPICO has contributed in the equity of 22 projects and has also financed 11 projects on a mark-up basis.

Level and growth of assets (RS million)

As at 31 December	1983	1984	1985
Net assets	286.779	565.045	840.596
Growth (per cent)	—	+97.03	+48.76

Profitability (RS thousand)

	1984	1985
Income	50.298	79.363
Expenditure	3.805	4.813
Profit	46.493	74.550

Number of employees

	1983	1984	1985
Executives	2	2	3
Management/supervisory	7	7	8
Non-supervisory	11	12	14
Total	20	21	25
Growth (per cent)	—	+5	+19.04

Capital structure (RS million)

Authorised capital	1,000
Paid-up capital	600

Future developments

SAPICO has made a considerable contribution to the industrial and agro-based industrial financing in the four years since its inception. The Company hopes to expand the scope of its operations and to establish a leasing company to expand the forms of Islamic financing.

Small Business Finance Corporation

Head office

National Bank of Pakistan Building
Civic Centre
PO Box 1587
Islamabad
Pakistan

Telephone/telex/cable

Tel: 821639, 820328, 825652, 825823, 828186
Cable: SMALBIZFIN

Other branches

Regional office, Hyderabad:
13 Saddar
PO Box 158
Hyderabad
Pakistan
Tel: 25467
Cable: SMALBIZFIN

Regional office, Lahore:
17 Edwards Road
Lahore
Pakistan
Tel: 54795
Cable: SMALBIZFIN

Regional office, Peshawar:
Hassan Building
3 Arab Road
Peshawar Cantt
Pakistan
Tel: 72524
Cable: SMALBIZFIN

Area office, Quetta:
Faiz Muhammad Road
PO Box 227
Quetta
Pakistan
Tel: 71156
Cable: SMALBIZFIN

Branches

Abbottabad:
Sherwan Road
Abbottabad
Pakistan
Tel: 4480
Cable: SMALBIZFIN
Bahalwalpur:
Seraiki Chowk
Bahalwalpur
Pakistan
Tel: 4739
Cable: SMALBIZFIN
Dadu:
Babar Centre Building
New Chowk
Pakistan
Tel: 845
Cable: SMALBIZFIN
Faisalabad:
272A People's Colony
Faisalabad
Pakistan
Tel: 40310
Cable: SMALBIZFIN
Gujranwala:
Kotwali Bazar
Gujranwala
Pakistan
Tel: 83399
Cable: SMALBIZFIN
Jhelum:
Railway Road
Jhelum
Pakistan
Tel: 2868
Cable: SMALBIZFIN
Karachi:
101 Al-Amna Plaza
M A Jinnah Road
Karachi
Pakistan
Tel: 712131

Khuzdar:
Hospital Road
Khuzdar
Pakistan
Tel: 477
Cable: SMALBIZFIN
Larkana:
Near Shah Latif Market
Larkana
Pakistan
Tel: 22629
Cable: SMALBIZFIN
Mardan:
Sarfraz Gunj
Mardan
Pakistan
Tel: 3234
Cable: SMALBIZFIN
Mingora:
Usman Building
G T Road
Mingora (Swat)
Pakistan
Tel: 4253
Cable: SMALBIZFIN
Multan:
Abid Shopping Centre
Hussain Agahi
PO Box 100
Multan
Pakistan
Tel: 42207
Cable: SMALBIZFIN
Muzafarrabad:
C M H Road
Muzaffarabad (AK)
Pakistan
Tel: 3083
Cable: SMALBIZFIN
Nawabshah:
Katchery Road
Nawabshah
Pakistan
Tel: 3050

Cable: SMALBIZFIN
Sahiwal:
271 Jinnah Road
Sahiwal
Pakistan
Tel: 4479
Cable: SMALBIZFIN
Sargodha:
3 Block A
Satellite Town
Sargodha
Pakistan
Tel: 63427
Cable: SMALBIZFIN
Sialkot:
Fine Art Building
Mujahid Road
Sialkot
Pakistan
Tel: 86278
Cable: SMALBIZFIN
Sukkur:
19 Mehran Markaz
Sukkur
Pakistan
Tel: 84144
Cable: SMALBIZFIN
Thatta:
Miskeen Shah Mohalla
Thatta
Pakistan
Tel: 701
Cable: SMALBIZFIN

Date of formation

13 October 1972.

Background

The Small Business Finance Corporation (SBFC) was set up under Parliament,
Act No XXIX of 1972 dated 13 October 1972. The Corporation started its
operations on 1 January 1973.

The main aim of setting up the Corporation was to render financial assistance
to persons of small means under the Islamic modes of financing, in order to
reduce unemployment particularly amongst the educated. The SBFC also

191

attempts to add to the production capacity of the economy.

Areas of operation

The SBFC provides financial assistance upon a hire purchase and a PLS basis to small business enterprises, individual transporters and entrepreneurs of cottage industries, clinics and small-scale hospitals in the private sector.

Directors

Mr Sadiq Sayeed Khan (Chairman)
Mr H A M Shaikh (Managing Director)
Mr Fasihuddin (Director)
Dr G M Samdani (Director)
Mr Usman Mahmood (Director)
Mr Humayum Akhter Adil (Director)
Mr Fasihuddin Khan (Director)
Mr Muhammad Abdur Razzaq (Secretary)

Objectives

The main aim is to promote and assist in the establishment and development of small business enterprises and small-scale/cottage industries in the country by providing financial assistance on an HP and PLS basis.

Level and growth of assets (RS million)

1983   134.72
1984   139.80 (+3.77 per cent)
1985   186.83 (+33.64 per cent)

Profitability (RS million)

	Net profit
1984	9.07
1985	10.13

Number of employees

1984   158
1985   163 (+3.16 per cent)

Capital structure (RS million)

Authorised capital   100
Paid-up capital   100

Future developments

In order to ease the unemployment problem in Pakistan the Corporation has recently started financing professional young men in different trades to help them start up business ventures, particularly in the rural areas of the country.

It is hoped that in the years to come the SBFC will prove useful in the implementation of government policy aimed at improving the standard of living of a large number of people engaged in small businesses all over the country.

United Bank Limited

Head office

State Life Building No 1
PO Box 4306
II Chundrigar Road
Karachi-2
Pakistan

Telephone/telex/cable

Tel: 227111 (10 lines)
Telex: 2834, 25312, 25313, 24732, 24734, 23182 (UBL PK)

Other branches

At the end of 1985 United Bank Ltd (UBL) had 1,584 branches; 1,559 domestic and 25 overseas.

The three major branches of UBL are:

II Chundrigar Road Branch
New Jubilee Insurance House
II Chundrigar Road
Karachi

Corporate branch
1st Floor
State Life Building No 1
II Chundrigar Road
Karachi
Bank Square Branch
Bank Square
Nila Gumbad
Lahore

Date of formation

Incorporated on 24 July 1959. Commenced operations on 7 November 1959.

Founders (first Board of Directors)

II Chundrigar (Chairman)
Mohd Sayeed Saigol (Director)
Abdul Razzak Dada (Director)

Mian M Yahya (Director)
Mohd Bashir Saigol (Director)
Mohd Rafique Saigol (Director)
Mohd Shafique Saigol (Managing Director)
Agha Hasan Abedi (Director and General Manager)

Directors

Tajammal Hussain (President)
K N Cheema (Director)
Muhammad Usman (Director)
M Saleem Malik (Director)
Muhammad Zaki (Director)
S Mojib Raza (Secretary)

Objectives

The aims of UBL are stated at length in its Memorandum of Association; however, its major aim is to carry out the business of a banking company as defined by the Companies Act of 1913 (Companies Ordinance 1984).

In particular, UBL is concerned with accepting deposits, providing loans and acting as a financial intermediary through which the Government can manage the economy.

Types of deposit accounts

PLS term deposits; PLS savings deposits; PLS special notice deposits; current deposits; foreign currency deposits: fixed, savings and current.

Islamic banking operations

The Bank utilises basically three modes of financing: (1) Financing by lending; (2) Trade-related modes of financing; (3) Investment type modes of financing.

PLS deposits increased by 60 per cent to Rs 6,793 million in 1984. These deposits further grew by 184 per cent to Rs 19,292 million due to conversion of all savings deposits to PLS from 1 July 1985 as per the policy of the Government.

Presently the bulk of the bank financing operations relating to trade-related modes are being conducted in the form of purchase and sale of goods to their clients at appropriate mark-up in price on deferred payment or otherwise under buy-back agreements. The purchase of trade bills and moveable and immoveable property is also being conducted on the above lines.

Level and growth of assets (RS)

	Total assets
1983	56,205,196,443.00
1984	59,787,008,779.00 (+6.37 per cent)
1985	70,931,353,333.00 (+18.64 per cent)

Profitability (RS)

Pre-tax profit
1983	183,950,576.00
1984	367,676,752.00
1985	237,917,020.00

Number of employees

1983	19.022
1984	18,966 (−0.29 per cent)
1985	19,196 (+1.21 per cent)

Capital structure (RS million)

Authorised capital	1,000
Paid-up capital	531

Reserves
1983	430
1984	740
1985	1,000

Future developments

The Bank plans to improve its performance in the light of the Charter for Banks announced by the Finance Minister in his Budget Speech for 1985–6. The Bank plans to take measures to achieve the targets given in the new Charter by reorganising its working and customer services, which should result in higher efficiency and greater profitability.

The Bank will continue to provide efficient banking services to its customers with the use of the most modern technology available.

QATAR

Qatar Islamic Bank (SAQ)

Head office

Electricity Road
PO Box 559
Doha
Qatar

Telephone/telex/cable

Tel: 438000 (5 lines)
Telex: 5176 ISLMFX DH — ISLAMB DH
Cable: ISLAMI DOHA
Telefax: 412700

Other branches: N/A

Date of formation

7 July 1983.

Background

Qatar Islamic Bank (QIB) is the first of its kind in Qatar and provides a full range of banking services in strict accordance with Islamic principles.

Areas of operation

QIB devotes time and effort to enriching the continuous development of Islamic economic theories and promoting co-operation between Islamic financial bodies. In this respect it has regularly attended meetings to exchange experiences and knowledge with Islamic financial institutions. It has also helped in the development of new Islamic bodies such as the Al Baraka Turkish Finance House and the Islamic Reinsurance Company in Bahrain.

Directors

Sheikh Abdul Rahman Abdulla Al Mahmoud (Chairman)
Sh Ali Bin Saud Bin Thani Al Thani (Deputy Chairman)
Mr Hassan Kasem Al Darwish Fakhroo (Managing Director)
Mr Abdul Rahman Essa Al Mannai (Member)
Mr Mohammed Bin Hamad Al Manaa (Member)
Sh Abdul Rahman Bin Nasir Al Thani (Member)
Mr Abdul Aziz Abdulla Turki (Member)
Mr Ali Mohammed Al Khatir (Member)
Mr Abdul Latif Hassan Al Jabir (Member)
Qasim M Qasim (General Manager and Chief Executive)

Supervisory board (legal control committee)

Dr Yousef Al Karadawy
Dr Ali Al Salous
Sheikh Abdullah Bin Abdul Aziz

Objectives

The aim of the Bank is to provide a full range of banking services in Qatar on a non-interest basis and in full accordance with the principles laid down in Islamic Sharia. Furthermore, QIB is interested in promoting the role of Islamic economics and banking. In this context the Bank has regularly hosted conferences on the progress of Islamic banking.

Types of deposit accounts

The Bank offers three major alternatives: (1) Current accounts; (2) Savings accounts; (3) Time investment deposit accounts.

Islamic banking operations

QIB specialises in Murabaha, Mudaraba and Musharaka with particular attention being put on Murabaha and Musharaka. Murabaha operations are the major involvement, where goods are imported on the basis of customer demand and then sold to them by instalment.

Level and growth of assets (QR)

	Total assets
1984	369,936,334
1985	605,169,137
1986	883,164,056

Number of employees

The Bank employed 50 people in 1986.

Capital structure (QR million)

Authorised capital	200
Paid-up capital	50
Reserves	15

Future developments

QIB is hoping to expand and open several branches in the near future.

SUDAN

Islamic Bank for Western Sudan

Head office

El Gamhuria Avenue
PO Box 3575
Khartoum
Sudan

Telephone/telex/cable

Tel: 79983, 79408, 79576, 79583, 79561
Telex: WISB SD 22382
Cable: BANK ALGHARB

Other branches

The Bank has a branch at Nyala which started operations in March 1985 (Tel: 2207, 2439, 2469).

Date of formation

Established in 1981, the Islamic Bank for Western Sudan commenced operations in August 1984.

Background

The establishment of the Islamic Bank for Western Sudan (IBWS) came as a culmination of the international Islamic initiation movement, and was undoubtedly influenced by the unprecedented success of other newly established Islamic financial instituations. The IBWS is clearly committed to the principles of Islamic Sharia in the conduct of all its financing operations and performance of its activities. In this context, the Bank conducts all relevant banking and economic activities that are void from usury benefits.

Areas of operation

The Bank utilises three main Islamic banking operations: Mudaraba, Musharaka and Murabaha.

In addition to these the Bank provides all the basic monetary activities one would expect: Current accounts; Saving accounts; Investment accounts; Internal and external exchange, letters of credit, letters of guarantee etc; Giving good loans relevant to the articles it forms.

Directors

Ibrahim Munim Mansour (Chairman)
Abdel Karim Hussein Gaafar (Deputy Chairman)
Dr Yahia Ahmed Mahmoud (Director)
Hassan Maki El Amin (Director)
Adam Yagoub (Director)
Mohamed Abdullah Gar el-Nabi (Director)
Ibrahim Ahmed Ibrahim Diraig (Director)
El Khair Ali Musa (Director)
El Tigani Mohamed El Hag (Director)
Representative, Faisal Islamic Bank, Egypt
Representative, International Islamic Bank, Egypt.
Representative, Tadamon Islamic Bank, Sudan.

Senior management

El Sharif El Khatim Mohamed (Governor)
Ibrahim Ahmed El Tahir (Deputy Governor)
Ali Taha (Director, Head of Main Branch)
Abdel-Hamid Ahmed Amin (Legal Advisor and Secretary)
Abdel-Halim Mohamed (Assistant Manager, Admin)
El Zahir Khalil Hamouda (Head of Investment Dept)
Abdel-Rahman Gameel Alla (Head of Accounting and Finance Dept)

Capital structure

LS 8 million, increased to LS 25 million in 1985.

Future developments

The Bank is hoping to set up a number of specialised companies to work in the industrial, commercial and insurance fields and to establish branches in order to extend into banking facilities all over the country.

Islamic Co-operative Development Bank

Head office

PO Box 62
Khartoum
Sudan

Telephone/telex/cable

Tel: 75234, 75366, 80223
Telex: 22906 ISCOB SD
Cable: ISCOBANK

Other branches

Port Sudan   Tel: 5449, PO Box 631
New Halfa   Tel: 2363, PO Box 15
Dongola   Tel: 2098, PO Box 38
Wad Medani   Tel: 668-647, PO Box 273
Atbara   Tel: 2295-2189, PO Box 240

Date of formation

June 1982.

Background

The Islamic Co-operative Development Bank was initiated as a joint venture between the Sudanese Government and the co-operative sector. It aims at the promotion, finance and development of the co-operative sector. The Bank also helps the private sector by providing banking services according to Islamic principles.

Areas of operation

The Bank commenced business in June 1983 and during this past short period it has achieved remarkable results. Its combined Musharaka, Mudaraba and Murabaha investments reached LS 10 million.

Directors

Tag El Sir Abdel Rahman (General Manager)
Hassan Mohamen Saleh (Deputy General Manager)
Bashir Musa (Assistant General Manager)
Ibrahim Hassan Idris (Assistant General Manager)
Mahmoud A Omrani (Khartoum Branch Manager)
Awadalla Elhadi Mabrouk (Wad Medani Manager)
Khalifa Mohamen Abdel Rahman (Port Sudan Manager)
Mohamed Ahmed Omer Elkalas (New Halfa Manager)
Hussain Mohamed Omer El Mufti (Dongola Manager)
Abdalla Bukhari Mohamed (Atbara Manager)

Objectives

The Bank's objectives are essentially, 'Consolidation, promotion and development of the co-operative sector by offering the necessary financing for the societies in their different fields and throughout the country'.

Capital structure (LS million)

Authorised capital   15
Paid-up capital   5

Of the paid-up capital, LS 3 million has been paid by the government and LS 2 million by the co-operative societies.

Future developments

The Bank's strategy is to give particular regard to small depositors and small investors and to spread its services throughout the country.

Faisal Islamic Bank (Sudan)

Head office

PO Box 10143
Khartoum
Sudan

Telephone/telex/cable

Tel: 81848, 81857
Telex: FIBS 22519 SD, FIBS 22164 SD
Cable: BANKISLAMI-KTM

Other branches

Capital branches

Main branch:
Fayha Building
PO Box 10143
Khartoum
Tel: 73717, 73566
Telex: FIBS 22164 SD, FIBS 22519 SD
Cable: BANKISLAMI-KTM
Central station:
PO Box 2415
Khartoum
Tel: 75590, 75586
Telex: FIBS 22164 SD
Cable: BANKISLAMI-KTM
United Nations Square:
PO Box 2415
Khartoum
Tel: 78957, 73774
Telex: FIBS 22519 SD
Cable: BANKISLAMI-KTM
Expatriates' branch:
PO Box 2415
Khartoum
Tel: 75367
Telex: FIBS 22163 SD
Cable BANKISLAMI-KTM
University of Khartoum:
Po Box 2415
Khartoum
Tel: 78691
Telex: FIBS 22519 SD
Cable: BANKISLAMI-KTM
Central Station, Omdurman:
PO Box 835
Omdurman
Tel: 51971, 53126
Telex: FIBS 28042 SD
Cable: BANKISLAMI-KTM

Craftsmen and Artisans, Omdurman:
PO Box 835
Omdurman
Tel: 50352, 56997
Telex: FIBS 28042 SD
Cable: BANKISLAMI-KTM
Al Saggana Khartoum South:
Tel: 47757, 47758
Cable: BANKISLAMI-KTM

Country branches

Port Sudan:
PO Box 877
Port Sudan
Tel: 4651, 4695
Cable: BANKISLAMI-PORT SUDAN
El Gadaref:
PO Box 324
Gadaref
Tel: 3503, 3403
Cable: BANKISLAMI-GADAREF
Kosti:
Faisal Islamic Bank
Kosti Branch
Kosti
Cable: BANKISLAMI-KOSTI
El Obied:
PO Box 239
El Obied
Tel: 2609
Cable: BANKISLAMI-EL OBIED
Atbara:
PO Box 42
Atbara
Tel: 3071, 3126
Cable: BANKISLAMI-ATBARA
Kassala:
PO Box 314
Kassala
Tel: 2044
Telegram: Bankislami — Kassala

Juba:
PO Box 25
Juba
Tel: 2389
Telegram: Bankislami — Juba
Damazin:
PO Box 106
Damazin
Tel: 2156
Telegram: Bankislami — Damazin
El Fasher:
Faisal Islamic Bank
El Fasher
Tel: 2238
Telegram: Bankislami — El Fasher
Dongla:
Tel: 2580, 2590
Telegram: Bankislami — Dongla

Subsidiary companies

Islamic Insurance Company:
PO Box 2776
Khartoum
Tel: 78287
Telex: TATA 22167 SD
Telegram: TATA — Khartoum
Islamic Trading and Service Co Ltd:
PO Box 2415
Khartoum
Tel: 81611, 81950, 81054
Telex: Tislm 22166 SD
Telegram: Tislm — Khartoum
Real Estate Development Co:
PO Box 2415
Khartoum
Tel: 80171
Telex: RECO 22943 SD
Telegram: RECO Khartoum

Date of formation

Established August 1977; commenced operations May 1978.

Background

FIB (Sudan) was established in August 1977 and started operations in May 1978 as a Sudanese public company.

The initial authorised capital was LS 6 million of which 40 per cent was allocated to Sudanese shareholders and 60 per cent to shareholders in Arab and other Muslim countries. In response to increasing demand the authorised capital was raised to LS 10 million in 1978, and thereafter to LS 50 million in 1981 and LS 100 million in 1983.

Areas of operation

The Bank provides normal banking services such as opening current and investment accounts, issuing letters of credit, letters of guarantee, foreign exchange operations, effecting transfers etc.

The Bank is also engaged in financing commercial and investment projects in accordance with Sharia modes of financing such as Mudaraba, Musharaka and Murabaha.

Directors

HRH Prince Mohamed Al Faisal Al Saud (Chairman)
Syd Ibrahim El Tyeb El Rayah
Sheikh Ahmed Salah Jamjoon
Dr Ahmed Abdel Aziz El Naggar
Sheikh Amin Ogeil Attas
Syd Bashir Hassan Bashir Osman
Syd Musa Hussein Dirar
Sheikh Mohamed Salih Baharith
Syd Mohamed Yousif Mohamed
Sheikh Abdel Hamid Abdel Razig El Obeid
Dr Abdalla Omer El Nasif
Dr Omer Abdel Rahman Azzam
Dr Abdel Aziz Abdalla El Fida
Syd Yassin Omer El Imam
Syd Youssif Abdel Rahman
Syd Abbas El Bakhiet Musa (Secretary)

Senior management

Syd Al Bagkir Yousif Mudawi (General Manager)
Syd El Haj Abdallah Khalid (Deputy General Manager)
Dr Ahmed Ibrahim El Turabi (General Manager's Assistant)
Dr Abdin Ahmed Salama (General Manager's Assistant)
Syd Rabie Hassan Ahmed (General Manager's Assistant)

Supervisory board

Prof El Siddig Mohamed Al Amin El Darir (President)
Sheikh Awadalla Salih (Member)
Sheikh Siddig Ahmed Abdel Hay (Member)

Dr Yousif Hamid El Alim (Member)
Syd Hassan Mohamed Ismail El Beili (Member)
Syd Mohamed Yousif Mohamed (Legal Advisor)
Syd Mohamed Abdel Halim and Co (Auditors)

Objectives

Faisal Islamic Bank (Sudan) was established with the objective of contributing to economic and social development within the framework of adherence to the principles of Islamic Sharia, particularly regarding the prohibition of giving or taking interest. It accordingly undertakes all commercial banking activities and other methods such as Ijara and leasing.

Profitability (LS thousand)

	Net profit
1983	26,154
1984	7,833

Capital structure (LS million)

Authorised capital   100
Paid-up capital   58.4

TURKEY

Faisal Finance Institution

Head office

Kemeralti Cad 46
Tophane is Hani Kat 6 No 703
Istanbul
Turkey

Telephone/telex/cable

Tel: 1.145 67 54 (5 lines), 1.149 99 45, 1.144 18 87
Telex: 25694 ffk tr (General), 25729 ffks tr (For Exch), 42793 hlal tr
Fax: 1.145 56 33

Other branches

The Institution has only Representative offices and no branches. There are five in Turkey: Ankara, Bursa, Izmir, Erzurum, Konya. Representative offices abroad are in Frankfurt and Jeddah.

Date of formation

9 October 1984.

Background

In 1984 the Government of the Republic of Turkey granted to Dar Al-Maal Al-Islami a licence to establish a bank operating on a profit and loss sharing basis dealing in Turkish lira (TL) and US dollars. Following this the Faisal Finance Institution AS Turkey was duly registered in Istanbul with an authorised capital of TL 5 billion. It was inaugurated on 14 December 1984 and started its activities in April 1985.

The capital is fully paid-up, each of the founders having paid a share.

Areas of operation

The FFI started operations with current and investment accounts in Turkish lira, US dollars and other foreign currencies which are available to Turkish and non-Turkish citizens. It is authorised to perform all banking transactions and offer financing through the accepted instruments for trading, commodities, mining and short-term projects, real estate and finance of foreign trade.

The FFI will participate with the Faisal Islamic Banks of Egypt and Sudan, DMI and MFI Bahrain through a real estate Mudaraba and for development of real estate, the objective of which is to re-invest funds for upgrading already constructed villas and apartments.

Founder members

Mohamed Al Faisal Al Saud
Dar Al-Maal Al-Islami Trust
Faisal Islamic Bank (Sudan)
Faisal Islamic Bank (Egypt)
Massraf Faisal Al-Islami, Bahrain
Salih Ozcan
Ahmet Tevfik Paksu

Directors

HRH Prince Mohamed Al Faisal Al Saud (Chairman)
Mr Saleh Ozcan (Deputy Chairman)
HRH Prince Saud Al-Abdallah Al-Faysal (Representing MFI, Bahrain)
Mr Omar Abdi Ali (Representing DMI Trust)
Dr Mahmoud El Helw (Representing FIB, Egypt)
M Al Bagkir Y Mudawi (Representing FIB, Sudan)
Mr Ahmed Tevfik Paksu (Representing Turkish shareholders)

Senior management

Mr Fehmi Akin (Acting General Manager)
Mr Gunduz Sevilgen (Assistant General Manager)
Mr Nazif Gurdogan (Assistant General Manager)
Mr Yunus Nacar (Assistant General Manager)

Supervisory board

Mr Halil Gonenc (Chairman)
Mr Mehmet Savas (Member)
Mr Cemil Ozcan (Member)

Objectives

The objective of the FFI is both to aid Turkey and the DMI Trust. It acts as an important link in the complex network of DMI Islamic financial institutions and at the same time helps Turkey by:

(1) bringing foreign capital into the country;
(2) providing export facilities and making finance available for foreign trade;
(3) pioneering the establishment of a profit-sharing system in a secular country;
(4) opening a window to the Islamic world which draws a lot of its consumer needs from Turkey;
(5) allowing the country to benefit from the international network of DMI Islamic financial institutions.

Types of deposit account

(A) Local currency deposit accounts
(B) Foreign currency deposit accounts

1. Special current accounts (Al-Amana contract)
2. Profit and loss sharing accounts (Al-Mudaraba contract)

A2 and B2: PLS accounts — 90 days maturity
PLS accounts — 180 days maturity
PLS accounts — 360 days maturity
PLS accounts — up to five years (not operating in practice)

Islamic banking operations

(1) Al-Mudaraba (Contract for profit and loss sharing)
(2) Al-Murabaha (Contract for purchase and sale)
(3) Al-Musharaka (Investment for contract for PLS)
(4) Al-Wadiah/Al-Amana (Contract for special current account)
(5) Qard Hassan (Interest free loan)

Islamic banking operations

For the last year the Faisal Finance Institution has utilised mostly Murabaha contracts for local and international purchasings and sellings. Mudaraba contracts are used between FFI and its depositors as well as FFI and its credit clients. Amana contracts are made between FFI and its current account holders. Qard has so far only been used for the employees of FFI. Musharaka is used for its subsidiary company, Faisal Foreign Trade and Marketing Co.

Profitability

1985 profit before tax: TL 1,235,615,646.

Number of employees

31 December 1985   63
31 March 1986   74

Capital structure

Authorised capital: TL 5 billion (all paid-up).

Future developments

The major future development will be to open domestic and overseas branches once a licence is granted. The Institution also aims to increase its capital and make use of the most up-to-date technology.

UNITED ARAB EMIRATES

Dubai Islamic Bank

Head office

Airport Road
PO Box 1080
Deira
Dubai
UAE

Telephone/telex/cable

Tel: 214888 (16 lines)
Telex: 45889 ISLAMI EM, 48772 ISLAMI EM
Cable: ISLAMI DUBAI

Other branches

Abu Dhabi:
Rashid Abdullah Al-Omran Building
Al-Salam Road
Al-Firdaus Roundabout
PO Box 3863
Abu Dhabi
UAE

Al-Ain:
PO Box 1232
Al-Ain
UAE

Murshid Bazar:
PO Box 7400
Deira
Dubai
UAE

Date of formation

10 March 1975.

Background

Dubai Islamic Bank, the first Islamic Bank in the world, was established in 1975 with the object of offering banking services to the public in general and to Muslims in particular in strict accordance with the principles of Islamic Sharia.

Areas of operation

The Bank offers all the normal services including current, savings, and investment accounts, remittances, letters of credit and guarantees, and provides financial assistance to commercial agricultural and industrial projects. The Bank is also involved in the sale and purchase of commodities and the participation in the capital of other Islamic financial institutions.

Directors

Mr Saeed Ahmad Lootah (Chairman)
Mr Sultan Ahmad Lootah (Deputy Chairman)
Mr Yousif Jasim Al Hijji
Mr Mohammad Abdul Aziz Al Khudairi
Mr Nasir Ahmad Lootah
Mr Yousuf Khalifa

Objectives

The main objective of the Dubai Islamic Bank is to help Muslims in their use of interest-free banking services. The major ambition of the Bank is to utilise its funds for the benefit of all in the public interest.

Profitability (dirhams)

	Net profit
1983	36,129,558
1984	49,009,799

Capital structure

50 million dirhams (fully paid-up).

Al Rajhi Company for Islamic Investments Limited

Head office

2 Copthall Avenue
London
EC2R 7JQ

Telephone/telex/cable

Tel: 01 588 8711
Telex: 8956196

Other branches: N/A

Date of formation

December 1980.

Founder members

Sheikh Saleh Al Abdulaziz Al Rajhi
Sheikh Abdullah Al Abdulaziz Al Rahji
Sheikh Sulaiman Al Abdulaziz Al Rajhi
Sheikh Mohammed Al Abdulaziz Al Rajhi

Directors

Sheikh Salaiman Al Abdulaziz Al Rajhi
Sulaiman Saleh Al Rajhi
Saleh Sulaiman Al Rajhi
Abdullah Sulaiman Al Rajhi
Elie El Hadj

Senior Management

B C Norton
J C Carney

Objectives

The stated objective is to provide Islamic investment advice to the Al Rahji Company for Currency Exchange and Commerce, Riyadh, Saudi Arabia.

Background

The Al Rajhi Company for Islamic Investments Limited is a UK registered company, established in December 1980 to render professional services to the Al Rajhi Company for Currency Exchange and Commerce in Saudi Arabia. These services include the worldwide identification of lending opportunities which comply with the theological prohibition on interest as well as investigation of the legal and tax implications of such transactions. It has a staff of 20 specialists in the various fields of financial operations.

The Al Rajhi Company for Currency Exchange and Commerce in Saudi is a general partnership, formed in 1978 by combining the individual businessmen of the four partners, Saleh, Abdullah, Sulaiman and Mohammad Al Abdulaziz Al Rahji, whose business origins date back to 1940. The Company now operates from a network of some 230 branches.

Part Three

Islamic Banking: Case Studies and Banking Laws

Introduction

All Muslim countries have practised Islamic banking to varying degrees. Interest-free banks have also been operating in several non-Muslim countries. The experience of the Islamic Republic of Iran and of Pakistan, the two countries that have recently attempted to implement Islamic banking on a comprehensive scale, is drawn upon here to assess the implications of this banking system. It is important to note that these two countries have approached the process of transformation from two different directions. The authorities in the Islamic Republic of Iran chose almost instantaneously to convert their banking system to one that is interest-free. Pakistan, on the other hand, chose to introduce an interest-free system in a gradual fashion.

Owing to these differences, the experiences of the two countries have, in several respects, been quite distinct. While both of them have opted for outwardly similar non-interest modes for deposit and asset generation to effect changes in the banking system, the characteristics and specific application of chosen instruments are sufficiently different to merit separate analysis for each country.

It is too soon to assess the full impact of the new regulations on the operations of the banking system, monetary policy, and the economy at large. Nevertheless it is clear that problems may have been encountered in moving away from traditional short-term trade financing operations and towards profit-sharing medium- and long-term equity-financing operations. Similarly, issues regarding bank financing of the government sector remain to be addressed. Banks have, in general, adapted well to the new procedures but speedy progress may have been hampered by the time-consuming process of retraining staff. The effectiveness of monetary policy in both countries has remained largely unaffected. It is recognised by the authorities however that a further transformation of the banking system — that is, toward equity-based profit and loss sharing operations — would not only entail considerable structural changes in the financial sector but also require a new legal framework and a change in the attitudes of banks, their clients, and the policy-makers implementing the new system.

1

The Islamic Republic of Iran

INTRODUCTION

Following the revolution in 1979, steps were taken to bring the banking system's operations into correspondence with the requirements of Islamic law. In February 1981, certain administrative steps were taken by the Bank Markazi (the Central Bank) to eliminate interest from banking operations, as a result of which interest on all asset-side transactions was replaced by a 4 per cent maximum service charge and by a 4–8 per cent minimum profit rate, depending on the type of economic activity. Interest on the deposits was also converted into a guaranteed minimum profit. In the meantime, preparations got underway for submission of comprehensive legislation to bring the operations of the entire banking system into compliance with the Sharia. The legislation, prepared by a high-level commission (composed of bankers, academics, businessmen and religious specialists), was passed by the Parliament in August 1983 as the Law for Usury-Free Banking (the Law). The Law required the banks to convert their deposits in line with the Sharia within one year, and their total operations within three years, from the date of the passage of the Law. The Law specifies the types of transactions that must constitute the basis for asset and liability acquisition by banks.

The implementation of the new system may have been constrained by diverse economic developments, caused by the weakening of the quality of banks' asset portfolios since the mid-1970s, political upheavals, freezing of assets, economic recession, and war. The banking system at the time of the Revolution was characterised by a large number of newly established banks, which were saddled with high levels of non-performing assets and of debt obligations to both the Bank Markazi and foreign creditors. The position of these banks reflected, in large part, a lack of banking and management experience and, probably, inadequate regulatory controls which existed in a previous system. The resulting inherent weakness of banks' asset portfolios, leading to lower overall profits, has continued to adversely affect the effective transformation of the banking system.[1]

CHARACTERISTICS OF BANK LIABILITIES AND ASSETS

The liability side of bank operations according to the new Law

According to the new Law, liabilities acquired by the banks must be based upon the following transactions.

(1) Qard al-Hasanah deposits

In the context of the Law, Qard al-Hasanah constitutes current and savings deposits (as in the conventional banking system), except that they earn no returns. The banks can, however, offer certain incentives in order to attract such savings deposits. These incentives can include one or all of the following: non-fixed prizes and bonuses in cash or in kind; an exemption from or a discount in, the payment of commission and/or fees; and priority in the use of banking facilities. The purpose of these accounts, from the point of view of the customers, would be to serve as a means of transactions, payments and liquidity. Moreover, the banks are to consider these deposits (both current and savings) as their own resources in their utilisation but no profits are to be returned to these accounts. The banks are required, however, to guarantee the full nominal value of these deposits.

(2) Term investments deposits

Banks are authorised to accept two types of investment deposits — short- and long-term. These deposits differ as regards the minimum required time limits, three months for the short-term and one year for long-term deposits, and with respect to the minimum amount required, Rls 2,000 for the short-term and Rls 5,000 for the long term accounts.

Although the banks can use their own resources, ie their capital plus Qard al-Hasanah deposits, the priority must be given to investment deposits, ie depositor resources. The banks can also use a combination of their own and depositor resources in an investment project, in which case the bank and the depositor share the resulting profits. A third possibility is for the bank to place the depositor's funds in an investment project, ie to serve as a trustee, in which case the entire resulting profits as well as any capital gains are returned to the depositors and the bank charges only a commission to cover the expense of administering the accounts. In this case the bank can guarantee and/or insure the principal amount of depositors' resources.

---

1. Steps were taken in 1979 through the Bank Nationalisation Act and the Bank Management Act to consolidate and reorganise the banking system. These Acts led to the reorganisation of the banking system into six commercial banks (previously 36) and three specialised banks. In addition, 22 provincial banks (one for each province) were established. The total number of banking units was reduced from 8,275 to 6,581.

In cases where combined resources of the bank and the depositors are invested, the return to depositors is, in principle, calculated in proportion to the total amount of investment deposits (while the required reserve portion is subtracted from the base amount). The banks are required to announce their profit rates at the end of each six months of their operation, at which time the shares of the depositors' profits are to be paid into each account. No profits are earned by deposits if they are either withdrawn before the minimum time required or reduced below the required minimum.

Financing and credit operations of the banks

The Law provides various modes of operation upon which the financing transactions of the banks must be based. A brief description of these modes follows.

(1) Partnership (Musharaka)

The Law recognises two different forms of partnerships: (i) *civil partnerships* and (ii) *legal partnerships*. The first is a project-specific partnership of short duration in commercial, production and service activities in which each partner provides a share of the necessary capital, and the assets and/or properties thus acquired are held as community property until the end of the life of the partnership. In these cases, the banks' share in the partnership cannot exceed the share of the manager-entrepreneur initiating and/or directing the project.

The second form of partnership is a firm-specific venture of longer duration in which the bank provides a portion of the total equity of a newly established firm or buys into an existing corporation. The banks can take equity positions in such partnerships only after the technical, economic and financial viability of the firm (or the project) has been appraised and the minimum expected rate of return from investment is deemed high enough to warrant such actions by the bank. Bank Markazi must determine the maximum amount of equity participation by the bank and the minimum amount of participation by other partners in the venture. The banks are allowed to sell shares which they have thus purchased whenever they deem it appropriate.

(2) Direct investment

Banks can undertake to invest directly in any economic activities which they choose so long as the following requirements are met: (i) banks cannot undertake to invest directly in projects in conjunction with the private sector and in projects that lead to the production of luxury and unnecessary commodities; (ii) the ratio of the initial capital of these ventures to total funds needed must not be less than 40 per cent; (iii) the total fixed capital necessary for undertaking these projects must be provided for by long-term financial resources; (iv) undertakings of direct investment by banks must be based on well documented evaluation and

219

appraisal of the project, and use of bank resources and investment deposits in direct investment projects is allowed if and only if the expected return from these projects is sufficient to meet the minimum required rate designated by Bank Markazi; (v) banks must report the amount of their own as well as depositors' resources allocated to direct investment projects to the Bank Markazi; (vi) once the projects in which the banks have directly invested have begun their productive activity, banks can sell shares to the public; (vii) the Bank Markazi is authorised to investigate and audit direct investment projects in which banks have invested.

(3) Mudaraba

This transaction is considered a short-term commercial, contractual partnership between a bank and an agent-entrepreneur according to which financial capital is provided by the bank and managerial effort by the entrepreneur in order to undertake a specific commercial project. Banks are required to give priority in their Mudaraba activities to cooperatives. Moreover, banks are not allowed to engage in Mudaraba financing of imports with the private sector.

(4) Salaf transactions

To provide firms with the needed working capital, banks can pre-purchase their future output so long as the product characteristics and specifications are determined at the time of the purchase and the agreed price does not exceed the market price of the product at the time of the transaction.[2] Banks, however, cannot sell the product until they have taken physical possession of the same. The date of the delivery of the product, which is to be established at the time of the transaction, cannot exceed one production cycle and in no case can it exceed one year.

(5) Instalment purchases

Banks are authorised to purchase raw materials, machinery and equipment for firms and resell the same to them on instalment. The volume of raw material cannot exceed that necessary for one production cycle and the repayment period for same cannot exceed one year. The price of the product subject to the transaction is to be determined on a cost-plus basis. The repayment period for machinery and equipment cannot exceed their useful life; this is considered to begin on the date of their utilisation in the production process for a duration to be determined by the Central Bank. Banks can also build and sell residential housing on an instalment basis.

---

2. Presumably the banks' margin is determined by the spread between the price negotiated between the producer and his bank and the going market price.

(6) Lease-purchase transactions

Banks can purchase the needed machinery and equipment, or other movable and immovable property and lease the same to firms. At the time the contract is entered into, firms have to guarantee to take possession of such property at the end of the contract period, if the conditions of the contract are fulfilled. The time period involved in this transaction cannot exceed the useful life of the property (to be determined by the Bank Markazi). Banks, however, cannot engage in transactions in which the useful life of the subject property is less than two years.

(7) Ju'ala (transactions based on commission)

Banks may provide or acquire services whenever they are needed and charge or pay commission or fees for such services. The service to be performed and the fee to be charged must be determined at the time of the transaction.

(8) Muzara'a

Banks may provide agricultural lands that they own or that are otherwise in their possession (eg as a trust) to farmers for the purpose of cultivation for a specific period and a predetermined share of the harvest. Banks may also provide seed and/or fertiliser along with the land if they so choose.

(9) Musaqat

Similarly, banks may provide orchards or trees which they own or that are otherwise in their possession (eg as a trust) to farmers for a specific period of time and a predetermined share of the harvest.

(10) Qard al-Hasanah loans

Banks are required to set aside a portion of their own resources in order to extend interest-free loans to: (i) small producers, entrepreneurs and farmers who would otherwise be unable to find alternative sources of financing investment and working capital; (ii) needy customers. Banks are permitted to charge a minimum service fee to cover the cost of administering these loans.

In addition to the above modes of financing, banks are permitted to purchase debt instruments of less than one year maturity, but only if these debts are issued against real assets.

General regulations governing asset acquisition by the banks

In addition to regulations covering specific modes of transactions, both the Law for Usury-Free Banking and its accompanying Articles of Implementation specify additional regulations that govern asset acquisition by the banks. The most important of these regulations are the following:

(1) Banks can only extend credits when they are reasonably assured that the principal sum granted and resulting profits are returned within a specific period of time.

(2) Banks are responsible for the control and supervision of the activity to which their own resources and/or the resources of their depositors are contractually committed.

(3) Credit can be extended, conditional upon observance of proper procedures that ensure the security of the financial resources extended by the banks.

(4) Banks must ensure that the value of physical assets obtained through the use of their resources by their clients and/or the value of collateral must be, at all times, equal to the remainder of outstanding principal. For this purpose, banks may take steps to ensure the value of such assets or collateral during the life-time of the project.

(5) While banks may engage in joint venture projects with other banks, one specific bank must assume the responsibility of supervision and control of the project undertaken.

(6) Banks must take necessary steps to ensure that their clients understand that contracts mutually consented to are binding legal documents and will be treated as such by the courts.

Supervision of the banking system

The law has placed the responsibility for the supervision of the banking system of the country in the Bank Markazi and accordingly it has specified the following means for exercising authority. The Bank Markazi is required to determine: (1) legal reserve requirements for various types of bank deposits of the banks; (2) bank-by-bank credit ceilings on aggregate and sectoral credit; (3) minimum and maximum expected rates of return from various facilities to the banks; (4) minimum and maximum profit shares for banks in their Mudaraba and Musharaka activities; (5) maximum rates of commission the banks are to charge for investment accounts for which they serve as trustees; (6) the minimum ratio of liquid assets to short-term liabilities; (7) the maximum amount of credit facility granted by banks to each applicant; (8) the ratio of credit facilities granted by each bank to that bank's capital; (9) the acceptable ratio of credit facilities granted by each bank to various deposits; and (10) the maximum amount of commitment made by each bank emanating from opening letters of credit, endorsements, issuing guarantees as well as the type and amount of collateral for such commitments.[3]

---

3. Insofar as the supervision of foreign banks is concerned, these banks are prohibited from engaging in banking operations in the Islamic Republic of Iran. They are allowed, however, to establish 'Representative Offices', but the operations of such offices are restricted to mainly advisory services provided for their Iranian clients (mostly importers and banks) and to their parent banks. Hence, supervision of these banks is limited to ensuring that they comply with the regulations.

Moreover, Bank Markazi is authorised to audit and inspect banks' accounts and documents. It is further empowered to devise additional regulations to enhance its supervisory authority as the need arises in order to ensure and safeguard against threats of banks' insolvency. Bank Markazi has developed procedures based on these guidelines for the commercial banks to follow in their transactions.

THE IMPLEMENTATION OF THE LAW

The Law for Usury-Free Banking implements the portion of Article 43 of the Constitution of the Islamic Republic of Iran that prohibits Riba (interest) in banking operations. Its most significant economic aspect is its attempt to forge a closer relationship between financial intermediation and real economic-asset creation without resort to using interest rates, while at the same time it has created safeguards designed to ensure sound banking practices. To this end, it has provided an apparatus that designates specific Islamic modes of financing which can facilitate necessary financing for needed transactions in various lines of economic activity. The modes corresponding to each line of activity are summarised in Table 3.1.1. Hence, the Law has made it the responsibility of the banking system to take a leadership role in implementing and fostering Islamic modes of financing throughout the economy. To this end, the role of the banking system has been broadened far beyond that which would be expected in a conventional banking system. This is a clear recognition that, at least throughout the transition phase, the banking sector will have to play a crucial role as a vehicle through which economic relationships can be transformed into Islamic forms. The centralisation of the banking system, facilitated through the Bank Nationalisation Act and the Bank Management Bill, provides managerial control to the Bank Markazi to direct the banking system in performance of this role.

Considering the comprehensive nature of the Law, it is too early to judge the effectiveness of its implementation, but the data available from the first full year of operation of the banking system under the provisions of the new Law permits analysis of some aspects of the implementation phase. Comparative figures for major items in the balance sheet of the banking system for the period 20 March 1984 to 20 March 1985 show that private sector deposits with the banking system increased by 5.7 per cent and that a major portion of old deposits were transferred into new accounts (Table 3.1.2). Although the banking system has been successful in converting its liabilities into Islamic forms, the asset side shows a much slower pace in this conversion. A more detailed breakdown of assets of banks (Table 3.1.3) indicates that the banking system in its first year of operation extended IRIs 754.7 billion in new banking facilities to the private sector, of which IRIs 591.3 billion was allocated from term investment deposits and the remainder from banks' resources (Qard al-Hasanah deposits).

Table 3.1.1: Islamic Republic of Iran: Summary of Various Forms of Permissible Transactions Corresponding to Types of Economic Activity.

Type of activity	Permissible mode
1. Production (industrial, mining, agricultural)	Musharaka, lease-purchase, Salaf transactions, instalment sales, direct investment, Muzara'ah, Musaqat, and Jo'alah.
2. Commercial	Mudaraba, Musharaka, Ju'alah.
3. Service	Lease-purchase, instalment sales, Ju'alah.
4. Housing	Lease-purchase, instalment, Qard al-Hasanah, Ju'alah.
5. Personal consumption	Instalment sales, Qard al-Hasanah.

Source: Bank Markazi, Jomhouri Islami Irana.

Table 3.1.2: Islamic Republic of Iran: Assets and Liabilities of the Banking System, 1984/85

Item	March 1984	March 1985
Private sector deposits	5,600.6	5,918.3
Sight	(1,955.8)	(2,509.0)
Non-sight	(3,644.8)	(3,409.3)
Old	3,644.8	1,087.9
Savings	(2,737.3)	(716.7)
Time	(907.5)	(371.2)
New		
Qard al-Hasanah	—	2,321.4
Savings	—	(780.0)
Term investment		
Short-term	—	(914.2)
Long-term	—	(627.2)
Credits to the private sector	4,256.6	4,500.7
Loan and credits (old)	4,256.6	3,746.0
Commercial banks	(2,819.2)	(2,288.4)
Specialised banks	(1,437.4)	(1,457.6)
New facilities	—	754.7
Commercial banks	—	(583.5)
Specialised banks	—	(171.2)

Source: Bank Markazi (1985), p. 10.
Unit: IRI billion

224

Table 3.1.3: Islamic Republic of Iran: Breakdown of New Banking Facilities Extended According to Various Islamic Contracts

Mode of transaction	Amount (IRI billion)	Share of each mode in total facility (per cent)
Lease-purchase	27.9	3.7
Instalment sale	247.5	32.8
Civil partnership	109.1	14.5
Mudaraba	134.6	17.8
Salaf transactions	26.8	3.5
Ju'alah	2.4	0.3
Legal partnership	37.0	4.9
Direct investment	4.4	0.6
Other	1.6	0.2
Total transactions affecting the profit of investment deposit	591.3	78.3
Debt purchasing	85.0	11.3
Qard al-Hasanah loans	78.4	10.4
Total transactions not affecting the profit of investment deposits	163.4	21.7
Total	754.7	100.0

Source: Bank Markazi (1985), p. 11.

Additionally, the commercial banks' share in extension of new banking facilities was 77.3 per cent of the total while that of the specialised banks was 22.7 per cent. This implies that, first, the banking system has been able to employ this IRIs 591.3 billion (about 38 per cent) of the available term investment deposits; second, of the credit facilities extended to the private sector, a major portion has been concentrated in short-term facilities, which indicates an allocation of financial resources largely to commercial and trade transactions.

Both of these factors can be explained by the various bottlenecks which exist in the system. The first and most important is the lack of trained personnel. The authorities have indicated that this is partly a problem inherited from the old system, in which the rapid growth of the banking system in years immediately preceding the Revolution did not permit orderly recruitment and training of bank personnel. Consequently, after the reorganisation of the banking system, Bank Markazi data suggests that only 7 per cent of the banks' personnel had college degrees, the majority had high school degrees or less, and 75 per cent had less than nine years of banking experience. By 20 March 1985, about one third of the personnel were trained in Islamic modes of banking. Although attempts have been made, through in-house training and the Bank Markazi's efforts, to speed up the training of the rest and although this bottleneck is only a short-run phenomenon, it is causing difficulty for banks to attract, appraise, and then finance investment projects in accordance with the provisions of the Law.

The best-trained personnel in terms of project evaluation appraisal and monitoring are concentrated in the specialised banks, but the Law has made it attractive for the commercial banks to attempt to attract trained personnel away from the specialised banks, thus exacerbating the personnel bottleneck problem. Traditionally, long-term investment financing in various sectors of the economy was concentrated in specialised banks. Hence,these banks were able to attract and train personnel for the purpose of project financing. Commercial banks were generally specialised in short-term financing and credit facilities. While the new Law permits all banks to engage in project financing, the extent of commercial bank activities in long-term investment financing is limited by the ability of their personnel, as well as their traditional organisational inertia in favour of short-term trade facilities. Additionally, and at least for the short run, banks are allowed to borrow funds at a fixed rate from the Bank Markazi and from one another. Hence this fixed rate establishes a minimum opportunity price for risk avoidance on the part of the commercial banks, thus making them reluctant to make resources available to the specialised banks either in a partnership or a joint venture basis.

The specialised banks, on the other hand, have found innovative means by which they have managed to package financing in a way that tailors funding to the needs of their clients. One such innovation has been for these specialised banks to break down the total financing requirements of a particular project into its various components, in accordance both with the size of each required amount of financing and with the gestation period. The component is then matched with a particular mode of financing.

EFFECTIVENESS OF THE MONETARY POLICY

Oil revenues and the budget policies of the government to a large extent determine the monetary base in the Iranian economy. During the post-Revolutionary period there has been an increasing reliance of the budget on central bank financing. The Bank Markazi data for 1973, for example, suggests that the three components of the monetary base-net foreign assets, central bank claims against the government, and the central bank's claim against the banking system were, respectively, 54.6 per cent, 28.3 per cent and 17.2 per cent of the total. The same data for 1984 suggests a major shift in the composition of the monetary base to 19.5 per cent, 68.1 per cent and 12.4 per cent respectively, for its three components. The combined effect of a reduction in central banks' claims against the commercial banks and an increase in its claims against the government implies an increase in the influence of fiscal policy in determining resource allocation. Historical data suggests further that the money multiplier, which can serve as another avenue for monetary policy influence (eg through variations in the reserve requirements) has remained historically stable. These results lead to the present conclusion that fiscal policy has dominated the conduct of monetary policy in recent years.

Monetary policy is formulated by the High Council on Money and Credit, which specifies the maximum level of credit expansion consistent with policy targets. Overall credit is then allocated between the government and the private sector, among banks and by economic activity. The Bank Markazi can supplement this allocation through variations in reserve ratios, moral suasion, and the 'modified open market operations' under which banks are required to hold 30 per cent of their assets in short-term government securities at a fixed rate of return. However, credit allocation, through which monetary policy and development policy objectives are co-ordinated, has remained the primary instrument of control (both before and after the introduction of Islamic banking) and its implementation has been enhanced by the nationalisation of banks. There have been no substantial changes in bank supervision but controls have become stronger since the introduction of the new system. The Bank Markazi has become more closely involved in the choice of asset portfolios by banks.

In combination with a restrained fiscal policy, which reduced government deficit, the restrictive credit policy helped in reducing inflation from 17.7 per cent in 1983 to 10.5 per cent in 1984 and an estimated 7.6 per cent in 1985.

Appendix: Islamic Banking Law in Iran

The Islamic Consultative Assembly of the Islamic Republic of Iran (the Majlis) approved a bill on 30 August 1983 for the formulation of a set of laws dealing with the legal framework for the implementation of interest free banking in Iran. Two days later (1 September) the bill was ratified by the Guardianship Council (Shuray-e-Nigabban).

Already, training courses had been devised for the bank employees to adopt the new system. According to an announcement by the Central Bank on 19 October 1983 as many as 20,000 bank employees had already attended these training courses. It was also announced that within the probation programme pending the approval of the bill the Iranian banks had already handled over 100 billion rials worth of banking transactions in accordance with the new system. The bill came into full effect on 21 January 1984.

1. THE LAW FOR USURY-(INTEREST) FREE BANKING (AUGUST 1983)[1]

Chapter I Objectives and duties of the banking system in the Islamic Republic of Iran

Article 1

The Objectives of Banking System:

(1) The establishment of a monetary and credit system based on rightness and justice (as delineated by Islamic jurisprudence) for the purpose of regulating the sound circulation of money and credit to enhance the health and growth of the country's economy.

(2) Availing itself of monetary and credit mechanisms, to engage in activities conducive to the attainment of the economic goals, policies and plans of the Government of the Islamic Republic.

(3) Creation of necessary facilities for the extension of cooperation and Gharz-al-hasaneh among the general public through the attraction and absorption of surplus funds, reserves, savings and deposits, and the mobilization thereof in provision of conditions and opportunities for gainful employment and investments, as stipulated in Clauses (2) and (9), Article (43) of the Constitution.

(4) Maintenance of the currency value and equilibrium in the balance of payments and facilitating the commercial exchanges.

---

1. Reproduced from Bank Markazi Jomhouri Islami Iran, *The Law for Usury-Free Banking* (Tehran, 1983).

(5) Facilitating payments and receipts, exchanges, transactions and other services to be performed by the banks, as determined by the Law.

Article 2

Duties of the Banking System:

(1) Issuance of notes and coins as legal tender, in conformity with the Law and regulations.

(2) Regulating, controlling and guidance of the circulation of money and credit, in accordance with the Law and regulations.

(3) Performance of all banking operations in foreign exchange and local currency, and undertaking or guaranteeing the foreign exchange payments of the Government, according to the Law and regulations.

(4) Supervision of transactions in gold and foreign exchange and the inflow or outflow of Iranian currency and foreign exchange, and the formulation of regulations governing thereof, in accordance with the Law.

(5) Performance of operations relating to valuable papers and documents according to the Law and regulations.

(6) Carrying out the monetary and credit policies, in accordance with the Law and regulations.

(7) Banking operations related to those parts of the approved economic plans which are to be conducted through the monetary and credit system.

(8) Opening of various Gharz-al-hasaneh (current and savings) accounts and accepting term investment deposits and issuance of relevant certificates, as required by the Law and regulations.

(9) Granting of loans and credits free of interest charges in accordance with the Law and regulations.

(10) Granting of loans and credits and provision of other banking services to the legally established cooperatives, for the realization of the provisions of Clause (2), Article (43) of the Constitution.

(11) Conducting transactions in gold and silver and holding and management of foreign exchange and gold reserves, with due observance of the relevant Law and regulations.

(12) Holding the Rial balances of international monetary and financial institutions or similar organizations and/or their affiliates, according to the Law and regulations.

(13) Entering into payments arrangements in order to effect monetary, trade and transit agreements concluded between the Government and other countries in accordance with the Law and regulations.

(14) Accepting and holding in trust of gold, silver, valuables, securities and official documents for real or legal persons and leasing of safe-deposit boxes.

(15) Issuance, confirmation and acceptance of Rial or foreign exchange guarantees for customers.

(16) Performance of the services of attorney or guardian, in accordance with the Law and regulations.

Chapter II Mobilization of monetary resources

Article 3

Banks are authorized to accept deposits under each of the following titles:

(A) Gharz-al-hasaneh Deposits.
    1 — Current
    2 — Saving
(B) Term Investment Deposits.
    Note: Term investment deposits, for the utilization of which the bank enjoys the power of attorney, shall be used in joint venture, Mozarebeh, hire-purchase, instalment transaction, Mozara-ah, Mosaqat, direct investment, forward dealings and Joaalah transactions.

Article 4

Banks are obliged to repay the principals of Gharz-al-hasaneh (saving and current) deposits and may undertake and/or insure the principals of the term investment deposits.

Article 5

Based on signed agreement, proceeds derived from activities stipulated in Note of Article (3) of this Law shall, in proportion to the term and the amounts of investment deposits and the bank's resources as a proportion to the aggregate resources used in such activities, be apportioned.

Article 6

In order to attract and mobilize deposits, the banks may, through promotional methods, give the following awards to the depositors:

(A) Non-fixed bonuses in cash or in kind to Gharz-al-hasaneh deposits.

(B) Exempting the depositors from, or granting discounts thereto, in payment of commissions and/or fees.

(C) According priority to depositors in the use of banking facilities as specified in Chapter III.

Chapter III Banking facilities

Article 7

In order to bring about the necessary conditions for the expansion of the activities of various productive, commercial and services sectors, the banks may, on the basis of partnership, provide a portion of the capital and/or resources required by these sectors.

Article 8

The banks may directly invest in productive and development projects or activities. Plans for such investments should be included in the State Annual Budget Bill to be approved by Majlis Shoaraye Eslami [The Islamic Consultative Assembly] and evaluation of the project should be indicative of no loss.

Note: The banks are by no means entitled to invest in the production of luxury and non-essential consumer goods.

Article 9

In order to provide facilities required for the expansion of commercial activities, the banks may, within the framework of the commercial policies of the government, put the necessary financial resources at the disposal of the customers on the basis of Mozarebeh, according priority to the legally established cooperatives.

Note: The banks shall not enter into Mozarebeh with the private sector for imports.

Article 10

For the purpose of providing facilities necessary for the expansion of housing activities, the banks may, in coordination with the Ministry of Housing and Town Planning, construct low-priced residential units for sale on instalment or hire-purchase.

Note:The banks are authorized to acquire land for the construction of low-priced residential units subject to Article (10), provided that they duly observe the Law Governing Lands Within City Limits.

Article 11

In order to create conditions necessary for the expansion of activities in industry, mining, agriculture and services, the banks are empowered, upon the request of the customer and his undertaking for the purchase, consumption and/or direct use of goods or commodity thus requested, to purchase movable property, and to sell them direct to the customer, on secured basis, on instalment.

Article 12

In order to create the necessary facilities for the expansion of services, agriculture, industrial and mining activities, banks may purchase movable and immovable properties, at the request of the client and his undertaking to hire-purchase the same for his own use, and place them at the disposal of the client in accordance with hire-purchase arrangements.

Article 13

In order to create the conditions required for the provision of working capital needed by the productive units, the banks may engage in any of the following operations:

(A) Upon the request of the productive units and their undertaking for the purchase and utilization of the raw materials and the spare parts thus requested, to purchase raw materials and spare parts needed by productive units and to resell them to the said units on credit.

(B) Upon the request of the productive units, to purchase, on a forward basis, the easy-to-sell products of the said units.

Article 14

For the realization of the aims contained in Clauses (2) and (9) of Article (43) of the Constitution, the banks are obliged to earmark a portion of their resources, as Gharz-al-hasaneh, to the applicants. The procedures for enforcement of this Article shall be drawn up by the Central Bank and approved by the Council of Ministers.

Article 15

All agreements concluded in pursuance of Articles (9), (11), (12), (13), and (14) of the present Law, shall, under the contract to be signed between the parties concerned, be considered binding documents and shall be subject to the Rules governing Legal Documents.

Article 16

In order to provide the necessary conditions for the expansion of productive, commercial and services activities, banks may engage in Joaalah.

Article 17

The banks may assign on Mozara-ah or Mosaqat agricultural lands and/or orchards which are at their disposal or in their possession.

Chapter IV Bank Markazi Jomhouri Islami Iran (BMJII) and monetary policy

Article 18

Bank Markazi Iran which shall be called Bank Markazi Jomhouri Islami Iran shall with respect to the state-owned corporations, the shares of which are not fully owned by the Government, conduct only those operations sanctioned by this Law.

Article 19

Policy for credit and short-term (one year) facilities shall be adopted upon recommendation by the General Assembly and approval by the Council of Ministers, and policy for credit and five-year and long-term facilities shall be incorporated in bills for five-year and long-term development plans and submitted to the Islamic Consultative Assembly for ratification.

Article 20

For the proper functioning of the monetary and credit system, BMJII, under Rules to be approved by the Council of Ministers, is empowered on the strength of Article 19, to intervene in, and supervise, the monetary and banking activities through the following instruments:

(A) Fixing a minimum and/or maximum ratio of profit for banks in their joint venture and Mozarebeh activities; these ratios may vary for different fields of activity.

(B) Designation of various fields for investment and partnership within the framework of the approved economic policies, and the fixing of a minimum prospective rate of profit for the various investment and partnership projects; the minimum prospective rate of profit may vary with respect to different branches of activity.

(C) Fixing a minimum and maximum margin of profit, as a proportion to the cost price of the goods transacted, for banks in instalment and hire-purchase transactions.

(D) Determination of types and the minimum and maximum amounts of commissions for banking services (provided that they do not exceed the expense of service rendered) and the fees charged for putting to use the deposits received by the banks.

(E) Determination of the types, amounts, minimum and maximum bonuses subject to Article (6), and the establishment of guidelines for advertisement by banks in the cases referred to.

(F) Determination of the minimum and maximum ratio in joint venture, Mozarebeh, investment, hire-purchase, instalment transactions, buying and selling on credit, forward deals, Mozara-ah, Mosaqat, Joaalah and Gharz-al-hasaneh for banks or any thereof with respect to various fields of activity; also fixing the maximum facility that can be granted to each customer.

Chapter V Miscellanea

Article 21

In its dealings with other banks, BMJII is not authorized to engage in banking operations which involve usury; nor are the banks among themselves.

Article 22

Upon authorization by BMJII, banks may engage in authorized banking operations with state-owned institutions, government-affiliated organizations and public corporations.

Article 23

The funds received as commissions and fees shall constitute the banks' income and cannot be divided among the depositors.

Article 24

Exemption from commercial tax and/or tax exemptions granted by law to factories and productive enterprises shall also apply to banks when replacing them in matters of imports or ownership.

Article 25

The units in which the banks have made investments and/or hold a share shall be governed by the Commercial Code, unless they are subject to another law.

Article 26

Consequent to the ratification of this Act, all contravening laws and regulations shall be null and void and all the powers and duties stipulated in the Monetary and Banking Law and the Bill for the Administration of the Banks and the amendments thereto, but under the present Law have been delegated to other authorized entities, shall be divested from the previous authorities.

Article 27

With the recommendations by the Bank Markazi Jomhouri Islami Iran, the Ministry of Economic Affairs and Finance shall draw up the By-Laws under this Law and put it into effect following its approval by the Council of Ministers. The drafting and approval of the By-Laws shall not exceed a four-month period.

This Law, containing twenty-seven Articles and four Notes, was ratified by Majlis Shoaraye Eslami (The Islamic Consultative Assembly) in its session held on Tuesday, Eight Sharivar 1362 and approved by the Council of Protectors on 10/6/1362.

Akbar Hashemi,
Speaker,
Majlis Shoaraye Eslami.

This is an unofficial translation of the original Farsi text which, in the case of any dispute, shall be controlling.

2. REGULATIONS RELATING TO THE LAW FOR USURY-FREE BANKING[2]

(a) Regulations Relating to the Mobilization of Monetary Resources (December 18, 1983)

Gharz-al-hasaneh deposits

Article 1

The banks accept Gharz-al-hasaneh deposits under the following titles:

a. Current
b. Savings

Article 2

The banks undertake and guarantee payment of the principal of Gharz-al-hasaneh deposits and are obliged to repay such principal on demand.

Article 3

In order to mobilize Gharz-al-hasaneh deposits, the banks may, at their discretion and without contractual obligation, grant to depositors one or more of the following rewards:

1. Non-fixed bonuses in cash or in kind.
2. Reduction or exemption from payment of commission for banking services.
3. Priority in the use of banking facilities.

The type, level, minimum and maximum of such rewards to be approved by the Money and Credit Council.

Article 4

Gharz-al-hasaneh deposits are considered as part of a 'bank's resources'.

Article 5

As of the date of enforcement of the Law, the banks are not authorized to accept funds of any kind for the credit of existing savings accounts. With the consent of the holders of existing savings accounts, the banks shall gradually convert such accounts into one of the deposit categories specified in Article 3 of the Law,

---

2. Unofficial translation of notifications by the Council of Ministers implementing the Law for Usury-Free Banking in the Islamic Republic of Iran.

before the end of the year 1363 [1984]. After the foregoing time limit, savings accounts which have not been converted into one of the new categories of accounts shall be deemed Gharz-al-hasaneh savings accounts.

Investment term deposits

Article 6

The banks accept investment term deposits as long-term and short-term investment deposits.

Article 7

The duration and other terms and conditions of short term and long-term investment deposits, as well as the rewards specified under Article 6 of the Law for such deposits, are to be approved by the Money and Credit Council.

Article 8

The banks undertake or insure at their own expense the repayment of the principals of the investment term deposits.

Article 9

As 'depositors' resources', investment term deposits shall be utilized by the banks in their capacity as attorneys, in equity participation, Mozarebeh, hire-purchase, instalment transaction, Mozaraah, Mosaghat, direct investment, forward delivery transaction ('Salaf') and Joaalah.

Note: Subject to the relevant regulations, acceptance of investment term deposits for use in a specified project is authorized. The application of Article 8 to such deposits is conditional upon its incorporation in the respective contract.

Article 10

No profit at a predetermined figure may be paid on investment term deposits. The profits derived from operations which are the subject of Article 9 shall be divided between the bank and the depositors, as per the concluded agreement, inclusive of proxy, in proportion to the amount of such investment deposits, net of statutory reserve requirements, and the duration thereof; and the amount of Bank's resources and the duration thereof, in relation to the total funds utilized in such operations.

Note 1: The Bank's remuneration for acting as attorney in utilizing the investment deposits shall be deducted from the depositors' share of profits. The minimum and maximum amount of such remuneration to be approved by the Money and Credit Council.

Note 2: In contracts between banks and depositors it is obligatory to stipulate the principle of compromise concerning sharing of profits, the undivided utilization of the deposit and the method of calculation and payment of profit.

236

Article 11

In providing the necessary resources for granting the facilities which are the subject of Article 9, the banks shall give priority to the utilization of 'depositors' resources'. In the event that the total amount of facilities granted, the subject of Article 9, is either less than, or, equal to the total volume of investment term deposits, net of statutory reserve requirements, then all of the profits, which are the subject of the said Article, shall be divided among such deposits. Should the total amount of facilities granted for such purposes exceed the total amount of such deposits, the balance shall constitute the share of bank's resources.

Article 12

Renewal, at maturity, of the existing fixed deposits with the banks is not permitted under the same category. In any event, if fixed deposits, with maturities extending beyond the end of Esfand 1363,[3] are not by the said date, with the consent of depositors, converted into one of the new categories, subject of Article 3 of the Law, such deposits shall be transferred into the Sundry Creditors Account. At the latest within one month after the maturity of those deposits which have not been converted into new categories, and also after the end of Esfand 1363 with respect to all those fixed deposits then existing which have been transferred to the Sundry Creditors Account, banks are obliged to notify the depositors in writing so that the position may be determined.

(b) Regulations Relating to the Granting
of Banking Facilities
(January 4, 1984)

General

Article 1

Banking facilities shall be granted in such a manner that the principal amount thereof as well as the expected profit thereon would, based on their respective projections, be capable of liquidation within a definite period of time.

Article 2

The criteria, for the determination of the rate of profit and/or the expected rate of return on the facilities granted by the banks, as well as the minimum and maximum rate of profit and/or the expected rate of return to be approved by the Money and Credit Council and endorsed by the Prime Minister.

---

3. Corresponding to 20 February–20 March 1984.

Article 3

The criteria, for the determination of the period for which the facilities are granted by the banks and the manner of the liquidation of the principal together with the profit arising therefrom to be approved by the Money and Credit Council.

Article 4

The banks shall implement the necessary and adequate supervision over the good performance of the contracts entered into, which are the subject of these present Regulations, in respect of both the manner of utilization and of the facilities granted. The banking operations in respect of the facilities granted shall be centered at the bank granting the facilities, at its discretion, and as may be warranted in each case.

Article 5

The provision of facilities shall be contingent upon, if deemed necessary, receipt by the banks of a certain amount of funds as 'Advance Deposit'. Determination of the cases when such 'Advanced Deposit' is necessary and the minimum amount thereof rests with the Money and Credit Council.

Article 6

At the bank's discretion, granting of facilities shall be contingent upon receiving adequate security, as deemed necessary, to safeguard the banks' interest and ensure the good performance of the respective contracts.

Note: In cases where facilities granted are in connection with goods which, in the judgement of the banks, have exclusive or limited use, and/or because of installation and operation, their further use is not economically viable, the banks shall require additional securities for granting of such facilities.

Article 7

The banks shall, if necessary, arrange for insuring annually in the banks' favour, the properties which are subjects of the facilities granted and/or the securities obtained in respect thereof, during the execution of the respective contracts for an amount at least equivalent to the outstanding balances due from the granting of such facilities.

Article 8

The granting of any one of the different types of facilities jointly by two banks or more to an individual or real persons or legal entities is authorized. In every case, the administration of such facilities shall be conducted by one bank, as chosen by the participating banks.

Article 9

All banking transactions connected with the facilities granted by banks are governed by the provisions of these Regulations and their relevant procedural instructions and shall, therefore, not be covered by the guidelines and regulations governing transactions pertaining to the banks' own supply requirements.

Note 1: Transactions relating to properties acquired by the banks as a result of the facilities granted and/or constructed by the banks, shall also be covered by the Rules of this Article.

Note 2: The period of the transaction and the disposal value of the acquired properties shall, according to the case, be determined by the banks.

Article 10

Effective from the date of the Law coming into force, the granting of the banks' new form of facilities shall be carried out based on the provisions of the Law for Usury-Free Banking and the Money and Banking Law, to the extent that it does not contravene the Law for Usury-Free Banking. With the consent of their customers, the banks are obliged to adjust, in the minimum time possible, the facilities granted previously, so as to conform with Islamic principles. In the event that adjustment of the banks' previous transactions and contracts so as to conform with the new banking transactions prove to be impossible, such transactions and contracts shall remain in force until their expiry date.

Article 11

In drafting contracts connected with operations in Mozarebeh, instalment transactions, hire-purchase, buying or selling on credit, forward delivery deals and Gharz-al-hasaneh, the banks are required to stipulate that on the basis of agreement reached, the said contracts are considered binding instruments and shall be governed by procedural Regulations relating to legal documents drawn and attested before Notaries Public.

Note: Those transactions which should be executed before a Notary Public, as required by laws and enacted regulations, shall continue to be so executed in conformity with the relevant procedures.

Article 12

In cases where the subject of the facilities granted involves the transfer of title to property, the banks are obliged to notify the customer of the cash value thereof, in accordance with the rules adopted by the Money and Credit Council.

Article 13

For the purpose of providing facilities necessary for expansion in the area of housing, the banks are empowered to engage in the construction of low-cost housing units.

Article 14

With due regard to the monetary policies, the subject of Article 20 of the Law, and in accord with the policy of the Ministry of Housing and Town Planning,

Bank Markazi Jomhouri Islami Iran shall formulate annually the program for building low-cost housing units by banks and shall communicate such program to the banks for implementation.

I. Gharz-al-hasaneh

Article 15

Gharz-al-hasaneh is a contract in which one (the lender) of the two parties relinquishes a specified portion of his possessions to the other party (the borrower) which the borrower is obliged to return to the lender in kind or, where not possible, its cash value.

Article 16

In order to accomplish the objectives set out in Clauses (2) and (9) of Article 43 of the Constitution and so as to satisfy the basic needs of individuals, the banks, in accordance with the rules to be adopted by the Money and Credit Council and endorsed by the Prime Minister, shall set aside a part of their resources and provide Gharz-al-hasaneh for the following purposes:

(a) to provide equipment, tools and other necessary resources so as to enable the creation of employment, in the form of cooperative bodies, for those who lack the necessary means;
(b) to enable expansion in production, with particular emphasis on agricultural, livestock and industrial products;
(c) to meet essential needs.

Article 17

The expenses incurred in the provision of Gharz-al-hasaneh shall be, in each case, calculated on the basis of the directives issued by Bank Markazi Jomhouri Islami Iran and collected from the borrower.

II. Civil partnership

Article 18

Civil partnership is based on the contribution of cash or non-cash capital by several real or legal persons to a common pool, on a contractual basis, for the purpose of making a profit.

Article 19

The banks shall undertake participation in civil partnership in order to provide the necessary facilities for productive, commercial and service activities. The object of partnership shall be specified.

Article 20

Civil Partnership will be considered as formed and effective when, on the basis of the contract, the partners pay their cash share in the capital into a special account opened at a bank in the name of the partnership, and in the event that all or part of the share is non-cash, it should be transferred to the Director or Directors of the civil partnership, in accordance with the rules of civil partnership.

Note: The share contribution of the partners in the civil partnership may be effected in instalments, as stipulated in the contract.

Article 21

Civil partnership shall dissolve and liquidate upon the accomplishment of the objectives of the partnership.

Article 22

In the contracts of civil partnership, the banks are required to stipulate that the Director or Directors of civil partnerships formed under these Regulations are not authorized to enter into transactions or to undertake financial commitments which exceed the combined total value of the cash capital paid into the account or non-cash capital transferred to the Director or Directors of the civil partnership.

III. Legal partnership

Article 23

The purpose of legal partnership is to provide a part of the capital of new joint-stock companies or to purchase part of the shares of existing joint-stock companies.

Article 24

In order to provide the necessary facilities for the expansion of the activities of various productive, commercial and service sectors, the banks may provide part of the capital needed by joint-stock companies which are and/or will be established for such purposes.

Article 25

Prior to their engaging in participation, the banks are obliged to assess and evaluate the companies whose shares are the subject of acquisition and/or the projects proposed for partnership, from the technical financial and economic aspects, insofar as the banks require. The participation of any bank, by drawing on its own resources and the investment deposits, is permissible only if the result of such assessment and evaluation evidences that the partnership is not anticipated to suffer a loss.

Note: At the outset of the partnership, the minimum ratio of the capital of the companies in which the banks intend to participate to the total financial resources of such companies, shall be determined by the Bank Markazi Jomhouri Islami Iran, if deemed necessary.

Article 26

The banks are authorized to sell the shares they hold in joint-stock companies.

Article 27

If deemed necessary, Bank Markazi Jomhouri Islami Iran may fix the ratio of participation, through the use of bank's resources and investment deposits, by one or several banks, in a newly established joint-stock company as well as the ratio of shares purchased in existing joint-stock companies by one or several banks by drawing on the above-mentioned resources.

IV. Direct investment

Article 28

Direct investment means the provision of capital by banks for the implementation of profit-making productive and development projects.

Note: The banks are not permitted to invest in the production of luxury or non-essential goods.

Article 29

The ratio of the capital to the total financial resources required for the implementation of a project, up to the point when it starts operation, should not be less than 40 per cent.

Note: 100 per cent of the fixed term investment required for the implementation of such projects must be provided in the form of long-term financial resources (whether from capital or other resources).

Article 30

Implementation of the projects which are the subject of Article 28 of the present Regulations is permissible through the establishment of joint-stock companies. The joint-stock companies which are established, independently of the banks, under these Regulations, shall be governed by their own Articles, rules and regulations.

Article 31

Prior to engaging in direct investment, the banks are obliged to assess and evaluate the proposed projects for investment from the economic, technical and financial aspects, insofar as the bank requires. Direct investment in such projects which require the use of the banks' own resources and investment deposits is permitted only if the result of the assessment and evaluation of any project is financially justifiable. The minimum profitability (rate of return) of any project shall be determined by the Money and Credit Council.

Article 32

In conformity with the relevant directives, the banks are required to report to Bank Markazi Jomhouri Islami Iran their plans for allocation of funds for direct investment, in order that such plans may be submitted, together with the State Annual Budget Bill, to Majlis Shoaraye Islami (the Islamic Consultative Assembly).

Article 33

In coordination with the High Council of Banks, the banks may offer to the public for sale part or all of their shares in companies which have been established through direct investment, once the said companies start operation.

Article 34

The banks are required to have the accounts and financial operations of the companies governed by the rules of direct investment audited annually by the auditing forms certified by the Ministry of Economic Affairs and Finance.

Note: Bank Markazi Jomhouri Islami Iran may, if deemed necessary, inspect the banks' direct investment operations.

Article 35

The banks are obliged to adjust their existing direct investments so as to comply with the provisions of these Regulations, no later than the end of the year 1365.

V. Mozarebeh

Article 36

Mozarebeh means a contract whereby one (the owner) of the two parties undertakes to provide capital (cash) on proviso that the other party (the agent) employs such capital in trade and that both parties share the resulting accrued profit.

Article 37

For the purpose of providing the facilities necessary for the expansion of commerce, the banks, as owners, may place the required cash capital (resources) at the disposal of the Agent, being either a real or legal person.

In providing such facilities, the banks shall give preference to the legally established cooperatives.

Article 38

The banks are not permitted to enter into Mozarebeh with the private sector for imports.

Article 39

The types of expenses acceptable in Mozarebeh shall be determined and declared by Bank Markazi Jomhouri Islami Iran.

VI. Forward delivery transactions

Article 40

Forward delivery transactions means the advance purchase for cash of products at a fixed price (with due observance of Shari'a laws).

Article 41

In order to provide the necessary facilities to raise working capital for the productive units, whether such units are owned by real or legal person, the banks may, solely on the request of such units, buy their products in advance of delivery.

Article 42

The banks are forbidden to sell the products so bought in advance before their date of delivery, unless the purchased products have been delivered to the bank before the date of delivery.

Article 43

The forward delivery purchase, under contract, by the banks of the products of the productive units is permitted only if such products:

    (a) are produced by the applicant productive units;
    (b) are not rapidly perishable (unless there exists the means of taking precautionary measures against spoilage during the period intervening between delivery and sale);
    (c) are readily saleable.
    Note: the phrase 'readily saleable', the subject of Clause (c), means that the banks, at the time of forward delivery purchase, should satisfy themselves that the products, the subject of the transaction, would be readily saleable at the date of delivery.

Article 44

The forward price of the products purchased by the banks shall be fixed by taking into account the price-determining factors including the forecast of the sale price of the products at their delivery date as well as the banks' own profits.

244

In any event, the forward purchase price of products should not exceed their cash price at the time of transaction.

Article 45

In transactions involving forward delivery purchase of products, the banks are required to observe the following points and to incorporate them in the respective contract:

(a) to identify the main specification of such products in such a manner that contributes to the determination of prices;
(b) to pay in full to the seller, at the time of transaction, the forward purchase price of the products bought forward;
(c) to specify the date of delivery;
(d) to specify the quantity, number, weight and other customary specifications of the products, the subject of the transaction;
(e) to specify the place of delivery of the products purchased forward.

Article 46

The banks are authorized to engage in forward delivery purchase of products only if the time for delivery of all the products to the bank (from the date of the transaction) is, at the most, equal to one production cycle, provided that in no circumstances does it exceed one year.

VII. Sale by instalment (credit sale) to provide working capital for productive units

Article 47

Sale by instalment means the surrender of a property by one party to another at a fixed price in such a manner that the whole or part of the said price will be received in equal or unequal instalments at a specified future date or dates.

Article 48

In order to provide the necessary facilities to raise working capital for the productive units, the banks may buy the raw materials, spare parts, working tools and other initial requisites needed by such units, solely upon the written request of applicants and on their undertaking to buy and utilize the above-mentioned items; and to sell them, on instalments, to such applicants. In estimating the requirements of the productive units, the volume of raw materials commensurate with the rate of production during one production cycle should be taken into consideration.

Article 49

The instalment sale price of the goods, the subject of Article 48, shall be determined by taking into consideration their cost price as well as the bank's profit.

Article 50

The period of collecting the value of the goods sold, the subject of Article 48, shall not exceed the duration of one production cycle or one year at the most.

Note: Where the sale by instalment is intended to provide working capital for new productive projects, the respective bank shall decide, on an individual case basis, upon payment period exceeding one year.

VIII Sale by instalment of the means of production, machinery and equipment

Article 51

The goods, the subject of this section, are the machinery and equipment with an effective life of more than one year according to a table to be drawn up by Bank Markazi Jomhouri Islami Iran.

Article 52

For the purpose of providing facilities for the expansion of activities in industry, mining, agriculture and services, the banks may purchase goods, the subject of Article 51, solely upon the written request of the applicants and their undertaking to purchase, consume and make direct use of such goods, and sell them to the applicants by instalments.

Article 53

The instalment sale price of the goods, the subject of Article 51, shall be determined according to their cost price as well as the bank's profit.

Article 54

The period for collecting the value of the goods sold by instalment, the subject of Article 51, shall not exceed the duration of the effective life of such goods as specified in the relevant table. The starting date of the productive operation, as determined by the bank, shall be regarded as the starting point for the purpose of calculation of the effective life.

IX. Sale by instalment — housing

Article 55

The banks may sell by instalment the housing units constructed, which are the subject of Article 13.

Article 56

The banks shall fix the sale price of the housing units on the basis of the cost price plus relevant expenses together with a reasonable profit for the bank.

Note 1: The rules governing the provision of facilities by the banks to those applying for the low-cost housing units constructed shall be adopted by the banks, on the basis of recommendations made by the Ministry of Housing and Town Planning and as approved by the Economic Council.

Note 2: In exceptional cases, as determined by the Prime Minister, the facilities required by the governmental organizations shall be provided by the use of the banks' own resources.

X. Hire-purchase

Article 57

Hire-purchase means a leasing contract wherein it is stipulated that the leaseholder, at the end of the period of the lease and upon fulfilling the conditions specified in the contract, will receive the title to the leased property.

Article 58

In order to provide the necessary facilities for the expansion of services, agricultural, industrial and mining activities, the banks may, as lessors, engage in hire-purchase transactions.

Article 59

Solely upon the written request of an applicant and his acceptance to undertake the hire-purchase for his personal use, the banks may purchase movable and immovable property for the purpose of providing the facilities set out in Article 58 and to place them at the disposal of the applicant by way of hire-purchase.

Article 60

The banks may sell the housing units constructed, which are the subject of Article 13, by way of hire-purchase.

Note 1: The banks are required to stipulate in the concluded contracts the obligation of the leaseholder to derive benefit from the hired goods, except in cases of emergency or force majeure, as determined by the banks.

Note 2: The rules governing the provision of facilities to those applying for the low-cost housing units constructed by the banks, shall be determined by the Economic Council.

Article 61

The period of hire-purchase shall not exceed the duration of the effective life of the properties, which are the subject of Articles 59 and 60. The starting date for the calculation of the effective life and the commencement of operations shall be determined by the bank.

Note: The banks are forbidden to engage in hire-purchase transactions in respect of properties with productive operation of less than two years.

Article 62

The amount of rent charged in respect of the properties purchased or housing units constructed, which are the subject of Article 13, shall be determined on the basis of the cost price, the period of the hire-purchase and a reasonable profit for the bank. In calculating the profit, allowance shall be made for the 'payment on account' which is the subject of Article 63.

Article 63

The banks are required to obtain as 'payment on account' at least 10 per cent of the total cost as part of the rental over the period of the hire-purchase.

Article 64

In the hire-purchase contracts it should be stipulated that at the end of the hiring period and after the last payment of the rental, the ownership of the property will be transferred to the leaseholder, provided that the leaseholder has fulfilled the conditions specified in the contract.

Note: If, prior to the end of the hiring period, the leaseholder pays and settles in full the balance of the rentals remaining due, the banks are authorized to transfer to the leaseholder the ownership of the property, in addition to giving an appropriate discount on the balance of rentals remaining due.

Article 65

The banks are required to specify in the hire-purchase contract the cases for termination and the method of settling accounts.

XI. Joaalah

Article 66

In these Regulations, Joaalah means an undertaking by one party, called 'Jael' or 'Employer', to pay a specified sum of money or wages (Joal) according to the contract in return for a specific service being rendered. The party rendering the service is called 'Amel' or 'Contractor'.

Article 67

In order to provide the necessary facilities for the expansion of productive, commercial and services activities the banks may engage by contract in Joaalah as Amel or, if deemed necessary, as Jael.

Article 68

Where a bank is the Amel in Joaalah, the bank's authority to entrust to another party, under the title of secondary Joaalah or any other title, the performance of a part of a specific action shall be stipulated in the Joaalah contract. In such cases, the banks are required to supervise the operations involved, the manner of consumption and the payment of funds.

Note: Where the bank acts as Jael in Joaalah, the Amel is permitted, subject to the bank's approval, to entrust to another party the performance of part of the service concerned.

Article 69

The responsibility for making initial preparations, procurement of materials, products and any other necessary equipment for performing the task can, by contract, be entrusted to Jael or Amel.

Article 70

In conformity with the regulations determined by the Money and Credit Council setting the minimum and/or maximum, the receipt of payment of part of the amount in the Joaalah contract, as 'payment on account' and/or 'advance payment', is permitted.

XII. Mozaraah

Article 71

Mozaraah is a contract under which one ('Mozare') of the two parties commits a particular plot of land for a specified period of time to another party ('Amel') to cultivate and the harvest to be divided between Mozare and Amel.

Article 72

In order to increase the productivity and the production of agricultural products, the banks may, as Mozare, commit, by contract, to Mozaraah the arable lands which they own or the lands which in one way or another they are entitled to possess or utilize.

Note: In addition to land, the banks may, by contract, provide other necessary elements such as water, seeds, fertilizers, pesticides, implements and means of production and transportation.

Article 73

By taking into consideration the share of each party in the harvest, the banks may, if deemed necessary, pay a certain amount of money in cash to Amel during the production cycle.

XIII. Mosaghat

Article 74

Mosaghat means a transaction between the owner of trees or the like and Amel, in return for a specified amount of common share in the produce. Produce includes fruit, leaves, flowers and the like.

Article 75

In order to increase the productivity and the production of agricultural products, the banks may commit to Mosaghat the orchards or fruiters which they own and/or to which they are beneficially entitled and/or are in one way or another entitled to possess or utilize.

Note: The banks may, by contract, provide other necessary elements such as water, fertilizers, pesticides and the means of production and transportation.

Article 76

By taking into consideration the share of each party in the harvest, the banks may, if deemed necessary, pay a certain amount of money in cash to Amel during the production cycle.

(c) Regulations relating to Chapter 4
of the Law for Usury-Free Banking
(March 7, 1984)

Article 1

Based on the country's general economic policies and priorities set, as well as taking into consideration its monetary situation, Bank Markazi Jomhouri Islami Iran shall formulate the general policy guidelines for credit and the provision of banking facilities, for the term of each plan, whether five years or longer, with due regard to their economic impact, so as to be submitted, subsequent to adoption by the Money and Credit Council, together with the bills on development plans, to Majlis Shoaraye Eslami for ratification.

Article 2

Based on the policies and priorities which are the subject of Article 1 of these Regulations, Bank Markazi Jomhouri Islami Iran shall formulate, with the approval of the Money and Credit Council, no later than the end of Aban of each year, a policy in respect of credit as well as a policy for the extension of short-term (one year) banking facilities for the following year, so as to be submitted to the General Assembly of Bank Markazi Jomhouri Islami Iran for proposal to the Council of Ministers for approval.

Article 3

For the effective implementation of the monetary and credit policies and the maintenance of currency value, Bank Markazi Jomhouri Islami Iran, in addition to using the instruments of monetary policy as outlined in the Monetary and Banking Law, to the extent that it shall not contravene the provisions of the Law for Usury-Free Banking, may intervene in, and supervise, the monetary and banking operations, with the approval of the Money and Credit Council, by availing itself of the following measures:

1. Determining the various fields for investment and partnership, with due regard to the economic policies approved by the Council of Ministers.

2. Determining the minimum projected rate of profit (return) for the purpose of selection of investments and/or partnership projects as well as stipulating the minimum and/or, if deemed necessary, the maximum projected rate of profit and/or the projected rate of return for other types of banking facilities.

3. Determining the minimum and/or maximum share of the profit for banks in Mozarabeh and in partnership.

4. The minimum and/or maximum ratios referred to in Clause 2 and 3 above may differ in various fields.

5. Determining the minimum and/or maximum amount of facilities provided by the banks, from the investment deposits and/or the banks' own resources, for each area of activity and, if deemed necessary, for each of the operations which are the subject of Article 9 of the Regulations relating to Mobilization of Monetary Resources (the subject of Cabinet Decree No. 81962 dated 12/10/1362), for all of the banks and/or any of them. The said limits shall be determined, at least once a year, in such a manner that will facilitate the implementation of the policies set out in Articles 1 and 2 of these Regulations.

6. Determining the maximum limit for each type of facility and/or total of facilities to be granted by one of several banks to any person, whether real or legal.

7. Determining the minimum and/or maximum limits of the remunerations of the various attorney functions in respect of the employment of investment deposits. Such attorney remuneration may include the banks' administrative expenses for the mobilization and management of the said deposits. No other amount whatsoever under any title shall be charged by the banks to the holders of investment deposits.

8. Determining the rules governing the minimum and/or maximum commissions for various banking services on the basis of the volume of tasks performed in respect of such services. The maximum rate of the said commissions shall not exceed the cost of tasks involved in rendering such services.

9. Determining the type, amount, minimum and/or maximum reward which are the subject of Article 6 of the Law, and introducing regulations governing the banks' promotional activities in this respect.

Article 4

With regard to the provision of banking facilities, Bank Markazi Jomhouri

Islami Iran is authorized to conduct banking operations with the government companies (whose capital equities are not owned 100 per cent by the government) solely in conformity with the requirements of the Law for Usury-Free Banking and these Regulations.

(d) Regulations Relating to Chapter 5
of the Law for Usury-Free Banking
(March 7, 1984)

Article 1

Bank Markazi Jomhouri Islami Iran may provide the banks with the necessary resources or accept to hold as deposits their surplus resources. The conditions governing the provision and/or acceptance of resources, as well as the period, profit margin and/or commission relating thereto shall be approved by the Money and Credit Council. The said profit margin and/or commission, however, shall be governed by the directives of the latter part of Article 4 of these Regulations.

Note: Subject to the conditions specified in Article 3, and its relevant Note, of these Regulations, Bank Markazi Jomhouri Islami Iran is authorized to accept resources drawn from investment term deposits.

Article 2

The banks may provide part of the resources needed by the other banks, using, according to priority, the depositors' and/or their own resources.

Article 3

Where the provision of resources by one bank to another is effected using the depositors' resources, the receiving bank, as the proxy, by right of substitution, on behalf of the providing bank, shall use the funds received solely for the purposes which are the subject of Article 9, in accordance with the rules governing the investment deposits as stipulated in the Regulations relating to the Mobilization of Monetary Resources (the subject of Cabinet Decree No. 81962 dated 12/10/1362).

Note: The remunerations for attorney functions in the employment of deposits shall be based upon the agreement reached between the transacting banks. The attorney remunerations collected from the holders of investment deposits shall not in total exceed the limit prescribed by Clause 4 of Article 20 of the Law.

Article 4

Where the provision of resources by one bank to another, in the form of loan and/or credit and the like, is supplied from the bank's own resources, the funds obtained by the receiving bank shall be considered as its own resources.

The profit and/or commission on these types of interbank transactions shall be applied as income to the account of the providing bank on the one hand and as expense to the account of the receiving bank on the other.

Article 5

The government, institutions, government-affiliated institutions, and government-owned companies are required to hold their funds exclusively with, and to conduct all their banking operations exclusively through Bank Markazi Jomhouri Islami Iran, except in cases where the said bank, by virtue of Article 22 of the Law, consents to the execution of part or all of the above-mentioned operations by other banks. In such cases, the banks may, subject to the relevant regulations, conduct authorized banking operations with such government institutions and companies.

Article 6

The directives and operational rules of these Regulations shall be drawn up by Bank Markazi Jomhouri Islami Iran and following their approval by the Money and Credit Council, shall be put into effect.

Note: Bank Markazi Jomhouri Islami Iran is obliged to communicate immediately to the Economic Council, the directives issued.

Article 7

The banks are required to act in accordance with the instructions and circulars which Bank Markazi Jomhouri Islami Iran will issue in accordance with the respective Laws and Regulations.

Article 8

As provided in Article 25 of the Law for Usury-Free Banking, the units with whom the banks have entered into partnership and/or have made investment, for any amount, or intend so to do, shall not be considered as government companies on account of such partnership and/or investments by banks.

2

Islamic Banking in Pakistan

Introduction

The process of Islamisation of the financial system in Pakistan was initiated in 1979/80 when the specialised credit institutions in the public sector reoriented their financial activities toward non-interest bearing operations. Effective from 1 January 1981, all domestic commercial banks were permitted to accept deposits on the basis of profit and loss sharing (PLS). Over the next three years, steps were taken to develop new non-interest bearing financial instruments in which PLS deposits could be invested. These include commodity operations of the government and its agencies, export bills, investment in shares, purchase of participation term certificates (PTCs), provision of loans to the specialised credit institutions (which had already moved to non-interest bearing operations), Musharaka (partnership) lending, hire-purchase, and Mudaraba certificates.

New steps were instituted on 1 January 1985 to formally transform the banking systems to a non-interest basis over the following six months, thereby completing the first phase of transforming the entire financial system on Islamic principles. As of that date, all finances provided by banks to the government, public sector corporations, and public or private joint stock companies were to be only on the basis of the specified Islamic (non-interest bearing) modes of financing.[1] However, transactions with the government are still interest-based; moreover, to the extent that the government has obtained financing through the sale of bonds whose purchase by the private sector is facilitated by the provision of bank credit at fixed rates, this provision with respect to financing the public sector does not appear to have been implemented fully. Effective from 1 April 1985, all finances provided to entities, including individuals, were also limited to the specified modes. As of 1 July 1985, no banks could accept any interest-

---

1. During transitional period 1 July–31 December 1984, lending for working capital purposes on interest was permitted but not to exceed six months in maturity.

bearing deposits, and all existing deposits became subject to PLS rules.[2] Deposits in current accounts have continued to be accepted as in the past, that is, at no share in the profits or losses of banks (equivalent to no interest previously). However, foreign currency deposits and loans from abroad would continue to be exempted from the new regulations. The State Bank of Pakistan specifies broad ranges of charges for the various modes of lending as guides for commercial banks; a formula is used to determine rates of return to depositors. The stress has been on introducing new modes of financing without, as far as possible, altering the basic functioning and structure of the banking system.

It is too soon to quantify the impact of new regulations on the operation of the banking system, economy, and monetary policy. However, the transformation of the banking system has led to the generation of a number of financial instruments, which have probably facilitated financial deepening and may have enhanced the potential for increased intermediation in the future. Moreover, there has been some deregulation of the banking system, especially with regard to the determination of charges on loans. Nevertheless, owing to institutional and legal constraints, banks have continued to concentrate as in the past on short-term finance and the provision of working capital on a mark-up basis. So far, there has been only limited progress toward the development of equity-oriented instruments, which is central to the growth of Islamic banking.

The introduction of the new modes of financing has required a shift in the procedures underlying lending operations of banks. However, the shift appears to have been effected without disruption to lending activity. The cautious pace of transition to the new system has facilitated the transformation. Nevertheless, owing to the introduction of more rigorous procedures and the enhanced monitoring by banks, there have been some difficulties in lending to smaller firms. By and large, corporate borrowers have insisted on ensuring that the net cost of borrowing should remain unchanged and banks, by opting for lending on a mark-up basis where mark-up rates are virtually identical to the interest rates prevailing prior to the introduction of the new system, have been able to accommodate their clients. Such accommodation is viewed by the authorities as essential for the orderly transition to the rigours of the new system. The elimination of interest rates has had no adverse effects on the accumulation of bank deposits, and the rates of return offered by banks have generally tended to be higher than deposit rates prevailing prior to the introduction of the new system.

There have been no changes in the instruments and effectiveness of monetary policy; bank supervisory and regulatory controls have also remained broadly unchanged. Based on guidelines issued by the State Bank of Pakistan, commercial banks have modified their procedures and practices in order to accommodate the new system.

---

2. However, deposits under the national savings schemes, which were the equivalent of over 11 per cent of deposits with commercial banks, have remained exempt from this provision.

The first phase of transformation, that is, shifting from interest based to non-interest-based banking, has been largely completed without major problems. However, further shifts toward a system based entirely on the PLS principles (rather than on mark-up), equity-participation, and without guarantees on deposits and loans, would entail basic changes in the economy and the society. This will be time-consuming and difficult to implement. Important prerequisites for such a transformation would be a further deregulation of the banking system and increased competition, changes in the attitudes of banks towards medium- and long-term lending, comprehensive retraining of staff to handle project-type lending operations, reform of the auditing systems in order to determine more accurately true profit levels, establishment of an efficient capital market, growth of a secondary financial market including specialised investment banking institutions, the establishment of an efficient judicial arbitration system, and a new legal framework to allow for speedy settlement of disputes and protection for borrowers.

FINANCING AND CREDIT OPERATIONS OF THE BANKS

While bank liabilities (other than foreign currency deposits) are composed of either current account deposits, on which no profit is distributed by the bank, or PLS deposits, three broad categories of non-interest modes of financing have been allowed to guide banks' asset operations. First, there is financing by lending, that is, loans not carrying any interest, on which the banks may recover a service charge, and also Qard al-Hasana, (interest-free loans on compassionate grounds). Second, there are trade-related modes of financing, including mark-up, purchase of trade bills, lending on the buy-back basis, leasing, hire-purchase, and financing for development of property on the basis of a development charge. Maximum and minimum rates of charges on these are fixed by the State Bank of Pakistan from time to time. Third, lending can take place under investment-type modes of financing which include Musharaka (partnership), equity participation and purchase of shares, participation term certificates (PTCs), Mudaraba certificates and rent-sharing. While the State Bank of Pakistan determines the ratio for sharing profits, losses are to be shared proportionately among all the financiers.

The following are the primary financing instruments that have evolved over the last four years.

(1) Participation term certificates (PTCs)

PTCs are transferable corporate instruments with maximum maturity of ten years and which allow for temporary partnership or Musharaka. There is, presently, no statutory definition of PTC but it may be viewed as a financial

256

arrangement between a financial institution and the business entity on the basis of profit-and-loss sharing over the maturity period of the certificate. It was introduced as an alternative to debentures (which typically carry a fixed rate of return) for raising medium-term financial resources.

Conceptually, since the financial and economic relationship envisaged under PTCs is that of a partner in a business venture, portfolio selection for the banks requires extensive knowledge and experience with businesses involved. Funds under a typical PTC arrangement may be obtained either from a single financial institution, including the specialised credit institutions, or from a consortium. The business entity is expected to pay to the financial institution or bank, provisionally on a semi-annual basis, an agreed percentage of anticipated profits with a provision for final adjustment at the end of the financial year. In the event of loss, the financial institution shall refund the share of profit received by it on a provisional basis. However, the loss sustained by an entity in any accounting year will first be adjusted against the reserves of the company, and the balance, if any, in the subsequent years shall be available for appropriation between the parties in agreed proportions. The financial institution is also permitted to convert up to 20 per cent of the principal amount of the PTC into ordinary shares at par value, so long as funds against PTCs are outstanding. Lending is secured by a legal mortgage on the fixed assets of the company.

So far, most PTC operations have been handled by the specialised credit institutions, including the Bankers' Equity Limited and the Investment Corporation of Pakistan. PTCs can be traded on the capital market.

(2) Musharaka

Like PTCs, no statutory definition of Musharaka has been specified. However, the Musharaka contract is bilateral between the financial institution and the user of funds. Moreover, the Musharaka contract is not documented in the form of a negotiable instrument and cannot be traded like other financial assets on the capital market.

While Musharaka companies are typically aimed at providing long-term capital for industrial investment, they have so far been used to meet the working capital requirements of the industrial and trade sectors on a non-loan basis. The funds provided for working capital purposes are akin to cash credit or overdraft accounts in which operations can be carried out by depositing and withdrawal of funds. Musharaka companies are deemed to be temporary partnerships in which the commercial bank and the client share in the profit or loss generated by the working capital supplied by each to the project. In practice, the profit-sharing arrangement is drawn up on the basis of future profit projections which, in turn, are based on past averages, duly adjusted according to the future plans and projections and overall state of the economy and the industry in which the firm operates. The client, for his managerial responsibilities, receives an agreed proportion of projected profits from the partnership, with the balance divided between the bank and the client in a mutually agreed ratio within the maximum and minimum ratios laid down by the State Bank of Pakistan. If a loss results, it is to be shared by the client and the bank in the ratio of their contributions to the funds employed in the project.[3] Musharaka agreements have occasionally accorded a greater weight to the bank than justified by contribution, thus enabling the bank to claim a higher percentage of profits compared with the actual investment. This is viewed as a safeguard to protect the interest of the investing bank. Banks also have the right to recall their investment earlier than the agreed period.

(3) Mudaraba

Under the law authorising the establishment of Mudaraba (commenda) companies, Mudaraba can be floated in order to meet the term financing needs of the private sector. Under this arrangement, subscribers participate with their funds, and the manager of funds with his efforts and skills. Profits on investments made out of Mudaraba funds are distributed among the subscribers on the basis of their contributions.

Conceptually, a Mudaraba is an investment fund for which resources are obtained through sale of certificates to subscribers. Commercial banks can serve either as managers or as subscribers. There can be two types of Mudaraba; (i) multi-purpose Mudaraba, that is, a Mudaraba having more than one specific purpose or objective; and (ii) specific purpose Mudaraba. However, all Mudarabas are to be independent of each other and none shall be liable for the liabilities of or be entitled to benefit from the assets of any other Mudaraba or of the Mudaraba company. These companies are subject to comprehensive regulations and safeguards under the Mudaraba Company Law including: (a) each must subscribe at least 10 per cent of the total amount of Mudaraba certificates offered for subscription; and (b) certificate holders must be provided with detailed balance sheets and profits and loss statements of the company at specified intervals.

So far, Mudarabas have primarily been managed by the specialised credit institutions, especially the Bankers' Equity Limited, and have been for single purposes. The first Mudaraba company in the private sector was incorporated in November 1982 and floated its first (multi-purpose) Mudaraba enterprise in early 1985 valued at PRs 25 million. Mudaraba certificates are to be traded and quoted on the stock exchange.

---

3. Once the liability towards the loss has been determined, the bank's share of investment would be reduced by the aggregate amount of its share of loss and the provisional profit earlier taken will also be refunded.

(4) Mark-up

In situations where financing on a PLS basis is not feasible owing to difficulties in determining profits or the short-term maturity of funds required, banks have been authorised to lend on the basis of mark-up. Under this arrangement, the margin of profit or mark-up to the seller is mutually agreed upon between the buyer and the seller in advance. The bank arranges for the purchase of goods requested by the customer and sells them to him on the basis of cost plus the agreed profit margin. The payment is deferred and is made either in a lump sum or in instalments over a specified period. The mark-up is mutually agreed, but must be within the minimum and maximum rates specified by the State Bank of Pakistan. Given the characteristics of banks' asset operations which are largely short-term and oriented towards financing domestic and import trade, as well as financing input requirements, they are amenable to mark-up lending operations. This is the most popular mode of financing in Pakistan at present.[4]

While banks are authorised to charge a mark-up within the limits specified by the State Bank of Pakistan, they cannot charge mark-up on mark-up in the event of delays in repayment; mark-up on mark-up is viewed as interest.

(5) Hire-purchase

Under this mode, banks and other financial institutions can provide funding for the purchase of fixed assets, which can be entirely owned by the financier or in joint ownership with the client; sole control and use of the fixed assets is, however, with the client. In addition to repayment of principal, banks receive rent or a share of the profits earned on the assets. After the amount of acquisition value and the agreed rent is paid in full, the ownership is passed on to the client. Given its nature, the hire-purchasing mode of financing has been used primarily for the acquisition of equipment, machinery, and consumer durables. Since banks cannot increase the amount of instalment to cover losses in the event of delays in payments, there is room for misuse of this mode, thus necessitating closer scrutiny of loan applications by banks.

(6) Other instruments

In addition to the instruments summarised above, banks and other financial

---

4. The mechanism of conducting mark-up transactions is similar to that followed for the cash credit accounts under the interest-based system. At the end of each quarter, the amount of mark-up payable by each account is worked out as banks did in the case of interest payable under the old system.

institutions are permitted to invest under leasing and buy-back arrangements. While the former is particularly useful for medium-and long-term financing, the latter is particularly suitable when profit and loss sharing and other alternatives are not feasible. This is especially relevant for meeting financial requirements for working capital of industry and agriculture as well as import trade financing.

(7) Choice of instruments

While modes of financing are to be determined by agreement between the bank and the client, the authorities have recommended certain preferred combinations of modes and types of transactions. Financing for trade and commerce, which is primarily of short-term nature, should preferably be handled through mark-up and mark-down operations, and through loan on commissions and service charges. Fixed investment in industry, trade, and commerce is to be financed through Musharaka, PTCs, leasing, and hire-purchase; working capital requirements are to be met through Musharaka and mark-up. Given the varied nature of financing requirements in agriculture, modes available for this sector cover a much broader spectrum than in other sectors. While short-term finance is to be provided largely on a mark-up basis, the choice of medium- and long-term lending modes depends upon the purpose. Leasing and hire-purchase are to be the primary instruments for purchase of machinery and equipment, and for dairy and poultry needs. Financing for the development of land, forestry etc, could be on the basis of development charges, mark-up, or PLS modes, depending on the nature of development undertaken. Advances for housing are to be on rent-sharing basis with flexible weights to banks' funds, or on a buy-back and mark-up basis; personal advances for consumer durables are to be on a hire-purchase basis. For purchasing consumption products, financing would be solely against tangible security with buy-back arrangements.

RATES OF RETURN AND CHARGES

Rates of return on deposits and charges on bank financing, including profit-sharing ratios, are ultimately to be determined by market forces. However, in order to ensure an orderly transition from the previous system, in which interest rates were closely regulated, the new system provides for a methodology to determine rates of return on PLS deposits and also lays down maximum and minimum charges for various types of financing modes; banks and clients are free to negotiate charges within these limits.

Banks and other financial institutions receiving PLS deposits are required to declare rates of profit on various types of liabilities, including PLS deposits on a half-yearly basis with prior authorisation of the State Bank of Pakistan. These rates are worked out by a formula that determined net profits accruing to the bank and allocates them to the renumerable liabilities according to their maturities. Allocations are based on differential weights assigned to liabilities according to their relative maturities: the smallest weight is accorded to special notice deposits followed by savings accounts, PLS call deposits from other banks, and term deposits. The highest weight is assigned to equity. In view of differences in the composition of liabilities and net profits, banks would offer different rates of return to depositors even if the average maturity structure were the same. Thus, more efficient banks would offer higher returns than other banks. The authorities believe that the differential rates of return would encourage competition. However, large variances in rates of return would be discouraged in order to avoid possible destabilising shifts in deposits among banks. Even though the depositor-bank relationships are based on PLS, there appears to be an implicit understanding between the bank and the depositor that the deposits will not incur any losses in practice. A comparison of interest rate and rates of return offered by banks on PLS deposit prevailing prior to Islamisation shows that the return on PLS deposits have been generally higher (Table 3.2.1). Rates of return offered by banks have shown variances of up to 10 per cent. Although no data are available on shifts in the size and maturity composition of individual banks' liabilities, differences in their rates of return may have generated transfer of funds among banks, thus encouraging competition.[5]

In order to protect the interests of both borrowers and lenders and to ensure a smooth transition from the highly regulated interest-based system to market-oriented financing, the State Bank of Pakistan is empowered to establish ranges within which financial institutions — including banks and the specialised credit institutions — and borrowers would be permitted to negotiate rates of charges and profit-sharing ratios. The determination of these ranges is also guided by considerations relating to sectoral credit allocation priorities and the need to minimise dislocations arising out of a sharp change in the cost of funding for borrowers. Therefore, the concern so far has been to keep the costs of funding as close to those prevailing under the interest-based system as possible, while allowing a greater role to market forces.

For financing by lending, where loans do not carry interest, banks may recover a service charge not exceeding the proportionate cost of the operations, excluding the cost of funds, provisions for bad and doubtful debts, Qard al-Hasanah and income taxation.[6] The State Bank of Pakistan also specifies ranges of profit that should guide banks and the specialised credit institutions in their lending operations under both trade-related and investment-type modes of

---

5. Some Pakistani banks have downplayed the importance of rates of return differentials in generating transfer of funds. They view quality of services provided to clients as equally (if not more) important in determining stability of the deposit base.

6. The service charge is calculated as a percentage ratio of net administrative expenditures to the average total assets of the bank for each accounting year. The State Bank of Pakistan scrutinises these charges to ensure fairness.

Table 3.2.1: Pakistan: Comparisons of Interest Rates and Rates of Return under PLS Deposits[1] 1981–85

		Notice deposits 7 days		Notice deposits 30 days		Saving deposits		Six-month deposits		One-year deposits		Two-year deposits		Three-year deposits		Four-year deposits		Five-year and above deposits	
		Non PLS	PLS	Non PLS	PLS	Non PLS	PLS	Non PLS	PLS	Non PLS	PLS	Non PLS	PLS	Non PLS	PLS	Non PLS	PLS	Non PLS	PLS
1981	June	5.3	–	...	–	7.6	8.6	9.4	10.9	10.4	12.2	10.5	12.7	11.2	13.7	12.0	14.2	12.0	14.7
	December	6.0	–	...	–	7.6	8.7	10.0	11.2	10.2	12.5	10.6	13.0	11.3	13.9	12.2	14.6	12.2	14.9
1982	June	5.8	–	...	–	7.6	8.6	9.8	10.8	10.3	12.0	11.1	12.7	12.0	13.6	12.3	14.1	12.4	14.6
	December	6.3	–	...	–	7.6	8.2	9.9	10.5	10.6	11.5	11.0	12.1	12.0	13.1	12.2	14.0	12.5	14.3
1983	June	6.3	–	...	–	7.6	8.3	9.9	10.5	10.5	11.6	10.8	12.2	11.8	13.0	12.4	13.6	12.4	14.1
	December	6.3	–	...	–	7.6	7.7	9.9	9.9	10.5	10.8	10.7	11.5	11.7	12.3	12.4	12.8	12.4	13.3
1984	June	5.5	–	6.5	–	7.6	7.5	9.9	9.5	10.5	10.5	11.1	11.0	11.8	12.5	12.5	12.5	12.5	13.5
	December	5.5	5.9	6.5	6.9	7.5	8.0	9.5	10.1	10.5	11.2	11.0	11.8	11.8	12.5	12.3	13.1	12.8	13.6
1985	June	–	5.4	–	6.2	–	8.3	–	10.8	–	11.1	–	12.2	–	13.2	–	14.2	–	15.2

Source: Data supplied by the authorities and the State Bank of Pakistan, *Bulletin*, May 1985.
[1] Rates of return offered by the nationalised banks which constitute about 95 per cent of the banking sector.

Table 3.2.2: Pakistan: Ranges of Profits on Trade Related and Investment
Type Modes of Financing

	Range of profit (%)	
	Minimum	Maximum
1. For exports under the Export Finance Scheme	—	6.0
2. Financing under the Scheme for Financing locally Manufactured Machinery		
(a) Local Sales	—	7.5
(b) Export sales		
(i) Pre-shipment stage	—	6.0
(ii) Post-shipment stage	7.0	no maximum
3. All other, not specified elsewhere		
(a) Trade-related finance	10.0	20.0
(b) Investment-related finance	10.0	no maximum

Source: State Bank of Pakistan, *BCD Circulars No. 23 and 24*, 25 May 1985.

financing. Estimated rates of profitability arising out of different modes serve
as a basis for determining these ranges. Table 3.2.2 summarises these ranges
as they apply presently. In principle, profits earned by a bank should not (actual
profits of the client permitting) be less than the specified minimum profit.
Should losses occur, they are to be shared by all the financiers in proportion to
the respective amounts provided by them. In the case of trade-related modes of
financing, there cannot be a compounding of overdue profit, mark-up, or service
charge. While, under the interest-based system, ceiling rates were specified for
a wide variety of loan operations, the new system accords considerable flexibility to the banks and their clients. None the less, according to banks, a large
proportion of financing has so far been provided at about the same cost as under
the previous system.

EXPERIENCE

It is too early to assess fully the impact of the new system on the operation of
banks in particular and the economy in general. For instance, detailed data are
not yet available on the shifts in banks' asset-liability structures. PLS deposits
have grown sharply since their inception in 1981 and stood at PRs 38 billion at
the end of June 1985, or the equivalent of 28 per cent of total deposits (Table
3.2.3); effective from 1 July 1985, all deposits were converted to a non-interest
basis. Time PLS deposits rose faster than demand deposits, accounting for 65
per cent of total PLS deposits at the end of June 1985. Moreover, most PLS
deposits up to the time of compulsory conversion to a PLS basis were personal
deposits.

Data on the use of PLS funds, available only for 1984, indicate that PLS
deposits were not fully utilised under the non-interest based modes of financing

Table 3.2.3: Pakistan: Growth of PLS Deposits, 1981–85

| | End-December | | | | End-June | |
	1981	1982	1983	1984	1984	1985
Total deposits	70.0	82.8	106.9	111.7	117.9	138.0
Return-bearing deposits	54.7	66.4	86.3	91.0	98.0	—
PLS deposits	6.5	12.9	19.9	29.7	22.1	38.1
PLS deposits/total deposits (per cent)	9.2	15.4	18.6	26.3	18.7	27.6
PLS deposits/return-bearing deposits (per cent)	11.9	19.4	23.1	32.3	22.6	—

Sources: Data supplied by the authorities; State Bank of Pakistan, *Bulletin*, November 1985; and State Bank of Pakistan, *Annual Report*, 1984–85.
Unit: PR billion

Table 3.2.4: Pakistan: Investment of PLS Funds by Commercial Banks[1] 1984

| Financing technique | June 1984 | | December 1984 | |
	Value	Share (%)	Value	Share (%)
Markup and markdown	17,318	86.7	16,263	83.0
Commodity operations	(14,687)	(73.6)	(11,426)	(58.3)
Trading operations	(727)	(3.6)	(2,755)	(14.1)
Documentary inland bills	(298)	(1.5)	(377)	(1.9)
Export bills	(705)	(3.5)	(953)	(4.9)
Import bills	(901)	(4.5)	(613)	(3.2)
Other	(—)	(—)	(139)	(0.7)
Musharaka	617	3.1	777	4.0
Hire-purchase	132	0.7	130	0.7
Rent-sharing (housing loans)	130	0.6	198	1.0
Investment (equity participation)	1,593	8.0	1,970	10.1
Others	176	0.9	249	1.3
Total	19,967	100.0	19,587	100.0
Memorandum items				
Total PLS deposits	22,088		29,684	
PLS financing/PLS deposits (per cent)	90.4		66.0	
Total bank credit and investments	140,206		147,928	
PLS financing/total bank credit and investments (per cent)	14.2	13.2		

Sources: Data supplied by the authorities; Government of Pakistan, *Annual Economic Survey*, 1984–85; and State Bank of Pakistan, *Monthly Bulletin*, November 1985.
[1] These data cover only nationalised banks which account for over 90 per cent of the total banking sector assets and liabilities.
Unit: PR million

(Table 3.2.4). This probably reflected limited experience with these modes of financing and the availability of interest-based alternatives. Nevertheless, PLS investments accounted for about 13 per cent of total bank credit and investments at the end of 1984. Over 80 per cent of such investments were, however, of a short-term nature and were undertaken on the basis of mark-up and mark-down methods of financing. Equity participation and Musharaka accounted for less than 15 per cent of the total, owing in part to a lack of appropriate institutional and legal infrastructure, experience, and trained staff needed to evaluate projects requiring participation by the banks. In view of the predominance of the short-term mark-up-based operations, bank managements did not encounter serious adjustment difficulties; the basis of banking operations has remained the bankers' knowledge of the client and familiarity with their creditworthiness rather than the expected profitability of the activity for which financing was sought.

The specialised credit institutions, which initiated the conversion of their operations toward non-interest-based modes much earlier than banks, have, by and large, transformed all of their operations to the Islamic system. The National Investment Trust (NIT), Investment Corporation of Pakistan (ICP) and the House-Building Finance Corporation (HBFC) were the first institutions that switched their operations from interest to PLS basis in July 1979. The HBFC shifted its new lending operations to sharing in the anticipated rental income of the property in proportion to its share in the investment instead of charging a fixed rate of interest. In order to safeguard its investment, the property is assigned to the HBFC under a deed of assignment for the maturity period of loan. As with the lending operations, if the co-owner falls behind in making payments of rental income, penalties are imposed; in delinquent cases, HBFC may foreclose on the property.

Since ceasing investment of its funds in interest-bearing securities in 1979, the NIT has confined its operations to equity participation. In particular, investments are concentrated in Mudaraba, Musharaka, PTCs, trading, and PLS accounts with commercial banks. Despite a slowdown in net sales after 1980 owing to declining demand, returns paid to subscribers continued to rise and stood at about 12.8 per cent in 1984, compared with 11.5 per cent prior to the Islamisation of its operations.

Transformation of the ICP followed a more gradual approach, reflecting the greater diversity of its financial operations. ICP's activities in the past had focused on: (1) the establishment and operation of closed-end mutual funds with the objectives of providing equity and debt financing to manufacturing firms and investment opportunities for small savers; (2) an investment management programme under which ICP managed the portfolios of individual private investors, while providing to the investor at interest margin loans up to one third the value of the portfolio; (3) the provision of bridging finance for new industrial undertakings through the underwriting of their shares and debentures; and (4) the arrangement of commercial bank lending consortia to meet the fixed investment and working capital financing needs of new industrial undertakings. In July 1979 the ICP mutual funds ceased purchasing interest-bearing assets and began to divest those in their portfolios; beginning 1 October 1980 a new programme was initiated to convert ICP's Investor Scheme to a Sharing Account Scheme that operated on a PLS basis. Under the new scheme the ICP undertakes joint investments with its account holders. Effective from 1 January 1981, the remaining operations of ICP, including underwriting of public issues, bridging loans and debenture financing, was replaced by PTCs.

The Small Business Finance Corporation (SBFC) also eliminated interest from its operations by converting to non-loan operations in June 1980. This was done through the introduction of hire-purchase arrangements and sales on a mark-up basis to finance machinery and equipment, as well as other PLS mechanisms such as the purchase of PTCs. Under the hire-purchase system, SBFC buys the equipment and rents it to the client against a 40 per cent downpayment. The client becomes the owner at the expiration of the specified period and the full payment of instalments. In the interim period, a monthly rental is paid, which at present is 11 per cent per annum. The Bankers Equity Limited (BEL), which was established in 1979 to meet the diverse requirements of industrial financing in the private sector and commenced its operations in January 1980, undertakes its lending operations through direct equity support, underwriting of public issues, purchases of PTCs, and Mudaraba. Most of its financing has so far been provided through PTCs.

IMPACT ON MONETARY POLICY AND BANK REGULATION

Monetary policy in Pakistan is characterised by direct and selective control of growth and distribution of domestic credit. Annual credit plans and specific credit targets are formulated on the basis of objectives underlying the annual development programme. Credit is allocated to the government and non-government sectors on the basis of annual credit plans. Given the predominance of direct controls on the creation and allocation of credit, little use is made of indirect instruments to regulate credit expansion. The minimum cash reserve requirements and liquidity ratios for the bank are utilised primarily for prudential purposes. Similarly, the re-discount rate policy of the State Bank of Pakistan has been of limited use since bank borrowing from the State Bank of Pakistan has, in general, been restricted to certain specific re-financing facilities. Accordingly, the bank rate has not been changed since June 1977.

The elimination of fixed interest rates has not weakened the effectiveness of monetary policy, which continues to be implemented through direct credit allocation. The bank rate policy has been replaced by a regulation that provides for State Bank of Pakistan financing on the basis of profit-and-loss sharing for commercial banks and the specialised credit institutions to ease temporary liquidity difficulties. The rate of profit derived by the State Bank of Pakistan from such finance is equal to the rate of return that the borrowing bank paid on its savings account. If the bank does not maintain any savings account, then the rate of profit shall be the rate of return paid on its deposits of six-month maturity. The State Bank of Pakistan can also provide finance to the specialised credit institutions on a PLS basis with appropriate weights for its funds (which in principle would be more than proportionate to its financial contribution). In the case of profits, they are to be shared by the various financiers based on relative weights attached to their financial contributions. In the event of loss, the amount of loss will be shared by all the financiers, including the State Bank of Pakistan, in proportion to their respective amounts contributed. If new government borrowing modes consistent with PLS principles are developed, this will doubtless affect the size and cost of borrowing thus requiring additional monetary as well as budgetary policy action.

The evolution of the banking system since the implementation of non-interest banking has not necessitated changes in procedures and regulations governing bank supervision. Most bank transactions continue to be short-term in nature and are based on mark-up rather than on taking long-term equity positions. The risk exposure of banks has therefore remained virtually unchanged. Hence, it has not been necessary to alter liquidity and cash reserve requirements. However, procedures for dealing with delays in repayment and delinquent loans have been changed. Under the former system, banks could impose interest on interest when there were delays in payments. The new system does not permit assessing mark-up on mark-up in the event of delays in payments. Instead, a system of fines for late payments is in effect to be imposed by the twelve Banking Tribunals, which are required to render their decisions within four months. Prospects of delays in payments and uncertainties regarding speedy settlement may lead to greater caution on the part of commercial banks. Moreover, an active legal machinery would be needed to implement speedily fines and decisions of the Banking Tribunals for the system to be effective. Even when they participate in Musharaka and Mudaraba operations, banks will continue to be authorised to obtain security and collateral in order to safeguard against defaults and misuse of resources. It is recognised that until such time as business ethics improve and the banks develop sufficient capability to monitor and audit enterprises so that they can be assured of the accuracy of their clients' financial statements, stricter security and collateral requirements will stay in place. The interbank market has not been affected by the new system except that transactions in this market will have to be based on non-interest-bearing instruments. Banks will have to negotiate the rate of return applicable to such transactions. So far this rate has been between the PLS savings rate and that paid on PTCs. The reporting requirements for banks have not been changed thus far.

The banks have been encouraged to develop their own procedure to implement broad guidelines issued by the State Bank of Pakistan. Since most of the transactions are on a mark-up basis, the banks have had little difficulty in accommodating their existing procedures. However, it is recognised that any

267

further transformation of the system requiring a shift in lending toward equity participation would require more substantial changes in procedures and acquisition of skills for designing and monitoring such operations. Similarly, stricter and more effective legal safeguards would be necessary to protect the interests of both lenders and borrowers.

Appendix: Islamic Banking Law in Pakistan

AN ORDINANCE

To provide for matters relating to registration of Modaraba companies and the flotation management and regulation of Modarabas

WHEREAS it is expedient to provide for matters relating to registration Modaraba companies and the flotation, management and regulation of Modarabas and for matters connected therewith or ancillary thereto;

AND WHEREAS the President is satisfied that circumstances exist which render it necessary to take immediate action;

NOW, THEREFORE, in pursuance of the Proclamation of the fifth day of July 1977, read with the Laws (Continuance in Force) Order, 1977 (CMLA Order No 1 of 1977), and in exercise of all powers enabling him in that behalf, the President is pleased to make and promulgate the following Ordinance:

PART 1 — PRELIMINARY

1. Short title, extent and commencement

(1) This Ordinance shall be called the Modaraba Companies and Modaraba (Flotation and Control) Ordinance, 1980.

(2) It extends to the whole of Pakistan.

(3) It shall come into force at once.

2. Definitions

(1) In this Ordinance, unless there is anything repugnant in the subject or context

(a) 'Modaraba' means a business in which a person participates with his money and another with his efforts or skill or both his efforts and skill and shall include Unit Trusts and Mutual Funds by whatever name called;

(b) 'Modaraba Certificate' means a certificate or definite denomination issued to the subscriber of the Modaraba acknowledging receipt of money subscribed by him;

(c) 'Modaraba company' means a company engaged in the business of floating and managing Modaraba;

(d) 'Modaraba fund' means a fund raised through flotation of Modaraba;

(e) 'prescribed' means prescribed by rules;

(f) 'Registrar' means the Registrar appointed under section 3;

(g) 'rules' means rules made under this Ordinance; and

(h) 'Tribunal' means a tribunal constituted under section 24.

(2) All terms and expressions used but not defined in this Ordinance shall have the same meaning as in the Companies Act, 1913 (VII of 1913).

3. Appointment of Registrar

The Federal Government may, by notification in the official Gazette, appoint a person to be the Registrar for the purpose of this Ordinance.

PART II — REGISTRATION OF MODARABA COMPANIES

4.

No company is to operate without registration — no Modaraba company shall operate without registration with the Registrar.

5. Eligibility for registration

(1) A company shall be eligible for registration as a Modaraba company if it fulfils the following conditions, namely:

(a) that it is registered under the Companies Act, 1913 (VII of 1913), or is a corporate body formed under any law in force and owned or controlled, whether directly or through a company or corporation, by the Federal Government or a Provincial Government;

(b) that, being a company solely engaged in the flotation and management of Modaraba, it has a paid-up capital of not less than five million rupees;

(c) that none of its directors, officers or employees has been convicted of fraud, breach of trust or of an offence involving moral turpitude;

(d) that none of its directors, officers or employees has been adjudged an insolvent or has suspended payment or has compounded with his creditors;

(e) that its promoters are, in the opinion of the Registrar, persons of means and integrity and have knowledge of matters which the company may have to deal with as a Modaraba company; and

(f) that, being a company also engaged in business other than flotation and management of Modaraba, it has a paid-up capital of such amount and of such nature as may be prescribed.

6. Application for registration

(1) A company which is eligible for registration as a Modaraba company may make an application for registration to the Registrar in such form and with such documents as may be prescribed.

(2) The Registrar, if he is satisfied after such enquiry and after obtaining such further information as he may consider necessary that the application is eligible for registration and that it is in the public interest to do so, may grant registration to such company on such conditions as he may deem fit.

(3) In particular and without prejudice to the generality of the powers conferred by sub-section 2, such conditions may include:

(a) investment to be made;
(b) information and returns to be furnished to the Registrar;
(c) business to be undertaken; and
(d) restriction on transfer of shares by promoters, sponsors or persons holding controlling interests.

PART III — PROVISIONS APPLICABLE TO MODARABAS

7. Types of Modaraba

(1) Modaraba may be of two descriptions:

(a) *Multipurpose Modaraba*: that is to say a Modaraba having more than one specific purpose or objective.
(b) *Specific purpose Modaraba*: that is to say a Modaraba having one specific purpose or objective.

(2) A Modaraba may be either for a fixed period or for an indefinite period.

8. Creation and maintenance of Modaraba

(1) A Modaraba company registered under section 4 shall apply to the Registrar, in such form and with such documents as may be prescribed, for permission to float Modaraba.

(2) An application for flotation of Modaraba shall be accompanied by a prospectus which shall contain, inter alia, the following information, namely:

(a) the name and type of Modaraba;
(b) the conditions and amounts of the Modaraba to be floated and the division thereof into Modaraba Certificates of fixed amounts;

271

(c) the business scheme, prospects and mode of distribution of profit;

(d) the amount to be subscribed by the Modaraba company to the Modaraba in its own name supported by evidence about its ability to meet the commitment;

(e) the form of the Modaraba Certificate; and

(f) such other matters as may be prescribed.

(3) The application, the prospectus and the documents filed therewith shall be authenticated by all the directors of the company.

9. Religious Board

The Federal Government shall, for the purpose of this Ordinance, constitute a Religious Board which shall consist of such members and shall have such functions, terms and conditions as may be prescribed.

10. Business of Modaraba

No Modaraba shall be a business which is opposed to the injunctions of Islam and the Registrar shall not permit the flotation of a Modaraba unless the Religious Board has certified in writing that the Modaraba is not a business opposed to the injunctions of Islam.

11. Authorisation

The Registrar may, after obtaining from the Religious Board a certificate to the effect mentioned in section 10 and on being satisfied that it is in the public interest so to do, grant a certificate in the prescribed form authorising the flotation of Modaraba on such conditions as he may deem fit, including conditions as to the business to be undertaken, expenses relating to the management of the Modaraba Fund, preservation of assets and other matters relating to the mode of management and distribution of profit.

Provided that, before issuing the certificate of authorisation, the Registrar may require the Modaraba company to make such modifications, additions or omissions in the prospectus as the Religious Board may have indicated or as he may deem fit.

12. Modaraba to be a legal person

(1) A Modaraba shall sue and be sued in its own name through the Modaraba company.

(2) The assets and liabilities of such Modaraba shall be separate and distinct from those of another Modaraba as also from those of the Modaraba company.

13. Conditions applicable to Modaraba

(1) No allotment of Modaraba Certificates shall be made unless a prospectus approved by the Registrar has been issued and the minimum amount stated in the prospectus to be the amount which must be raised in order to provide for the business operations and expenses has been subscribed.

(2) All moneys received from the applicants for Modaraba Certificates for a Modaraba shall be deposited and kept in a separate account in a scheduled bank as defined in the State Bank of Pakistan Act, 1956 (XXXIII of 1956), until they are refunded in accordance with the provisions of subsection 3 or until it is certified by the Registrar that Modaraba Certificates have been allotted in an amount not less than the minimum amount referred to in subsection 1.

(3) If the subscription referred to in subsection 1 has not been received from the applicants it shall be refunded to them within fifteen days of the said date and the Modaraba company and the directors thereof shall be jointly and severally liable to repay the money which is not so refunded.

(4) The Modaraba company shall issue Modaraba Certificates within thirty days from the date of allotment.

(5) The Modaraba company shall maintain a register of holders of Modaraba Certificates in such form and in such manner as may be prescribed.

(6) The Modaraba company shall maintain separate bank account, funds, assets and liabilities of each Modaraba.

(7) No Modaraba shall be liable for the liabilities, or be entitled to benefit from the assets, of any other Modaraba company.

(8) Modaraba Certificates shall be transferable in the manner provided for in the prospectus of the Modaraba.

14. Preparation and circulation of annual accounts, reports etc

(1) The Modaraba company shall, within six months from the close of the accounting year of the Modaraba, prepare and circulate to the holders of Modaraba Certificates:

(a) annual balance sheet and profit and loss account in such form and manner as may be prescribed;
(b) a report of the auditor on the balance sheet and profit and loss account;
(c) a report by the Modaraba company on the state of affairs, activities and business prospects of the Modaraba and the amount of profits to be distributed to the certificate holders.

273

(2) In addition to the documents referred to in subsection 1, the Modaraba company shall furnish to the Registrar and to the holders of Modaraba Certificates such reports, accounts and information as may be prescribed or as the Registrar may, at any time by an order in writing require.

(3) The Modaraba company shall submit five copies of the accounts, statements and reports referred to in subsections 1 and 2 to the Registrar simultaneously with the circulation of these documents to the holders of Modaraba Certificates.

15. Audit of accounts

(1) The accounts of a Modaraba shall be audited by an auditor who is a chartered accountant within the meanings of the Chartered Accounts Ordinance, 1961 (X of 1961), appointed by the Modaraba company with the approval of the Registrar and such auditor shall have the same power, duties and liabilities as an auditor of a company has under the Companies Act, 1913 (VII of 1913) and such other powers, duties and liabilities as are, or may be, provided in this Ordinance and the rules.

(2) In addition to other matters, the auditor shall also state in his report whether in his opinion the business conducted, investments made and expenditures incurred by the Modaraba are in accordance with the objects, terms and conditions of the Modaraba.

16. Prohibition of false statement etc

No Modaraba company, director, officer, employee or agent or auditor thereof shall, in any document, prospectus, report, return, accounts,information or explanation required to be furnished in pursuance of this Ordinance or the rules, or in any application made under this Ordinance or the rules, make any statement or give any information which he knows or has reasonable cause to believe to be false or incorrect or omit any material fact thereof.

17. Conditions applicable to Modaraba company

(1) No Modaraba company shall engage in any business which is of the same nature and competes with the business carried on by a Modaraba floated or controlled by it.

(2) No Modaraba company or any of its directors or officers or their relatives shall obtain a loan, advance or credit from the funds of the Modaraba or on the security of the assets of the Modaraba. *Explanation*: In this subsection, 'relative', in relation to a director or officer, means the spouse, brother or sister

or any of the lineal ascendants or descendants of the director or officer.

(3) A Modaraba company shall subscribe in each Modaraba floated by it not less than 10 per cent of the total amount of Modaraba Certificates offered for subscription.

18. Remuneration of Modaraba company

The remuneration of a Modaraba company in respect of a Modaraba floated by it shall be a fixed percentage of the net annual profits of the Modaraba and shall not exceed 10 per cent of such net annual profits computed in the manner to be prescribed.

19. Cancellation of registration

(1) Where the Registrar is of the opinion that a Modaraba company has contravened or has failed to comply with any provision of this Ordinance or the rules or with any direction made or given thereunder, he may, if he considers necessary in the public interest so to do, by order in writing:

(a) cancel the registration of the Modaraba company; and
(b) remove the Modaraba company from the management of the Modaraba floated by it; provided that no such order shall be made without giving the Modaraba company an opportunity of being heard.

(2) The Modaraba company removed from the management of a Modaraba under clause (b) of subsection (1) shall not be entitled to or be paid any compensation or damages for loss or termination of office.

(3) A Modaraba company removed from the management of a Modaraba under clause (b) of subsection (1) shall not be entitled to float any Modaraba.

(4) A Modaraba company aggrieved by an order of the Registrar under subsection (1) may prefer an appeal to the Federal Government within thirty days of the date of the order.

20. Appointment of Administrator

(1) If:

(a) the Registrar has reason to believe that a moderate company has been conducting the affairs of a Modaraba in a manner prejudicial to the interest of the Modaraba or the holders of Modaraba Certificates or in a fraudulent or unlawful manner or has committed a default in complying

275

with the provisions of this Ordinance or the rules or with any direction made or given thereunder or any condition of the Modaraba;

(b) the registration of a Modaraba company has been cancelled; or

(c) any other Modaraba under the management of the Modaraba company has been ordered to be wound up by the Tribunal, the Registrar, after affording the Modaraba company an opportunity of being heard, may, without prejudice to any other action under the law, by order in writing:

(i) appoint an administrator to take over and manage the Modaraba in place of the Modaraba company for such period as the Registrar may specify; or

(ii) require the Modaraba company to carry out such changes in the management and procedure as may be specified; and

(iii) remove the Modaraba company and appoint another Modaraba company in its place to manage the Modaraba.

(2) The Registrar shall not make an order under subsection (1) without the approval of the Federal Government.

21. Enquiries

(1) The Registrar may, on his own motivation or on an application made by the holders of Modaraba Certificates the value of which is not less than 10 per cent of the total subscribed amount of the Modaraba, by an order in writing cause an enquiry to be made by a person appointed by him in this behalf into the affairs of a Modaraba company or the Modaraba or any business transaction thereof.

(2) Where any enquiry under subsection (1) has been ordered every director, manager or other officer of the Modaraba company to which the enquiry relates and every other person who has had any dealing with such Modaraba company or director or officer shall furnish such information or document in his custody or power or within his knowledge relating to or having a bearing on the subject matter of the enquiry as the person conducting the enquiry may by notice in writing require.

(3) The person conducting the enquiry under subsection (1) may for the purpose of such enquiry enter into any premises belonging to or in occupation of the Modaraba company or of the person to whom the enquiry relates and may call for, inspect and seize books of accounts and documents in possession of any such Modaraba company, director, manager or any other officer or employee thereof.

(4) The person holding an enquiry under subsection (1) shall, for the purpose of such enquiry, have the same powers as are vested in a court under the Code of Civil Procedure, 1908 (Act V of 1908), when trying a suit in respect of the following matters, namely:

(a) enforcing the attendance of a person and examining him on oath or affirmation;

(b) compelling the discovery and production of documents; and

(c) issuing commissions for the examination of witnesses.

(5) On receipt of the report of the person conducting the enquiry, the Registrar shall take such action as he may consider necessary on the basis of the report.

22. Circumstances in which Modarabas may be wound up voluntarily

(1) A Modaraba floated for a fixed period or for a specific purpose shall be wound up by the Modaraba company itself on the expiry of the period fixed for the Modaraba or the accomplishment of the purpose of the Modaraba, as the case may be, provided the following conditions are fulfilled, namely:

(a) all the directors of the Modaraba company shall make a declaration verified by an affidavit to the effect that they have made a full enquiry about the affairs of the Modaraba and, having done so, have formed the opinion that the Modaraba will be able to discharge its liabilities, pay the amount subscribed by the holders of Modaraba Certificates and all their other dues in full within a period of twelve months from the date of expiry of the period fixed for the Modaraba or the accomplishment of the purpose of the Modaraba, as the case may be;

(b) the declaration referred to in clause (a) shall be supported by a report of the auditor of the Modaraba on the affairs of the Modaraba and shall have no effect unless it is filed with and approved by the Registrar within ninety days of the date of expiry of the period fixed for the Modaraba or the accomplishment of the purpose of the Modaraba, as the case may be.

(2) Any person aggrieved by the decision of the Registrar under clause (b) of subsection (1) may prefer an appeal to the Federal government within thirty days of the day on which the decision is given.

23. Circumstances in which Modaraba may be wound up by the Tribunal

(1) A Modaraba shall be wound up by the Tribunal on the application made by the Registrar if:

(a) in the case of a Modaraba for a fixed period on the expiry of that period or, in the case of a Modaraba for a specific purpose on the accomplishment of its purpose, the declaration referred to in section 22 has not been filed with the Registrar within the period specified in that section;

(b) in the case of any Modaraba, the Registrar has declared that:

(i) the Modaraba is unable to discharge its liabilities;

(ii) the accumulated losses of the Modaraba exceed 50 per cent of the total amount subscribed by the holders of the Modaraba Certificates; or

(iii) the business of the Modaraba is being, or has been, conducted for a fraudulent purpose or with intent to defraud the holders of the Modaraba Certificates, or its creditors or any other person.

(c) the Tribunal is of the opinion that it is just and equitable that the Modaraba should be wound up.

(2) The Registrar may make an application to the Tribunal for the winding up of a Modaraba on receipt of an application under subsection (1) of section 21 or of the report of an enquiry under that section relating to the Modaraba.

(3) No application shall be made by the Registrar under subsection (1) or (2) without giving the Modaraba company an opportunity of being heard.

24. Constitution of Tribunal

(1) The Federal Government may, by notification, in the official Gazette, constitute one or more Tribunals for the purpose of this Ordinance and, where it constitutes more than one Tribunal, shall specify in the notification the area within which, or the cause of cases in respect of which, each such Tribunal shall exercise jurisdiction under this Ordinance.

(2) A Tribunal shall consist of a person who is, or has been, or is qualified to be a judge of High Court.

25. Powers of a Tribunal

(1) A Tribunal shall:

(a) in the exercise of its civil jurisdiction, have in respect of a claim filed by a holder of Modaraba Certificates against the Modaraba company or by a Modaraba company against any other party with whom it has entered into business transactions relating to Modaraba Fund, or in respect of an application by the Registrar for the winding up of a Modaraba company, all the powers vested in a civil court under the code of Civil Procedure, 1908 (Act V of 1908);

(b) in the exercise of its criminal jurisdiction, try the offences punishable under this ordinance and shall, for that purpose, have the same powers as are vested in the Court of a Sessions Judge under the Code of Criminal Procedure, 1898 (Act V of 1898).

Provided that a Tribunal shall not take cognisance of any offence punishable under this Ordinance except on a complaint in writing made by the Registrar or an officer authorised by him in writing; and

(c) exercise and perform such other powers and functions as are, or may be, conferred upon or assigned to it by or under this Ordinance.

(2) All proceedings before a Tribunal shall be deemed to be judicial proceedings within the meaning of sections 193 and 228 of the Pakistan Penal Code (Act XLV of 1860), and the Tribunal should be deemed to be a court for the purpose of sections 480 and 482 of the Code of Criminal Procedure, 1898 (Act V of 1898).

(3) No court other than the Tribunal shall have or exercise any jurisdiction with respect of any matter to which the jurisdiction of the Tribunal extends under this Ordinance.

26. Procedure of the Tribunal

(1) Matters before the Tribunal shall come up for regular hearing as expeditiously as possible and, except in extraordinary circumstances and on grounds to be recorded, the Tribunal shall hear the cases from day to day.

(2) In the exercise of its civil jurisdiction, the Tribunal shall, in all suits before it, including suits for recovery of moneys, follow the summary procedure provided for in Order XXXVII of the First Schedule to the Code of Civil Procedure, 1908 (Act V of 1908).

27. Powers of Tribunal on hearing application for winding up of Modaraba

(1) If, after hearing the application for winding up of a Modaraba, the Tribunal decides to wind up the same it shall appoint a liquidator in consultation with the Registrar and approve a general scheme of winding up.

(2) After a winding up order has been passed by the Tribunal, the Modaraba company shall forthwith hand over charge of the Modaraba to the liquidator and furnish him with such statements, documents, records, information and other material as may be required by him.

(3) The liquidator shall conduct the winding up of proceedings in the prescribed manner under the control and directions of the Tribunal.

(4) The winding up proceedings shall be completed within a period of one

year from the date of appointment of the liquidator, unless the Tribunal, for special reasons to be recorded in writing, extends the period.

(5) During the winding up proceedings, the Tribunal may allow the administrator appointed by the Registrar under section 20, if any, to continue to function or may appoint an administrator to manage the Modaraba until the disposal of the proceedings.

28. Judgement and decree

(1) A Tribunal shall, after the case has been heard, pronounce judgement as early as practicable and on such judgement a decree shall follow forthwith.

(2) The Tribunal shall, on the application of the decree-holder, forthwith order execution of the decree:

Provided that, if the decree is for money, the recovery in execution thereof shall be made as arrears of land revenue.

29. Finality of orders

Subject to the provisions for appeals as provided in section 30, no court or other authority shall call or permit to be called in question any order, judgement or sentence of the Tribunal or the legality or propriety of anything done or intended to be done by the Tribunal under this Ordinance.

30. Appeals

(1) Any person aggrieved by any order, judgement, decree or sentence of the Tribunal may, within thirty days of such order, judgement, decree or sentence, prefer an appeal to the High Court within whose jurisdiction the order, judge-ment, decree or sentence is passed;

Provided that no appeal shall lie from an interlocutory order which does not dispose of the entire case before the Tribunal.

(2) An appeal under subsection (1) shall be heard by a bench of two judges of the High Court and shall lie on any one of the following grounds, namely:

(a) the decision being contrary to law or to some usage having the force of law; or

(b) the decision having failed to determine a material issue of law or usage having the force of law; or

(c) a substantial error apparent in the procedure provided by or under this Ordinance, which may possibly have led to an error in the decision.

(3) An appeal may be preferred under this section from a decision made ex-parte.

31. Punishment

(1) Whoever contravenes the provisions of sections 4, 10, 13, 14, 16 or 17 shall be punishable with imprisonment of either description for a term which may extend to three years and with a fine which may extend to five hundred thousand rupees.

(2) Where the contravention referred to in subsection (1) has caused loss to the Modaraba or any other person, a further fine to the extent of the loss shall be imposed.

32. Penalty

If any person:

(a) refuses or fails to furnish any documents, return or information which he is required to furnish by or under this Ordinance; or

(b) refuses or fails to comply with any condition imposed or made by the Federal Government or direction made or given under this Ordinance or the rules; or

(c) contravenes or otherwise fails to comply with any provision of this Ordinance or the rules other than those referred to in subsection (1) of section 31, the Registrar may, if he is satisfied, after giving the person an opportunity of being heard, that the refusal, failure or contravention was wilful, by order, direct that such person shall pay to the Federal Government by way of penalty such sum not exceeding one hundred thousand rupees as may be specified in the order and, in the case of continuing default, a further sum calculated at a rate not exceeding one thousand rupees for every day after the issue of such order during which the refusal, failure or contravention continues.

33. Liability of director, manager or officer of a company

(1) Where the person guilty of an offence referred to in subsection (1) of section 31 or in section 32 is a company or other body corporate, every director, manager, or other officer responsible for the conduct of its affairs shall, unless he proves that the offence was committed without his knowledge, or that he exercised all diligence to prevent its commission, be deemed to be guilty of the offence.

(2) Any sum directed to be paid under section 32 shall be recoverable as an arrear of land revenue.

(3) No prosecution for an offence against this Ordinance or the rules shall be instituted in respect of the same facts on which a penalty has been imposed under section 32.

34. Powers of the Registrar in relation to certain proceedings

In any proceedings under section 32, the Registrar shall have the same powers as are vested in a court under the Code of Civil Procedure, 1908 (Act V of 1908), when trying a suit in respect of the following matters, namely:

(a) enforcing attendance of a person and examining him on oath or affirmation; and

(b) compelling the discovery and production of documents.

35. Application of fine

The Tribunal imposing any fine under this Ordinance may direct that the whole or any part thereof shall be applied in or towards:

(a) payment of costs of the proceedings;

(b) payment to an aggrieved party of compensation for any loss caused by the offence;

(c) payment of compensation for any loss mentioned in subsection (2) of section 31.

36. Enforcement of provisions of the Ordinance etc

(1) If a Modaraba company makes default in complying with any provisions of this Ordinance or a direction made or given under this Ordinance and fails to make good the default within thirty days of the service of a notice to the Modaraba company requiring it to do so, the Tribunal may, on an application made to the Tribunal by the Registrar, make an order directing the Modaraba company and any director or officer thereof to make good the default within such period as may be specified in the order.

(2) Nothing in this section shall be deemed to prejudice the operation of any provision of this Ordinance providing for the imposition of penalties on the Modaraba company or its directors and officers in respect of any such default as aforesaid.

37. Exemption from tax

The income of a Modaraba shall be exempt from tax under the Income Tax Ordinance, 1979 (XXXI of 1979), if not less than ninety per cent of its profits in a year is distributed to the holders of the Modaraba Certificates.

38. Power of Federal Government to exempt etc

The Federal Government may, by notification in the official Gazette, exempt from the requirements of subsection (1) and (3) of section 17 a company or a body corporate formed under any law and owned or controlled by the Federal Government or a Provincial Government, whether directly or through a company or corporations set up by such Government.

39.

Delegation Registrar may, by notification in the official Gazette, delegate, subject to such limitations, restrictions or conditions, if any, as he may, from time to time specify, such of his powers and functions under this Ordinance as he may deem fit to any officer subordinate to him.

40. Indemnity

No suit, prosecution or other legal proceeding shall lie against the Federal Government or the Registrar or any other officer for anything which is in good faith done or intended to be done under this Ordinance or any rules.

41. Power to make rules

(1) The Federal Government may, by notification in the official Gazette, make rules for carrying out the purposes of this Ordinance.

(2) In particular and without prejudice to the generality of the foregoing power, such rules may include:

(a) the duties and functions of the Registrar;
(b) terms and conditions of a Tribunal;
(c) procedure relating to a Tribunal;
(d) composition, terms and conditions of the Religious Board;
(e) procedure relating to the Religious Board;
(f) form, contents and other requirements of a prospectus;

283

(g)   issue and allotment of Modaraba Certificates;

(h)   maintenance of Modaraba accounts and funds;

(i)   form of balance sheet and profit and loss account;

(j)   audit and auditor's certificate;

(k)   annual and periodical accounts and reports;

(l)   inspection of record and supply of copies of documents;

(m)   matters and procedures relating to enquiries;

(n)   charging and determination of fees payable under this Ordinance;

(o)   such other matters as are to be or may be prescribed.

42. Act to override other laws

The provisions of this Ordinance shall have effect notwithstanding anything contained in the Companies Act, 1913 (VII of 1913), or any other law for the time being in force.

43. Removal of difficulties

If any difficulty arises in giving effect to any provision of this Ordinance, the Federal Government may make such order, not inconsistent with the provisions of this Ordinance, as may appear to it to be necessary for the purpose of removing the difficulty.

General M Zia-Ul-Haq
President

THE ELIMINATION OF INTEREST RATES

The law governing operations of the banking system (Banking Companies Ordinance, 1962) has remained unchanged; several measures have been introduced to phase out fixed interest rate as the basis for financial transactions. Reproduced below are three primary circulars issued by the State Bank of Pakistan that aim at eliminating interest rate.

State Bank of Pakistan, Banking Control Department, Central Directorate, Karachi.

BCD Circular No. 13, 20 June 1984

Elimination of 'Riba' from the banking system

1. As has been announced by the Finance Minister, it is the intention of Government that the Banking System should shift over to Islamic modes of financing during the course of the next financial year. These modes of financing have been described in Annexure I. This shift will take place according to the following program.

(i) As from the 1st July, 1984, all banking companies will be free to make finances available in any of the modes of financing listed in Annexure I. However, as a transitional arrangement, they will also be free to lend on the basis of interest, provided that no accommodation for working capital will be provided or renewed on interest basis for a period of more than six months.

(ii) As from the 1st January, 1985, all finances provided by a banking company to the Federal Government, Provincial Governments, public sector corporations and public or private joint stock companies shall be only in any one of the modes indicated in Annexure I.

(iii) As from the 1st April 1985, all finances provided by a banking company to all entities, including individuals, shall be on the same basis as mentioned in (ii) above.

(iv) The appropriate mode of financing to be adopted in any particular case will be settled by agreement between the banking company and the client. Some possible modes of financing for various transactions have been shown in Annexure II.

(v) As from the 1st July, 1985, no banking company shall accept any interest-bearing deposits. As from that date, all deposits accepted by a banking company shall be on the basis of participation in profit and loss of the banking company, except deposits received in Current Account on which no interest or profit shall be given by the banking company.

2. The instructions contained in items (i), (ii), and (iii) above shall, however, not apply to on-lending of foreign loans which will continue to be governed by the terms of the loans. Likewise, the instructions contained in item (v) above shall not apply to foreign currency deposits.

3. The above instructions are being issued under the Banking Companies Ordinance 1962. Further instructions, where necessary, will follow.

Permissible modes of financing

(A) Financing by lending:

(i) Loans not carrying any interest on which the banks may recover a service charge not exceeding the proportionate cost of the operation, excluding the cost of funds and provision for bad and doubtful debts. The maximum service charge permissible to each bank will be determined by the State Bank from time to time.

(ii) Qard-e-Hasana loans given on compassionate ground free of any interest or service charge and repayable if and when the borrower is able to pay.

(B) Trade-related modes of financing including the following:

(i) Purchase of goods by banks and their sale to clients at appropriate mark-up in price on deferred payment basis. In case of default, there should be no mark-up on mark-up.
(ii) Purchase of trade bills.
(iii) Purchase of moveable or immoveable property by the banks from their clients with Buy-Back agreement or otherwise.
(iv) Leasing.
(v) Hire-purchase.
(vi) Financing for development of property on the basis of a development charge.

The maximum and minimum rates of return to be derived by the banks from these modes of financing will be as may be determined by the State Bank from time to time.

(C) Investment type modes of financing. These modes include the following:

(i) Musharika or profit and loss sharing.
(ii) Equity participation and purchase of shares.
(iii) Purchase of participation term certificates and Modaraba Certificates.
(iv) Rent-sharing.

The maximum and minimum rates of profit to be derived by the banks from such transactions will be as may be prescribed by the State Bank from time to time. However, should any losses occur, they will have to be proportionately shared among all the financiers.

Possible modes of financing for various transactions

Nature of Business   *Basis of Financing*
I.   *Trade and Commerce*
      (a) Commodity operations of   Mark-up price.
          the Federal and Provincial
          Governments and their
          agencies.

286

(b) Export Bills purchased/ negotiated under Letters of Credit (other than those under reserve).

(i) Exchange rate differential in the case of foreign currency bills.

(ii) Commission or mark-down in the case of Rupee bills.

(c) Documentary Inland Bills drawn against Letters of Credit purchased/ discounted

Mark-down in price.

(d) Import Bills drawn under Letters of Credit.

Mark-up in price.

(e) Financing of exports under the State Bank's Export Finance Scheme and the Scheme for Financing Locally Manufactured Machinery.

Service charge/Concessional service charge.

(f) Other items of trade and commerce.

Fixed investment
Equity participation, PTCs, leasing or hire-purchase.
Working capital
Profit and loss sharing or mark-up.

II.   *Industry*

Fixed investment
Equity participation, PTCs, Modaraba certificates, leasing, hire-purchase or mark-up.
Working capital
Profit and loss sharing or mark-up.

III.   *Agriculture and Fisheries*
       (a) Short-term finance

Mark-up. In the case of small farmers and small fishermen who are at present eligible for interest-free loans finance for the specified inputs, etc., up to the prescribed amount may also be on mark-up basis. The mark-up amount may however be waived in the case of those who repay the finance within the stipulated period and payment of the mark-up made by the State Banks by debit to Federal Government Account.

(b) Medium- and Long-Term
Finance

(i) Tubewells and other wells	Leasing or hire-purchase in addition to ownership of machinery, banks may create charge on the land in their favor as in the case of other loans to the farmers under the Passbook System.
(ii) Tractors, trailers and other farm machinery and transport (including fishing boats, solar energy plants, etc.)	Hire-purchase or leasing.
(iii) Plough cattle, milk cattle, and other livestock	
(iv) Dairy and poultry	PLS/mark-up/hire-purchase leasing.
(v) Storage and other farm construction (viz., sheds for animals, fencing, etc.)	Leasing or rent-sharing basis with flexible weightage to the bank's funds.
(vi) Land development	Development charge.
(vii) Orchards, including nurseries	Mark-up, development charge, or PLS basis.
(viii) Forestry	Mark-up, development charge, or PLS.
(ix) Water course improvement	Development charge.

IV. *Housing* — Rent sharing with flexible weightage to bank's funds or buy-back cum mark-up.

V. *Personal Advances* (other than those for business purposes and housing)

(a) Consumer durables (cars, motorcycles, scooters and household goods).	Hire-purchase.
(b) For consumption purposes.	Against tangible security buy-back arrangement.

BCD Circulation No. 26, 26 November 1984

Elimination of 'riba' from the banking system — rate of service charge recoverable on finances provided by way of lending other than 'Qard-e-Hasana'

1. Please refer to item (A)(i) of Annexure I to BCD Circular No. 13 dated the 20th June, 1984.

2. The maximum rate of service charge which a bank/development finance institution may recover on its loans other than 'Qard-e-Hasana' during an accounting year shall be calculated by dividing the total of its expenses excluding cost of funds and expenditure relating to bad assets and income taxation by the mean of its total assets at the beginning and end of the year and rounding off the result to the nearest decimal of a percentage point. An illustration of this is given in the annexure.

3. A bank/DFI may recover service charge during an accounting year on the basis of the rate determined by it which shall be communicated by it to each of its branches, as also intimated to the State Bank at least a week before commencement of each accounting year. However, immediately after its accounts for an accounting year are audited, it shall work out the maximum rate at which service charge was recoverable during that accounting year on the basis of the methodology laid down in paragraph 2 above and in case the rate so worked out is less than the rate determined for the year earlier, it shall refund the excess recoveries if any, to its clients concerned within one month of audit of the accounts. It shall also submit to the State Bank for post-facto audit, within five months of the close of the accounting year, the rate worked out as above along with a certificate, in case the rate is lower than the one determined earlier for the year, to the effect that excess recoveries have been refunded to the clients concerned.

4. The above instructions are being issued under the Banking Companies Ordinance, 1962.

Annexure to BCD circular no. 26, 26 November 1984

Name of Bank _____

Maximum rate of Service Charge recoverable for the year ended _____

Calculation Sheet

(Figures in Millions
of Rs)
For the above year

1. Total expenditure (total income less balance of profit, i.e., gross profit, as per audited Profit and Loss Account) — 4,775

2. Less:
    (i) Interest and return on deposits, borrowings, etc. — 3,600
    (ii) Income taxation and provision for it if charged to Expenses Account — 50
    (iii) Bad assets provision and write-offs by direct debit to Expenses Account — 25
    (iv) Total of (i) to (iii) — 3,675
3. Administrative expendiuture (1 minus 2(iv)) — 1,100
4. Total Assets at the beginning of the year — 29,000
5. Total Assets at the end of the year — 35,000
6. Average of the total assets at the beginning and end of the year — 32,000

Service Charge in percentage terms
to the nearest decimal point

$$(3 \text{ divided by } 6 \text{ and multiplied by } 100) = \frac{1,100 \times 100}{32,000} = 3.4\%$$

BCD Circular No. 34, 26 November 1984

Elimination of 'riba' from the banking system — determination of rates of profit on various types of PLS liabilities of the banks and development finance institutions

1. In exercise of the powers vested in it under the Banking Companies Ordinance, 1962, the State Bank of Pakistan is pleased to direct that a banking company or development finance institution receiving PLS deposits shall declare rates of profit on various types of its PLS deposits on a half yearly basis for the half year ending 30th June and the half year ending 31st December each year after obtaining clearance from the State Bank in regard to the rates of profit proposed to be declared. The proposed rates should be worked out after compiling the relevant information in the enclosed proformae 'A', 'B', 'C', 'D', and

'E' which also give numerical illustrations for guidance in determining the rates. Proposals along with information in the aforesaid proformae in regard to the rates proposed to be declared for each half year shall be submitted to the State Bank by the 20th of the month succeeding the half year.

2. As explained in the proforma 'E' enclosed, while distributed noninterest income in the manner spelt out therein, the following weightages will be given to PLS deposits, PLS borrowings, and equity:

Type and Maturity	Weightage to be given
A. Deposits:	
I. Special notice deposits:	
(i) Withdrawal at 7 to 29 days' notice	0.65
(ii) Withdrawal at notice of 30 days or over	0.75
II. Savings accounts	1.00
III. PLS Call Deposits from other banks	Weightage as agreed to by the banks concerned.
IV. Term deposits:	
(i) For terms up to and inclusive of 6 months	1.00 + 0.05 for each month of the term of the deposit.
(ii) For terms in excess of 6 months	1.3 for the first six months plus 0.01 for each subsequent month of the term of the deposit, subject to a maximum of 2.08.
B. PLS Borrowings	Borrowings of various maturities will be given weightages as for term deposits of corresponding maturities.
C. Equity	Not exceeding 5 as may be determined by the concerned bank.

The amount of non-interest income distributable on PLS deposits of each type/maturity will be converted into an annual percentage rate of profit and the rate rounded off to the nearest one-tenth of a percentage point as illustrated in proforma 'E'.

3. It would appear that if the non-interest earning assets are low as compared to PLS deposits, the rate of return on such deposits will be low as in such a situation as part of the funds will remain unutilized. The Banks/DFIs should carefully watch the growth of PLS deposits and ensure that their investments in non-interest bearing assets are substantially higher than the deposits. If for any reason this is not feasible at any stage, the unutilized funds should be deposited

with the State Bank on PLS basis as already permitted under BCD Circular No. 27 dated the 24th December, 1980 in the case of banks, which facility is being extended to DFIs also.

4. The figures in the annexed Statements should pertain only to the domestic operations of the nationalized commercial banks. The part of the cost of head office organization attributable only to external operations will be secluded from domestic costs. Similarly, the cost of foreign banks organizations meant only for external operations will have to be distributed among the branches abroad and the share attributable to branches in Pakistan taken into account. The figures for these cost calculations as well as the provisions for bad and doubtful debts will have to be finally estimated by the State Bank of Pakistan for distribution of profits. This will, however, be without prejudice to the figures adopted by Income Tax authorities in due course which will be the basis of taxation of banks and allowing remittance of profits by foreign bank branches located in Pakistan.

Statement A

(Name of the Bank)

Average funds employed on earning assets during the six months ended ....

(Rs .... 000)

I. Funds employed on the basis of interest

Particulars	Average	
(i) Loans and Advances	80,000	
(ii) Balances held abroad	5,000	
(iii) Investments	35,000	120,000

II. Funds employed on non-interest basis

(i) Assets based on trade-related modes of financing	100,000	
(ii) Assets based on investment type modes of financing	110,000	
(iii) PLS deposits with other banks	20,000	
(iv) Funds employed on the basis of other modes, if any	10,000	240,000
	Total	360,000

The following assets will not be included in this statement:
  (i) Loans on the basis of service charge
  (ii) Qard-e-Hasana
  (iii) Assets on which interest or return is not being taken to income account

292

Statement B

_____

(Name of the Bank)

Income for the six months ended _____

(Rs .... 000)

I. Interest-Based Income
   Income from   *Amount of income*

    (i) Loans and Advances   4,800
    (ii) Balances held abroad   300
    (iii) Investments   2,100

    (iv) Total   7,200

II. Non-Interest Income
   Income from   *Amount of income*

    (i) Assets based on trade-related modes of financing   7,000
    (ii) Assets based on investment type modes of
        financing   6,600
    (iii) PLS deposits with other banks   1,000
    (iv) Non-fund based income   800
    (v) Other non-interest sources   200

    (vi) Total   15,600

    (vii) Less:
        (a) Proportionate Admn. cost as per Statement 'D'   4,930
        (b) Provision for Bad/Doubtful non-interest based
            assets   380
                        5,310

    (viii) Balance ((vi) minus (vii))   10,290
    (ix) Less management fee not exceeding 10% of (viii)   1,029

    (x) Net non-interest income ((viii) minus (ix))   9,261

Statement C

_____

(Name of the Bank)

Average remunerable liabilities
for the six months ended _____

(Rs .... 000)

Particulars	Average	
I. Interest-Bearing Liabilites		
(i) Deposits	70,000	
(ii) Borrowings	10,000	80,000
II. PLS Liabilities		
(i) Deposits	140,000	
(ii) Borrowings	20,000	160,000
III. Equity		
(i) Capital	20,000	
(ii) Reserves	10,000	
(iii) Balance of Profit and Loss Account	—	30,000
	Total	270,000

Statement D

_____

(Name of the Bank)

Administrative cost for the six months
ended _____
and its allocation between interest-based
income and non-interest income

(Rs .... 000)

	Amount	
I. Administrative Cost		
Particulars		
Total expenditure excluding taxes on income		18,000
Less:		
(i) Interest and/or return on deposits,		
borrowings, etc.	10,500	
(ii) Bad and doubtful assets written off directly	295	10,795
Administrative cost		7,205

II. Allocation of the Administrative Cost

(i)	Non-interest income as per statement 'B'	15,600
(ii)	Interest-based income as per statement 'B'	7,200
(iii)	Total	22,800
(iv)	Ratio of (i) to (iii)	13:19
(v)	Administrative cost allocable to non-interest income (cost multiplied by the ratio, i.e., 13/19)	4,930

Statement E

_____

(Name of the Bank)

(Rs .... 000)

Distribution of net non-interest income (item II (x) of Statement 'B') for the six months ended _____

1. Average earning assets as per statement 'A'	360,000
2. Average remunerable liabilities as per statement 'C'	270,000
3. Ratio of 2 to 1 above	3:4
4. Total non-interest assets as per statement 'A'	240,000
5. Total non-interest assets deflated by the ratio at 3	180,000

6. Manner of distribution of non-interest income:
   (i) If the figure at 5 above is less than or equal to the average PLS deposits as per statement 'C' the entire net non-interest income as per statement 'B' will be distributed on the PLS deposits.
   (ii) If the figure at 5 above is more than the average of PLS deposits as per statement 'C' but less than or equal to the sum of average PLS deposits and PLS borrowings, the non-interest income will be applied to remunerate the entire PLS deposits plus such portion of the PLS borrowings, which together with PLS deposits is equal to the amount at 5 above.
   (iii) If the figure at 5 above is more than the average of PLS deposits and PLS borrowings but less than or equal to the sum of PLS deposits, PLS borrowings and equity as per statement 'C', only such portion of non-interest income will be applied to remunerate the whole of PLS deposits and PLS borrowings and such portion of equity which together with PLS deposits and PLS borrowings is equal to the amount at 5 above.

(iv) If the figure at 5 above is more than the sum of average PLS deposits and PLS borrowings and equity as per statement 'C', only such portion of non-interest income will be applied to these items as bears the same ratio to the total non-interest income as the sum of PLS deposits, PLS borrowings, and equity bears to the amount at item 5 above.

(v) The distribution of non-interest income to the various remunerable liabilities will be made after giving the following weights to various items:

Particulars	*Weightage*
I. Deposits	
1. Special Notice Deposits	
(i) Withdrawable at 7 to 29 days' notice	0.65
(ii) Withdrawable at notice of 30 days or more	0.75
2. Savings Accounts	1.00
3. PLS call deposits from other banks	Weightage as agreed to by the banks concerned.
4. Term Deposits	
(i) For terms up to and inclusive of 6 months	1.00 + 0.05 for each month of the term of the deposit.
(ii) For terms in excess of 6 months	1.3 for the first six months plus 0.01 for each subsequent month of the term of the deposit, subject to a maximum of 2.08.
II. PLS Borrowings	Borrowings of various maturities will be given weightages as for term deposits of corresponding maturities indicated above.
III. Equity	Not exceeding 5 as may be determined by the concerned bank.

Net non-interest income (Rs 9,261,000) would thus be distributed as in the Annexure.

Annexure to Statement E

Type and maturity of non-interest liabilities	Average	Weightage	Weighted average liabilities	Income allocation	Annual rate of return in terms of percentage	Rate of return rounded off to the nearest one tenth of a percentage point
I. Deposits						
1. Special notice deposits						
(i) 7 to 29 days' notice	30,000	0.65	19,500	828	5.25%	5.5%
(ii) Over 30 days' notice	20,000	0.75	15,000	637	6.37%	6.4%
2. Savings accounts	30,000	1.00	30,000	1,273	8.49%	8.5%
3. PLS call deposits	20,000	1.00	20,000	849	8.49%	8.5%
4. Term deposits						
(i) 3 months	10,000	1.15	11,500	488	9.76%	9.8%
(ii) 6 months	10,000	1.30	13,000	552	11.04%	11.0%
(iii) 1 year	10,000	1.36	13,600	577	11.54%	11.5%
(iv) 5 years	10,000	1.84	18,400	781	15.62%	15.6%
II. Borrowings						
Borrowings (1 year)	20,000	1.36	27,200	1,154	11.54%	11.5%
III. Equity	20,000	2.50	50,000	2,122	21.22%	21.2%
Total	180,000		218,000	9,261		

3

Major Issues of Transition in Islamic Banking

Islamic banking must be considered an integral part of a functioning Islamic economic system. The Islamic economic system is only part of an Islamic social system that possesses well identified characteristics whose existence is a prerequisite to assessing the efficiency with which its individual components functions. Above all, it is the full implementation of Islamic law in a society that establishes the criteria by which the optimality of a system claiming to be Islamic can be measured. When the society as a whole expresses its willingness to adopt and implement an Islamic banking system, it becomes necessary to internalise the relevant value system, composed of such elements as honesty in business dealings, faithfulness to contracts, and the duty of sharing with others. The implementation process requires considerable time, effort, and discipline on the part of all segments of the society, particularly when the society is accustomed to carrying out its day-to-day affairs on the basis of a value system which to a great degree cannot accommodate Islamic values. Herein lies the primary constraint on effectively implementing Islamic banking.

TRANSITIONAL ISSUES IN THE ISLAMIC REPUBLICS OF IRAN AND PAKISTAN

Notwithstanding different approaches to the Islamisation process, the Islamic Republics of Iran and Pakistan have encountered a number of common problems. The authorities in the two countries are cognisant of these. For example, in both countries, banks' lending has so far been concentrated on short-term trade financing modes rather than a shift toward PLS-type assets, which is contrary to the intentions of the new system. Similarly, owing to problems in devising appropriate modes of financing budgetary deficits that would be consistent with the Sharia, government borrowing requirements had to be met effectively on an interest basis. At the bank level, difficulties have been encountered in lending to small-scale enterprises — owing to increases in perceived risks — and this tends to skew the distribution of credit in favour of large-scale enterprises.

Moreover, there has been a slower adjustment to new modes of financing than to those of deposits, in part owing to the fact that adjustments to new lending procedures and the requisite training of staff are time-consuming. Therefore, the cost of banking may have gone up. Bankers have also felt that there are insufficient instruments available in the market for asset diversification at present.

Apart from these common issues, effective implementation of the new system in the two countries may have been constrained by particular economic and legal environments. For example, in Pakistan the absence of precise legal definitions of various modes of financing is likely to influence the future evolution of the system. Similarly, the dispute settlement system will have to be closely watched to ensure the rights of banks and borrowers and to avoid defaults. Some banks also view the formula determining profit-sharing ratios for depositors as arbitrary, which could lead to a destabilising movement of deposits between banks. There is also a need for more financing instruments to take care of the diverse needs of the private sector. In the case of the Islamic Republic of Iran, the build-up of excess liquidity in the banking system has probably been caused by difficulties in quickly adjusting to the new modes of financing and in lending to the small-scale sector. So far, returns on deposits and profit-sharing ratios have been determined exogenously. Decisions with respect to rates of return have been guided by a desire to ensure adequate rewards to savers rather than the actual profits of banks. The absence of a law explicitly defining property rights may also complicate the process of transition.

Asset concentration

As indicated earlier, bank assets in both countries are concentrated primarily on a few short-term and trade-financing instruments such as mark-up, instalment sales, and short-term partnerships rather than PLS-oriented transactions. Apart from being inconsistent with the objectives of the Islamisation process, the heavy concentration on a few assets might adversely affect the stability of banks' asset portfolios and increase risk.

Several factors have been instrumental in this development. First, the short-term modes of financing are more akin to interest-based banking, thus requiring the least modifications of the old lending procedures. Second, as in most developing countries, the basis for lending continues to be the banker's knowledge of the client and his creditworthiness rather than the profitability of the project, and banks do not have a high degree of expertise in the evaluation of project financing.[1] The inability to evaluate exposure, thus profitability of

---

1. While creditworthiness is also a significant factor in bank loan evaluation in more developed financial markets, financial institutions in these markets are far better equipped to analyse the profitabilities of prospective investments than are banks in the typical developing country.

projects, has tended to militate against investment-type lending; persistence of this situation may retard the development process. Thirdly, borrowers have not yet fully reconciled themselves to the changed environment. Their immediate concern has been to ensure that the cost of credit does not increase; short-term lending operations such as mark-up, instalment sales, lease-purchase, and the short-term Mudaraba permitted them and the banks to ensure this. Moreover, borrowers have been reluctant to agree to the sharing of information about their business with banks; yet this is an inevitable prerequisite for longer-term and investment-oriented financing operations. Fourth, shortcomings in business ethics make it difficult to establish closer bank-client relationships — a precondition for the successful application of Islamic banking. For example, clients either do not keep adequate records or keep fraudulent records of their operations. Until such time as business ethics improve and the banks develop sufficient capability of monitoring and auditing enterprises, such that they are assured of the accuracy of the reports on business activities, they will be reluctant to take equity positions in enterprise.

Finally, and most importantly, particularly in Pakistan, the perception of 'unfair' taxation, and the consequent tax evasion, has tended to exacerbate the problem of business ethics, thus making it even more difficult for banks to participate in modes other than short-term trade financing. In order to evade taxation, businesses are believed to under-report the size of their operations and income. Under these circumstances, they are unlikely to be honest with their financiers, thus discouraging investment-type lending operations. In the Islamic Republic of Iran, the general economic slowdown and uncertainties regarding medium-term prospects have also encouraged a concentration on short-term assets.

Institutional structures are also not fully developed to facilitate the growth of investment-type lending. In particular, the private capital markets in the two countries have neither the depth nor the breadth to accommodate transactions in such instruments on a large scale.

Government borrowing

Difficulties have been encountered in devising means and instruments for financing the budget deficit without violating the prohibition of interest. Resolution of this problem is central to a further evolution of the Islamic banking system since the government accounts for a major component of demand for credit. In the case of the Islamic Republic of Iran, it has been decreed that financial transactions between and among the elements of the public sector, including the Bank Markazi and commercial banks which are wholly nationalised, can take place on the basis of a fixed rate of return; such a fixed return is not viewed as interest. Therefore, the government can borrow from the nationalised banking system without violating the injunctions of the Law. While no preferential rates are charged on lending to the government in Pakistan, not all government financing is being handled through non-interest modes. To a large extent, this reflects difficulties of the government in raising additional revenues and containing expenditures. In addition, problems in devising non-interest based instruments of financing have also been responsible for the emergence of this apparent conflict between fiscal policy objectives and the Islamisation of the financial system. Continued borrowing on a fixed-rate basis by the government would inevitably index bank charges to this rate rather than to the actual profits of borrowing entities.

Country specific issues

Lending to small-scale enterprises

Given the comprehensive criteria to be followed in granting loans and monitoring their use by banks, small scale enterprises have, in general, encountered greater difficulties in obtaining financing than their large-scale counterparts in the Islamic Republic of Iran. This has been particularly relevant for the construction and service sectors, which have a large share in the GDP. The service sector is made up of many small producers for whom the banking sector has not been able to provide sufficient financing. Many of these small producers, who traditionally were able to obtain interest-based credit facilities on the basis of collateral, are now finding it difficult to raise funds for their operations. Although in the case of bankruptcy the lender can claim a share of the remaining assets of a failed company corresponding to the share of his investment in total capital, the commercial banks do face an element of moral hazard due to the non-existence of systematic book-keeping in this sector. Additionally, the reluctance of small producers to submit their operations to bank audits and the perceived enormous cost of auditing and monitoring relative to the small sizes of potential credits leads to an unwillingness of the banks to extend credit to these small producers on the basis of the new modes of financing. The reduced lending to small producers may also explain the existence of excess liquidity in the banking system.

Legal issues

Although the Law establishing interest-free banking in the Islamic Republic of Iran is comprehensive, the lack of a proper definition of property rights may have constrained bank lending. Thus far, there has been no precise legislative and legal expression of what is viewed as 'lawful and conditional' private property rights. This may also have militated against investment lending in agricultural and industrial sectors and thus encouraged increased concentration of assets on short-term trade-financing instruments.

In the case of Pakistan, the new system has been introduced without fundamental changes in the existing laws governing contracts, mortgages and pledges. Similarly, no laws have been introduced to define modes of participatory financing, that is, Musharaka and PTCs. It is presumed that wherever there is a conflict between the Islamic banking framework and the existing law, the latter would prevail. In essence, therefore, the relationship between the bank and the client is left unchanged as specified by the existing law; that is, that of a creditor and a debtor. This may be a useful solution to the short-term problems of transition, but an orderly evolution would require concordance between the law and the banking framework. The existing banking law was developed to protect mainly the credit transactions; its application to other modes of financing results in the treatment of those modes as credit transactions also. Doubts have been expressed by banks whether some contracts, though consistent with the Islamic banking framework, would be acceptable in the courts. Hence, incentives exist for default and abuse. The authorities recognise the potential problems arising out of this legal inconsistency and are keeping this issue under constant review so as to seek solutions when and if needed. By contrast, in the Islamic Republic of Iran all permissible financing modes are explicitly defined, the bank-client relationship is clear, and all contracts are legally enforceable.

Determination of rates of return and charges

The rates of return on deposits and charges on financing operations in the Islamic Republic of Iran are at present determined exogenously, based on those prevailing prior to the introduction of the new system, which could lead to misallocation of resources. While each bank is, in principle, expected to announce rates of return on investment deposits based on its profits, so far uniform rates of return have been decreed for all banks, irrespective of their profit levels. This was intended to avoid a withdrawal of deposits and also to avoid large-scale deposit migration among banks. Similarly, minimum and maximum rates of profit-sharing applying to various modes of financing are, at present, fixed on the basis of rates of interest prevailing prior to the introduction of the new system; these rates may therefore be inconsistent with sectoral growth priorities and credit demand pressures. The authorities are aware of this problem.

In Pakistan, some commercial banks have contended that the formula determining profit-sharing ratios between banks and depositors is arbitrary and may lead to destabilising deposit flows between banks. The weighting system that determines returns to liabilities according to their maturity structure leads to higher rates of return from banks with a relatively larger share of equity. These concerns have been voiced particularly by foreign banks, which are characterised by a relatively higher share of equity in their liabilities. So far no such migration of deposits has been observed, but persistently higher returns in some banks, simply because of their maturity structure of liabilities, could be destabilising.

Dispute settlement procedures

Guarantees for banks and dispute settlement procedures may also adversely affect the operation of the new system in Pakistan. Understandably, security of banks' investments and depositors' interest needs to be guaranteed in the transitional period, but such guarantees may be counterproductive. For example, in the event of losses under the PTC arrangement, the financial institution is protected by the fact that the borrowing entity sustaining losses shall adjust them first against the reserves of the entity and only the remaining losses shall be apportioned. While such a measure may be viewed as a deterrent against malpractices, it may also be viewed by borrowers as unfair and aimed at protecting the financial institutions against all losses. Similarly, attachment or more than proportionate weights to banks in sharing profits under Musharaka arrangements may be viewed as inconsistent with equal treatment of partners in an enterprise. While such unequal treatment may be deemed as desirable in the transitional period, it could become institutionalised, in which case it would be inimical to the growth of Musharaka in the future.

Apart from the establishment of twelve banking tribunals in Pakistan which are required to resolve disputes relating to delays in repayments under mark-up mode of financing, the dispute settlement system has been left unchanged. While little is known about the experience of the tribunals in settling disputes and ensuring speedy repayments, their small numbers may lead to a lack of sufficient speed in rendering decisions and may generate a premium on defaults. Hence, the success of the new system will hinge on the availability of legal recourse to the banks and borrowers as a safeguard against defaults and other abuses.

SOURCES OF PROBLEMS AND SUGGESTED SOLUTIONS

There are three primary reasons for the difficulties faced by the two countries as enumerated above. These relate to the legal framework, fiscal policy objectives and instruments, and the inadequacy of financial infrastructure required to implement the system fully. Successful implementation of an Islamic banking system will, therefore, require correction of these inherent problems. Specific solutions would naturally be shaped by the institutional characteristics of each country.

Legal framework

Some of the problems faced by both the Islamic Republic of Iran and Pakistan stem from the lack of a well defined legal system, specifying the domain and limitations of property rights and of contracts, that fully corresponds to the established special banking system and the Islamic law. In both countries, this lack has strengthened the environment of uncertainty, limited long-term

303

investment, and forced the banking system to concentrate its asset portfolios in short-term transactions.

This problem appears in two different forms in the two countries. In Pakistan, it has forced the Government to establish special banking tribunals to deal with contracts based on Islamic modes, since the regular court system, as well as existing contract and corporate law, cannot handle Islamic-based contracts. This a short-term remedy and the problem will continue to persist and become more complex until the legal system and the underlying corporate and contract law have become more attuned to the legal requirements of the new banking system. In the Islamic Republic of Iran, where the legal system is fundamentally based on the Islamic law, the difficulty lies in the absence of a legislative definition of the rights and limitations of private property which would explicitly determine the extent and intensity of the private enterprise activities in the economy. Although the existing banking regulations require that all banks must make it clear to all their customers that all contracts mutually agreed to by both parties are presentable to the courts as legal documents, lack of a clear and legislatively sanctioned definition of rights and limitations of private property has induced a reluctance on the part of both the entrepreneurs and the banking system to engage in long-term and Islamic-based profit-sharing project activities. Hence, there is a need for a law explicitly defining individuals' property rights.

Government deficit financing

Another problem faced by the two countries, and one which until now has proved to be quite intractable, has been the inability to formulate, non-interest-based instruments for financing budget deficits, thus leading to a position where the government, which is the major exponent of the implementation of the Islamic system, is forced to raise funds through borrowing on the basis of a fixed rate of return. Islam requires an efficient and responsible fiscal policy under which the government can justify and rationalise all its expenditures. Under such a fiscal policy, there is a clear distinction between a government's general expenditure and its 'welfare' expenditure. The welfare expenditure is to be financed through mandatory levies imposed on income and wealth of the individual members of the society, based on the Islamic law. If the resources raised in this manner are deemed insufficient, the state is empowered to meet the resource gap through additional taxes. The revenues needed for the undertaking of general expenditures are to be raised through the management and operation of the society's resources which the Islamic law has placed at the disposal of the state, eg underground mineral resources. Writers on an Islamic fiscal system are of the opinion that if the government were to conduct its affairs strictly in accordance with Islamic prescriptions, if ordinances regarding the duty of sharing were to be strictly observed, and efficiency and waste were to be eliminated from government expenditures, such a government would carry not only a much smaller fiscal burden than at present, but would have to justify all expenditures. If it still becomes necessary for governments to finance deficits from borrowing, the question becomes one of devising proper non-interest-based instruments that can be used to raise the necessary funds.

Much thought has been given to the idea of devising instruments that would allow government borrowing on the basis of a non-fixed rate of return. Briefly, these suggestions include: (1) to permit the central bank to make available to the government a portion of demand deposits on non-interest basis; (2) to remove the fixed rate of return on government borrowing by providing a variable rate of return that is tied to the rate of growth of the nominal GDP; (3) to create a mutual fund pool out of a class of government-financed projects and use their average rate of return as a basis of reward to the lenders; (4) to float nominal-value-indexed bonds adjusted to various indices such as the value of the US dollar, gold, SDR or some other index; and (5) to issue bonds for investors in higher income brackets with large tax liabilities, and borrow that money at the cost of a tax, ie the lender would not be taxed for income invested in these bonds if he holds them for a specific period of time. This last measure may not only solve the problem of borrowing at no interest, but also help shrink the size of the informal market. These bonds could be transacted in the market place.[2]

Whereas the question of proper procedure and instruments needed to finance government borrowing is crucial, the more fundamental problem is the structure of taxes and their rationalisation. This problem is particularly acute in Pakistan, where tax evasion has created the underlying motivation on the part of businessmen for maintenance of multiple books of accounts and nondisclosure of their true profits. In turn, it has led to reluctance and risk aversion behaviour on the part of the banks to undertake projects on a profit-sharing basis. Thus the problems of moral hazard and of monitoring, which tend to be characteristic of principal-agent type contracts epitomised by Islamic-based and profit-sharing arrangements, are made even more complex with these additional constraints. The authorities in Pakistan are aware of the need for tax reform and its beneficial effects on the Islamisation process. A Taxation Reform Commission has been established to pursue this matter.

The economic consequence of the moral hazard problem is potentially serious in that (1) it can lead to allocation of credit and of financial resources away from long-term investment projects and towards short-term trade financing arrangements; (2) it can lead to financial disintermediation away from the banking system and to the growth of informal financial markets particularly when the service sector is a major contributor to the GDP; and (3) it strengthens and perpetuates the existing bias of the banking system towards large enterprises and against small and indigenous entrepreneurs. If the financial needs of small

---

2. Methods (2), (3), (4) have been rejected by some Muslim scholars on the grounds that they are incompatible with the Sharia. See Z. Ahmed (1984).

305

businesses are not accommodated by the banking system, they will be forced to seek sources of financing in the informal sector. This will not only perpetuate interest-based financing in the private sector but may also weaken the effectiveness of monetary policy. The remedy — besides tax rationalisation, provision of the necessary legal framework, and the removal of incentives for tax evasion — is an improved monitoring and auditing system, which can be undertaken only at heavy initial cost. This can be effected by setting up banking and financial institutions, perhaps in the form of subsidiaries to the existing commercial banks, which can specialise in the provision of credit and financing to the service sector and small business. Such institutions, whose operations may need to be subsidised initially, can then concentrate on dealing with the particular problems of these sectors. This action would need to be concomitantly supplemented by legislative action, which would provide sanctions against financial transactions on an interest base in the private sector in order to guard against the growth of the informal sector and financial disintermediation.

Infrastructure

This problem has both general and specific dimensions. Its general dimension relates to the lack of familiarity of businessmen and entrepreneurs with the requisites of Islamic business ethics which, in turn, emanates from their lack of knowledge regarding Islamic ethical rules. Its specific dimension relates to the long-standing problem of inadequate education and training on the part of the staff and personnel within the banking system. Even though the latter problem is formidable by itself, the former is by far the most difficult and complex, requiring enormous time and effort to overcome. The authorities believe that it will, perhaps, take a considerable period of time before Islamic business ethics can be inculcated in the market participants but it is clear that without the internalisation of the rules and norms of economic behaviour that Islam requires, the intervention in, and guidance of, the economy by the state will be extensive.

The specific dimension of the problem and the extent of the necessary commitment to its solution has been recognised by the authorities in both countries. In order to carry out detailed project appraisals and to monitor these projects when undertaken, the banking personnel must not only have a high degree of expertise in banking and finance, they must also be familiar with various modes of Islamic financial transactions and their requirements. It is likely that, for a considerable period during the transition, banking personnel will have to play a major role in informing and educating their clients in the various modes of Islamic transactions and in providing financing packages most suitable to their clients' needs. At present, the major share of the burden of this training has been carried out by the banks in both Pakistan and the Islamic Republic of Iran on an in-house basis. In the latter, the Bank Markazi undertook the initial phase of the training of personnel of the banking system in Islamic modes of finance and, through the combined efforts of Bank Markazi, commercial banks, and specialised banks, almost one-third of the banking personnel have been trained and the training of the rest is continuing. The technical training in portfolio management and in project appraisal and monitoring have not been formally undertaken.

It is also important to undertake steps aimed at resolving technical difficulties in developing and utilising new instruments, so as to facilitate a more diversified approach toward asset portfolio management for the banks. These instruments should cover all maturities and be marketable enough so that the problems of excess liquidity and asset management is resolved.

SUMMARY AND CONCLUSIONS

The central requirement of the Islamic financial system is the replacement of the rate of interest with the rate of return on real activities as a mechanism for allocating financial resources. While prohibiting interest, Islam permits profit-sharing. A variety of modes of transactions have been devised to support a well-functioning financial system without resort to contracts based on fixed interest. Models of Islamic banking decompose the bulk of the liabilities of banks into demand and investment deposits. The nominal value of demand deposits is guaranteed by the banks, but these deposits earn no return. Investment deposits, on the other hand, share in the profits earned by the banks. On the asset side, the banks provide financing to agent-entrepreneurs on the basis of profit-sharing with explicitly stated sharing rules specified beforehand; the most important forms of such financing arrangements are Mudaraba and Musharaka. As the sharing of risk and incentive is a fundamental premise of Islamic banking, models of this banking system provide for the accumulation by banks of loss-compensating balances in periods of high profit, as well as for deposit insurance, asset diversification, and monitoring of projects to reduce the risk borne by investment depositors.

Theoretical models of Islamic banking foresee no reduction in the effectiveness of monetary policy or of central banks in the performance of their traditional roles. With the exception of the discount rate, all other traditional tools of monetary policy would be available to the central bank.[2] Moreover, these models propose manipulation of the ratios that determine profit-sharing between banks and depositors, as well as between banks and the agent-entrepreneurs, as an additional monetary policy tool at the disposal of the central bank. These models also foresee that, in an Islamic banking system, the central bank could

---

2. In economies in which capital markets are imperfect and interest-based monetary policy tools are in extensive use, there may be a need for instruments for influencing net international capital movements possibly including a greater role for the exchange rate and flexible use of central bank control over banks' profit-sharing ratio.

invest directly in the real sector and so long as securities did not have par value features and represent real assets, the central bank would have the ability to buy and sell securities, ie engage in open market operations.

The Islamic banking system is, in principle, compatible with a close correspondence between financial and real rates of return and an efficient allocation of resources. Moreover, it could be adopted without harming the effectiveness of official supervision of financial intermediation. It is, however, recognised that the efficient working of such a financial system requires properly organised primary and secondary markets.

All Muslim countries practice Islamic banking to varying degrees and interest-free banks have been operating in some non-Muslim countries. However, Islamic banking is intended to operate within a totally Islamic system. Hence a distinction can be made between interest-free banking operating within systems that lack essential characteristics of an entirely Islamic system and Islamic banking as an organic part of such a system.

For purposes of analysing the operation of Islamic banking in practice, this sections draws upon the experience of the Islamic Republics of Iran and Pakistan, which have recently attempted to introduce Islamic banking on a comprehensive basis. Each has chosen a different path toward the achievement of its objective. Pakistan has chosen the route of gradual Islamisation, ie a step-by-step replacement of its present economic instruments and institutions with their Islamic counterparts, beginning with the banking system. The Islamic Republic of Iran, on the other hand, has chosen the path of a complete, once-and-for-all transformation of the existing system into an Islamic one. Its experience with implementation of full Islamic banking has been shorter than that of Pakistan and has been constrained by enormous exogenous shocks to the economy. Even though it is far too soon to discern fully the impact of the adoption of the new system, the two countries' experience of the last few years appears to indicate that they have been able to replace the interest rate mechanism with non-interest based modes of financial resource allocation without disrupting either the financial stability of the system or the effectiveness of monetary policy. There has been a general acceptance of the new modes of financing and deposit instruments. Private sector deposits have continued to rise despite a shift from fixed interest to variable rates of return on deposits. However, progress on the development of non-interest based modes of financing has been slower owing, mainly, to the need for changes in banks' procedures and delays in the acquisition of new skills required for applying such modes; resolution of this constraint would be crucial to the further development of the financial system.

The implementation of the new system has been cautious and attempts have been made to avoid unnecessary disruptions in the orderly operation of the banking system. There has been some deregulation of the banking system insofar as rates of return and charges on lending within broad ranges are to be determined according to certain objective criteria rather than by the monetary authorities. When diversified non-interest-based modes of financing become available, the capacity to influence credit creation and its allocation is likely to increase to the extent that the monetary authorities can alter profit-sharing ratios. Owing to the deviation between the requirements of an Islamic banking framework and the existing institutional and legal structures, the Islamic Republic of Iran and Pakistan has encountered, or are likely to encounter, difficulties in the effective implementation of the new banking system. Although many of their problems are different, they do share a set of common problems that have been investigated in this paper. These include concentration on short-term assets, difficulties in the acceptance of instruments based on the principle of profit-and-loss-sharing rather than on a fixed rate of return, possible disintermediation for small-scale business, and difficulties in devising appropriate non-interest-based instruments for financing the government budget.

There are basically three important sources of these problems: (1) the lack of a legal framework that unambiguously specifies the domain and limitations of property rights and of contracts in accordance with an Islamic banking system; (2) difficulties in devising non-interest-based sources for financing government deficits; and (3) the lack of adequate financial infrastructure, including trained banking staff, and more generally the means for dealing with higher information and transaction costs to both depositors and banks.[3] The existence of these constraints can create acute uncertainties reducing the scope of long-term investment financing and leading to a further strengthening of the observed concentration of the portfolio of the banking system in short-term assets. At stake is the stimulation and maintenance of a flow of financial intermediation high enough to support a rate of long-term fixed capital formation that fully exploits available social rates of return to long-term investment. Moreover, since both economies are characterised by market and informational imperfections, further persistence of these problems will increase the cost information gathering, monitoring, and auditing for the banks. These higher operating costs require a larger spread between rates of return to the banks and to their depositors, thus undermining the full implementation of Islamic banking through a process of disintermediation away from the banking system and strengthening of the parallel markets. Moreover, business attitudes would have to change in order to allow for a transition toward investment-orientated financing, which is the ultimate objective of the Islamic system.

Finally, distortions underlying the existence of large fiscal deficits would have to be corrected. Fixed rate charges (eg interest paid by the government debt), while having no relationship to the productivity of expenditure financed by borrowed funds, would act as a floor for bank charges on other financing operations. Therefore, appropriate expenditure policies and tax rationalisation

---

3. It must be kept in mind that the transactions and information costs in the conventional system are largely reduced through government insurance and supervision. It is likely that a depositor in an interest-based conventional system but with no such insurance and supervision would face similar costs.

would be needed so as to establish a closer relationship between rates of return and charges and thus promote a movement toward the acceptance of profit/loss-sharing which is essential for the growth of long-term financing by commercial banks.

Appendix A: Islamic Banking Law in Malaysia

Islamic banking in Malaysia is governed by the Islamic Banking Act 1983 which is known as Act No 276 and which provides for the licensing and regulation of Islamic banking business in Malaysia.

Consequent upon the passage of this Act the Bank Islam Malaysia was established with an authorised capital of US $500 million (of which US $100 million is paid-up initially). Dr Abdul Halim Ismail, the former Chief Economist of Bank Bumiputraa, is the Managing Director of this new bank. Initially the capital of the bank is subscribed by the Federal Bank, the Islamic related agencies and the Government bodies. The Central Government holds 30 per cent of the shares, the Pilgrims Management and Fund Board 10 per cent, the Muslim Welfare Organisation (Perkin) 5 per cent, the State Islamic Affairs Department 25 per cent and the State Islamic Agencies (like Islamic Economic Foundations and Baitul Maal) 10 per cent, while such bodies as Felda and the Armed Forces Fund Board hold 10 per cent of the shares and the remaining 10 per cent have been subscribed by other Islamic organisations.

The Malaysian Prime Minister has indicated that while the new bank is wholly Malaysian it will seek business links with Islamic banks elsewhere.

The following is the text of the Act dealing with Islamic Banking in Malaysia.

Act 276: Islamic Banking Act 1983

An act to provide for the licensing and regulation of Islamic banking business.

BE IT ENACTED by the Duli Yang Maha Mulia Seri Paduikia Baginda Yang Agong with the advice and consent of the Dewan Negara and Dewan Rakyat in Parliament assembled, and by the authority of the same, as follows:

PART I — PRELIMINARY

1.

(1) This Act may be cited as the Islamic Banking Act 1983 and shall come into force on such date as the Minister may appoint by notification in the *Gazette*.

(2) This Act shall apply throughout Malaysia.

2.

In this Act, unless the context otherwise requires:

'branch' in relation to an Islamic bank includes a mobile branch of the bank and a branch established and maintained for a limited period only.

'Central Bank' means the Central Bank of Malaysia established by the Central Bank of Malaysia Ordinance 1958;

'company' has the meaning assigned to it by the Companies Act 1965;

'corporation' has the meaning assigned to it by the Companies Act 1965;

'depositor' means a person who has an account at an Islamic bank, whether the account is a current account, a savings account, an investment account or any other deposit account;

'Islamic bank' means any company which carries on Islamic banking business and holds a valid licence; and all the offices and branches in Malaysia of such a bank shall be deemed to be one bank;

'Islamic banking business' means banking business whose aims and operations do not involve any element which is not approved by the Religion of Islam;

'Investment account liabilities' in relation to an Islamic bank means the deposit liabilities at that bank in respect of funds placed by a depositor with that bank for a fixed period of time under an agreement to share the profits and losses of that bank on the investment of such funds;

'licence' means a licence granted under section 3;

'other deposit liabilities' in relation to an Islamic bank means the deposit liabilities at that bank other than savings account, investment account, sight and time liabilities from any other Islamic bank, any licensed bank under the Banking Act 1973 or the Central Bank.

'public company' has the meaning assigned to it by the Companies Act 1965;

'savings account liabilities' in relation to an Islamic bank means the total deposits at that bank which normally require the presentation of passbooks or other such documents in lieu of passbooks as approved by the Central Bank for the deposit or withdrawal of moneys;

'share' means share in the share capital of a corporation and includes stock, except where a distinction between stock and share is expressed or implied;

'subsidiary' has the meaning assigned to it under section 5 of the Companies Act 1965;

'time liabilities' in relation to an Islamic bank means the total deposits at that bank which are repayable otherwise than on demand, but does not include savings account liabilities or deposits of any other Islamic bank, any licensed bank under the Banking Act 1973 or the Central Bank.

PART II — LICENSING OF ISLAMIC BANKS

3.

(1) Islamic banking business shall not be transacted in Malaysia except by a company which is in the possession of a licence in writing from the Minister authorising it to do so.

(2) A company which desires authority to carry on Islamic banking business in Malaysia shall apply in writing through the Central Bank to the Minister for a licence under this section and shall supply:

    (a) a copy of the memorandum of association and articles of association or other instrument under which the company is incorporated, duly verified by a statutory declaration made by a senior officer of the company; and

    (b) such other documents or information as may be called upon by the Minister.

(3) Upon receiving an application under subsection (2) the Central Bank shall consider the application and make a recommendation to the Minister stating whether a licence should be granted or not and the conditions, if any, to be attached to the licence.

(4) Upon receiving an application under subsection (2) and the recommendations of the Central Bank under subsection (3) the Minister may, subject to section 4, grant a licence, with or without conditions, or refuse a licence.

(5) The Central Bank shall not recommend the granting of a licence, and the Minister shall not grant a licence, unless the Central Bank or the Minister, as the case may be, is satisfied:

    (a) that the aims and operations of the banking business which it is desired to carry on will not involve any element which is not approved by the Religion of Islam; and

    (b) that there is, in the articles of association of the bank concerned, provision for the establishment of a Shariah advisory body to advise the bank on the operations of its banking business in order to ensure that they do not involve any element which is not approved by the Religion of Islam.

(6) Any person who contravenes the provisions of this section shall be guilty of an offence and shall on conviction be liable to a fine not exceeding twenty thousand ringgit or to imprisonment for a term not exceeding three years or to both such fine and imprisonment.

4.

(1) The Minister may at any time, on the recommendation of the Central Bank, vary or revoke any existing condition of a licence or impose conditions or additional conditions.

(2) The Minister shall, prior to any action under subsection (1), notify his intention in writing to take such action to the Islamic bank concerned and shall give the bank an opportunity to submit within such period, being not less than fourteen days, as may be specified in the notification reasons why the condition of the licence should not be varied or revoked or conditions or additional conditions should not be imposed.

(3) Where a licence is subject to conditions, the Islamic bank shall comply with those conditions.

(4) Any Islamic bank which fails to comply with any condition of its licence shall be guilty of an offence and shall on conviction be liable to a fine not exceeding twenty thousand ringgit.

5.

(1) No company shall be granted a licence under section 3 nor shall any company licensed thereunder carry on business in Malaysia without the written consent of the Minister if its capital funds, unimpaired by losses or otherwise, are less than the minimum amount.

(2) For the purposes of this section:

'capital funds' means paid-up capital and reserves and any other sources of capital as may be defined and computed in such manner as may be prescribed by notice in writing from time to time by the Central Bank.

'minimum amount' means such amount of capital funds to be maintained by an Islamic bank as may be prescribed by the Minister on the recommendation of the Central Bank by notification in the *Gazette*.

(3) The prescription of the minimum amount to be maintained under subsection (2) shall be complied with within such uniform period of grace being not less than three months as may be specified in the notification.

6.

(1) No company shall be granted or shall hold a licence if the Minister is satisfied that it is or has become foreign-owned or controlled.

(2) For the purposes of this section, a company shall be deemed to be foreign-owned or controlled if fifty per cent or more of its capital issued and paid-up is owned by or on behalf of persons who are not citizens of Malaysia,

or if a majority of the persons having the direction, control or management of the company are not citizens of Malaysia.

7.

Except with the consent in writing of the Central Bank, no Islamic bank may open a new branch, agency or office in any part of Malaysia or outside Malaysia.

8.

(1) Subject to subsection (2), every Islamic bank may establish a correspondent banking relationship with any bank outside Malaysia.

(2) The Central Bank may prescribe by notice in writing that no Islamic bank shall, except with the approval of the Minister on the recommendations of the Central Bank, establish a correspondent banking relationship with any bank established in any of the countries specified in the notification or with any bank owned or controlled by the government or any agency of the government of any such country.

9.

Every Islamic bank shall pay to the Central Bank such annual licence fees as the Minister, on the recommendation of the Central Bank, may by notification in the *Gazette* prescribe.

10.

Except with the consent in writing of the Minister, no Islamic bank shall be licensed by a name which includes any of the words 'Central', 'Commonwealth', 'Federal', 'Federation', 'Malaysia', 'Malaysian', 'National', 'Reserve' or 'State' either in the National Language or in English or in any other language.

11.

(1) Subject to subsection (2), if any Islamic bank:
  (a) is pursuing aims, or carrying on operations, involving any element which is not approved by the Religion of Islam;

    (b) is carrying on its business in a manner detrimental to the interests of its depositors and other creditors;

    (c) has sufficient assets to cover its liabilities to the public;

    (d) is contravening any provisions of this Act; or

    (e) has ceased to carry on banking in Malaysia,

the Minister may, on the recommendation of the Central Bank, revoke any licence issued to such bank.

(2) The Minister shall, prior to any such revocation, notify his intention to take such action to the Islamic bank concerned and shall give the bank an opportunity to submit within such period, being not less than twenty-one days, as may be specified in the notification reasons why the licence should not be revoked.

(3) Where the licence of an Islamic bank has been revoked under subsection (1), the bank may within thirty days of the revocation appeal against the revocation to the High Court, which may make such order thereon as it thinks proper, including any direction as to the costs of the appeal.

(4) The Central Bank shall be entitled to be heard on any such appeal.

(5) The making of an appeal under this section shall in no way affect the exercise of the powers and duties of the Central Bank under sections 37, 39 and 40.

12.

(1) Where an order of revocation becomes effective under section 11:

    (a) notice of the revocation shall be published in the *Gazette*; and

    (b) the Islamic bank shall as from the date of the notice cease to transact any banking business in Malaysia except as may be approved by the Minister on the recommendation of the Central Bank for the purposes of winding up of its banking business.

(2) The provisions of paragraph (b) of subsection (1) shall not prejudice the enforcement by any person of any right or claim against the bank or by the bank of any right or claim against any person.

13.

The Central Bank shall cause to be published in the *Gazette* in each year a list of all Islamic banks to which licences have been issued under this Act, and if any licence is issued, revoked or surrendered during the interval between the publication of two such lists, notice thereof shall also be caused to be published in the *Gazette*.

PART III — FINANCIAL REQUIREMENTS AND DUTIES OF ISLAMIC BANKS

14.

(1) The Central Bank may require an Islamic bank to maintain capital funds, unimpaired by losses or otherwise, in such proportion to the assets of its branches and offices both in Malaysia and outside Malaysia or only of its branches and offices in Malaysia as may be prescribed from time to time by the Central Bank by notice in writing.

15.

(1) Every Islamic bank:
    (a)   shall maintain a reserve fund; and
    (b)   before any dividend is declared shall transfer to the reserve fund out of the net profits of each year, after due provision has been made for zakat or taxation
        (i) so long as the amount of the reserve fund is less than fifty per cent of the paid-up capital, a sum equal to not less than fifty per cent of the net profits;
        (ii) so long as the amount of the reserve fund is fifty per cent but less than one hundred per cent of the paid-up capital, a sum equal to not less than twenty five per cent of the net profits.
(2) If the Central Bank is satisfied that the aggregate reserve fund of an Islamic bank is adequate for its business, it may by order in writing exempt the bank from the provisions of subsection (1) for a period of one year.

16.

(1) The Central Bank may from time to time prescribe by notice in writing to each Islamic bank a minimum amount or amounts of liquid assets to be held by the bank at all times.
(2) The minimum amount or amounts of the assets so prescribed to be held shall be expressed in the form of:
    (a)   a percentage or percentages which such assets shall bear to be sight, savings account, time and other deposit liabilities of each Islamic bank and such other liabilities as may be determined by the Central Bank, either jointly or separately; and
    (b)   a percentage which such assets shall bear to the investment account of each Islamic bank;

317

and such percentage or percentages may be varied by the Central Bank from time to time by notice in writing to the bank.

(3) Whenever the Central Bank issues a notice under subsection (1) each Islamic bank shall be allowed such uniform period of grace, being not less than one week, as may be specified in that notice in which to comply with the provision thereof.

(4) An Islamic bank shall not, during any period in which it has failed to comply with any notice under subsection (1), without the approval of the Central Bank, lend or advance any money to any person.

(5) For the purpose of computing the minimum amount or amounts of liquid assets under this section and sight, savings account, investment account, time and other deposit liabilities of an Islamic bank carrying on business in Malaysia and elsewhere and such other liabilities of such bank as may be determined by the Central Bank in Malaysia shall be deemed to constitute a separate bank carrying on business in Malaysia.

(6) For the purposes of this section liquid assets shall be:

    (a)   notes and coins which are legal tender in Malaysia;

    (b)   balances at the Central Bank, not including the reserve specified in paragraph (c) of subsection (1) of section 37 of the Central Bank of Malaysia Ordinance 1958;

    (c)   investment certificates issued under the Government Investment Act 1983; and

    (d)   such other assets as may be approved by the Minister on the recommendation of the Central Bank.

(7) The Central Bank may by notice in writing require each Islamic bank to render such return or returns as the Central Bank deems necessary for the implementation of this section.

(8) Any Islamic bank which fails to comply with any of the provisions of this section shall be liable to pay, on being called upon to do so by the Central Bank, a penalty of not more than one-tenth of one per cent of the amount of the deficiency for every day during which the deficiency continues.

(9) Any Islamic bank which fails or refuses to pay a penalty under subsection (8) shall be guilty of an offence under this Act.

17.

(1) Notwithstanding the provisions of the Companies Act 1965, every Islamic bank shall appoint annually an auditor approved by the Minister.

(2) The Minister on the recommendation of the Central Bank may appoint an auditor:

    (a)   if the Islamic bank fails to appoint an auditor; or

    (b)   if he considers it desirable that another auditor should act with the auditor appointed under subsection (1).

and may fix the remuneration to be paid by the Islamic bank to that auditor.

(3) The duties of the auditor appointed under subsections (1) and (2) for an Islamic bank shall be to make a report in accordance with section 174 of the Companies Act 1965 upon the annual balance sheet and profit and loss account of the bank.

(4) The report of the auditor referred to in paragraph (b) of subsection (3) shall be laid together with the report of the directors of the Islamic bank at the annual general meeting of the bank; and a statutory declaration made by a senior officer of the bank to the effect that the report was so laid shall accompany the documents forwarded under paragraph (c) of subsection (1) of section 18.

(5) No person having an interest in an Islamic bank otherwise than as a shareholder, and no director or officer of that bank, shall be eligible for appointment as an auditor for that bank; and any person appointed as auditor to an Islamic bank who after such appointment acquires such interest or becomes a director or an officer of that bank shall forthwith cease to be the auditor.

(6) The duties, powers and liabilities imposed and conferred by section 33 in relation to an investigation by the Central Bank of the affairs of an Islamic bank under section 31 or 32 are hereby imposed and conferred in relation to auditors appointed under this section.

(7) Any Islamic bank which fails to comply with the requirements of subsection (4) shall be guilty of an offence and shall on conviction be liable to a fine not exceeding twenty thousand ringgit.

18.

(1) Every Islamic bank shall:
    (a) exhibit in a conspicuous position in every office or place of business in Malaysia:

        (i) a copy of each of its latest audited annual balance sheet, profit and loss account, together with any note thereon, and the report of the auditor;

        (ii) the full names of all its directors; and

        (iii) the names of all subsidiaries for the time being of the bank;

    (b) within fourteen days of the laying of its accounts at its annual general meeting publish in at least two daily newspapers published in Malaysia and approved by the Central Bank a copy each of its latest audited annual balance sheet, profit and loss statement, together with any note thereon, and the report of the auditor; and

    (c) within six months after the close of each financial year or such

319

further period as the Central Bank may approve, forward to the Central Bank:

(i) two copies of each of its latest audited annual balance sheet, profit and loss account, together with any note thereon, and the reports of the auditor and the directors;

(ii) in the case of an Islamic bank with branches outside Malaysia, two copies of each of its latest audited annual balance sheet and profit and loss account in respect of its operations in Malaysia, and two copies each of its latest audited annual balance sheet and profit and loss account in respect of its operations in each country outside Malaysia.

(2) The form and content of the balance sheet and profit and loss account shall, together with the report of the directors, be as approved by the Central Bank.

(3) The Central Bank may require any Islamic bank to submit such further or additional information as it may deem necessary either by way of explanation, amplification or otherwise with regard to the balance sheets and profit and loss accounts forwarded by that bank under paragraph (c) of subsection (1) and that information shall be submitted within such period and in such manner as the Central Bank may require.

(4) Any Islamic bank which fails to comply with the provisions of this section shall be guilty of an offence and shall on conviction be liable to a fine not exceeding twenty thousand ringgit.

19.

(1) Every Islamic Bank shall send to the Central Bank in such form as may be prescribed by the Central Bank:

(a) a statement showing the liabilities and assets of its banking offices and branches in Malaysia at the close of business on the last business day of each month within such period as may be prescribed by notice in writing from time to time by the Central Bank;

(b) a statement giving an analysis of loans, advances and investment of its banking offices and branches in Malaysia as at such intervals and within such period as may be prescribed by notice from time to time by the Central Bank;

(c) not later than six months after the close of its financial year, a statement showing the income and expenditure in respect of its business in Malaysia;

(d) notwithstanding the provisions of subsection (3) of section 34, a statement showing such credit information of its customers as is required for the purposes of the credit bureau established under section 30 (1) (iii) of the Central Bank of Malaysia Ordinance 1958 at such intervals and within such period as may be prescribed by notice in writing from time to time by the Central Bank; and

(e) any such statistical information as may be requested by the Central Bank.

(2) Except for the purposes of paragraph (d) of subsection (1), any information received from a bank under this section shall be regarded as secret between that bank and the Central bank.

(3) Any Islamic bank which fails to comply with any requirement set out in subsection (1) shall be guilty of an offence and shall on conviction be liable to a fine not exceeding four thousand ringgit for every day during which the default continues.

(4) It shall be the responsibility of the Central Bank to prepare and publish consolidated statements aggregating the figures in the returns furnished under paragraphs (a) and (b) of subsection (1).

20.

An Islamic bank which operates branch offices or agencies outside Malaysia shall furnish to the Central Bank any information relating to the operations of such offices or agencies as may be requested by the Central Bank.

PART IV — OWNERSHIP, CONTROL AND MANAGEMENT OF ISLAMIC BANKS

21.

(1) Whenever a change is about to occur in the control of any Islamic bank, the bank shall report the proposed change to the Central Bank.

(2) Whenever a loan or advance is made by any Islamic bank secured in the aggregate by twenty per cent or more of the paid-up capital shares of any other Islamic bank or of any licensed bank under the Banking Act 1973 incorporated in Malaysia or of any finance company licensed under the Finance Companies Act 1969, the Islamic bank shall report the fact to the Central Bank.

(3) The reports required to be made under subsection (2) shall contain the following:

(i) the names and addresses of borrowers;

(ii) the name of the Islamic bank, the licensed bank, or finance company issuing the shares by which the loan or advance is secured;

(iii) the number of shares by which the loan or advance is secured; and

(iv) the amount of the loan or advance.

(4) The reports under subsections (1) and (2) shall be in addition to any report

which may be required pursuant to the provisions of any other written law.

(5) For the purposes of this section, the expression 'control' in relation to an Islamic bank means the possession directly or indirectly of the power to direct or cause the direction of the management and policy of the bank.

(6) Any Islamic bank which fails to comply with the provisions of subsection (1) or (2) shall be guilty of an offence and shall on conviction be liable to a fine not exceeding twenty thousand ringgit.

22.

(1) Every Islamic bank shall obtain the approval of the Minister of any proposed:
    (a) arrangement or agreement:
        (i) for the sale or disposal of its share or business; or
        (ii) affecting voting power, management or other matters, which will result in a change in the control or management of the bank; and
    (b) scheme:
        (i) for reconstruction of the bank; or
        (ii) for amalgamation, merger or otherwise between the bank and any other corporation.
Wherein the whole or any part of the undertaking or the property of the bank is to be transferred to another corporation.

(2) The Minister, on the recommendation of the Central Bank, may approve or refuse to allow the proposed arrangement, agreement or scheme, but the approval of the Minister shall not be unreasonably withheld.

23.

(1) Without prejudice to anything contained in the Companies Act, 1965, any person who is a director, manager, secretary or other officer concerned in the management of an Islamic bank shall cease to hold office:
    (a) if he becomes bankrupt, suspends payment or compounds with his creditors; or
    (b) if he is convicted of an offence involving dishonesty or fraud.

(2) No person who has been a director of, or directly concerned in the management of, an Islamic bank, or a licensed bank under the Banking Act 1973 which has been wound up by a court shall, without the express authority of the Minister, act or continue to act as a director of, or be directly concerned in the management of, any Islamic bank.

(3) Any person who acts in contravention of subsection (1) or (2) shall be guilty of an offence and shall on conviction be liable to a fine not

exceeding twenty thousand ringgit or to imprisonment for a term not exceeding three years or to both such fine and imprisonment.

PART V — RESTRICTIONS ON BUSINESS

24.

(1) No Islamic bank shall:
    (a) pay any dividend on its shares until all its capitalised expenditure (including preliminary expenses, organisation expenses, share-selling commission, brokerage, amounts of losses incurred and any other item of expenditure not represented by tangible assets) has been completely written off;
    (b) grant an advance, loan or credit facility against the security of its own shares; or
    (c) grant unsecured advances, unsecured loans or unsecured credit facilities in excess of, in the aggregate and outstanding at any one time, ten thousand ringgit to any corporation which is deemed to be related to the bank as described in section 6 of the Companies Act, 1965, other than an Islamic bank, a licensed bank under the Banking Act, 1983, a finance company licensed under the Finance Companies Act, 1969, or any other financial institution approved by the Central Bank.

(2) For the purpose of this section 'unsecured advances', 'unsecured loans' and 'unsecured credit facilities' mean respectively advances, loans and credit facilities made without security, or, in respect of any advance loan and credit facility made with security, any portion thereof which at any time exceeds the market value of the assets constituting the security of, where the Central Bank is satisfied that there is no established market value, the value made on the basis of a valuation approved by the Central Bank.

25.

(1) Except as provided under paragraph (c) of subsection (1) of section 24 and subsection 2 of this section, no Islamic bank shall grant advances, loans or credit facilities to:
    (a) any of its directors, officers or employees or other persons being persons receiving remuneration from it (other than accountants, advocates and solicitors, architects, estate agents, doctors and any other persons receiving remuneration from it in respect of their professional services);

    (b)   any firm in which any of its directors, officers or employees is interested as partner, manager, agent or guarantor;

    (c)   any corporation in which any of its officers or employees is a director, manager, agent or guarantor, or any corporation in the shares of which any of its officers or employees has any material interest as determined by the Central Bank.

    (d)   any corporation in which any of its directors (not being an executive director), he being within the ambit of the provisions of paragraph (c) pursuant to subsection (3) is a member, director, manager, agent or guarantor, or any corporation in the shares of which any such director of the Islamic bank has any interest whatsoever directly or indirectly; or

    (e)   any individual for whom any of its directors, officers or employees is a guarantor.

(2) An Islamic bank may grant to any of its officers or employees loans which are provided under its appropriate scheme of service and, where the bank is satisfied that special or compassionate circumstances exist, a loan not exceeding at any one time six months' remuneration of that officer or employee on such terms and conditions as the bank thinks fit.

(3) The provisions of paragraph (c) of subsection (1) and of subsection (2) shall also apply to the executive directors of Islamic banks.

(4) The provisions of paragraph (d) of subsection (1) shall not apply to the granting of advances, loans or credit facilities by an Islamic bank to:

    (a)   a corporation which is listed on a recognised stock exchange and in the shares of which no director of that Islamic bank has, directly or indirectly, any material interest as determined by the Central Bank; and

    (b)   a public company in which a director of that Islamic bank has no interest in his personal capacity, as determined by the Central Bank.

Provided that for the purposes of this subsection the director concerned is not an executive director of that Islamic bank.

(5) For the purpose of this section, 'director', 'officer' or 'employee' includes a spouse, parent or child of a director, an officer or employee.

26.

No Islamic bank shall grant any advance, loan or credit facility under the exemption referred to in subsection (4) of section 25 unless the following conditions are satisfied:

(a) that the advance, loan or credit facility meets the standards of creditworthiness required of other applicant borrowers;

(b) that the terms of the advance, loan or credit facility are not less favourable to the bank that those offered to others;

(c) that the grant of the advance, loan or credit facility will serve the best interest of the bank; and

(d) that the advance, loan or credit facility has been approved by the votes of not less than two-thirds of all the other directors of the bank at a duly constituted meeting of the full board of directors and the approval has been recorded in the minutes of that meeting.

27.

(1) No Islamic bank shall grant any customer any credit facilities or incur any liabilities on his behalf to an aggregate amount in excess of such percentage as may be determined from time to time by the Central Bank in relation to such bank's capital funds unimpaired by losses or otherwise.

(2) Subsection (1) shall not apply to:

    (a) transactions with other Islamic banks, with licensed banks under the Banking Act, 1973 and with finance companies licensed under the Finance Companies Act, 1969;

    (b) any facilities granted in respect of imports into or exports from Malaysia or trade within Malaysia against letters of credit or bills of exchange; or

    (c) any other transactions which the Central Bank may approve from time to time.

(3) for the purposes of subsection (1), the expression 'capital funds' shall have the meaning assigned to it by subsection (2) of section 5.

28.

(1) Every director of an Islamic bank who is in any manner whatsoever, whether directly or indirectly, interested in an advance, loan or credit facility or proposed advance, loan or credit facility from that Islamic bank shall as soon as practicable declare the nature of his interest to the Board of Directors of that Islamic bank and the secretary of that Islamic bank shall cause such declaration to be circulated forthwith to all the directors.

(2) The requirements of subsection (1) shall not apply in any case where the interest of the director consists only in being a member or creditor of a corporation which is interested in an advance, loan or credit facility or proposed advance, loan or credit facility from that Islamic bank if the interest of the director may properly be regarded as not being a material interest.

(3) For the purposes of subsection (1), a general notice given to the board of directors of an Islamic bank by a director to the effect that he is an officer

or member of a specified firm or a member of a specified corporation and he is to be regarded as interested in any advance, loan or credit facility which may, after the date of the notice, be made to that firm or corporation shall be deemed to be a sufficient declaration of interest in relation to any advance, loan or credit facility so made if:

    (a) it specifies the nature and extent of his interest in a specified form or corporation;

    (b) his interest shall not be different in nature or greater in extent than the nature and extent so specified in the notice at the time any advance, loan or credit facility is made; and

    (c) it is given at the meeting of the directors or the director takes reasonable steps to ensure that it is brought up and read at the next meeting of the directors after it is given.

(4) Every director of an Islamic bank who holds any office or possesses any property whereby whether directly or indirectly duties or interest might be created in conflict with his duties or interest as a director shall declare at a meeting of the directors of the Islamic bank the fact and the nature, character and extent of the conflict.

(5) The declaration referred to in subsection (4) shall be made at the first meeting of the directors held:

    (a) after he becomes a director of the Islamic bank; or

    (b) (if already a director) after he commenced to hold office or to possess the property as the case may require.

(6) The Secretary of the Islamic bank shall cause to be brought up and read any declaration made under subsection (1) or (4) at the next meeting of the directors after it is given, and shall record any declaration made under this section in the minutes of the meeting at which it was made or at which it was brought up and read.

(7) Any director who acts in contravention of subsection (1) or (4) shall be guilty of an offence and shall on conviction be liable to a fine not exceeding twenty thousand ringgit or to imprisonment for a term not exceeding three years or to both such fine and imprisonment.

29.

(1) Any credit facility granted by any Islamic bank to any person for the purpose of financing the purchase or the holding of shares shall not exceed such percentage of the market value of the shares at the time the credit facility is granted, as may be directed by the Central Bank in writing.

(2) A credit facility under this section to any person shall be accounted for in an account separate from that kept for any other credit facility granted to him.

(3) The Central Bank may give direction in writing to any Islamic bank in

respect of the following matters, that is to say:

(a) the basis and method for determining the market value of shares held as security for such credit facility;

(b) the withdrawal of funds or shares by the persons to whom such facility was granted;

(c) the substitution of other shares held as security for such credit facility; and

(d) such other matters as may be deemed necessary.

(4) Any Islamic bank which acts in contravention of the provisions of this section or any direction given under this section shall be guilty of an offence under this Act.

30.

Any Islamic bank, if at any time called upon in writing by the Central Bank to do so, shall satisfy it by the production of such evidence or information as it may require that the bank is not acting in contravention of any of the provisions 24, 25, 26, 27 and 29.

PART VI — POWERS OF SUPERVISION AND CONTROL OVER ISLAMIC BANKS

31.

The Central Bank shall from time to time investigate, under conditions of secrecy the books, accounts and transactions of each Islamic bank and of any branch, agency or office outside Malaysia opened by an Islamic bank.

32.

The Minister may at any time direct the Central Bank to make an investigation, under conditions of secrecy, of the books, accounts and transactions of an Islamic bank, if he has reason to believe such Islamic bank is carrying on its business in a manner detrimental to the interests of its depositors and other creditors, or has insufficient assets to cover its liabilities to the public, or is contravening the provisions of this Act or of the Central Bank of Malaysia Ordinance, 1958.

33.

(1) Subject to subsection (2), for the purposes of an investigation under section 31 or 32, an Islamic bank shall afford the Central Bank access to its books, accounts and documents and shall give such information and facilities as may be required to conduct the investigation.

(2) Books, accounts and documents shall not be required to be produced at such times and at such places as shall interfere with the proper conduct of the normal daily business of the bank concerned.

Appendix B: Islamic Banking Law in Turkey

Islamic banking in Turkey has been sanctioned by a Decree of the Government passed on 16 December 1983 by the Council of Ministers and is known as the Decree No 83/7506 dealing with the foundation, operation and liquidation of Special Finance Institutions.

The following two communiques from the Undersecretariat of Treasury and Foreign Trade of the Prime Ministry and the Central Bank of Turkey (the Bank) respectively lay down the complete details, laws and procedures relating to the Institutions and operation of the Islamic financial Institutions in Turkey.

COMMUNIQUE

From: Undersecretariat of Treasury and Foreign Trade of the Prime Ministry

Communique Related to Decree Attached to Decree Number 83/7506 *Regarding the Foundation of Special Finance Institutions*

The Foundation, operation and liquidation of Special Finance Institutions are subject to the provisions below, in accordance with the covenants of the Council of Ministers' Decree dated 16 December 1983 and number 83/7506 related to foundation of Special Finance Institutions and the authority and responsibility vested upon Prime Ministry by Law Number 1567 regarding the Preservation of the Value of the Turkish currency.

Scope

Article 1

According to Decree Law dated 16.12.83 and number 83/7506 Special Finance Institutions founded or to be founded in Turkey are subject to the provision of this Communique.

Abbreviations and Definitions

Article 2

Some of the expressions used in this Communique shall have the meaning defined below:

(a) Institution: Special Finance Institution.

(b) Undersecretariat: Undersecretariat of Treasury and Foreign Trade of the Prime Ministry.

(c) Bank: Central Bank of the Republic of Turkey.

(d) Current Account: Special Current Account.

(e) Participation Account: Account giving the right to participate in Profit and Loss.

(f) Accounts: Current Account and Participation Account.

(g) Special Current Accounts: Funds opened in Turkish lira or foreign exchange, bearing no interest or profit, deposited by real and legal persons which can be partially or totally withdrawn upon demand.

(h) Profit and Loss Participation Accounts: Funds deposited with the Finance Institution against a 'Contract for Profit and Loss Participation Account', for a maximum period of five years, opened by real and legal persons which will lead to sharing profit and loss resulting from the placement of these funds in conformity with principles set forth in Communique.

(i) Contract for Profit and Loss Participation Account: A uniform, written contract regulating legal and financial relations between the Institution and account holder who deposits funds in the profit and loss participation account. The fundamentals of this Contract shall be determined by the Bank.

(j) Contract for Profit and Loss Participation Account: A uniform, written contract regulating legal and financial relations between the Institution and real and legal persons who were placed with funds for certain periods by the Institution, with the intention of participating in their profit and loss. The fundamentals of this Contract shall be determined by the Bank.

(k) Sale Purchase Contract: A contract organising the advance purchase of immobiles, raw and semi-finished products and machinery and equipment for those who apply to secure the same for regulating enterprises from third parties and time-sale of said goods to such applicants.

Institutions shall complete the sale purchase contract within free contracting but at the same time.

(l) Rent Contract (Leasing): Renting equipment producing goods and services to enterprises within free contracting but keeping the titles thereof in the Institution.

(m) Unit Account Value: Daily or weekly amount, expressed in Turkish lira, calculated by multiplying 'Unit Value' by 'Account Value' and one which owners of the Contract for Profit and Loss Participation Investment have a right to claim. A sample regarding the determination of Unit Account Value is attached.

(n) Unit Value: A unit varies according to profit and loss incurred. Unit value, accepted as 100 for the first day, is a 'weight' unit, calculated and announced daily or weekly, being found out during booking of profit and loss by division of total value of assets existing in each segregated fund as per terms to the total Account Value of the proceeding day.

(o) Account Value: A ratio of participation of real and legal persons, who have deposited to Profit and Loss Participation Accounts, in the assets existing in such funds. This ratio is specified in the special section of Contract Form of Profit and Loss Participation Account. Considering that this ratio will vary at the time of deposits to and withdrawals from this account, the new ratio replaces the former ratio on the contract form. Account value is calculated on the first day the Institution accepts funds by dividing the amount deposited by the account holder by unit value as assumed 100. Calculation of Account Value in the following days is carried out in the manner written below:

The new account value is computed by adding to or subtracting from the existing Account Value of the Account Holder, the amount which is calculated by dividing the amount deposited or withdrawn to the Unit Value.

(p) Institution Account: An account that shall be kept by the Institution as a joint stock company in accordance with Turkish Commercial Law and other related legislation. These accounts are booked separately from Islamic Current Accounts and Profit and Loss Participation Accounts.

Exception Clause: Besides the covenants above the adoption of principles relating to the calculation of profit and loss is subject to the proposal of Institution, affirmative approach of the Bank and the approval of Undersecretariat.

Establishment

Article 3

Institutions must be established as joint companies with a minimum of 100 shareholders, at least 5 of which should be founding partners; total paid up capital shall not be less than 5 billion Turkish lira. Institutions shall be liable to pay ¼ of the company capital at once in cash and the balance in six months, in cash. Undersecretariat shall specify the terms of payment of portions of capital over 5 billion Turkish lira of those Institutions established with a capital of more than the minimum capital of 5 billion Turkish lira. Foreign partners are required to bring regulating capital share in Turkey in cash and in foreign exchange, subject to purchase and sale by the Bank.

Institutions shall allocate capital to be defined by Undersecretariat under the above conditions for each new branch to be opened (in addition to the head office).

The founders of Institutions should be neither bankrupt nor have been sentenced for ethical or moral offences.

Specialities of the share certificates

Article 4

Certificates of the joint stock companies which are established to operate according to this Communique shall be as follows:

(1) Certificates shall be issued to the name and against cash.
(2) Nominal values shall not be less than TL 100.000,-.
(3) Non-resident participants may own the whole of the share capital. In case such shareholders transfer their share to persons residing in Turkey, the revenue gained shall, after being converted to foreign exchange at the current rate, be blocked for five years in accordance with the provisions of the Law on the Preservation of the Value of Turkish Currency.

Authority of permission and application

Article 5

The founders are required to obtain permission from the Council of Ministers, the approval of the Bank and Undersecretariat in accordance with the provisions of Decree Number 83/7506 and of this Communique.

The founders shall apply in writing to the bank to obtain permission. The principles and procedures regarding the application are specified by the Bank.

Declaration to be submitted after the establishment

Article 6

After having been granted a licence by the Council of Ministers for establishment and having completed the procedures connected with the establishment in compliance with the provisions of Turkish Commercial Law, and after establishment has been approved by the Commercial Court, registered at the Trade Registry Office and announced duly, institutions are required to obtain special permission to commence their operations by submitting a declaration to the Bank.

The content of the declaration to be submitted shall be specified by the Bank.

Opening branches

Article 7

Institutions shall obtain permission from the Undersecretariat through the Bank for each branch office to be opened.

Institutions wishing to liquidate or to suspend operations of one or more of their branches must notify the Undersecretariat through the Bank within 15 days from the date of the decision taken by the Board of Directors.

Granting and cancelling of the authority to collect funds and to utilise funds

Article 8

Upon submission of the application as per Article 6, the Bank shall verify if the parties concerned have fulfilled the requirements set forth in this Communique, and if the Institution has acquired the specialist skills deemed necessary to operate by the regulations; it shall give the necessary permission within one month (at the maximum) following the date of submission of the declaration. The Bank shall inform the Undersecretariat of the institution granted permission to operate.

A time period of two months shall be given to rectify the omissions to those submissions not approved. Applications of those who do not rectify the omissions within the given period are considered to have been refused.

Should the operations of institutions who obtained permission according to covenants above be then found inappropriate, such institutions shall be prohibited from operating temporarily or permanently by a Council of Ministers' Decree processed upon the application of the Undersecretariat after obtaining the view of the Bank.

The Board of Directors

Article 11

The Board of Directors shall consist of seven members elected at the General Assembly of Shareholders. The members shall designate one of the members as the Chairman. Members of the Board of Directors shall hold office for three years.

Decisions taken by the Board shall be recorded daily in a register with subsequently numbered pages, which is approved in accordance with the provision of Turkish Commercial Law on registers, in chronological and numerical order without leaving any blanks and without any additions between the lines, and under each decision the Members of the Board shall sign.

If the Board deems it necessary, a second copy of this register can also be kept in a foreign language, but this will not constitute legal documentation.

Operating structures

Article 10

Operating structure of the Institution consists of the General Meeting of Shareholders, the Board of Directors and the Committee of Auditors.

Voting rights in the General Assembly of Shareholders

Article 11

Each share of TL 1,000.000 permits single voting. Shareholders possessing shares of less than TL 1,000.000 in value can get the right to vote by combining their shares and delegating authority to one shareholder.

The Chairman and Members of the Board of Directors and those who are vested with the authority of first category signature may not vote by proxy. The sum total of votes used for his own and by proxy by a person who does not fall within the scope of this paragraph, may not exceed 10 per cent of the share capital.

General Director

Article 12

Line activities of the Institution are executed by a General Director appointed by the Board.

The General Director is responsible to the Board for the execution of these decisions. The General Director is a natural Member of the Board but may not vote at these meetings of the Board. Of the General Manager or his assistants at least one should be domiciled in Turkey or be a Turkish citizen.

Committee of Auditors

Article 13

The Committee of Auditors shall consist of three members elected by the General Assembly of Shareholders.

The Committee of Auditors shall be chosen from real and legal persons who have knowledge and experience in the fields of finance, economy, law and accounting. Two of the auditors must be Turkish citizens.

Members of the Committee of Auditors shall notify cases contradictory to regulations and to the Articles of Incorporation, with a report to the General Assembly of Shareholders, the Undersecretariat, and the Bank together with documentary evidence.

Types of funds acceptable by the Institution

Article 14

Institutions can collect funds in two types of accounts which are 'Current Accounts' and 'Participation Accounts'. Institutions are obliged to keep current accounts and participation accounts separately from the accounts of the Institution and to keep participation accounts independently according to different terms.

The Institution is required to take all the necessary technical measures to keep its accounts. In order for a Licence of Performance to be given in accordance with Article 8, certification that these measures have been taken is required.

The Institution is authorised to maintain, on microfilm, in accordance with the principles to be set up by the Undersecretariat, the books and other accounts and documents that it has to keep in accordance with Article 68 of Turkish Commercial Code and Tax Procedure Law.

Current Accounts

Article 15

It is an account to be opened in Turkish lira or in foreign exchange according to provisions to be set forth by Communiques and being payable partially or totally on demand; the account holder receives no interest, profit or other proceeds under whatever name they may be; the funds do not fall within the scope of the Savings Accounts Insurance Fund.

Specialities of Current Accounts

Article 16

Current accounts are booked and operated independently of Institution accounts and participation accounts and are booked and operated individually as Turkish lira accounts.

The Institution transfers the profit and the loss incurred from the utilisation of funds accumulated in this account to its own accounts.

Current account creditors are first-priority creditors of the assets corresponding to current accounts as well as the capital and the reserve of the Institution for the total amount they have deposited.

The maximum amount the Institution can collect in its current account is determined by the Bank.

Utilisation of funds accumulated in Current Accounts

Article 17

A minimum of 10 per cent of the funds accumulated in these accounts shall be kept in cash or as deposits in commercial banks. An additional 10 per cent shall be kept in the bank either in cash or as liquid assets to be specified by the Bank. These percentages can be changed by the Bank.

The remainder of the funds can be utilised to finance commercial activities of real or legal persons, 50 per cent of which have a term of longer than one year. Eighty per cent of funds utilised shall be collected in cash when due and 20 per cent at the most can be participated to the profit and loss of the real or legal persons using the fund in accordance with the covenants of Contract for Profit and Loss Participation. The share the Institution receives from profit and loss and, if necessary, the securities the Institution takes shall be clearly expressed in the Contract for Profit and Loss Participation investment.

The amount of a fund which can be associated with a single, real or legal person from these amounts shall be determined by the Bank.

Foreign exchange accumulated in these accounts can, furthermore, be utilised in Turkish banks and in international monetary and commercial markets.

Participation Accounts

Article 18

Such accounts entitle participation in profit and loss arising from the utilisation of funds deposited with the Institution in Turkish lira or foreign exchange by real or legal persons against 'Contract for Profit and Loss Participation Accounts'. These types of accounts can be opened with a minimum of TL 100.000.

Features of Participation Accounts

Article 19

Participation Accounts have the following features:

(a) No interest or fixed income is paid to the account holder and the repayment of the deposited principal is not guaranteed. The obligation of the Finance Institution and the claim of the Account Holder will be the amount corresponding to the Unit Value. Incomes to be accrued to the benefit of the account holders shall be considered dividends from the point of view of taxation regulations.

(b) These accounts are divided into four alternative terms, being 90 days, 180 days, 360 days and longer. Each group is administered as a segregated pool and each is operated and booked separately. The Bank has the authority to re-establish the terms.

(c) Funds in these accounts are booked according to Unit Account Values, and are not carried in Accounts of the Institution. The Institution is required to prepare a status of accounts of these funds twice a year, and to inform the public.

(d) Third party creditors of the Institution can have claims only on the capital, the reserves and the undistributed profits of the Institution; they cannot have any rights on the funds accumulated in these accounts.

(e) All expenses incurred through the operation of these accounts are paid by the Institution.

(f) The share of the Institution in the profit or loss resulting from the placement of the funds in these accounts cannot be more than 20 per cent. The change of the ratio set by the Institution being within the 20 per cent margin is subject to the permission of the Bank. The Institution can carry on its balance sheet only its share of profit and loss and expenses incurred as a result of the operation of these accounts. The Institution transfers its share from the loss or profit to its accounts daily or weekly.

(g) Funds accumulated in these accounts do not fall within the scope of the Savings Account Insurance Fund.

Utilisation of funds accumulated in Participation Accounts

Article 20

The funds accumulated in these accounts shall be used as follows:

(a) An amount to be determined by the Bank not in excess of 50 per cent of those amounts retained in the Bank as per Article 17, paragraph 1, shall be blocked in the Bank as per provisions set forth in the said article.

(b) The non-blocked funds may be allocated to the use of real and legal persons in the following manners:

Production Assistance
This will be realised through buying the necessary goods and equipment and real estate from third parties in cash and selling these on credit to those who apply for the provision of real estate, raw or semi-finished material and machinery and equipment for their enterprises. The finance house is required to complete the purchase and sale contracts simultaneously in accordance with the freedom of entry into contracts.
Utilisation of funds by participation in profit and loss
In order to place the participation funds in profit and loss, the Institution shall sign a 'Contract for Profit and Loss Participation Investment' with real and legal persons who will use these funds. Participation in profit and loss can either cover all activities or only one activity of the fund-user of the profit and loss resulting from buying and selling of a specified amount of goods. The Institution can have a claim on the profits at a ratio specified in the Contract of real and legal persons using these funds; in the case of loss, the Institution participates in the loss according to the maximum amount allocated that activity.
Rental contract (leasing)
This is the leasing of equipment to be utilised in the production of goods and services to enterprises while retaining the title of such equipment in the Institution.
Placement of funds upon documentary letters of credit
This type of placement is relevant only for the activities permitted by the Foreign Trade Regulation.
    A contract is signed between the House and the fund-user which regulates purchasing of the document by the Institution in cash and reselling it to the fund-user at a higher price on credit.

(c) Funds not utilised in the ways specified above can be kept in the banks.
(d) The Institution is required to allocate, starting from the second year of activity, a minimum of 25 per cent of the funds accumulated in Participation Accounts to activities earning foreign exchange.

(e) The Bank determines the maximum amount of funds which will be used by a single real or legal person from the funds accumulated in each pool.

Early withdrawal from Participation Accounts

Article 21

Money can be drawn from Participation Accounts before the due date provided a notice of 30 days shall be given to that effect. The maximum amount to be drawn early is the sum total deposited by the account owner until that date if the term-pool wherein the fund is deposited shows profit; should the related term-pool show loss, the amount to be drawn is Unit Account Value.

The difference between the amount drawn and the sum total corresponding to 'Unit Account Value' of the amount drawn on the date of such draw shall be accounted as profit to the related term-pool.

Depositing to accounts

Article 22

Real and legal persons domiciled in Turkey may deposit Turkish lira and foreign exchange funds to current accounts and participation accounts and real and legal persons domiciled abroad may deposit foreign exchange funds to these accounts.

The foreign exchange funds deposited to Participation Accounts shall be operated in a single account regardless of the kind of foreign exchange and terms and independent of other accounts. Foreign exchange funds deposited to Current Accounts are also operated and booked independently. Foreign exchange accumulated in these accounts shall comply with the provisions of this Communique and procedures to be specified by the Bank and meet primarily the country's needs.

Closing the Participation Accounts

Article 23

Accounts that are not closed within five working days after maturity shall be deemed to have been renewed with the same term. Notice may be given beforehand that the account shall not be renewed after maturity. In the event of closing the Account, the amount claimed by the Account Holder shall be equivalent to the Unit Account Value on the maturity day.

Prescription of Current Islamic Accounts and Profit and Loss Participation

Article 24

The Sum of the Account, together with a certificate covering the name, identity and address of the Account Holder, shall be transferred to the Bank to the order of treasury, if, regarding Current Accounts, ten years pass after the date of last transaction or last written instruction of the Account Holder after the date of first maturity.

The Institution, with the aim of notifying the Account Holders who will be subject to the ten years prescription, should prepare twice a year a list of such account holders whose ten-year period shall expire in a year; it should keep the list at branches and announce that such lists are ready for inspection in one of five newspapers having the highest circulation in Turkey and in cities and countries that the Institution deems necessary.

On those accounts opened in the name of minors with a condition that payments should solely be made to them, the prescription periods referred to in the Article commence on the date the minors become of age.

Other services Institutions may offer

Article 25

Institutions may render the following services:

(a) To rent safe deposits;
(b) To conclude transfers and assignments to order;
(c) To prepare feasibility studies;
(d) Other services to be approved by the Bank.

Institutions may also render the following services provided they obtain special permission from the Undersecretariat through the Bank Principal; procedures regarding such activities shall be specified separately by the Undersecretariat.

(a) To issue Letters of Guarantee;
(b) To enter into partnership in activities out of the areas specified by order of this Communique;
(c) To purchase and sell real estate with commercial purposes;
(d) To establish and operate enterprises in agro-industry with the funds accumulated in the participation accounts;
(e) To collect funds in independent accounts to finance special projects and allocate such funds in these projects.

Booking of profit and loss, arising from placement of the parties

Article 26

Temporary profit arising from the placement of funds to real and legal persons by the Institution shall be paid to the Institution by those real and legal persons or the loss shall be collected from the Institution. The amounts paid because of profit by the real and legal persons using these funds shall be booked as expenditures by those persons and the amount which the real and legal persons receive due to the loss shall be carried to the profit and loss accounts. The Institution shall book losses paid and profits collected by itself in accordance with the provisions of this Communique.

Except for the above regulations, calculations of profit and loss and auditing procedures shall be determined by the parties in the Profit and Loss Investment Contract.

All obligations arising from Turkish Commercial Law and from Taxation Laws regarding those operations shall be deemed to be the liability and obligation of real and legal persons using funds.

Provisions related to foreign exchange

Article 27

Institutions can hold foreign exchange positions and can render foreign exchange operations; the principles and conditions of pursuing exchange positions shall be specified by the Undersecretariat.

Transformation of profits into capital

Article 28

From the net profit obtained by the Institution, the profit shares due to non-resident shareholders can, with the demand of the Institution and decision of the Undersecretariat, be added totally or partially to the capital or can be invested in other enterprises and areas within the framework of existing regulations.

Enterprises and participation of the Institution

Article 29

An Institution may not establish an independent enterprise or become a participant of an enterprise by placing capital from the funds accumulated in Islamic Current Accounts and Profit and Loss Participation Accounts. The total amount of funds which can be placed in enterprises either by the Institution or its shareholders from these accounts is limited to a maximum 20 per cent of the funds accumulated in these accounts.

The Undersecretariat may decide to increase this ratio for the placement of Participation account funds to some special project.

Transfer of profit, capital share and funds deposited to accounts abroad

Article 30

The following are the rights of those capital owners who are domiciled abroad and paid in foreign exchange and those capital owners of Turkish nationality who work abroad and gain foreign exchange income:

(a) net profits due to their shares;
(b) the amounts which are transferred into cash from their share of assets at the liquidation of the Institution;
(c) proceeds of the total or partial sale of capital shares, which are changed to foreign exchange at the rate of the date of such sale and kept blocked for five years and regain the right of transfer following the completion of the said period.

Amounts payable to the account owners who are domiciled abroad and paid in foreign exchange and to account owners of Turkish nationality who earn foreign exchange working abroad shall be transferred freely.

Prevailing regulations shall be applied to other matters related to transfer.

The Undersecretariat may audit tax returns and records of demanded profit remittances if deemed necessary; it always has the authority of examining the conformity of other amounts to the books and records of the Institution and to the results of liquidation.

Public agencies authorised to audit

Article 31

Operations and accounts of Institutions are audited by the Bank. The Undersecretariat is always authorised to audit these Institutions.

Measures

Article 32

Should the operations and state of being of an Institution be found to be contrary to the regulations, purpose and principles of the enterprise at the end of audits done in accordance with Article 31, a reasonable time period shall be given by the Undersecretariat which should obtain the view of the Bank as to the conformity with the Law, purpose and principles of the enterprise.

As a consequence, Institutions may be prohibited from functioning temporarily or permanently in accordance with Article 12 of the Decree should it be established that the necessary measures are not taken and ameliorations are not realised by the Institution in a given period.

Liquidation of Institutions

Article 33

(A) If Institutions operating in Turkey wish to go into liquidation they shall inform the Undersecretariat. On request for liquidation by an Institution, the Undersecretariat should inspect whether the Institution's activities are in conformity with the regulations, aims and principles of the establishment with the assistance of inspectors of Finance and Customs, tax accountants and bank examiners. At the end of the inspection the following procedures will be carried out:

(1) If the state of the Institution is found to be in conformity with the aim and principles and regulations of the establishment, the Institution has notification to liquidate itself in a given period. Liquidation shall be realised at a maximum of two years under the supervision of the Undersecretariat or a bank appointed by the Ministry.

(2) If the Institution is not found to be in conformity with the aims and principles of the establishment and of regulations, or cannot liquidate itself in the given period, the Prime Ministry applies to the Council of Ministers to take a decision for gradual liquidation.

Gradual liquidation of the Institution is carried out by a Bank appointed by the Undersecretariat. The Bank and the Undersecretariat shall be informed of the state of gradual liquidation by a report prepared every six months. Provisions of Turkish Commercial Law, Execution and Bankruptcy Law and other legislation relating to liquidation shall not be applied to the decision for and execution of liquidation. Liquidation procedures shall be determined by the Undersecretariat.

(B) Liquidation is carried out for Current Accounts, Participation Accounts and Accounts of the Institution separately:

(1) *Liquidation of Current Accounts*: Assets corresponding to the existing capital and reserves of the Institution to be liquidated as well as assets corresponding to the Current Accounts are primarily allocated to meet the obligations arising from current accounts.

These funds shall be transferred to an account opened in a bank and the bank shall become a privileged creditor over these funds. The completion of liquidation shall not wait for payments to be made to current account holders from these funds.

(2) *Liquidation of Participation Accounts*: Liquidation of these accounts is realised individually for each segregated pool. However the accounts of foreign exchange shall be liquidated separately. Assets which exist in foreign exchange account and assets which exist in each pool are transferred to the Bank appointed for liquidation on the condition that they shall be paid according to the 'Unit Account Value' to the holders of Participation Account.

(3) *Liquidation of Accounts of the Institution*: Assets of the Institution, other than those allocated for the liabilities in connection with the payment of Current Account, are paid to other creditors of the Institution. Assets remaining after all these operations are divided in accordance with their capital shares among the shareholders.

The expenditures of the bank responsible for liquidation are met by the assets other than those in the Current Accounts and Participation Accounts of the Institution subject to liquidation. In the case where funds in the Accounts of the Institution are not enough to cover these expenses, the shareholders will be responsible jointly and individually for the remaining amount.

Legal proceedings

Article 34

Opening of judicial enquiry on grounds of contrary actions to Decrees relating to Institutions issued by the Council of Ministers and to Communiques issued related thereto is carried out by the Undersecretariat, obtaining also the view of the Bank through written application to the Public Prosecutor. The Ministry becomes a joint Plaintiff by this application at the same time.

Public prosecutors who are informed that actions contrary to decrees relating to Institutions issued by the Council of Ministers and Communiques issued by the Undersecretariat and the Bank have taken place, notify Undersecretariat and require investigation.

Should the public prosecutor decide on a refusal of trial, the Undersecretariat is authorised to object to this decision.

Validity

Article 35

This Communique comes into effect on 19 February 1984.

THE CENTRAL BANK COMMUNIQUE — NR 1

Scope

Article 1

Founders of the Special Finance Houses, which will be established in Turkey according to the Decree of the Council of Ministers number 83/7506 and the Communique of the Undersecretary for Treasury and Foreign Trade, shall apply to the Central Bank of the Republic of Turkey in a written form, in order to get a licence for establishment and permission for commencing their operations.

Abbreviations

Article 2

The following expressions used in this Communique shall have the meaning assigned in this article:

(a) House: Special Finance House,
(b) Undersecretary: Undersecretary of Treasury and Foreign Trade,
(c) Current Account: Special Current Account,
(d) Participation Account: Profit and Loss Participation Account,
(e) Accounts: Current Account and Participation Account.

I — REGULATIONS CONCERNING THE LICENCE

Application for getting a licence

Article 3

To get a licence from the Council of Ministers the founders have to send an application in written form to the address of Turkiye Cumhuriyet Merkez Bankasi, Bankacilik Genel Mudurlugu, Sermaye Piyasasi Mudurlugu, Ankara.
  Documents to be sent:

(a) The indenture of the House prepared in accordance with the provisions of the Decreee of the Council of Ministers number 83/7506 and the Communique of the Undersecretary published on 25 February 1984 in the official Gazette number 18323 and of other Legislation.
(b) A draft report, including the suggestions of the house on the necessary staff, technical appliances, organisation and other issues deemed necessary by the House, to enable the House to operate productively and in compliance with the Decree, Communique and other legislation.
(c) Personal Status Form accepted by authorised bodies, which shall also be signed by the Turkish Consulate if the founder is not a Turkish citizen.

In the Personal Status form there shall be:

- full name and residence address;
- previous occupations and their duration until the date of application;
- whether sentenced to pay indemnity personally or by companies managed by himself, as a consequence of commercial disputes; if so, the amount;
- document showing that the founder is not insolvent and was not sentenced because of the offences defined as disgraceful in the Turkish penal Law;
- amount of Certificates he guarantees to buy.

II — REGULATIONS CONCERNING THE PERMISSION FOR COMMENCEMENT OF OPERATIONS

Application for commencement of operations

Article 4

To the application to get permission for commencement of operations, after having been granted a licence by the Council of Ministers for establishing the House and completing the procedures in connection with the establishment in compliance with the provisions of Turkish Commercial Law, the below mentioned documents and information shall be attached:

(1) Official Gazette, in which the decision of the Council of Ministers regarding the establishment of the House is published;
(2) the approval of the establishment by the Commercial Court;
(3) Turkiye Ticaret Sicili Gazetesi (Trade Registry Paper of Turkey), in which the indenture was published;
(4) balance sheet at the time of establishment;
(5) documents assuring that all necessary measures have been taken to realise the operations and bookings;
(6) location of the head office and branch offices in Turkey;
(7) amount of the capital paid up in cash and all at once for the head office and the branch offices;
(8) amounts of various reserve funds, if there are any;
(9) type of business they intend to carry out;
(10) specimen of contract for Profit and Loss Participation Account and Contract for Special Current Account.

Permission for commencement of operations

Article 5

Houses, which are found to satisfy the conditions, after the documents given by the House according to Article 4 having been examined by the Central Bank, shall be given the necessary permission within a month after their application to the Central Bank. Two more months shall be given for the completion of applications not satisfying the necessary conditions. Applications which are not completed in this period will be taken as rejected.

Application for special activities

Article 6

Houses have to get additional permission from the Undersecretary in order to realise activities other than those clearly mentioned in the Decree and the Communique. Applications on this issue shall also be given to the Bank.

III — PROVISIONS REGARDING THE UTILISATION OF FOREIGN CURRENCY ACCUMULATED IN ACCOUNTS

Provisions regarding foreign currency

Article 7

Foreign currency accumulated in the Accounts shall be used according to the provisions of the Communique published by the Undersecretary on 25 February 1984. Provisions of the related current circular of the Central Bank apply to cases which are not covered in the above mentioned Communique.

IV — GENERAL PROVISIONS

The maximum amount in current accounts

Article 8

The maximum amount the House can collect in its current accounts may not exceed ten times of its net worth.

The ceiling of funds placed from current accounts

Article 9

The maximum amount of funds which can be placed from current accounts to a single real or legal person is limited to ten per cent of the net worth.

Blockage

Article 10

10 per cent of the funds accumulated in current accounts shall be kept as tellers' cash or in banks. An additional 10 per cent of the funds collected in current accounts and 1 per cent of the funds accumulated in participation accounts, will be blocked in the Central Bank. The blockage will be realised either in cash or in liquid security accepted by the Central Bank.

Maximum amount of funds to be placed from participation accounts

Article 11

The maximum amount of funds which can be placed to a single real or legal person from the funds accumulated in each pool is not subject to any limitation.

Maturity in participation accounts

Article 12

Participation accounts can be opened with maturities of 90 days, 360 days and longer.

Profit share of the House from participation accounts

Article 13

Profit share of the House from the accruing profit or loss after the placement of funds accumulated in participation accounts, will be determined by the House separately for each maturity pool and this percentage will apply to every account in the same pool. The change of the profit and loss share is subject to the approval of the Central Bank.

Calculation of the profit to be distributed

Article 14

The profit and loss to be distributed will be calculated according to the Unit Account Value. Other forms of profit and loss distribution are subject to the decision of the Undersecretary after the approval of the Central Bank.

Minimum requirements in the contracts

Article 15

The necessary requirements in the Contract of Profit and Loss Participation Account, Contract of Profit and Loss Participation Investment and Contract of Current Account is mentioned in Annexes 1, 2 and 3.

Necessity of information

Article 16

The House is obliged to send a copy of each realised Contract of Profit and Loss Participation Investment, due to its placement of funds by participation in profit and loss of the fund user, the annual results of the balance sheet, profit and loss account, current accounts and the results of each pool in the participation accounts quarterly at the end of March, June, September and December within 15 days after their realisation to the Central Bank.

Auditing

Article 17

Operations and accounts of the House shall be audited by the Central Bank.

Validity

Article 18

This Communique comes into effect with its publication.

ANNEX 1

ITEMS TO BE MENTIONED IN THE CONTRACT FOR PROFIT AND LOSS ACCOUNT

(1) A statement to explain that the account holder will participate in profit and loss which will occur through placement of funds with the same maturity.
(2) Regarding the bearer accounts the open title of the House and the word 'bearer' written in a clear way; regarding accounts opened in names, open titles of both sides and their names.
(3) The address of the House and also the address of the account holder, if the fund is deposited in names.
(4) The signatures of the House and the account holder, in case that the account is opened in names.
(5) Place for registration of deposited and withdrawn funds:
    TL: Foreign Currency:
(6) Account number.
(7) Maturity of the account.

(8) A statement to explain that the House has the right to place funds accumulated in different pools with different maturity, together, in which case the profit share of each pool is determined according to its contribution and the claim of the account holder is limited to his share in the profit of the pool, in which the fund is deposited.

(9) A statement to explain that all expenses occurring from utilisation of funds will be borne by the House.

(10) A statement to explain that in this account, besides the profit and loss sharing, no other advantage to the account holder can be given.

(11) A statement to explain that the House's share from profit and loss occurring from the placement of the funds accumulated in this account is . . . per cent in case of profit and . . . per cent in case of loss; the amount the account holder can lose may not exceed the amount he deposited.

(12) A statement to explain that the claim of the account holder is not on the difference between funds he deposited and withdrew but is on the unit account value at the date of maturity.

(13) A statement to explain that the unit account value will be calculated through the multiplication of the unit value and the account value.

(14) A statement to explain that the unit value is 100 prior to the commencement of operations and will be calculated through the division of total value of assets in each term of participation account, to the total account value of the preceding day; and a statement to explain the choice of the House regarding the calculation of unit value (daily or weekly).

(15) A statement to explain that the account value is calculated by adding or subtracting the value found out by the division of the deposited or withdrawn amount through unit value, to or from the initial account value of the account holder, according to deposits or withdrawals.

(16) A statement to explain that the account value will be written on the contract and will be renewed on the contract at the date of each new deposit.

(17) A statement to explain that the account is to be closed within five days after maturity; if no notice is given to the House beforehand that the account will not be renewed, it will be automatically renewed with the same maturity beginning at the first day after expiration of maturity of the account.

(18) A statement to explain that the maximum amount subject to early withdrawal (upon notice to be given 30 days before) shall correspond, in the case that the pool in which the fund was deposited shows a profit, to the total deposited by the account holder, and in case of a loss to the unit account value.

(19) A statement to explain that the earnings of the account holders shall be considered as interest earnings and are subject to withholding tax.

(20) A statement to explain that funds accumulated in these accounts are not covered by the Saving Deposit Insurance Fund.

(21) A statement to explain that the sum of the account shall be transferred to the Central Bank, to the order of treasury, if ten years pass without any operation and investigation of the account holder; and an explanation that regarding accounts under the names of children — opened with the condition that only they are allowed to withdraw money — the prescription period of ten years begins on the date on which the child has attained his majority.

(22) A statement to explain that, if the contract form is lost, the account holder will receive a copy of it from the House after fulfilling the obligations of advertisement.

(23) Amount of the capital of the House.

(24) Duration of operations of the House.

(25) Dates of registration and modifications of the indenture of the House.

(26) Date and number of official gazette in which the decision of the Council of Ministers for granting the licence was published.

(27) Date and number of the permission for commencement of operations given by the Central Bank.

ANNEX 2

ITEMS TO BE MENTIONED IN THE CONTRACT FOR PROFIT AND LOSS INVESTMENT

(1) Open titles of the House and the fund user and names of authorised persons signing the contact.

(2) Addresses of both parties.

(3) Signatures: House and the fund user.

(4) Amount of the fund to be placed:
TL:
Foreign currency:

(5) Share of the House in profit and loss of the fund user:
Profit share: %
Loss share : %

(6) The amount the House will pay in case of a loss may not exceed the amount the House placed.

(7) If the participation covers all the activities or only a few specific activities of the fund user.

(8) If the participation covers only a few specific activities, the exact description of these activities.

(9) Duration of profit and loss participation.

ANNEX 3

ITEMS TO BE MENTIONED IN THE CONTRACT FOR SPECIAL CURRENT ACCOUNT

(1) A statement to explain that no profit share or interest will be paid to these accounts.

(2) Regarding the bearers accounts, the open title of the House and the word 'bearer' written in a clear way; regarding accounts opened in names, open titles of both sides and their names.

(3) The address of the House and also the address of the account holder, if the fund is deposited in names.

(4) The signatures of the House and the account holder, in the case when the account is opened in names.

(5) Place for registration of deposited and withdrawn funds:
TL:
Foreign currency:

(6) Account number.

(7) A statement to explain that the total amount of the account can be partially or totally withdrawn on demand, by the account holder or by the person authorised by the account holder.

(8) A statement to explain that, in case of liquidation, current account depositors are first priority creditors on assets corresponding to capital and reserves of the House as well as on assets corresponding to current accounts.

(9) A statement to explain that funds accumulated in these accounts are not covered by the Savings Deposits Insurance Fund.

(10) A statement to explain that the sum of the account will be transferred to the Central Bank to the order of treasury if ten years pass without any transaction or written instruction of the account holder.

(11) Amount of capital of the House.

(12) Duration of operations of the House.

(13) Dates of registration and modifications of the indenture of the House.

(14) Date and number of official gazette in which the decision of the Council of Ministers for granting the licence was published.

(15) Date and number of the permission for commencement of operations given by the Central Bank.

(16) A statement to explain that, if the contract form is lost the account holder will receive a copy of it from the House after fulfilling the obligations of advertisement.

ٱلْحَمْدُ لِلَّهِ

LIVING UP TO YOUR CONFIDENCE

More than 1400 branches in Pakistan and 27 branches in commercial centres of the world in addition to associates and representative offices.

NBP has played a leading role in Pakistan's development and served trade and industry in a wide sphere.

BRANCHES AT FINANCIAL CENTRES
NEW YORK, CHICAGO, WASHINGTON, BAHAMAS, LONDON, PARIS, FRANKFURT, CAIRO, BAHRAIN, HONG KONG, TOKYO.
Also at: Birmingham, Bradford, Edinburgh, Glasgow, Knightsbridge, London, Manchester, Sheffield

JOINT VENTURE: Bank Al Jazira, Kaki Building, Airport Road, Jeddah, Saudi Arabia.

SERVING IN MANY LANDS FOR MANY YEARS
National Bank of Pakistan
18, Finsbury Circus, London EC2M 7BJ
Telex: 883398. Cables: Millatbank
Telephone: 01-588 1511

WE CARE

Three hospitals with sophisticated medical equipment and four pharmaceutical companies constitute our present achievement in the medical field. Which we are proud of. Not only from an investment point of view, but also from a humamitarian one.

TOTAL BALANCE SHEET	US$2,053.4 MILLION
TOTAL DEPOSITS	US$1,542.2 MILLION
TOTAL INVESTMENTS	US$1,613.9 MILLION
SHAREHOLDERS' EQUITY	US$97.6 MILLION

Faisal Islamic Bank of Egypt

Address, Head Office & Cairo Branch:
1113 Cornish el Nil, CAIRO
P.O. Box 2446, CAIRO
Tel: 753109-753165-742113-743364
Telex: 93877-93878 FBANK-UN
Management:
Dr. Mahmoud M. El Helw, Governor
Mr. Ahmed A. Kamal, Deputy-Governor
Branches:
10 Operating Branches. Plus 13 more under establishment.

UMMA FINANCE GROUP

EXTENDING THE FRONTIERS
OF ISLAMIC BANKING
AROUND THE WORLD

UMMA FUND
INTERNATIONAL ISLAMIC UNIT TRUST

MANAGED BY A GROUP OF
PROFESSIONAL ISLAMIC
BANKERS, INTERNATIONAL
FINANCIAL EXPERTS AND
RENOWNED FUQAHA OF ISLAM.

Holding Company:
International Modaraba Holding Co.
Ltd., Dehands House, Second
Terrace, West Collins Avenue,
Centreville, Nassau, Bahamas.

Subsidiary:
Umma Fund Management Ltd.,
Havelet House, South Esplanade,
St. Peter Port, Guernsey,
Channel Islands.

Subsidiary:
Umma Finance House Ltd.,
108 Fenchurch Street,
London Ec3 ☎ 01-488 4298
Telex: 8814439 GBC G.